With Ossie and Ruby

Ex Libris

With Ossie and Ruby: In This Life Together

OSSIE DAVIS AND RUBY DEE

Perennial

An Imprint of HarperCollinsPublishers

First Quill edition published 2000.

Reprinted in Perennial 2004.

Designed by Bernard Klein

The Library of Congress has catalogued the hardcover edition as follows:

Davis, Ossie.
    With Ossie and Ruby : in this life together / by Ossie Davis and
Ruby Dee. — 1st ed.
        p.   cm.
    Includes index.
    ISBN 0-688-15396-8
    1. Davis, Ossie.   2. Dee, Ruby.   3. Actors—United States—
Biography.   I. Dee, Ruby.   II. Title.
PN2285.D28   1998
792'.028'092273
[B]—DC21   98-35621
                                                                  CIP

ISBN 0-688-17582-1 (pbk.)

05 06 07 08 QW 10 9 8 7 6 5 4 3

To our children, Nora, Guy, and Hasna;

and to our grandchildren,

Ihsaana, Muta'Ali, Jihaad, Brian, Jammal, Imani, and Martial.

To our brothers and sisters,

those with us and gone,

and their children.

To all the spouses;

to aunts and uncles and cousins,

those with us and gone.

And to our parents—

Edward, Emma, Kince, and Laura.

ACKNOWLEDGMENTS

We began this book not fully realizing the enormous amount of time, work, and commitment it would take to complete. With an already full schedule, the task would have been impossible without our editor, Sydné Mahone, who worked with us so faithfully and diligently. She helped us immeasurably with the organization of all the material as fast as we could get it to her, no matter the order. We appreciate her patience, her sound judgment, and her ability to blend, balance, and intertwine our separate and collective accounts; to pack two lives into one book is a formidable accomplishment indeed.

How fortunate we are to have a daughter like Nora, who can almost go inside each of our minds and help us to articulate our thoughts as well as we can, who helped us to remember with greater accuracy events that happened when she herself was still very young; for helping Sydné work even better with us; for reading and rereading when we couldn't. For leaving her family and her job in Atlanta a number of times to travel to New York and to Canada to help us pick our relatives' brains, and for just being a gifted and loving human being.

To Hasna, though eyeball deep in working on her doctorate, to Guy, and to Mama for the stories and the memories; to Ruby's sister, Angelina, and to her husband, Carl Roach, who helped her enormously in untangling the early years. To Tommy, her nephew, who supplied a picture of Ruby's tree; to Ruby's cousins, Madelyn Bohanon and Jean Burns, who also remembered much about the beginnings—we offer thanks. To God above all, egged on by Kince, Emma, Ed, and all from whose loins we descended, a prayer of thanksgiving for all the Spirit help, and a dance of joy that this summation of the lives of two people in one book is done.

To those in our office and in our home who helped us manage on

Acknowledgments

so many levels—Ms. Deborah McGee, Ms. Latifah Salahuddin, and her brother, Mr. Rahim Salahuddin; Ms. Arminda Thomas, our researcher—we offer profound thanks.

We are deeply grateful to Paul Bresnick, executive editor at William Morrow, who decided that an account of our lives would make good reading. We appreciate so much the vote of confidence. Thanks for hearing us out on this and that, even when you may have disagreed. We also thank Paul's assistant, Ben Schafer, for his support of our efforts.

For their encouragement and enthusiasm, which strengthened our resolve to go forward with this exploration, we thank our agents, Bettye McCartt and Susan Crawford.

CONTENTS

Contents

Be not deceived,
The Struggle is far from over,
The best of being Black is yet to be—
So said the Ones who Died to set you free.

—OSSIE DAVIS

Prologue

RUBY: It was 1995. Ossie and I were having dinner in the presidential dining room. I was sitting next to Bill, and Ossie was sitting at another table with Hillary. And I said to the President, "Bill, I'm sure tomorrow I'll think of a million things I will wish that I'd discussed with you." And he said, "Well, all right, Ruby. If anything occurs to you, just give me a ring." I wanted to tell him what had happened on our way to this auspicious occasion. I changed my mind. But let me tell *you* what happened.

The truth is we almost didn't go. I remember the day when we received this beautifully engraved invitation from the White House asking us to attend a ceremony at which we would be honored with the President's National Medal of the Arts. I said, well, maybe the Secret Service hasn't done its job and brought out our dossiers and showed them to the people who make these choices. Because when they find out who we really are, maybe they'll go to the post office and snatch that invitation back. On the heels of the excitement came the doubts and questions. Should we go? Remember, Ossie? What had we done to merit such an honor? Then, because we saw the delight and the anticipation build in the children, and with your Mama and some of the nieces and nephews, we decided to make the trip to the White House.

OSSIE: President and Mrs. Clinton were gracious, warm, and most reassuring.

RUBY: Indeed, they were. They gave no indication that they were aware of our shady past. The only trouble I had was with the dog.

OSSIE: Maybe the dog was a Republican?

RUBY: Republican or not, there were questions in his eye that made us both very uneasy, remember?

OSSIE: The weather was not generous at all. It rained upon our journey to the Rose Garden, where the ceremony was to take place under a tent. High culture, coming to the circus.

RUBY: We gathered with our fellow awardees: Licia Albanese, soprano and founder of the Puccini Foundation; poet Gwendolyn Brooks; arts patrons Iris and Bernie Cantor; composer David Diamond; James Ingo Freed, the architect; Bob Hope, the comedian; the artist Roy Lichtenstein; the choreographer and founder of Dance Theatre of Harlem, Arthur Mitchell; musician Bill Monroe; and a representative of Urban Gateways. Preceding the main event, however, was the rendezvous with the Presidential Dog. All of us were ushered into a bus and ferried to the White House for a private reception with the First Couple of our native land.

OSSIE: On the bus, the conversation was subdued but heady in anticipation of what lay before us. There was a good feeling and much laughter as we discussed many things, above all, the implications of a presidential salute to the arts and all that that could mean in terms of funding and support.

RUBY: It made us feel important—exemplars, we were, of the best the national culture had to offer. When we arrived at the White House, we were stopped by the guards, who took a perfunctory look at our various forms of photoidentification: driver's licenses, birth certificates, passports—anything to prove that we were who we said we were. Then we got back onto the bus for the short shuttle to the side entrance.

Before the bus pulled away, a strange thing happened: An executive-looking dog of a wolverine variety with an air of business about him, with an equally authoritative-looking man attendant, leaped onto the bus and proceeded down the aisle, sniffing each of the dignitaries—knees, crotch, hands, and the air around us. Needless to say, we were all surprised and suddenly silent.

As the dog made his way to the rear where we were seated, I began to squirm. Sweat popped out on our foreheads. Here was something, silently but relentlessly accusatory, that we had not expected. Could that dog know about that night at Crystal Lake when we dodged the witch-hunter's subpoena by hiding out backstage? Could we explain on the spot that we were never found guilty of subversive activities, but merely accused of being misguided pinkos and fellow travelers?

OSSIE: We looked at each other, living again for the moment an ancient nightmare, but smiling away our panic.

Just before he reached us, the dog stopped in his tracks and, with eyes gleaming, bared his canines and growled a low growl. Suddenly from everywhere, the Secret Service, all looking like Dick Tracy in black, hurriedly boarded the bus, lifted us to our feet, and ushered us off the vehicle and into a steady, beating rain.

We could hear the cries of surprise from our fellow awardees: "What did they do? What did they do? Will they go to jail? Get shot? What?" And us? Standing, staring at the retreating bus, disgraced. Our very best award-ceremony clothes becoming soggy, we waved weakly toward the receding bus speeding the truly deserving to glory. Then we trudged along the road in squishy shoes, hoping to thumb a ride back from ignominy.

RUBY: Naw, naw, naw—that's not what really happened. That's what we were thinking. The truth is that the dog barely noticed us, let alone bared his canines. But that story—that lie—gives us an excuse, a good reason to write a joint-life tale.

OSSIE: We've never been, to our knowledge, guilty of anything— other than being black—that might upset anybody. But perhaps the time has come to set the record straight; to prove to the President's dog at least that our lives were indeed forged in danger, struggle, and escape, and rate more than a cursory sniff.

RUBY: We also need to reassure ourselves, our friends, and those who think well of us that we truly did merit that National Medal of the Arts.

OSSIE: The question of merit may be open to debate. Still, we were there, at the White House—Mama; Nora; Guy; Hasna; Gail and Sharón, Ruby's brother's children; and Karen, my sister's child. We were there and nobody, including the President's dog, was about to throw us out.

> *"Ruby and Ossie are ready to testify, sir, standing by in the dock."*
> *"Well, well, well,"* the spirit of Senator McCarthy might very well be saying. *"We've been looking forward to this for a long time. Swear them suckers in!"*

PART ONE

Before We Met

CHAPTER 1

Ruby Is Born
at Seven

I remember consciously acknowledging myself, the fact of myself as a girl and a part of a family, as I stood alone facing the window in apartment 24. I was wearing a brown dress and I had been looking at my hands because just a few minutes before, in the kitchen, my mother was explaining to a neighbor, Marie Taylor, who was rubbing some cream on them, that as I got older, the hands would probably get softer and smoother.

"Yeah," Ms. Taylor said, "children with these kind of dried-out, wrinkly hands are old souls come back with work to do."

"If you're a woman, don't care what kind of hands, you got work to do," Mother said.

They laughed as Ms. Taylor screwed the lid back on the jar and rubbed her own hands, as if putting on gloves. I felt bad about my hands. My mother and Ms. Taylor had pretty hands. Mine were ugly.

I put the incident out of my mind. Standing, looking out the window, I announced out loud, "I am seven years old. I am one, two, three, four, five, six, seven years old." A kind of excitement came over me.

Since that realization, snatches and bits of life before age seven crop up in my mind—but are unclear. To this day, it seems as if most of my life, I've drifted through waves of experience—like an embryo in amniotic fluid—accommodating tides, brushing by sensations, reaching out to stimuli, but not certain enough to grab and hold on. I am plagued by long gaps of unremembered years, fuzzy focus, and doubts about even my strengths. I believe deeply, however, that each generation must share some of its experiences with the next generation. I tell myself that it is time to find focus, get solid, and to be a fully conscious traveler on this trip that doesn't repeat.

I almost didn't get to make the trip. It was the third pregnancy for the teenagers, my parents. Two had already been born—a boy when my father was seventeen years old and my mother fifteen, a girl eleven months later—and now this. What, again! Everybody had a remedy. Potions, lotions, oils, and prayers. Everything ever heard of, short of knitting needles was applied to the condition, but I came anyway.

That was the end of school for Edward Nathaniel Wallace and Gladys Hightower in Cleveland, Ohio. Get a girl pregnant, you married her. By the end of about three years, though, Gladys had found religion. She left her husband and her brood to follow a preacher man, a way-shower to glory, forgiveness, and salvation.

Grandma Wallace introduced my father to his next wife, Emma Amelia Benson. Emma was thirteen years older than Edward, but they hit it off. They genuinely liked each other, and they needed each other. He and his mother wanted to keep the family together. Emma always said her heart went out to this young man with his three children. Having grown up on a farm, riding horses all her life, her insides were severely damaged; but she wanted children. "I married your father for the sake of you children," she would repeat for many years.

Emma Amelia Benson had gone to Atlanta University and had studied under W.E.B. Du Bois, one of the nation's greatest philosophers and historians; she had been a teacher and had saved money to continue her studies at Columbia University. But there was this young man and his three children, whose mother had deserted them, and she knew what to do for these children. With the money she had saved, she paid for his divorce, bought an apartment for $500 on Seventh Avenue in a just-turning-colored neighborhood, and sent for and married the man, with the hope and expectation that he would finish high school, and maybe go on to college.

According to my sister Angelina, Grandma Wallace brought the babies—Thomas Edward, aged four; Angelina, three; and Ruby, not quite one—from Cleveland, Ohio, on a dark, wood-paneled, chandeliered, and red-velvet-curtained train to New York; to the good woman Emma, to the good address, the Rangely Court, 2340 Seventh Avenue, in Harlem.

There was some complication with the divorce, however, that put the legitimacy of this marriage in question. Daddy had to make several trips back to Cleveland to deal with legalities. During one such trip, Grandma Wallace revealed to Emma that there was another baby about to be born to Gladys. Despite Daddy's raging denials, and Emma's tears, arguments, and accusations, she demanded that he bring her that baby, too. His children must be raised together, she decreed. Gladys got to at least name the baby before she let her go.

Three months later, the divorce and other parental issues were resolved, and baby LaVerne arrived at the good address. All I remember about the time is a wicker baby buggy with big wheels.

Looking back is tricky business. It is seeing through time, people, events; it's remembering subtleties and attitudes. It's getting the facts straight, even though the facts may have little to do with "telling the truth." So much depends on who does the looking back and why. What is the condition of the vision mechanism—one-eyed, shortsighted, farsighted, or no-sighted, blind?

I want to, need to, look back though, like Lena in the play by Athol Fugard, *Boesman and Lena.* Lena had to know the towns in South Africa from which she and Boesman had been forced to flee. Her meaning as a human being, her sanity, depended upon getting all the towns in the right sequence. The truth of the order of things, in immediate terms, centered her in the cosmos. She needed to know that her life mattered.

Perhaps that is why I, Ruby Ann Wallace Davis, known as Ruby Dee, must offer this account of myself. Also, I may have something of use to share with people who, like me, sometimes process information in peculiar ways.

One of the dilemmas of my life is that I can arrive at a point of view, a solid conclusion, and in the blink of an eye, betray it in favor of an opposite and equally compelling conclusion. Another dilemma: Maybe my story has already been told. Much of my life is like the lives of others. Only the names have changed. Your memory, Ruby, is like your vision was for many years—fuzzy and unreliable—I tell myself.

I believe that God puts every creature on earth for a particular reason, and looking back, even a blind person can see and can have impressions, can connect the dots of recognition and make a picture. So relying on my family and friends, calling out to the dead to visit me in dreams, and especially calling on God in prayer, I take on this task of lighting up the territory of myself.

CHAPTER 2

Ossie Is Still a Mistake

I was born to laugh. The midwife who introduced me into existence by slapping my behind expected me to cry. And cry I did. But, knowing me, I probably cried to keep from laughing.

The first child of Kince and Laura Davis, I was born into a world of jokesters, black and white, waiting to tickle my feet. Take, for example, the matter of my first name. I was named after my father's father, Raiford Chatman Davis. (He put twenty-five cents in my fat little hand for the privilege.) In the South, we tend to use initials. So when the clerk at the Clinch County courthouse asked Mama who I was, she said, "R. C. Davis." He thought she said, "Ossie Davis," and wrote it down that way. Mama would not have argued with him. The man was white. Mama and I were black and down in deepest Georgia. So the matter of identification was settled. Ossie it was, and Ossie it is till this very day.

Cogdell, the little town in Georgia where I was born, was home to some four hundred souls, mostly black, who lived under the civic paternity of Alex K. Sessoms, the white man who owned Cogdell and everything in it, including the Waycross and Western, a little railroad that ran twenty-three miles from Cogdell to Waycross. It had one jitney, which had once been a streetcar that seldom carried passengers; a donkey steam engine; some boxcars and some flatcars, most of which carried timber from the swamps and stumps, and sometimes cattle, off to Waycross.

My daddy, who couldn't write his name, helped to build the Waycross and Western. I don't mean that he just labored with picks and shovels, crossties and sledgehammers; Daddy was a self-taught railway and construction engineer. He could build a railroad line from scratch, which in that day and age was a white man's job. Daddy, of course, was black but was not afraid and didn't give a damn about the Ku Klux Klan. The bad blood between them was the source of my first adventure.

Daddy had moved the family to Zirkle, Georgia, for a while, to help another white man build a small railroad, which ran right in front of the shack in which we lived. I was but three or four years old and ran outdoors early one morning to play in the yard. There I found a long, tall stick driven into the ground. The stick was split at the top with a folded sheet of paper stuck in the split. I took the paper into the house and showed it to Mama, who looked at it and let me look, too. Somebody had drawn a pistol in red ink, firing a stream of red bullets into a big, black heart from which red drops of blood were falling into a coffin. I didn't know what it meant, but Mama did. "Oh my God, the Ku Klux Klan!"

She called a neighbor to watch me and my baby sister, put on a pretty dress, and stuck the letter and my father's pistol in her bosom. Then she walked out into the middle of the railroad track—the one my daddy and his crew were building—and started up the road as fast as she could go, to the spot a couple of miles away where Daddy and his men were working.

Everybody loved my daddy, Kince Charles Davis. Everybody except the Klan. At least that's what I thought. Daddy was a local legend, the hero of many a story told by black and white folks. It was common knowledge that he had once spent time on the chain gang for shooting a preacher in Kissimmee, Florida, it was rumored; the preacher, it was said, had made Mama leave the church in the middle of his sermon because I was crying too loud.

My first memory of him was as a presence looming out of the myth and mystery that always surrounded him. Mama was sitting on the floor in the back of a horse and buggy giving me lunch from her breast. Daddy was sitting in the driver's seat next to Grandpa Sam, Mama's father. Cradled in her arms, I was slurping away as the old horse farted along. I remember looking up at my daddy's big broad shoulders spread across the horizon, and knowing, just from that look, that I would never die.

There were stories about Daddy told by the men who worked in his construction gang. There were stories Daddy told of himself, some of which were not quite satisfactory. For example, when we asked why he didn't have a left forefinger, like other people, he'd laugh and tell us that a bullfrog had bitten it off. Some of his men said that he had lost it long ago in a gunfight. Daddy refused to clarify the matter when we pressed. Rather he'd laugh, pick up his guitar, and play a funny tune.

The letter in the split stick was to warn him to run for his life. But Daddy didn't run. He was big and strong and easy, and laughter trailed after him like a long, warm scarf in the wintertime. Everybody looked up to him and laughed a lot when he did. Everybody knew that Daddy wasn't scared of anybody, black or white. But when he got angry, a great silence could be heard in his vicinity.

The crew of men, who called him "Chief," built a big fire in the yard and kept watch all night. I was the little, big-eyed boy allowed to stay up with the rest of the men standing guard. Daddy went inside and went to sleep with his pistol on the bed right next to his hand.

The Klan never came. But that was not surprising. A black man with Daddy's skill was a rare and precious commodity to Sessoms and the other big men who ran things. They didn't mind giving him a white man's job as long as they didn't have to give him a white man's pay. It was all right for the Klan to try and run him off, but they didn't dare touch him, not while he worked for Sessoms. Daddy knew that as well as they did.

The job in Zirkle was only temporary, and when it was over, Daddy moved us back to Cogdell. As I remember it, Cogdell was a warm, country world, full of family—Grandpa and Grandma, a whole lot of uncles and aunts, but no cousins yet. I was the first grandchild, a boy, and everyone must have been waiting. They loved me to death.

Cogdell had one country store where the railroad and the dirt road intersected. It had two or three churches for black folks, a lot of woods and paths and gatherings of shanties here and there where the black folks lived. Most everybody, black and white, worked for Alex Sessoms.

Sessoms had a scientific bent and had gone all the way to France to bring back the latest method of distilling the gum from pine trees into turpentine. He also planted acres and acres of sweet potatoes; the leaves from the growing sweet potato vine were fed to his cattle while the potatoes under the ground were left for his Negroes. Cogdell was Sessoms's industrial and agricultural base, but it had no school for black folks. So off I had to go, at the age of five, in search of an education.

Grandpa Sam had moved away from Cogdell after Coot, Mama's Mama, died. He now lived in Waycross with a newly acquired wife, a schoolteacher who had little use for any of Grandpa Sam's children, including Mama. They sent me there. I remember Mama telling Grandma that she was my mother. Then Grandma took me away.

Grandpa Sam was a Methodist preacher. I don't remember ever hearing him preach. What I do remember is that he was also a carpenter, and that he called me "Jack," and enjoyed very much showing me how to use his tools.

I remember even less about my grandmother, Martha, or Coot, as they used to call her. My only memory of her places me somewhere along a country road, walking with her and two of her women friends. They had on long, colorful dresses that covered their high-buttoned shoes. I am told that when she was buried, I was found somewhere close to the graveyard chasing a rabbit. Somehow, even now, I know that I was special to her, that she loved me, and that I returned that love with all my heart.

Cogdell, of course, has vanished; it is no more, gone with the wind carrying down with it all the small things that made it seem that some-day it might be a city as big and as important as Homerville, including the cemetery. Nobody knows now where Coot lies buried, not even Mama. Her resting place is grown over now with grass and brush and trees, as so many southern black cemeteries are when a city gives up the ghost and the people who inhabited it move on. I certainly wish I knew where to find her grave. But I don't.

Still, wherever she is, I hope the spot is quiet and peaceful, with some sense of respect for the love, suffering, and sacrifice that must have filled her bosom. I hope she knows that her first grandchild would like to know her again, now that he has come to some understanding of who you really are, Coot. You and Daddy's Mama, deep people of the shadows, were the backbone of the black man's survival and exis-tence. No one yet has chronicled the peculiar woman's price you paid that kept us all alive. Coot, wherever you are and wherever lie your remains, you are still very much a part of the family.

CHAPTER 3

Under One Roof

The REAL children were all together now under one roof, with a mother and a daddy. Ruby, Edward, Angelina, and LaVerne. As Edward pointed out one day, "The first letters of our first names spell REAL."

Before this gathering together under one roof, in Harlem in the early 1920s, we children had often stayed with relatives—with Grandma Wallace, with some of Daddy's older half-brothers and half-sisters—and with neighbors, sleeping where there was a spare bed, or on a pallet on the floor. I understand that once my bed was a dresser drawer.

Edward and Angelina had come to our new home with a few memories of times past. Dim memories of Daddy and Gladys living in a one-room kitchenette apartment on East Forty-third Street in Cleveland; of one day hearing Daddy yell upstairs to Gladys to bring him his overcoat, and her opening the window and throwing it down. Of him coming upstairs and ordering the two of them in the closet; of hearing the bumping and fumbling and angry voices and silences that accented Gladys being beaten. Edward and Angelina had memories of standing at a chair that served as a table and of eating from one plate.

One day in the Harlem apartment, Edward ran crying to Daddy that "that lady hit me." Daddy explained that "that lady" was his and Angelina's new mother; that from now on they must call her "Mother," that "that lady" was his new wife who loved them and who would have to whip them when they didn't behave; and that they must never talk about Gladys anymore to anyone.

LaVerne and I had no memories of the Gladys times. We grew up to be teenagers before we learned about our relationship to Gladys, who kept writing to us through the years, sending candy, gifts, and letters that were given to us, often with pieces torn from the bottom where her signature would have been.

I get the impression that Gladys's family wasn't poor. There is a small photograph of the Hightower children. Uncle Raymond, the eldest, with a very high forehead, became a Christian Science minister. His son, Ray, Jr., one of my favorite cousins, also became a minister and hypnotherapist. There is Aunt Ruby, after whom I'm named, and Gladys, whom we all thought of as some kind of fanatic. We understood that some time in her life, she sold things, like needles and pencils, on street corners. In the photograph, they are well dressed, wearing black shoes and stockings. The girls wear big bows in their long hair.

By the time Gladys was twenty-two years old and she'd brought four babies into the world, one could conclude that something was wrong. After all, it was not the Stone Age. Where were the family support systems, the community assistance programs?

By the time I got to be a teenager, near grown, full of myself and impressed with my own wisdom and knowledge, judgment came swiftly, easily, and harshly. Armed with the information that the woman Gladys had given birth to me and three others, and had abandoned us all to follow some preacher, I found myself under the influence of a new attitude—contempt. How dare she keep on writing to us, sending candy and stuff to rot our teeth? Through the years, we received stupid letters about religion and Communist devils, spaceships, and God's vengeance. Once or twice a year, there were phone calls from Gladys, even after I was grown and married with babies of my own. Her sudden surprise visits were my only personal encounters—five in all, as I recall.

My baby sister, LaVerne, told me that even before we knew Gladys was our mother, Daddy had taken us to Cleveland for a visit with her. Where we stayed seemed dark. Light curtains fluttered against a window. She brought us acidophilus milk. She baked a pretty chocolate cake. It didn't taste good. We didn't eat it. She asked a lot of questions. We spent two nights. Maybe Daddy was doing Gladys a favor by taking us to visit. She may have wanted to claim us for a little while, and he made it possible. It sounds like him.

Gladys seemed to appear out of the ether, uninvited, when I was in my late teens and married for the first time to Frank Brown. Before the visit was over, I gave her a gold watch I was wearing, which I later discovered she promptly pawned. I don't remember how she got to New York, to the brownstone where I lived, where she stayed, if she stayed, or when she left.

First of all, I didn't think there was any resemblance between us, and I wondered why. I was struck by the ill-fitting false teeth. They looked crooked in her mouth. A too-pink gum arrangement seemed lopsided, and the teeth, off center. It occurred to me that perhaps she'd bought them secondhand. Straight black hair in a sloppy bun was loosely pulled back from a pecan brown face with the high forehead. Big eyes protruded under long lashes. Maybe my nose looked like hers, except for the very arched nostrils. Conversation was uncomfortable. She smiled a lot. I felt uneasy. The visit was short and I was relieved as she tried to hug me, then hurriedly left.

It seems strange that both mothers, Emma and Gladys, had been injured by horses. Gladys had a plate in her head, having been kicked by a horse. She wasn't considered "quite right." I watched her descend the steps and go down the street. She had an odd walk. The shoulders moved with a deliberate motion from front to back. They seemed to reflect the way she spoke—quickly and in non sequiturs, as if speaking in one dimension and thinking in another. As I grow older, I sometimes think I speak and move as I remember her. My sister Angelina reminds me most of her, in the way she speaks. But I know now that Gladys lives in all of us. I see her even in my children and grandchildren.

Some years later, about 1955, after Ossie and I were married and two of our children were born, Gladys appeared again in Mount Vernon, New York. She had brought some kind of gift wrapped in brown paper. I think it was something for the children. Although she seemed edgy, uncomfortable, I remember, I tried to put her at ease, wanting to ask questions and almost being glad to see her. She had come to New York to visit her daughter, Tondelayo. She seemed in a hurry, but before she left, she asked to take Nora and Guy, our children, for a short walk. She wanted to buy them something. We agreed that she could take Nora.

On that walk, Nora remembers, Gladys said, "I want you to do something for me. Will you do something for me?" Repetitions were typical of the way she spoke. "Will you call me 'Grandma'? While we walk, let me hear you call me 'Grandma.' Call me 'Grandma Gladys.'" And Nora did. We hadn't planned to tell the children the truth about Gladys. So when Nora asked about her new friend, "Grandma" Gladys, I warned her, "Just don't let Grandma Wallace hear you say that."

Gladys had married again, and borne two more sons: Raymond, named after her Christian Scientist brother who was to die from a simple ailment because he didn't believe in orthodox medicine, and Charles. Tondelayo resulted from a third liaison.

While I was on the road with the play *Anna Lucasta* in 1946, Monty Hawley, one of the actors, told me that he had met my sister. "Which one?" I asked.

"Tondelayo," he said. "She hangs out in Small's Paradise."

"Small's Paradise in Harlem?" I asked.

"Not but one Small's," he said, realizing he was telling me something I didn't know. Yes, I had heard about Tondelayo. I had met her twice.

One afternoon in Small's Paradise Lounge, I joined her on a barstool. She asked me for a picture. I was more curious about her than anything else. We looked like sisters, except for her rather heavy mustache, of which she seemed proud. I had sent her a publicity single from the play, care of Small's, signed, "To My Sister, Tondelayo." That was the eight-by-ten-inch photo she had shown Monty. During our visit, several men stopped to greet her or to chat with her. She would introduce me as her sister.

That afternoon, before we parted, she told me that if I ever heard of her being dead, I must send a wreath shaped like a question mark to the funeral home. A few years later, there was an article in the *Amsterdam News:* Tondelayo had been shot and her body dumped in the Harlem River. The murderer was never apprehended. My father paid for the funeral. Gladys didn't come. I couldn't go, but I sent that wreath shaped like a question mark.

Through the years, Gladys continued to write to the four of us, Edward, Angelina, LaVerne, and me. She called us, too, from time to time. It was always the wrong time, a major distraction for me, when her calls came. Too often, I was abrupt and dismissive, particularly one day in October 1965, when she called to insist that I visit her that weekend because she was leaving on a spaceship and wanted to talk with me. She wasn't making sense, as usual. Less than two weeks after that call, she dropped dead in the ladies' room of a movie theater. I understand she went to movies a lot, especially in winter. Many of the letters she wrote to us were on the stationery of various hotels.

Gladys died on October 21, 1965. LaVerne and I went to Detroit to arrange the funeral. We had her cremated and gave the ashes to one of her sons. Angelina and Edward did not come.

Among her belongings were packets of needles, which I think she may have peddled along with other such small objects we found in her bag. There was also a silver medal of the Virgin Mary, and a copy of *Jet* magazine with a cover photo of me as Kate and John Cunningham as Petruchio in *The Taming of the Shrew*, which we had performed during the summer of '65 at the American Shakespeare Festival Theatre in Stratford, Connecticut.

Emma Amelia was a light-skinned colored woman with long, straight black hair. Her mother was a black Native American who looked like the one on the buffalo nickel. Her father looked like Santa Claus and smelled of tobacco, horses, and sweat; it was a good smell. We'd often watch her make two long braids, which she coiled into buns and fastened on each side of her head with big bone hairpins. She always seemed to be working so hard—washing, ironing, cooking, sewing, scrubbing. She often had headaches, and would put a Stanback powder in water, swallow it, and lie down.

Soon after we were all under one roof, it was discovered that I had rickets, and was subject to convulsions. Somebody would tell Mother, "Ruby's shaking." Mother would put me in the bathtub. I remember lying on my back kicking like a frog with something cold on my tongue.

I didn't know that Emma wasn't my real mother until I was eleven. It was a gray day, and I was standing near the piano in the living room when my brother Edward said, "She's not your real mother, you know. Gladys Hightower is your real mother." I didn't believe him. He explained the history to LaVerne and me as best he could. Until then, I had thought I looked like her, more so than the other children. How they kept the truth from me and LaVerne so long is due, I think, largely to my father. Besides, almost everyone said I looked like Mother. Nevertheless, there was a distance between Emma and us children. She wasn't the kind of mother into whose arms we rushed; she didn't grab and tickle us or laugh out loud and play with us. She rarely hugged, kissed, or showed her affection, but I believe she loved us.

One Christmas, when I was perhaps four years old, I dropped my brand-new china doll and the head smashed to pieces. I remember the sobs that wracked me as I looked at Mother and Daddy, as first one and then the other hugged, patted, and tried to console me. "Santa Claus will just have to get you a new doll," Daddy said. "We'll see if he can't get one tomorrow." Their reassurance lifted the grief as Mother swept up the broken pieces. At that moment, I sensed their love for me.

Another time, so sick I didn't come to dinner, I crawled up in a chair. "Where's Ruby?" I heard her ask. Then she came in the living room, touching my forehead with her cheek as she picked me up and carried me to her bed. I must have had a fever. I stood watching as she cleaned the vomit from me and the bed, and changed my clothes. I put my arm around her neck and she helped me back to bed.

One day, LaVerne and I were playing with our tea set near a chair where she sat sewing. We were pretending we had company. I heard her laugh; then she got up and brought us some goodies, which she put in our teacups.

Emma was a good mother. She saw to it that we went to Sunday School and church at Mother Zion A.M.E. She read to us, introduced us to poetry, and encouraged us. At the time, we, like most people we knew, had some kind of piano in the house. We took piano, violin, and dancing lessons. She gloried in our achievements at school. When Angelina and I began to write poetry, she submitted the work to magazines and newspapers.

She was a no-nonsense mother. We folded our clothes and kept our spaces in order. Mostly when we disobeyed, she would report us to Daddy, who would whip us. When company came, before we could be excused, we had to exhibit some accomplishment—play the piano, recite, or show our report cards. My brother and I would play a violin duet.

Daddy worked as a waiter on the Pennsylvania Railroad. Most of his income came from tips. I remember well the times when he would dump his leather bag of coins on the bed and watch us count them. For some reason, he lost that job and worked at odd jobs from time to time.

One such job was assisting the director of a funeral home. He was to have taken the exam to become an undertaker himself, but confusion about the date caused him to miss the test. Soon afterward, his youngest brother, Marshall, a prizefighter, was killed by gangsters. They were never apprehended. Daddy sobbed uncontrollably when the telegram came. We had never seen him cry, or seen Mother minister to him so tenderly. Subsequently, he took his brother's name, became Marshall E. Wallace, and returned to work on the railroad.

Emma was a resourceful woman. She continued to make ends meet by renting rooms in our apartment. She was also lucky playing numbers, and when she'd hit big, she'd rent another apartment in 2340 and sublet it to roomers. Several times she rented houses for the same purposes.

Hotels didn't cater to black people, so such rentals served many kinds of people looking for temporary housing. More permanent places, both furnished or unfurnished accommodations, were advertised in the *Amsterdam News,* and specified the kind of person being sought—married couple; single woman; single man; families with one or two children, no animals, no children—and amenities offered—kitchen privileges, breakfast provided, and so on. Sometimes just plain ROOM FOR RENT signs along with an apartment number would be placed in the lobby or elevator.

Among the famous people who rented rooms from Mother for their relatives and associates on short stays in Harlem, I most remember the jazz musician Fletcher Henderson, and his beautiful wife and daughter. One lady who was a friend of Joe Louis caught my adolescent attention because she had so many pairs of beautiful shoes. One day when she was out, I crept into her room to admire them and all the beautiful clothes.

CHAPTER 4

The Waycross Years

I don't remember my first day at school, who the teacher was, or how I behaved. It was only during my second year that school and books, and a beautiful teacher named Mary Lee Hall, brought it all alive. I loved it all because I thought she did.

The next year, my whole family—Mama, my sister Essie Mae, and my brother Kenneth—moved to Waycross, but Daddy still worked for Sessoms in Cogdell. And every Monday morning, he would drive whatever old car he possessed back to Cogdell to meet his men and his occupation.

Waycross was big, 15,000 people, and no whiff at all of what life had been like in Cogdell. The Atlantic Coast Line Railroad had a switchyard where big engines could be overhauled and repaired. Some of the most important black men in Waycross had jobs there. Waycross, black and white, thought of itself as a city of some importance. And it was here that I first began to dawn on myself as a person.

The first school I attended was Northside Elementary, and it was there that I had my first experience as a racist—it didn't last long. There was a boy in school who may have been Chinese—he certainly looked it. I used to see him at recess playing with the kids, running, shouting, having fun. He seemed to be friendly and all us kids liked him. One day I ran up to him, singing out loud what I had heard the other children sing: "Chink, Chink, Chinaman." I thought it would make him like me, as he liked the other kids. He looked at me, hit me in the face, knocked me to the ground, then went on running and playing. I never called him that again. And nobody had to tell me why. I knew.

Few of my childhood adventures led to fisticuffs. I was smart and likable, probably the teacher's pet. At any rate, I had an aunt in a higher grade who made it her business to look after me. Skinny little Florence Cooper could beat anybody on the playground, boy or girl, and often did.

In third grade, I ran into racism from another source. We had a geography book that taught us about the world and all its people. The chapter on Africa had no relevance to me or to my classmates. We related only to the references to Ethiopia, because that was in the Bible. The book was full of pictures, of Eskimos, Indians, Europeans, and, in the one short chapter about Africa, there was a full-page picture of a little African boy with a mouth full of teeth, and under it a caption: "Limweechee smiles." We laughed and made jokes about Limweechee. It never entered our heads that he was kin to us.

We played a lot, in school and out—my friends, my brother, my sister, and I. There was always something to do, or something to build. We'd go hunting with homemade slingshots, go fishing, and play games we made up ourselves. We used to build wagons from boxes, wheels, and ropes, then hitch them up to a billy goat somebody had near the edge of the city. In summer, we made popguns.

Most people had dirt yards, and every Saturday, some of us boys would cut some gallberry bushes, fashion them into a broom, and go out sweeping yards. People would give us a dime for our labor, and by the afternoon, we would have saved enough to go downtown to the picture show and see the cowboy pictures. Some were talkies and others were silent. Tom Mix was my favorite, he and his horse, Tony.

In my fantasy, I was always on my horse, riding to the rescue of some white girl, just like Tom Mix, Hoot Gibson, and Art Accord. Often these films had Negro characters in them, people like Stepin Fetchit, who were always the target of our ridicule. We'd talk back to the screen and join the white audience laughing.

On our way home, each of us would take turns imitating the white hero as he fought off the villains, or we'd imitate the black clowns and buffoons—laughing, laughing, laughing long and loud as a way of disassociating ourselves from them.

I liked the movies but not nearly as much as I liked reading. I read anything I could get my hands on, filling my head with stories from my books as well as from the neighborhood storytellers—Daddy, of course, being among the best of them. Yet none of what I heard or read could match the stories I made up myself.

Books more than anything else taught me to be a drunkard long before I knew how to drink. The state of drunkenness—that extended sense of well-being and power that floods the soul and makes it hard to walk straight, or to think straight at all—became a familiar one to me as I imbibed a heady brew of literary glories—and was equally intoxicated by magazines, newspapers, movies, wherever stories were found, all stewing around in my mind in a wash of dreams. And out of it all, I almost became a writer. Almost, but not quite.

Oh, yes, when I was a boy, my favorite place to hide was in my mind. That was where I found the magic. There, surrounded by memory, crowding in, always trying to have the last word, imagination bubbling over stories made up on the fly, and speculations on other unfinished business a boy might have, I would sit enthralled for hours, all by myself, swept along from story to story, a willing prisoner, trapped in a world that never existed. Reality had no say unless it pretended it was a daydream. So vivid was the pageantry that filled my head that I was blind to the rest of the world. There was plenty of time for me to be free and alone, which ultimately came to mean one and the same thing, with little occasion for my daydreams to be disciplined by the facts of life.

Somewhere along the way, I abandoned life in the real world—and most of the rules by which it was lived. And much of what I am today, the good and the bad, springs from that fact. In a daydream, there's no such thing as success or failure. I suspect that, in the final analysis, I am much of both.

To this day, I hate necessity as I hate a tyrant. I am too lazy and indifferent to separate fact from fiction, and will never willingly undertake it, except under duress. I am therefore a most unreliable witness to things that happen in time and space. Most of my adventures wind up as perjured testimony. I cannot practice recall without lying a little; improving the story, throwing out the unpleasantness, reducing it first to anecdote then finally to a gag—for which I supply the punch line. And that alone makes life really real. I would make a perfect absentminded professor.

Images, even now, churn around in my head like peas in a boiling pot, and are seldom brought to order. Ideas move about on their own business, under their own steam and instigation. My function at these times is to not disturb the traffic of my thoughts, but to quietly find myself a seat somewhere in the back of my mind and enjoy the show. I must have been the busiest—and certainly the happiest—little black boy in all the world.

In the summer, I would go out to Cogdell with Daddy and work picking up spikes. Daddy and I would leave Waycross in the early morning and drive the twenty-three miles to Cogdell before sunrise. Met by his crew, Daddy and I would then transfer to a lever car, a lightweight contraption about five feet long and four feet wide that had handlebars at both ends. It was operated by two men who would stand and pump the handlebars up and down, engaging the gears that made the lever car move. The two men chosen were usually proud, playful, and competitive; by the rapidity of their motion, they could move the car along at tremendous speeds.

One rainy morning, a man was waiting for Daddy with an urgent message.

"Kince," he said, "Mr. Satterfield say this job belongs to him, and if you ain't out of Cogdell for good by tonight, the Klan's going to find you and shoot you down like a dog."

Daddy let his raincoat flop loose in the front, so the man could see the pistol he was wearing in his belt. "You tell Mr. Satterfield that I said to come right ahead," Daddy said. "But tell him that when he shoots, he better shoot straight. I don't intend to give him a second chance. Come on, son. Let's go."

I climbed onto a box on the lever car, and off we went. Daddy didn't seem the least bit scared, and neither was I. I took my cue from him, like a boy will do.

Now, Daddy was brave enough. I have no doubt that had the Klan showed up, there would have been a shoot-out. But Daddy knew which side his bread was buttered on. And the Klan did, too. Years later in Valdosta, I saw Mr. Satterfield and Daddy sitting on a porch, talking together as quietly—and respectfully—as you please.

Daddy and I would stay in Cogdell till Friday, which was payday, then drive back to Waycross, rejoin the family for the weekend, then, come Monday, do it all over again. During the workweek, Daddy and I would sleep in a caboose, and at night, he would get out the Bible and ask me to read.

My job was quite simple: to retrieve ten railroad spikes a day. But Homer, the cook, allowed me to help him, too. Daddy and his crew might be working anywhere there was a need along the tracks. Homer had set up his pots, pans, and ovens in a shanty. At lunchtime, he and I would load the pots onto the lever car, then carry the food to wherever the men were working. On these occasions, Homer let me pump the handlebar along with him. And that to me was pure heaven.

I loved to ride on that lever car more than I loved my honor or my safety. Daddy, knowing my addiction, had given me strict orders to stay off the lever car unless he was present. I really meant to obey him, but the minute his back was turned, two of the crew, having a short trip to make, offered to take me with them. They knew Daddy's rule, but always promised me we'd be back before Daddy returned. One day, however, we got delayed somehow and when we got back to the camp, there was Daddy, waiting. He looked at me and I looked at him, with never a word between us.

I was so ashamed to have betrayed his trust that, with tears rolling down my cheeks, I looked forward to the whipping I knew was coming. He reached behind him, yanked up a little tree about five feet tall, and struck me once across my back. We looked at each other again; then he dropped the little tree and walked away. That was the only time my Daddy touched me.

As I grew older, sex introduced itself into my daydreams. Things I kept hearing from other boys and from eavesdropping on the older men about what was supposed to happen between a man and a woman became matters of increasing concern. Sex acquired its own mystique, and nobody—certainly no grown-up—ever discussed it openly. My cousin, Sammy Barr, who worked as one of Daddy's crewmen, once asked me if I had ever had a woman. I told him no. He took me to meet his girlfriend, who lived with him in a shack near the railroad, and told her to fix me up.

There was also an old lady from one of the farms nearby who, once in a while, would come to Homer and sell him a chicken, a pig, some eggs, or other produce. Sometimes they would go into Homer's cabin, where she would supply him with sex. Later, on the way home, if I asked her, she would supply me, too.

The most exciting events of the year always occurred during Negro History Week, as it was called then, when all of us students would appear before an audience of our parents, family, friends, and neighbors to recite poems, stories, orations, dramatic sketches, or essays. We had to master whatever text the teacher assigned. Then, when the time came and everybody was assembled in the auditorium, we had to stand and deliver.

My most memorable appearance was the time I had to recite "De Cone Pone's Hot," a poem by Paul Laurence Dunbar. In the middle of the poem, my mind suddenly went blank and I forgot the next stanza. Without hesitation, I improvised another stanza so cleverly that only my teacher—standing in the wings, holding her breath till I got back on track—knew what I was doing.

None of these boyhood peccadilloes, no matter how innocent they seemed, was totally free of guilt; there was a pervading sense that everything we thought or did was open to the inspection of God. I went to Sunday School every Sunday along with Mama and Daddy, and I read the Bible regularly enough to know the meaning of fornication, which was one of those sins that could lead a young soul straight to Hell. Certainly in church on Sunday morning, Reverend Whitaker would make very plain the nature of the punishment that was awaiting me.

The community, in many ways, shared a common belief in the wondrous way the universe worked. First off, there was God, who was always deeply concerned with and deeply involved in our lives, and deeply hurt by what we humans were doing. We were the major topic of His concern. Opposed to God in every way possible was the devil, old Satan, whose main preoccupation was trying to trap people into sinning so he could send them to hell. In the center of this gigantic turmoil was you.

The struggle came to a head every Sunday morning as I sat there, a miserable sinner, with Reverend Whitaker, who represented God, looking straight at me. There, with Mama and Daddy, and all the neighbors looking on, Reverend Whitaker would act out, step by step, the great fight God and His Son, Jesus, were putting up on my behalf. It scared me to death, while at the same time, it stimulated my imagination and made me feel important. The whole universe was privy to this knock-down-drag-out fight over me and my soul!

Another time I thought my soul was in the balance and Judgment Day was at hand was one evening just after sunset. Mama and I were hurrying along the railroad track trying to get home when, up ahead—we knew not from where—came a flash of light, sweeping across the dark horizon. Mama and I, not knowing *what* it was, wondered if it heralded the end of time and the Judgment Day. Every minute or so, the flash would sweep across the horizon directly ahead of us. Under normal circumstances, we might have turned and run in an effort to make our getaway. But home was in the same direction from which the strange light came, and that's where the rest of the family was. Nothing for us to do but grit our teeth, duck our heads, and plow on ahead.

Later we learned that Waycross had just acquired an airport and that the sweeping light served as a beacon to the pilots who might get lost in the night. We laughed in relief when we found out and filed the incident away with the growing collection of stories peculiar to the Davis family.

God was the head of everything in the universe, but His authority and His wrath were expressed in the Davis household directly through Daddy. Daddy was calm and reasonable, never forbidding or even judgmental. Take sex. He and I never discussed sex directly, but we did go round and round on fornication more than once. He led me from one statement in the Bible to the other, inviting my opinion every step of the way, like a friendly lawyer leading a friendly witness.

By the time we were through, he would indicate on the evidence that—fornication or not—I was a sinner. But everybody else was also a sinner. Only God's love, expressed through His only begotten Son, saved us all from hell. In my own mind, I was convicted. Little by little, I became aware that life and death choices always lay before me. I could remain a sinner with the rest of the sinners in Cogdell and Waycross, or I could choose to join the church, be baptized, and become a Christian.

The preponderance of the evidence as laid out by Daddy and Reverend Whitaker, plus my being scared of dying and going to hell, burning in flames forever—especially the vivid hell that was painted by Reverend Whitaker—pointed in only one logical direction: At eight years of age, when I was in the third grade, Reverend Whitaker baptized me in a pond beside the dirt road. And when I climbed up out of the water, I was a Christian, sworn to keep old Fornication as far from my door as possible!

My life in grade school with my friends comes back to me now in bits and pieces. I'm on a search for a little boy who never appears quite clearly, but keeps darting in and out of my memory—laughing, playing, having the time of his life; knowing himself loved and appreciated, aware of his own abilities as a student and the praise those abilities merited. I'm aware of having been different in the best of ways, of being accepted and even looked up to by my playmates; of being liked by teachers and grown-ups; of being pointed out as Kince's boy; and of the special, mostly inarticulate bond between me and my father.

I was the eldest boy and after me came Essie, my sister, who was probably—and deliberately—smarter than I was, which produced in her a kind of cunning. Then came Kenneth and Willie and, much later, James.

Mama was pretty and capable. She could make dresses for Essie and herself, and she made underwear from discarded flour sacks for all her children. Daddy smoked King Edward cigars and always owned some approximation of an automobile. He was not skilled at mechanics, and I never saw him with a hammer or a saw in his hands. But cars, in those days, were very simply constructed. His cooking was primitive and, I'm sure, without Mama's skill in the kitchen, he would have died early at his own hands.

We children were rambunctious and full of energy, noise, and laughter. There was all of outdoors to play in, so Mama didn't hesitate to drive all of us out of the house when she had had enough. We each had our own circle of friends, roughly our own age.

Family gatherings were always fun, and playing didn't stop at the dinner table in spite of Mama's commands. Daddy would say the blessing, Mama would put the dishes on the table, and we would all dive in and eat as much as we could. Daddy usually provided a serving of news from the outside world, although Mama occasionally led things off. There was always horseplay and laughter, usually brought on by one of Daddy's stories, except when the news was bad. Somebody was dead, or dying, or had been lynched. Then there would be silence, and Mama's special groans, after which would come some serious discussion.

The dinner table was the intellectual, spiritual, and social center of our lives. It was where the day was headed and it was about as close to heavenly satisfaction as a poor man could expect to get. Some of us black folks owned property, but not all. What clothes we might take pride in were reserved for Sunday display. No, the glory of every day was in every household's dinner table time. That's what living well was all about.

In 1929, the stock market crashed, and in 1930, I graduated from Northside and went to Center High. I don't think anybody paid much attention to either event. I know I didn't.

CHAPTER 5

From the Fire Escape

Mother didn't allow us to play in the streets when we were little. We climbed out the living room window of our apartment and played on the fire escape. From there we saw the world. Long black cars would streak down Seventh Avenue, and once I remember seeing a boy hit by a car and bounced in the air with his bicycle. Once some man leaned out of a moving car and shot a gun at the car in front. I understand that there were frequent confrontations between the black gangsters who lived in the community and the white ones trying to take over Harlem.

Apartment 24 in the Rangely Court is on the corner, facing Seventh Avenue and 137th Street, between Seventh and Eighth Avenues. Anchoring the block, Abyssinia Baptist Church is on the east side of Seventh Avenue at 138th Street, and Mother Zion, the Methodist church, is roughly in the same location on 137th Street.

Parades, marching bands, and funeral processions were a part of the spectacle and excitement from the fire escape. The happenings, the horses, the smells, the elegance, the music—all are part of the scene finely etched in my memory. From the fire escape, perched above the teeming life on the street, we could see far in both directions.

Sometimes Edward would get on the fire escape ladder, somehow jump down and go next door to the Sugar Bowl, an ice cream parlor, to buy treats—sometimes with money we had taken from the roomers' purses when they'd go to the bathroom—then he'd leap back up the ladder, and Mother never knew. We'd watch the comings and goings, wave, and talk with the children who were allowed out.

The iceman delivered a twenty-five-cent or a fifty-cent block of ice, carried on his shoulder protected by newspapers and leather; he slung it into the ice box while Mother held the remains of the last piece to fit in over the new piece. "Let me chip you a piece of ice," she'd say to visitors when offering them a plain glass of water, especially in the summer heat.

In the summertime, Daddy and Mother would buy bushel baskets of grapes and make wine in crocks that would be stored under the kitchen table. There would be the mashing and Daddy's big hands squeezing the mash through cheesecloth. The house smelled happy with the activity. One year, Edward got into the wine mash and was found passed out behind the sofa. Daddy thought that was so funny. Later, when the wine was "right"—maybe around Christmastime—a few of the neighbors would come over, and Mother and Daddy would laugh, tell jokes, drink the wine, and smoke Spud cigarettes. Mother never let us see her smoke. Much later, Daddy told us that on rare occasions, she would.

At the store, bread was five cents a loaf and a quart of milk was dipped from a big pail into your little pail. Pickles, salt fish, beans, and rice came out of barrels and kegs; chickens were selected from live chicken markets and dressed on the spot. Horse-drawn wagons brought watermelons for a nickel apiece, fresh-baked bread, pies, fresh fish, fresh vegetables, or a man who sharpened your knives. If the salesman wasn't too busy, Mother would call her order from the window, get the price, and watch as one of us went to fetch whatever it was. Sometimes after the salesmen were gone, it would be our job to scoop up the horse droppings that she mixed with the soil for her plants.

At the Sugar Bowl, we bought penny candy and ice cream, but we also received emergency telephone calls there because no one had a private telephone. That service cost a little something, though, because Jimmy had to leave the counter and close the store, if the owner wasn't there, and either tell the elevator man to give you a message or come to your apartment to get you.

Christmas was a delightful time. They'd take us to the armory where there would be a big Christmas tree, and we'd get toys and lots of walnuts. We'd have our own Christmas tree, too, for which we'd make ornaments to add to those yet unbroken from previous years. I remember when getting an orange, some nuts, and hard candies in our stockings was a real treat. We made gifts for each other as well. Especially do I remember my brother's rings made out of peach pits, hollowed out in the middle where the seed had been, with a bead glued in the stem end.

Once while trying to make a bracelet for me out of a tin can, he cut his left hand and two fingers to the bone. He was rushed to the hospital, where it took many stitches to close the wounds, the scars from which he bore all his life.

For several Christmases after that, his gifts to us became more lavish—roller skates, jewelry, handkerchiefs. Edward had begun to shop at Woolworth's—the five-and-ten-cent store—without any money. He had begun to steal. Seldom do I go into a five-and-ten-cent store that I don't think about Edward teaching us the art of shopping without money. Teaching me and Angelina to steal. We'd had some limited experience on our own, robbing the roomers, but more about that later.

Edward had a paper route, ran errands, and did odd jobs, so Mother and Daddy accepted the fact that he handled money. They didn't talk about the improved quality of his gifts, and luckily he was never arrested for his forays into free acquisition, so the opportunity to discuss honesty didn't present itself.

A strong shopping bag was a must, plus sharp eyes and a busy store. And, of course, luck. I was nearsighted in my days as a thief, so I must have been lucky in luck. But it made me nervous, made my heart pound, and made me want to pee.

One night during the Christmas heist period, I had to go to the bathroom. One aspect of life I totally hated was having to go down the dark hallway to the toilet in the middle of the night. One reason, I suspect, was the vivid memory of my sister LaVerne, who slept between Angelina and me, wetting the bed. Mother would sit her on a potty-chair (poor baby) with the wet pajamas tied under her nose and her big gray eyes spilling tears, as mother changed our nightclothes and the bed linen. Sometimes LaVerne would try to make one of us go with her down the dark hall. If we were too mean or too sleepy, the inevitable would happen and we'd all suffer. Mostly, Angelina would serve as escort.

On one occasion, after a particularly trying time earlier in the day with Edward and thief duty, night mercifully came and I'd not been caught, killed, or incarcerated. Just as I speedily finished answering nature's call and was standing to leave the commode, long bony fingers grabbed both my arms and pinned me to the cold tile wall between the tub and the toilet. With my mouth open wide enough to split the corners, I screamed, but no sound came. I tried to free my arms, but the wall claimed me like a magnet and wouldn't let go. Mouth wouldn't close, feet couldn't run, and tears didn't flow. Only eyes rolled around in my head.

"I ain't gon' do it anymore. Please. Please. I ain't gon' do it anymore," my tongue tried to say. Just then, whatever had me, let me go. I fell against the opposite wall of the narrow bathroom and ran back to bed. That was the first of several remarkable experiences I would have in my life.

It is ridiculous how far that experience, and a few others, have put me off stealing. I mean, I quit stealing. If air cost a quarter and I didn't have it, I wouldn't even steal a breath. Buck naked and broke in a lingerie shop, I wouldn't steal a pair of drawers. No lock on a box with a million dollars in small change, not a dime would I claim to be mine. Could be the finest man in the world who loved me and I loved him, but if he belonged to somebody else, I wouldn't let him touch me with a ten-foot pole. Even today, if I come home with a hotel hanger in my luggage by mistake, I've got to call somebody.

"Look, lady," a hotel manager once said, "please just keep the hanger. What's the cost? Three-fifty; maybe five dollars? Madam, I don't know who to tell you to send the check to. Just forget it. Let it be a gift."

"But I didn't steal it! It is written, Thou shalt not steal!"

He whispered into the phone, "Now that is a really complicated order for all of us 'one nation under God' people, wouldn't you say?" Click. He hung up.

This poem, included in *My One Good Nerve,* a collection of my short stories, poems, and essays, reflects some of the perspectives to which my thoughts on stealing have led me:

COMPARED

The pocketbook and body snatchers
Masked, desperate, terrible creatures
Sneaking through the night
Are as babies compared to the
Easy smiling, correctly suited
Thieves and killers of our world
Dealing through the day.

Daddy would leave early for Sunnyside, Long Island, where he boarded the train he worked on as a waiter and later as a cook. The runs would last anywhere from two to four or more days. There would be "layovers" and "double-headers." He worked the sleek, new trains with their Pullman sleeping cars, like the Silver Cloud.

When I was about eleven years old, he took me with him on a trip to Cleveland, where I met some of the men with whom he worked. I slept that night in a curtained lower berth, and the next morning ate in the dining car behind another curtain.

I was by myself, watching the countryside whiz by as I sat at the most beautiful table I had ever seen. The tablecloth was a dazzling white. The glass from which I drank was so beautiful; the water and ice in it was so clear, and it made a lovely tinkling sound as the train moved along. The silverware, the sugar bowl, and the salt and pepper shakers sparkled as if they were brand-new.

Daddy's coworkers were very attentive. They first brought me soup in an exquisite bowl, followed by little plates of food and then ice cream that tasted better than any I could remember. I was glad no one could see me behind the curtain. I wanted to giggle and cry at the same time.

Daddy came to take me back to my seat, which was no longer a bed, but two seats facing each other. So this is where he worked. When he used to let me put the sugar and the milk in his coffee in the early, early morning, this was the magical place to which he was coming. He brought me some magazines, and before he turned to go, I reached up and hugged him. I felt happy.

Mother sewed and I wanted to sew. I wasn't allowed to use needles, so to make doll clothes, I tied thread to straight pins and forced the head of the pin through the fabric. In kindergarten, I made a little jacket that I wanted to wear to school. Mother let me wear it. I'd hear her whispering to her friends, Miz Taylor and Miz Tanks, about various marvelous things I'd done; they'd laugh and I'd feel very special.

Miz Megan, the numbers lady, wore dangling earrings with little gold horseshoes attached. I remember watching the earrings shake and dance as she laughed and talked with Mother. At first, LaVerne and I would split peanuts just enough to pinch our earlobes and we'd spend the whole day being ladies wearing earrings. Peanuts in the shell were not always available, so we used to put beads on strings and put the strings over our ears.

One morning, as Mother was braiding my hair, getting us ready for school, she saw something dangling from my ears. Figuring that I was planning to go to school with the play earrings, she tried to fling them off. She couldn't. She almost broke my neck, though, to get a better look at what I had done. "Oh, my God," she said; then she ordered Angelina to get Marie Taylor "to step over here a minute." She came on the run.

Very late the previous night, I had taken a chair to the bathroom mirror and carefully forced two medium-sized safety pins through my earlobes and fastened them. One lobe was in fine shape. The pin was beautiful. The other lobe was red, swollen, and oozing something.

Nothing hurt, so the excitement and attention surprised me. Miz Taylor got everyone else off to school as Mother took me to Harlem Hospital, where the ear was dressed, and the whole side of my head, looked like, was bandaged.

No one could persuade Mother to allow me to have my ears pierced or to let me wear my hair cut in bangs. Once Daddy even asked her to let Mr. Spillman, their friend and a hairdresser, cut bangs to cover my very high forehead. She didn't see the sense of filling my head up with earrings and bangs. "Get something *in* her head, not so much outside it," she said.

But the word was out. "Aw, look at that. Ain't she cute?" Inside P.S. 119, my elementary school, while playing around under the coatracks where the classes lined up before the bell, two big girls startled me as I ran out from under all the coats.

"Come here, come here," one of them said. "She's so cute."

The other girl chimed in, "Oh, yeah, look at those little dimples. Come here, little girl, what's your name? You so cute." I looked up at them with my head down, warming to their attention, then ran to get in line for the orderly procession to our classrooms. But something had struck me. I knew I was cute.

Not only am I cute, I've got dimples, I am smart, and I get good report cards. Edward and Angelina say I'm Mother's favorite. I'd hear Mother or Daddy say to them, "Ruby wouldn't do such and such," or "Just look at this report card; look at those grades." Edward once told them, "Ruby doesn't spend her money on candy because she's afraid you'll ask her what she did with it."

My first secret piggy bank was a small jar that held four pennies—one was shiny; the others were old Indian head pennies. I made sure no one saw me hide it, as far back as I could push it on the ledge behind our upright piano. A few years later when we moved from Apartment 24 to 52, I recovered my jar and put it with the rest of my things. I remember feeling what I now recognize as a great sense of security.

Mother and Daddy praised me for my wisdom and thrift. In retrospect, I think what a terrible thing parents do when they put one child on a pedestal in front of the other children. Such praise always made me uncomfortable.

•

When Daddy would be gone for days at a time, one of Mother's refrains was "Just wait till your father gets back here. He'll take care of you. No, I'm not going to whip you. I'll just report that to your father." Daddy wouldn't be home very long before he'd have to get to his whipping chores.

Angelina didn't get many whippings, as I recall. Occasionally, he took his belt off to me and LaVerne, but it was our brother who bore the brunt of Daddy's fatigue and frustration as he'd lash into Edward with his belt, sometimes using the buckle end in his fury. Edward would try not to cry, but soon low sounds of anguish would come from the other room. The three of us girls would cry. Often Mother would go in. "That's enough, Ed," she'd say quietly. "That's enough!"

Edward didn't read well, didn't get good grades. Sometimes I'd hear Mother or Daddy call him a dummy. He might ask a question that didn't make sense to one of them, and the answer would come back, "No, dummy" or "Yes, dummy." He'd give a little grin, almost as if he'd accepted the appraisal of him.

A policeman came to our house one day to tell us that something was interfering with radio signals and the problem had brought them to our door. Edward and his friend from across the street had rigged up a telephone contraption and had been talking to each other. Part of the mechanism was on the roof.

Edward was always tinkering—with lamps, clocks, busted radios, bicycles, and so forth. It was only a small surprise to see a policeman at our front door on account of his telephone. He'd been wiring our apartment for a long time, hooking us girls up on the other end of some kind of phone system. It all started out with long strings attached to cups. When we finally abandoned the flatirons that we had to set on the stove to heat in order to iron clothes, and graduated to the electric iron, he would fix the cords when they broke, splicing wires and attaching new plugs.

After the incident with the policeman, Mother decided to take Edward out of regular public school and send him to a vocational school. There was some stigma attached; it was said that mostly black boys were put in vocational school. Nevertheless, he seemed to do better.

After World War II, and occasionally during the war, I met a number of men who served with my brother. They'd say, in effect, to a man, "Eddie's a genius. Anything went wrong with the equipment—anything, you name it—Eddie could fix it. If he didn't know what the problem was, he'd invent a diagnosis nobody had heard of, then go to work, find out what was really wrong and fix the damn thing."

I loved going to school. In assembly, we marched, sang, and learned new songs most every week. Because I was little, I suppose, I sat in the front row of the class, and stood at the front of most lines, as they were usually formed according to height. One day while Miss Peace was conducting the glee club, her eyes fell on me. She suddenly smiled, patted my cheek, and kept on conducting. I felt very special.

There were classes in sewing where I learned to make patches and buttonholes, aprons and stuffed rag dolls. I learned how to turn a hem, make a French seam, tool leather to decorate a purse, and attach metal snaps.

In addition to sewing, Mother taught us much about keeping house—how to iron handkerchiefs and pillowcases, how to make a bed, clean a bathroom, freshen woodwork, make patchwork quilts, and so much else that became a part of me.

"Everybody ought to know something about keeping house," she'd say, "not just colored people. A man ought not to have to marry just to get someone to sew a button or cook him a meal." The talk was that children in Harlem, and colored school-age children everywhere, were mostly being encouraged to become domestics and low-wage laborers.

At home and at school, I also learned about food—how to prepare and serve it. At school, I enjoyed the spelling bees and the music appreciation classes. Many of the skills I learned then have never left me.

There is this photograph of me on a beach, posing with my feet far apart, arms raised, fists clenched, forcing the muscles to bulge in my skinny upper arms. I am strong and tough. Look at me, it says. LaVerne looks vulnerable and seductive. Angelina's on the beach, too, both of them getting plenty of attention from the boys.

I remember one time when the three of us were walking down the street, and some boys were following us, teasing. "Oh-oh-oh," said one. "Sure wish the one on that end was mine." Another said, "Man, I want the one on this end." And the third boy said, "No, man. I want the one on this end. You can have the one in the middle." The one in the middle would be me.

I was short, skinny, and rusty. My fuzzy hair was usually up in braids that all went in different directions, accentuating my high forehead. My sisters were beautiful. Angelina was pecan-brown and wore her long black hair in curls. She curled her hair by dipping a hairbrush in water and twirling sections of hair around a rung from a discarded chair. The rung, carefully removed from the damp hair, formed her lovely curls.

I would curl LaVerne's soft brown hair the same way. Her big gray eyes seemed to change color—gray to greenish-brown. She could be described as "high yaller," and she seemed, somehow, frail. She was the tallest of us girls, so she would have to sit while I fashioned her hair. She was the baby, and I often gave her a hard time, bossing her around; I don't remember hitting her, but I probably did. Many of my after-school fights would be to protect her, though.

"I'm gonna get you, girl."

"Oh. You think you cute, huh?"

"You better git your fis' out my face."

"I will kick your ass off!"

Girl fights. On Seventh Avenue, between P.S. 119 on 133rd Street and where I lived on 137th Street. It seems that most of the fights broke out between 134th and 135th streets. Always on Seventh Avenue. I took some hard hits sometimes, but I don't remember being whipped. I only remember beating up people, fists flying at the end of arms whirling in circles.

I knock people to the sidewalk, straddle them, and punch as hard as I can. If a girl scrambles up, I chase and punch some more. Fists balled up. Huffing, puffing, snarling, and looking ba-a-d! Girls, mostly, circle around, egging us on, taking sides. I get a nosebleed now and then. Pull hair. Snatch and throw books on the sidewalk.

"You better leave me alone. I will tear your behind up! I dare you. I double-dare you. You bet' not put your hands on *me*." Out of my mind with righteous wrath. Wouldn't even know if I got killed. Sometimes, some grown-up pulls us warriors apart and stops the battle, to everyone's relief.

Edward was very protective of us and would fight for us, too. I didn't hit Angelina, perhaps because she would be in charge when we were alone. She was bossy, though, and once I picked up the piano bench and threw it at her, aiming to do serious damage, after she had turned her back on me during an argument and walked off down the hall.

I overheard Mother and Daddy talking about my bad temper. I had kicked at a policeman who had been talking with Mother in the street. Perhaps he had been warning her about something or had been impatient in some way. I felt hurt and sad to hear them say they would have to watch me because I had a "bad temper." I had heard people call me cute and smart, but that was the first time I heard anybody say I had a bad temper.

CHAPTER 6

Center High School and Valdosta, 1930–1934

Going from Northside to Center High was my rite of passage, my first step toward becoming my own man. In the first place, Center High had always been something special. Back in 1926, black parents keenly felt the lack of higher education for their children, so they built their own high school; they paid the teachers out of their own pockets, and they hired the best. Later, Center High was taken over by the state of Georgia, but it remained a source of special pride to black people.

By the time I got there, I knew that the purpose of my life would center around words and stories.

In the South, people tell stories at the drop of a hat. Everybody knew the stories about Br'er Rabbit, slavery time, and ghosts. Those tales were part of a floating sufficiency that constantly fed the community. My father and my mother told stories based on their own experiences.

One of Daddy's best stories was about a time when he was young and just released from the chain gang. He went to visit his sister, who was living near the railroad in the little town of Argyle, Georgia. No-body was home to receive him, but the door was open, as was the custom, so he went on in and made himself right at home.

He went into the kitchen and though there was no cooked food to satisfy his hunger, there was an untouched pound cake sitting in the wire-covered safe that kept the food away from the flies. He took almost half of that pound cake, as he was sure his sister would expect him to do, then went and sat in a rocking chair on the porch to wait till she came home.

After a while, an old acquaintance rode up in his mule-drawn wagon and, seeing Dad, stopped to talk.

"Good God Amighty, Kince, ain't seen you in a coon's age. How you been doing, fellow? What you got to say for yourself?"

"White man still on top," Daddy replied and laughed. They con-tinued their conversation until the friend just had to go.

"Sure is good to have you back in Argyle, Kince, but I got to be on my way. Be sure to take care of yourself." He clucked his teeth, slapped the reins on the mule's rump, and started off. Then he stopped.

"Oh, Kince, I forgot to tell you; your sister don't live here no more."

"She don't?" asked Daddy, his mouth still full of cake.

"No, she don't. As a matter of fact, white folks live here now. Well, so long, boy. You take care of yourself, you hear?" And he was gone.

Daddy said his heart almost stopped; he almost choked on the cake, and the sweat popped out on his forehead. A black man, sitting on the white folks' porch, eating cake he had taken from their kitchen without permission. That could get you killed.

He got off the porch and out into the street as fast as he could. His impulse was to run like hell, but the sight of a black man running through town at top speed with nobody chasing him was bound to bring out the dogs and that would be the end, for sure. He walked, slowly and casually, to the edge of the town—*then* he ran.

My imagination produced so many stories that I couldn't possibly keep up with them. I am still not a disciplined writer. I tend to work on two or three things at the same time, with no set procedure for tackling any one. As time went by, I became my own editor and in-head librarian, as I chose among the many contenders for my attention. I decided that someday I must write them down in a book, like other stories, or else they would get away from me. The way was opening up for me to become a writer, but something else of deepest import was happening to me.

When I became my own editor, I also became my own censor. I wasn't just a boy anymore; I was a Negro boy surrounded by white hoods, burning crosses, and stories that brought the smell of burning flesh. No longer could I hide myself in the safe and secret folds of my fancies. The outer world, where race and color were decisive, intruded upon my daydreams and began to wrestle with them.

I wonder, even now, who it was that first taught me the black man's basic fear of, and deep, perverse attraction to, the white man's prized possession, the white woman? Was it something Daddy said? Or Mama? Was it an uncle or an aunt who struck the tribal fear of God into my trembling soul on this subject? Whoever did it, did a thorough job. Without even knowing it, Mama's bright little boy was becoming not only a failure as a writer, but in many unsuspected ways, a failure as a man. He was, in fact, becoming a nigger—a development that, for the black man, begins with mother's milk.

One day when I was still at Northside, no more than six or seven years old, I was on my way home from school when two policemen called out to me from their car, "Come here, boy. Come over here." They told me to get in the car, I got in, and they carried me down to the precinct. There was no sense of threat or intimidation in them. I was not afraid; neither was I upset. They laughed at me, but the laughter didn't seem mean or vindictive. They kept me there for about an hour. No attempt was made to call Mama, who might very well have been worried that I had not come home from school. We didn't even have a phone at the time.

Anyway, going along with the white game of black emasculation seemed to come naturally. Later, in their joshing around, one of them reached for a jar of cane syrup and poured it over my head. They laughed as if it was the funniest thing in the world, and I laughed, too. Then the joke was over, the ritual was complete. They gave me several hunks of peanut brittle and let me go.

I ate up the candy right away and went home. I never told Mama or Daddy. It didn't seem all that important. For whatever reason, I decided to keep the entire incident to myself. They were just having some innocent fun at the expense of a little nigger boy. And yet, I knew I had been violated. Something very wrong had been done to me, something I never forgot.

The process of niggerization is always a two-sided one, shared by two consenting individuals, one black, one white. The price of consent exacted from the black person, however, can be his life, livelihood, and all that he holds dear. The ritual is never fixed or certain, but must be renegotiated at every turn. Is that what was happening to me?

But what about them? Was it mere serendipity? Or perhaps, without knowing it themselves, were they testing me to see what kind of nigger I was going to make? What were they seeking from me? Perhaps they were soliciting, not only my acquiescence, but also my approval, so as to validate their treatment of Negroes. The encounter was like an initiation, a form of hazing akin to the rituals of fraternities. We now had a shared experience and I accepted my part of the bargain.

But why did I never tell anyone? Perhaps even then I feared that such information would force Daddy into a confrontation that he couldn't win and might even leave him dead. I think my silence was derived from the fact that I was completely not at home in the real world. I saw no value in living in an outside world of mean white policemen. If I kept quiet, Mama and Daddy would be spared all the trouble that could arise for black folks who had a grievance against the police. I learned to evade reality whenever possible—a dangerous habit indeed.

The real world, no matter how my imagination finessed it, was strictly divided into black and white. The white woman who lurked in my imagination, breeding nightmares, helped me to learn how to negotiate the tricky passage between fantasy and reality.

In high school, I should have been transformed from a boy who dreamt into a man who took action. That never happened to me. There was no imperative to separate fact from fiction, so I never learned. Nothing and no one pushed me to decide what I wanted to do with my life. Dreams are fine, but they are always insufficient. High school should have helped me learn how to fashion my dreams into reality; not only to write, but to publish and produce the writing. It did not.

But Center High was not at fault; its mandate had led it in the opposite direction. Their job, of course, was to turn us into men; but black folks didn't define manhood in the South, white folks did. To them, a black man could never be a real man; all he could be was a nigger man.

The image of manliness that our teachers gave us was consistent with those virtues and values set forth in highly concentrated form during Negro History Week. Frederick Douglass, Toussaint L'Ouverture, and Booker T. Washington had been men. But our teachers knew that for a black man to approximate those images in the outside world was to invite damnation. Whatever our definition, it had to contain enough nigger to appease the white man's continuing fear and envy.

The dangerous realities of ritual lynchings and the Ku Klux Klan's reign of terror had an insidious effect upon the educational imperative at Center High. Instead of teaching me to walk softly but carry a big stick, like the white man did, it taught me to walk softly, but took the stick out of my hand. Reality was too dangerous, so I was encouraged to dream for the dreamer's sake, but not to take action, to be neither assertive nor competitive. The only way to avoid danger was to disavow that action, and in short, Center High prepared me to always defer to the white man.

I didn't know all this was being done to me in the name of survival by my parents, teachers, and preachers, and they may not have known it themselves. But in the end, they did what they had to do. And left me crippled forever.

None of these thoughts were on my mind the day I ran across the Center High campus for the first time, found my teacher and my classroom, took my seat, and answered my first roll call.

"Ossie Davis?"

"Here!" I was now a full-fledged freshman at Center High. That meant I was a star!

Meanwhile, things had changed profoundly with the family. Daddy, in the middle of the Depression, up and quit his job with Alex Sessoms. He went into the woods and dug up roots, which he put into the family washpot together with gallons of water; to this he added sulfur, ginger, magnesium sulfate, and boiled this concoction for hours until the whole mixture turned purple. Then he poured it up into five-gallon jugs to let it cool. Finally, from the jugs he filled at least two dozen bottles, corked them, and slapped on a label that read K. C. DAVIS' HERB REMEDY.

Daddy put the bottles, plus reserve jugs of the precious liquid, into his car and drove out into the countryside, where the people knew him. At last, he had become the healer he had dreamt of being all his life. No more a railroad man, but an herb doctor, out on his own— independent, self-sufficient, and broke! He never worked for a white man, nor for anybody else, again in his life.

It didn't happen all at once, of course. For years, he had been treating people with his remedies, which had been left him by his father. His tonics, teas, salves, ointments, and liniments were known far and wide among the blacks who lived way back in the country without access to any doctor at all.

In the beginning, his patients were as poor as he was. They had no money, but they did have pigs, chickens, eggs, corn, tomatoes, okra, cane syrup, and sweet potatoes, which they would give instead of cash. At the end of each week, Daddy would return to Waycross with very little money but with enough produce to last us for the week.

Mama kept the home fires burning. She stretched the food as far as it would go, and did some washing for the white folks, in secret, because Daddy didn't permit his wife to do such a thing.

Once, when Daddy was off on the road, and we had run out of food, a young white farmer driving a pickup truck came through our street. He had a cowhead which he was trying to sell for a quarter. Mama didn't have a quarter, but promised the man she'd pay him as soon as her husband got back, if he'd let her have it on credit. The farmer reduced the price to fifteen cents, but Mama didn't even have that. The farmer, disgusted, hopped back into his truck and sped away.

A few feet from our house was a little wooden bridge covering a gully that ran under the dirt road. When the truck hit the bridge, it bounced, and the cowhead leaped up and fell into the ditch. Almost before it hit the ground, my brother and I grabbed it and ran into the house.

Mama had us fire up the old wood-burning stove, washed off the cowhead under the pump in the backyard, half filled the iron pot with water, and when it came to a boil, she dumped in the cowhead. The tongue had been removed, but the cow's eyes—two pitiful eyes—were still in their sockets looking up at us as we danced around in the kitchen in hungry anticipation.

Mama added some tomatoes and okra, and cooked some rice as we set the table. Mama is a great cook, but she had never dealt with a cowhead before and had no idea how long it would take before the little meat left on the bones and the gristle would be ready for consumption. The head boiled . . . and boiled . . . and boiled—the whole day and far into the night—before it was tender enough to eat. It took us less than fifteen minutes to pick that cowhead clean, pitiful eyes and all, laughing with every mouthful.

That was one of the little miracles that happened almost every day to us and to our neighbors during the Great Depression, and I took them as a matter of course by the time I finally arrived at Center High.

At Center High, I could not wait to get my hands on my textbooks, which I read from top to bottom as soon as they fell into my hands. Wilhelmina Gaines was my English teacher. She spoke as if her words tasted sweet, and because of her, I learned the joys of listening to speech and language in a different way. She was tall, and brown, with long, black hair that fell to her shoulders. I think she wore glasses, and some of her teeth were gold. In her company, you felt ashamed not to be dressed as well as she was, not to be as clean, to smell as fresh, and not to sparkle as brightly in the eye as she did. We all loved Mrs. Gaines. We couldn't help ourselves.

Then there was Professor Jackson, who taught physics and chemistry, and coached the football team. He also played the piano, and often his rendition of "China Doll"—I'm not sure if Jack knew any other song—would ring through all the classrooms when he had a notion to play.

Jack was a different kind of man than my father was. He too was a leader; he inspired us, and the team thought he was God. But Jack was a part of the world of school, which is always slightly artificial and distanced from the real world. He wasn't as real to us as our fathers and mothers were. He had come from north Georgia to teach at Center High and usually wore a sweater with a big number stitched on the back. It was from him that we got our first idea of going on to college.

I was much too thin and not aggressive enough to make the team as a player, so during football season Jack made me the water boy and took me with the team when they went on the road.

I was also Jack's assistant in the chemistry lab. In my junior year, a friend and I distilled alcohol from a fermented mix of cornmeal, water, and sugar; we drank it and were promptly expelled. It was Jack's impassioned plea, as well as Mama's and my other teachers', that got us reinstated.

My experience in the art of public speaking had begun when I was a child in Sunday school and had continued on into Negro History Week at Northside. When I arrived at Center High, it was natural for me to join my classmates in the plays, operettas, and pageants staged by the teachers. I remember playing the "Melancholy Jacques" in Shakespeare's *As You Like It*. After that, I read Shakespeare for the fun of it. Somewhere along the way, I became aware that I could write plays just like the ones that we performed in the auditorium.

To prepare my homework was nothing; preparing to meet my friends and classmates the next day was what excited my nights. I lay down in gladness and woke up in joy. I'd hop out of bed, wash my face, put on my clothes, eat my breakfast, snatch up my books, and dash off, knowing I'd meet some of my classmates on the way. Waving, running, and shouting, I couldn't wait to get onto the schoolyard to watch the quick and wonderful unfolding of my life. I couldn't wait to see what would happen next and neither could they.

Little by little, Daddy's practice grew. People came to him from far away along with some of the people in Waycross. Of course, Waycross had its own Negro upper class, to which the Davises did not belong. Material worth was not the only decisive factor in determining social status, as there was always another way for a black man to be outstanding. Membership in the church greatly affected the way your neighbors viewed you. Daddy was a deacon in the Baptist church, and that meant a great deal.

Class certainly did not pertain to life at Center High. There, we belonged to each other—teachers and students—in fierce and self-protective confraternity. The fact that Daddy was an herb doctor who had no degree and no license was barely noticed. Though he was illiterate and had never gone beyond the third grade, he was entirely comfortable with who he was, and he was middle-class in his ambition. The only difference between him and the other big shots was that they had gone to school and he had not. He believed most fervently that education separated the sheep from the goats, white or black, and set about making himself into his own version of a businessman.

He managed somehow to get a trademark from Washington, D.C., to protect his products and his dream of someday owning a drugstore where his medicines would be dispensed across the counter. The thing about Daddy that remained unchanged was his great love of the Bible. When I went with him on his selling trips, after he'd treated the patients, he would often wind up after dinner discussing Bible matters with his hosts, who oftentimes invited us to spend the night.

He knew the book from top to bottom and could quote long passages from memory. Often to back up a point he was making, he'd turn to me and say, "Son, let's go to 37 Psalm, verse 10 and see what it says." Turning to the Bible, I would quickly find the reference and read it aloud to the people in the room, some of whom had come only to hear him talk. Far into the night these discussions would go on with me reading by lamplight. Daddy's mind was never very far from his main preoccupation—the King James Version of the Holy Bible.

Sometimes he would venture deep into the woods in search of roots, herbs, barks, and other growing things from which to make his medicines, me walking in his wake through the underbrush, carrying a grubbing hoe and a crocus sack. Daddy would talk to me and I would listen. But before long, his focus would drift away from me, and out toward the rest of the universe, private as a prayer, from which I would gradually find myself excluded. But I always knew how to listen, to give him praying space, to hold my peace in the presence of this deep communion between Daddy and his God.

And there was much for Daddy to pray about. It wasn't easy being poor and black way down in the backwoods of Georgia, with a family to take care of, and with folks in the community in immediate need of something, and looking to you. A sickness, a lynching, or some other sorrow—Daddy would bring these things to God's attention, and keep on walking, in such a way as not to be disturbed.

Daddy's therapy was simple and to the point. He believed that many illnesses of the body could be relieved by a good sweat to purge the blood of impurities, and a good tonic to put the body back in working order. He'd explain to the patient exactly what he was doing and why, then put him or her to bed, under a mountain of covers, and give large doses of his remedy, as hot as the patient could bear. Then he'd sit beside the bed for an hour or two. When the sweating was over, the patient would be bathed and given food and water, and would usually feel much better.

It was hard not to feel better if you truly listened to Daddy talk. Something about him came from the God we all believed in; his comfort was spiritual as well as medicinal. I've seen him cure ulcers with his ointments, backaches with his liniment, and troubled spirits by his conversation.

At the top of the black social ladder in Waycross were the Harrises, who owned a drugstore down on Tebeau Street. Both graduates of Tuskegee Institute, they had a big house and a Cadillac. Their son, Robert, was my friend and classmate. He spent his summers in New York and when he returned to class, he would fill us in on the exciting lives of black folks living up North. What we heard made us all vow to see Harlem before we died. He talked about seeing people in the flesh whom we read about in the weekly *Pittsburgh Courier*, a major black paper distributed nationally, or heard on the radio.

Radio was rapidly becoming all the rage. We had no set in our house; we didn't even have electricity, but some of my classmates did. We heard the music of Duke Ellington, Cab Calloway, and Louis Armstrong. Some of the better homes had gramophones, of course, and they would play recordings such as Louis Armstrong singing "I'll Be Glad When You're Dead, You Rascal, You" or Cab Calloway singing "St. James Infirmary."

In 1933, my junior year, Daddy and the rest of the family moved to Valdosta, about sixty miles west of Waycross, and I was left with my Aunt Bina, Mama's sister, while I finished out the term. Aunt Bina lived by herself and spent most of her time cooking for white folks. To all intents and purposes, I was alone, but I was about to need my family very badly.

Robert Harris was accused, by a girl in a lower class, of being the father of her unborn child. He denied it and his parents backed him up. The case went to court and Robert was put on trial. His lawyer, in order to dispute the girl's accusation, decided to call witnesses. Robert's parents persuaded me to go into court and swear that I had had sex with the girl. Of course, I had done no such thing. I knew that what I was doing was wrong, but I had no idea how to say no to Robert's parents, who also convinced me not to tell anybody, not even my Aunt Bina.

Almost as if hypnotized, I felt I had no power at all to control my own actions. They were grown-ups, the most important black people in Waycross, and as such had a right to expect obedience from me and all us children. But only up to a point. This was wrong, over the line, and I knew it. Had Daddy and Mama been there, the matter would have been settled. But they weren't there; they were far away in Valdosta.

I didn't know what to do, and so—as was to become a habit with me when faced with difficult choices—I did nothing. I allowed myself to be used without any resistance whatsoever, a dangerous habit that has followed me to this day. I closed my moral eyes, treating reality just as I had treated my daydreams—as if they had no consequence, except to be indulged and then forgotten.

I went into court and lied under oath, saying that I'd had sex with a girl I barely knew. My description of my transgression was so clumsy that even the lawyers laughed. Obviously the Harrises were to blame; they took advantage of the fact that I was only fifteen years old. But some of the blame was mine. I should have refused, and reported them to Daddy and Mama; but I didn't. Not only was I a dreamer and not a doer, but I was under a cultural mandate to become a nigger. A certain unmanliness was already at work, set up to guarantee my safety in a white man's world.

My courtroom misadventure affected nobody at all. It was as if it had never happened. We covered it up. I finished out the term, said good-bye, and rejoined my family in Valdosta.

There I met new friends. My sister and my brothers had settled into their new school, Dasher High, and were now the center of the town's attention. I was the stranger. In September, I registered at Dasher High, intent upon finishing out my senior year. But that was not to be.

After two weeks, some of my teachers from Center High came to Valdosta to get me. It would be a shame, they thought, for me to have come this far at Center High and not graduate. They talked to Daddy and Mama and arranged for me to return to Waycross and graduate from there. I went to live for the year with Mary Lee Hall, my first-grade teacher at Northside.

My senior year at Center High was anticlimactic. For me, it was a kind of celebration, as if I were a visitor. All I can remember about the graduation ceremony was our class motto: "Tonight we launch; where shall we anchor?" And, for some reason, my burgundy graduation gown was wrinkled. Mama was in the audience, having come all the way from Valdosta. None of the rest of the family could afford to come.

I had two scholarships, one to Savannah State College and the other to Tuskegee Institute in Alabama. I couldn't afford to go to either school. I spent the year instead helping Daddy, who managed to rent an ice cream parlor, where I was the clerk. Of course, Daddy's interest was in dispensing not ice cream but his medicines, which by now had acquired a reputation in south Georgia and in north Florida. In Valdosta, he was known as Dr. K. C. Davis, and business was never better.

Curfew was ten o'clock for most young folks in Valdosta, which wasn't such a hardship since there wasn't much going on at that time of night. I was out of school but most of the boys I associated with were not. Still, once in a while, hanging on the corner, talking, I would lose sight of the time and have to run like crazy to make Daddy's deadline. Mostly, he was away on business peddling his medicines and healing in one place or another. But on one occasion, Daddy was home, and he and Mama were already in bed when I ran up on the porch and tried to open the door as quietly as I could, but I couldn't—the door was locked. I had no key, so after mumbling to myself in prayer, I shook the door again.

"Who's there?" Daddy's voice boomed out into the night.

"It's me, Daddy."

"It's me, who?"

"It's Ossie, Daddy, me, your son."

"Ossie don't live here anymore." And that was the end of that. Nothing for me to do but curl up in the porch swing and try and get some sleep. And that's the way it was until Mama got up a little later, opened the door, and quietly let me in.

I had absolutely no ambition that I can remember, no desire to be anything more than I was, whatever that was.

Everybody took it for granted that I was going to be something out of the ordinary, and so did I. I knew I didn't want to teach, preach, work in the post office or on the railroad, or be a colored undertaker. I most certainly did not want to be a doctor and follow in my father's footsteps, though I knew how happy that would have made him. I knew I had to go on to college—Daddy made that clear—but where or when was not at first decided.

My classmates were busy choosing professions and schools where they could prepare themselves. Not me. I already knew exactly what I was going to be—a writer—and nothing in the world could have changed that. So dazzled was I at the simple joys of being alive, that I had no time or inclination to plan for the future. I didn't need ambition and I still don't. Just being alive was the answer to all my questions. The world was full to the brim with now, right now.

There seemed no hurry for us to grow up and find a job, marry, and settle down, and make something of ourselves, and above all, be a credit to the Negro race. We boys knew that that was part of the bargain; such aspirations were proper enough during school and the wintertime—but not now, not yet, not during those green seeming generous days of summer.

The year was 1934. Franklin Roosevelt had come to power and that event changed people's attitudes during the Depression. Our rent was paid, our clothes were clean, and there was food on the table. The New Deal had brought excitement and we knew—Roosevelt himself kept saying so—that things would soon be better for everybody. But there was a persistent shortage of cash. How then to get me off to college?

What I did have was two aunts living in Washington, D.C. If I could get there, my aunts could at least provide me with room and board. So, the family agreed that I should stay out of school for a year and save enough money to pay tuition at Howard University in the nation's capital.

There was no job to be had for a kid like me. We had to see what Daddy and his medicines could do. Not very much, it turned out.

In August of 1935, Mama took a ten-dollar bill, which she had managed to save, and pinned it to my underwear. She also gave me a brown paper bag with some gingerbread in it, I think, and a piece of hot sausage. The family gathered on the front porch to see me off. My sister and my three brothers were excited to see me go, indulging in horseplay up to the last minute. Mama overbusied herself, checking and double-checking everything to hide her own anxiety.

"Be sure you got the address," she said, as she pinned a note to the other side of my underwear.

Daddy sat and rocked in his rocking chair, smiling a little, but not saying a word. When it was time to leave, I went over to him to say good-bye. He didn't answer, but I think he shook my hand. What I am certain of is that, down from one eye, a single teardrop fell. I had never seen my Daddy cry before.

It was early enough, on a Monday morning, and I, of course, was anxious to be gone. So I walked swiftly to the corner, about two or three houses away, then turned and waved. They were all there exactly as I had left them, and they all waved right back.

And then I was gone. On my way, walking to Washington, D.C., hitchhiking. On my way to meet Ruby Dee. But many things were to happen before that fateful event would take place.

CHAPTER 7

Ruby's Harlem

Poverty comes with different personalities. There's that po', po', pitiful po': no money, no food, no pot to piss in, nor window to throw it out of. There's suicide po' when you roll on into the ocean in your Rolls-Royce after the stock market crashes and the bottom drops out. I guess the worst kind of po' is the kind joined to spiritual poverty. But unemployment and the Depression were systemic, broad-based realities; we all sort of belonged to them and they belonged to us. There was no particular stigma attached to being poor. Everybody was.

Angelina recalls, "I wasn't sent to stand in line to get the relief cans of hash. You and LaVerne used to go." She had just come home from the hospital, where she'd spent several months receiving treatment for pleurisy, an infection of the covering of the lungs.

I clearly remember being in some kind of line with my head tilted as far back on my neck as possible, walking slowly and staring up at a bedbug as it crawled along in the folds of a man's white shirt until my turn came in the line and a can of something was given to me. There were lines at a milk station where each child was given a cup of milk before proceeding to another room to get a dose of cod liver oil, which tasted sweet, as if mixed with molasses. Then we were given containers of milk and cod liver oil to take home. Mother gave us cod liver oil every single morning and castor oil twice a year.

Mother seemed always to be at war with dirt. "I can't stand filth," she'd say. I see her scrubbing, scouring, flipping on lights to squash bugs that sucked our blood in the nights. She would have us help get mattresses to the roof, where she'd spray, air, and whisk the seams. Sinks were filled with bedding and laundry to wash, the table covered with clothes to sprinkle and iron with flatirons heated on the stove and grabbed with padded rags. The sweat, sweat, sweat that plastered her hair to her face and dripped from the end of her nose added to the sizzle of dampened clothes being attacked by the heavy irons.

Mother frequently had nightmares and Nurse Dickerson, who lived in the lovely Dunbar apartments (named after the poet), showed us all what to do. We were to awaken her by lifting her head and neck together so her head would not flop over. My heart would race to hear the soft, but piercing cry mingled with a high wail.

A poem written by Samuel Allen, entitled "View from the Corner," begins: "Now what the Negro has GOT to do/I looked from my uncle to my dad . . ." That was typical of the talk in our house, too. Such discussions might be fueled by newspaper headlines, street corner orators, by poets like Dunbar and Countee Cullen or the writings of Du Bois and Frederick Douglass reprinted especially during Negro History Week. The IBPOE—the International Brotherhood and Protective Order of the Elks—was prominent in many parades up Seventh Avenue. Every year they sponsored an Oratorical Contest.

Mother, who had been an elocutionist, encouraged me to compete. I have three medals that I won in these contests. After two honorable mentions, I won second prize for speeches about Negroes and slavery. Finally, I won first prize for a speech titled "John Marshall and the Constitution." Mother hired a coach and we rehearsed at the YMCA. It was a thrilling victory even though my speech didn't have anything to do with Negroes.

Other events that fueled the talk about "Now what the Negro has got to do" were publicized by loudspeakers on cars and trucks that would often announce a meeting after an atrocity had been perpetrated against a Negro. There were protests against job discrimination in the stores on 125th Street, the main shopping area in Harlem.

Among my earliest recollections of Harlem was a community fighting and struggling so hard to get jobs. The heart of the shopping district and the center of much activity and unrest was 125th Street. Its largest store was Blumstein's Department Store. Mrs. Blumstein, along with the other merchants on the street, had for years refused to hire colored people as salesclerks or in any capacity other than as maintenance workers. It wasn't my first time on a picket line when the four of us children walked in protest with my mother and a group of people she knew outside Blumstein's. We were also given pamphlets to distribute after Sunday School, explaining the actions being taken and urging support.

At the forefront, organizing the protests were some clergy; socially prominent women, like Mrs. Marion Day; Mr. L. A. Austin, who may have been related to our landlord; Arthur Reid, a relative of our family doctor, I believe; and Ida Kemp, a well-respected activist in Harlem and citywide politics. Their efforts were not always supported and understood by some of the clergy and other members of the community.

A pamphlet issued by the newly formed Harlem Labor Union stated, "Nationalistic women and men from Lenox Avenue, unselfishly dragged picket signs in fair weather and foul, and a head whipping squad showed Negroes, who insisted on buying in Blumstein, the error of their ways." The Harlem Labor Union kept on with the fight. Street corner speakers and the press worked hard to educate the community about what was at stake.

It seems incredible now that the pawnshops, restaurants, clothing and shoe stores, and jewelry stores had refused to hire people living in the community, and that the people accepted the exclusion and continued to patronize those stores. Shopping at Blumstein's used to be the highlight of a Saturday afternoon on 125th Street. I missed going there. It was the first store targeted, however. It complied only after great pressure, and remained off limits to us for a very long time.

The major labor unions reluctantly got involved, mostly because they wanted to block the existence of the independent Harlem Labor Union, and they later succeeded in destroying it by forcing its members to join the CIO. I believe that the Harlem Merchants Association came into existence about that time.

I remember the excitement in 1935 following what was called a riot. I don't remember the details, except that it had been preceded by voices from loudspeakers up and down Seventh Avenue, repeating, "Don't buy where you can't work!"

Harlem uprisings occurred from time to time, instigated deliberately, it was said, to make some political point, to increase the sale of newspapers in the summertime, to allow the community to vent its resentment of injustices, or as a smoke screen for some white folks' skulduggery. At any rate, at such times of riot, the tension index went up. People were injured and some were killed.

I think I always knew that if you were a Negro, you couldn't own or work in stores on 125th Street, that you had to sit in the back of the bus in the South, and that you had to ride on the trains in the Jim Crow section, behind the engine.

Sometimes Mother would stop and we'd listen to speeches on street corners. There were Garveyites, Communists, and Holy Rollers, among many others. Whatever the topic—Jesus, the government, Judgment Day, Negroes, or the wickedness of white folks—the speeches were highly emotional. Sometimes the listeners would argue and dispute among themselves or with the speaker. Occasionally it would get violent.

Once, from the fire escape, I saw a policeman hold a man up by the collar and head-whip him with his billy club. The man held one arm over his head and the other one flailed in the air trying to avert the blows. I was transfixed and watched until the cop dragged him against the wall of the funeral parlor and walked off.

I would have other transfixions in my life where I would stare at images, people, or objects until they seemed to etch themselves into my soul to stay with me always. One day, in the *Amsterdam News* or *Pittsburgh Courier,* there was a photograph, now a classic, of two young men who had been lynched. In it, white people were gathered around, some looking up at the hanging corpses with expressions of wonder, glee, or anger. A few looked sad. There was an inset of another young man tied like an animal, faceup, lying horizontally over what had been a fire; he had been tarred, feathered, and horribly burned. On another day, there was a drawing of three people who had been hanged—one was a woman whose belly had been slit open and the unborn baby was hanging out.

These images were connected with the talk about "what the Negro has got to do," the talk about rallies and raising money, about folks hiding out, and my own father trying to get train fare together for some man who had come to our house in the middle of the night.

That night, lights came on and there was much scurrying around. We children were told, "Just go on back to sleep." There were whispers and drawers opening; Mother making coffee. Mother, Daddy, and the stranger tiptoeing down the hall, then the sound of the front door opening and closing. The lights were quickly turned off as Mother and Daddy whispered, "Go back to bed." Years 1ater, Daddy told us the man was a cousin escaping a hanging because it was said that he had killed somebody.

The photographs and drawings broke through all the talk and spoke to me in deeply personal ways. I felt such anguish for the people killed with hands tied behind them, whose heads were oddly angled, as their feet hung in the air; for those who were burned alive, and for the babies who had been stomped.

From hiding four pennies behind the piano, I became a hoarder of secret funds that I might need for myself, a relative, or a friend in the middle of the night. As I grew older, I became a stasher of survival stuff—water, beans, millet, canned goods, first-aid items, and cooking and lighting paraphernalia. I daydreamed of secret hiding places equipped with protection mechanisms including guns and pepper spray for bloodhounds and traps for rats. I put aside stuff to pawn in case flight led to foreign soil where dollars wouldn't cut it.

In the two houses Ossie and I bought, I located spaces that could be walled up from the inside or the outside with undetectable breathing outlets—my secret walls. When the children got old enough, I left notes telling them where various necessities could be found in case they were home or could get home to effect a happy ending to some Mission Impossible event.

I wanted my children, and now I want my grandchildren, to realize that being a Negro can be a dangerous, scary, unpredictable affair. I want us all to be determined that no one will split our bellies open, burn us alive, or cut our bodies down from some tree.

There came a time when diligence and determination couldn't make up for unpaid bills and lack of jobs. One by one, Mother's rental properties were forfeited. Daddy wasn't doing well on the road and we became delinquent in our rent. Mother would send us to answer the doorbell and we were to ask, "Who is it?" If it was the landlord or an expected bill collector, we were to say, "I'm sorry, but my mother's not in." We began to receive dispossess notices, which ordered us to vacate the premises by a given date.

Mr. Austin was one of the black landlords who invested in Harlem when the whites for whom the area was intended didn't want to move so far uptown. A man from the West Indies, he seemed to like our family and to understand something about Mother that pleased him.

Once when we were several months behind in our rent, and the final eviction notice was upon us, Mr. Austin made an appointment with Mother and Daddy, but Daddy couldn't be home at the time. Angelina and I were practicing a piano duet when Mother led him down the hall to the living room. Mother told us that we could be excused, but Mr. Austin insisted that we keep playing and he stood in the doorway until we finished. As we were leaving the room, I almost knocked over a little lamp that was next to the piano. Mother kept the lamp from tumbling over, at the same time offering Mr. Austin a seat, and explaining that Edward had made the lamp, that he was quite good with handicrafts and electrical work, too.

"I've got to go along," he said. "I only want to be sure you know how serious the situation is. You put me in a very bad position."

From the kitchen, where we were all huddled, we heard Mother say, "I'll be making another payment as soon as my husband returns next week from this trip."

"I'm afraid I can't take any more payments. It's well past time for full payment of all that is owed, Mrs. Wallace."

As they continued down the hall, she pleaded, "I hope you can see your way clear to give me two more weeks. In two weeks, we'll be able to do just that. In full."

We heard the door close and Mother came back up the hall. She blew her nose in a white handkerchief as she ushered us back to the living room.

"Go on, go on. Finish practicing," she said. Angelina and I went back to the duet, looking sheepishly at Mother because we could see her nose was red. We'd never seen her cry.

A few days later, we saw her cry again after Edward brought her a letter that had been stuck under the door. While she was reading it, she uttered noises that sounded something like her nightmares. She kept saying, "Oh, ho Jesus! Thank you! Thank you, Jesus! Oh, ho Jesus! Thank you! Thank you, Jesus!"

That same night, Daddy came home and she showed him the letter. I guess they thought we were asleep. He hugged her and said, "That's a good man; that Mr. Austin is a good man." Our landlord had told Mr. and Mrs. Wallace that they didn't have to pay the past three months' rent. Then they talked and talked about "what we need to do now is . . . ." Mother said, "We can't go through this anymore, Ed."

"Believe me, you won't have to, baby. Longest day I got to live, I promise you that," Daddy said.

Mother tiptoed to the kitchen where Edward slept, then back through the living room where we three girls slept. She had two glasses in her hand. We heard them pouring up some of the last year's wine they had made. Daddy tamped the cork back in the bottle. The last thing I heard was the sound of two glasses clinked together.

Later I thought about Mother's threats to her tenants when they couldn't or didn't pay the rent, and the advice from her friends, "Well,

Emma, you're just too good. You're just going to have to put them out. Get the sheriff and evict them." There was much talk about So-and-so, who had just got set out in the street. Mother would say to her tenants, "How do you expect me to pay my bills if you strut around owing me?" The fact is, for all the good luck Mother had with playing numbers and securing properties, she lost them all. Hard times stomped down all over Harlem. And to paraphrase, "Wasn't for hard luck, a whole lot of people wouldn't have no luck at all."

I don't remember Mother ever putting anybody out, but it was being done all over Harlem. Sofas, mattresses, cribs, tables, chairs, rugs, pianos, pots and pans, books, shoes, and clothes—sitting on the sidewalks, right outside our building on Seventh Avenue, on Eighth Avenue, Lenox—any avenue you can name. People were thrown out in the street in the rain, in the snow, in the boiling sun. Streets bloomed with people's belongings.

If you were lucky, there would be somebody to shoo off the thieves; maybe even a stranger would spread an oilcloth over as much as it could cover. If you were lucky, the protection would consist of a painter's drop cloth; it was bigger. If you were smart, there'd be a vehicle to collect the stuff and put it all in storage before it hit the ground. I heard, for some people, it was too much. Some people took a look at their life's accumulation of worldly goods, and went mad, or hit the bricks and never looked back.

I remember staring at those monuments to poverty and feeling my heart hurt—wishing and daydreaming about what I could do. Feeling nervous and very thankful, I said to myself, "Wouldn't be for Mr. Austin, we could have been set out in the streets, too."

Our school was named for the author of *Uncle Tom's Cabin,* Harriet Beecher Stowe Junior High, Public School 136. All girls, we wore white middy blouses, blue skirts, and blue, red, or black ties, depending on your grade level. Blouses were worn over the skirt, loose, knotted on the ends or inside; short sleeves, long sleeves; dingy, blinding white, starched to cut, or rough dry. The navy blue skirts could boast of almost as much variety—pleated, plain, shiny, pilly, cotton, wool, well hung, or lopsided. Ties, too, could vary: bows, strings, scarves, or hanging triangles. Each morning or evening, little time was spent deciding what to wear.

When graduation day arrived, we wore white middy blouses and skirts with black ties, and added black shoes and stockings. Paul Spillman, the hairdresser, had fixed my hair so that my high forehead felt naked. Somebody took a photograph, which I saw later, and in it I was forcing a little smile and clutching my diploma. I didn't look happy.

The diploma, for me and my friends, meant that we wouldn't be walking to school anymore. We would be taking the subway every day to someplace else. I and my friends—Carlotta Henderson, Barbara Smith, Mary Harrison, Jean Piper, Winifred Murray, and Carolyn Johnson—had been accepted into Hunter College High School. We'd be leaving home.

We had an inkling, but we really didn't know yet how much Harlem was home; was where we belonged; where we knew and were known in return; where we felt most alive; where, if need be, *somebody had to take us in.* Harlem defined us, claiming our consciousness and, I suspect, our subconsciousness. It was the place where pain was understood without explanation; where joy was an undercurrent when it wasn't out loud and raucous; where spirit was tested, and knowledge grew up through cement; where danger got its pulse and peace passed understanding. Overcoming was the name of the game. We plunged into the hot middle of things when picking around the cool edges got tiresome. There we could holler on the street corner without necessarily getting locked up; ideas could find wings and maybe fly. There love was perched to refuel on redemption.

In Harlem, the gangsters, after their fashion, looked after the neighborhoods where they lived and sent their children to school until Dutch Schultz and the Cosa Nostra bumped them off and left the streets exposed. It was where the pimps, politicians, and crooks counted on the guilelessness and the yearning, the trust and the hope of the people.

Right then, though, the diploma meant that it was time to get out of the house, and to acquaint our lungs and our brains with a different kind of air.

I had not grown up thinking of Harlem as a "ghetto" or "slum." I didn't know those words. I didn't even think of it as an enclave of segregation, despite all the evidence of brutality and injustice that noisied up the atmosphere and people's lives.

Many years were to pass before I learned how many people had joined forces to split the cocoon that sent us nine wriggling, wide-eyed girls out of Harlem and into the big ol' white world and other wider definitions of ourselves.

Most of the girls who graduated from junior high schools in neighborhoods like Harlem went to Julia Richmond, Wadleigh, or to industrial or commercial high schools. They were good schools, but they didn't offer the demanding academic curriculum; nor did they have Hunter High School's reputation for providing direct access to Hunter College.

It so happened, however, that Mrs. Madelyn Henderson, the mother of my friend, Carlotta, felt that the children of Harlem were being shortchanged. She had a master's degree in clinical psychology and taught mentally challenged children in the Little Italy section of New York City. Although fair-skinned, she never denied being black, but her associates considered her to be one of them, and so she often fielded slurs and innuendos about colored people. Active in the NAACP and the Urban League, she would form a group of children and take them downtown to solicit memberships and donations on the streets. Small wonder that she became president of the Parent Teacher Association at P.S. 136.

The fact that inner-city children were being shunted to less demanding schools impelled her to do something about it. She encouraged teachers and parents to insist on the right to compete for admission to the best schools available. Why not make it possible for students at P.S. 136 to take the entrance examination for Hunter High, a school known for its academic rigor, excellence, and concern? Surely those students on the rapid track, who had finished junior high in two rather than three years should automatically take the test.

I was among those students in the rapid classes. My mother knew of the exams in algebra and English that were required for acceptance at Hunter College High School. She had not known that students at

P.S. 136 were not given the option to take them. She had taken it for granted that every junior high would be made aware of the exams. She was counting on it. She never said, *if* you go to Hunter; she always said *when*. The high school, in her mind, was a stepping stone to Hunter College, and my attendance there, a foregone conclusion.

Mother, therefore, was first among those parents fervently supporting Mrs. Henderson's position: Our children needed to be prepared to compete with students anywhere in this world.

With the involvement of the teachers, parents, community, and especially the church leaders, P.S. 136 voted to enter students in the Hunter High School competition. And so the teachers, some of whom were black, selected nine of us from the rapid track.

After a preliminary exam, one of the math teachers, Ms. Chitrarro, let it be known that we were deficient in math. Mrs. Timmerman, who had taught the rapid grades, had not been aware of the schedule and had presented us with the regular math curriculum instead of the advanced one, and so it was decided that we nine girls should stay after school three days per week during the ninth grade to be tutored in the advanced math. We were drilled and grilled until finally it was time to go downtown for the real exam.

Hunter College High School was located in an old building on East 68th Street. Two teachers were in the room, one in front and one in back. The exam papers were facedown. We were instructed to turn them over at the appropriate signal, to begin addressing the questions immediately, and to stop at the signal. My hands felt cold. My right knee trembled; I put my hand on it and willed it to stop. Most of the girls taking the tests were white. Barbara and I were the only colored girls in the room. The other seven girls were scattered in other rooms. As I went from question to question, choice to choice, problem to problem, a peace came over me. I had been prepared well.

There had been tension in the air at P.S. 136 beginning the week before the test, and it lasted until about a week later, when we received the results. Not only had all nine of us passed, but we were ranked in the top percentile in the whole of New York City! When I got the news, I sat riveted to my seat; I couldn't move. Teachers scurried out from their classrooms into the hallways to hug each other. They were ecstatic. They even compared Barbara Smith's paper with mine. Had we copied from each other? No! "Why," they asked, "was this question answered incorrectly? But for this and this, she would have scored one hundred. I realize that it is only four points, but we covered this. . . ." It was as if they were reliving a hard-fought battle. They tried to be reserved, but their joy burst forth like firecrackers.

I wanted to scream, run home, hug Mother, and shout, "Mother, Mother! I passed. I passed. Thank you, Jesus, I passed!" Later when I did tell her the news, she was pleased, I could tell. She smiled, went on with what she was doing at the sink, dried her hands, and said, "It'll make it easier now to get to the college."

In the fall of 1936, I attended my first class at Hunter College High School. I was enormously impressed by my new classmates. They seemed so very sure of themselves. They were well dressed, and they seemed to have everything, I thought. Some of them went on vacations with their parents in the summers. In the winters, they went on holidays and returned to school all tanned and glowing. I'm sure there were many poor girls, too, but I don't remember them. Above all, they seemed to know so much already and they were smart.

Among other things, we learned to paint and draw. Lillian and Barbara could already draw very well, and the teacher was impressed with their work. Once we went outdoors to draw a certain tree. I liked their versions of the tree so much better than mine; my tree seemed fuzzy and pale.

It was discovered that I was very nearsighted, and I was examined and fitted with new eyeglasses. My first night wearing them, I looked out over the Polo Grounds, and for the first time, I saw all the separate lights glowing sharply against the dark night. I saw distinctly the people in the streets below—walking, running, getting into cars and off of buses. I walked down the long hallway of our apartment and observed the details of the curtained French doors, behind which stood our upright piano against the wall. All this I could see clearly at last. The gold cap on Mother's front tooth shone. She had freckles and little lines on her throat, I noticed.

No wonder my tree had looked fuzzy. The miracle of the eyeglasses! From now on, I'd draw my trees, faces, everything, brightly, sharply, and realistically.

The fuzziness, however, crept into other aspects of my life and personality where eyeglasses were of little use.

"Men are just dogs." I don't remember hearing that *some* men were dogs or that *that* man was a dog. All the talk that preceded the pronouncement escaped me. But I knew for sure that Marie Taylor's husband was a dog because she regularly came from her apartment to ours, pleading, "Open the door, Wallace." The chain would be hastily removed, locks unlocked, and there would be Mrs. Taylor, sometimes bleeding. Mother would console her as she worked on repairing the damage.

One night Emile, her husband, had banged her head so hard against the lock as she was trying to leave that they had to get her to the hospital for stitches. For the rest of her life, she suffered with headaches and impaired vision. Sometimes the police would come, but that would only make matters worse. They never took him to jail. "Oh, that man is a dog."

"If I leave him, where am I going, Wallace?" Mrs. Taylor cried, "He swears he's not going to drink anymore. You know how good he is without that liquor in him."

"You can't go on like this, Marie," Mother would say. "At the rate he's going, one day, he will kill you." But it was Emile who died first. Marie Taylor lived to be ninety-nine.

Mother's niece, also named Marie, had a husband, Uncle Joe, who was another dog. He, too, beat his wife. Mother would counsel Aunt Marie and threaten Uncle Joe with arrest. "Make no mistake about it, if any harm comes to Marie"—we'd stop playing with our cousins, Gloria and Benson, long enough to hear the warning—"I'll have you thrown so deep in jail . . ." Then there would be silence except for Mother adding, "And I mean that thing, too." I don't know exactly how, but my father got to be one of the dogs, too.

~ ~ ~

Looking back, I realize that Daddy was just a kid himself when he became a father. There was no time for him to sow wild oats, to get to know himself, or to go to school for very long. From the few letters I've received, I believe he was a romantic who could have been a poet. From what he told me during his last days, women demonstrated sexual interest in him even as a young boy. I sensed their attraction when I was growing up. Women would change in his presence; their voices pitched higher and their mannerisms would liquefy. This was so even among Mother's friends, though she didn't seem to notice; or if she did notice, she seemed not to care.

More than once, I heard her say, "Love. Love—go on away from me talking about love. I married you for the sake of these children."

"Oh, come on now, Em," Daddy would tease, "don't tell me you didn't love me."

"Shoot," she'd say and push him away as he playfully tried to hug or kiss her.

"You mean you didn't love me just a little bit? Not just a little bit?" He'd make an inch measure with his fingers, and say, "Well, you coulda fooled me!" He'd laugh and leave her alone.

Then came the time in our lives when Mother began to accuse Daddy of "women."

"You and your women," she'd say. "Tell 'em don't be calling here for you. I'm not going to have it."

Denials and counteraccusations followed. For his part, Daddy thought he had reason to believe that the hairdresser, Paul Spillman, was flirting with Mother. I suspect they were just friends.

There was a rough argument once and Daddy hit Mother. She had him arrested. He missed work, and stayed away from home. She changed the locks on the door and wouldn't let him in.

"You don't sleep in my bed when you are whoring around." There was talk about somebody in the hospital having Daddy's baby. Of these times, my memory becomes crystal clear. Daddy gets a gun. We knew because Edward saw it. Mother goes to Ms. Buckley, a spiritualist, who advises her. Daddy gets in the house, scares us all, waving the gun around.

Later, Mother encourages Angelina to find the gun. When she does, Edward removes the bullets and puts the gun back where they found it. Daddy gets on his knees and begs Mother to let him come back. She relents and lets him come back.

LaVerne and I take Mother's side. I say I hate my father, and one day, he kicks at me when I'm on my knees praying. I suspect the prayer posture was judgmental, dramatic, and smart-alecky.

In the middle of one night, somebody we don't know is having a baby and there is some complication. Can Daddy come right away? Mother tries to get one of my teachers to help stage a running away from home. The teacher refuses, but at Mother's instruction, LaVerne and I go to the American Society for the Prevention of Cruelty to Children on 110th Street where we spend two nights in a long room with many other children. The beds are arranged in rows.

Mother comes to get us and takes us to a first-floor apartment in a house on Edgecombe Avenue. Daddy is served with papers. Mother wins a separation and custody of me and LaVerne. (Angelina has gone away to school in the South.) Mother sues Daddy for child support and because he is delinquent, he spends more time in jail, and his salary is garnisheed.

Daddy finds us on Edgecombe Avenue. He and Mother have a severe argument during which he accuses her of stealing his children. My heart hurts for him when they go to the door and I hear him crying, begging, "Don't leave me, Em. Don't leave me."

"I warned you. I told you," Mother tries to whisper. "I don't know how many times I told you, I just can't have that. You want your women. You need your women. They need you. Well, now, you'll be free."

"See here now, this time, I promise. I know I've promised before, but this time I promise on my knees. On the Bible. On my mother's grave. On anything you say, Em."

"Go on, Ed. Just go on. We've talked like this too many times before. Let me close this door now." And she gently pushes the door against him until it closes, and locks the locks. I imagine him still standing there.

When Mother files for divorce, some of her friends try to talk her out of it. "I'm just not like that," she'd say. "I'm not one of those women who's just got to have a man, no matter what. I wasn't raised that way."

We move again. Up on Sugar Hill, we live now at 938 St. Nicholas Avenue, apartment 38, another "good address," with white-liveried elevator operators and doormen. As black people move in, whites move out. The large elevator with its elegant wrought-iron folding gates is replaced by a much smaller automatic self-service elevator. Rents are raised. Roomers once again make Sugar Hill affordable. The elevator operators and doormen disappear. The huge gated entrance to the building is cemented up to accommodate a much less elegant doorway to the courtyard.

Daddy has another apartment and Edward lives with him. I don't remember where the apartment is because we never visit him. He comes to the house a lot. Sometimes he cooks, sometimes spends the night. Their relationship seems good; they laugh and Daddy teases Mother, "Told you not to leave me. You know you love me."

"You better get out of my face talking about love. Love. What love? Time for you to get on out of here, now. I don't need love. All I want is some respect. I married you for the sake—"

And Daddy would join in, "Of these four children."

"That's all," Mother would continue. "I've worked and sacrificed the best years of my life and I don't need you flaunting—"

"I didn't flaunt," Daddy would interrupt.

"What do you call women waking me up in the middle of the night? What do you call somebody sending me pictures of babies they claim—"

"Aw, Emma, do you have to keep rehashing all that stuff? Look, I'm leaving. If I don't see you for a while—"

"Wouldn't be any different from all the times past," she'd finish.

Through the years, he came to see her, sometimes at our house. They were arguing and teasing until the moment she died one July evening in 1970. Daddy cried and cried and cried.

CHAPTER 8

The Howard Years,
1935–1939

When I arrived in Washington, D.C., Mama's two sisters, Florence and Effie, opened their hearts and the cramped quarters of their little apartment so that "Brother," their favorite nephew, Kince and Laura's boy, might stay with them and go to school. Both aunts did day work for the white folks when they could get it. Uncle Leo, Florence's husband, was put out to sleep in his old Cadillac, not only because it provided space for me, but also as a way to prevent thieves from stealing his car. I stayed with them for about a year, until I was able to move into a room of my own, walking away as a boy will do, and never looking back.

A few years later during the early 1940s, they both died of tuberculosis, one after the other, when my back was turned and I was far away. I have no pictures of them in my mind. I only know that without them, I doubt I would have made it. I hope they forgive me and my carelessness.

As I moved about Washington, D.C., making a bumpkin's inventory, I was aware not only of a new kind of city with its impressive buildings made of stone and brick that stretched for miles in every direction, but also of a new kind of people, white and black. They moved along in a hurry, some almost running, not paying any attention to each other, and certainly not to me. Nobody took the time to say, "Good morning," to ask me who I might be, to inquire into my health and well-being, or to comment on the weather, as they certainly would have done back home, where protocol and good manners required one to at least stop, if only for a moment, and pass the time of day.

Just as in South Africa under apartheid, a black man might have been required to show his passbook to any white man who might have challenged him, so in America, a black man might be required to show his grin—and for the same reason—to reassure the passing white folks that they had nothing to fear. But something was different about these black people in Washington, D.C. They walked as if the white man had not yet been invented.

Early the following week, still gawking like a tourist, I took the Georgia Avenue streetcar, got off at U Street, and walked a couple of blocks to the bottom of a hill. I looked up and saw, "Reared against the eastern sky," as sung in the alma mater, a most impressive sight— Howard University. In a haze of sweet surprise, I was dazzled by it all.

On campus, a smiling man with glasses, J. Sinclair Price, seemed to make it his business to like all freshmen, including me. I was not the only southern black boy trying to get in school with no money or much of anything else. Somebody had to take us all under wing and guide us through the entry process, and that he did. When school officially opened, I was a freshman not only duly registered, but also possessed of a National Youth Administration scholarship, and a job working in the library every day.

I couldn't wait for classes to begin because there I was in my element. I knew exactly how to call attention to myself and to my brilliance, with just enough eccentricity to be charming. In fact, my being poor and different—and from the Deep South—gave me an edge. I had seen my Daddy use his poverty to make fools of men who were much higher up the social ladder then he. The problems that I faced, large and small, were challenges I was glad to meet. And meet them I did, mostly out of pure mother wit and simple commonsense invention.

For example, I had no schoolbooks or money with which to buy them, so I simply went to the Library of Congress after class, pulled up the textbook, and used it to do my homework, committing most of what I read to memory. The next day, I was better prepared than most of my classmates, who acted for the most part as if classwork was, if not beneath them, the very last thing in the world on their minds. They sometimes boasted of their lack of being prepared. Serious attention to books was for squares, dummies, and country bumpkins, like me. Some of the students, boys and girls, even had cars of their own, and that impressed me. It impressed me, but it did not intimidate me.

I was the first child in my family to have the chance to go to college, and I knew Daddy and Mama would have sacrificed anything to keep me in school. Still, once I got to college, it was up to me. I wanted to be a writer, and I wanted to write plays, so I majored in English, soaking myself in all the plays of Shakespeare, wallowing in the glories of the white man's mother tongue—a tongue not really for me, but I didn't care.

Reading Shakespeare, I walked among the Elizabethans and found myself at home. As a Bible caddy for Daddy, and as a Sunday School teacher myself, I knew a good piece of iambic pentameter when I saw it. I sensed my mission and began to find my voice—a voice that sounded like the biblical King David and like Shakespeare.

After *Beowulf* and Chaucer, John Milton, Oscar Wilde, and the Romantics—Byron, Coleridge, Wordsworth, Shelley, and Keats—were paraded before me as role models. I reveled in them all, but nothing about them set me afire like "Marlowe's mighty line," which became my poetic home address. None of them bothered to rhyme anymore, let alone write passionate sonnets to their loved ones. While my greedy assault on the kingdom of English lit answered my compulsion to read, in truth, I was waiting to hear the voice that would father mine, waiting to get my assignment from the Muse.

That same year I registered for a course in Negro literature under Sterling Brown, where I was introduced to the works of Langston Hughes, Countee Cullen, and Sterling himself, all of whom quickly replaced Paul Laurence Dunbar and Phillis Wheatley. No longer were the cowboy and the gangster the principal performers in my fantasy life. I became inundated with a new kind of subject matter in which the interest of my people was at stake, and I could only be a hero by serving their urgent cause. The Struggle opened a new chapter in my imagination.

I was tempted to try my hand at poetry, and on one occasion put a few of my verses under Sterling's door. He was very kind, but left me under no illusions that I would be the next Hughes or Cullen.

I loved the Negro poets, but we didn't really share language. I mean I never wanted their sound to be my sound. Their idiom, though modern and black, was not for me. The poet's learning process begins with imitation of the master poets. I couldn't have imitated their cadence and rhythm even if I tried.

It was only in the garden of the white Anglo-Saxon Protestants that I found my fruit; only the voices of another race and another generation were speaking to me. But not all of them. Chaucer, Spenser, and Milton were foreigners. They were talking far above my head and beyond my interests. It was the Romantics, especially Keats, striding off the page, like fairy princes, who stooped to kiss a little black boy awake.

I sensed the contradiction from the very beginning. They were very white, and I was black; and in the end, they did not speak the language demanded by the Struggle. But laughter was always there, looking over my shoulder, helping me to find a way around it. The great Romantics gave me access, but only Shakespeare, and Solomon, Paul, and David from the Bible gave me rest.

This was to pose a serious problem for the writer I longed to be in later years. But at the time, I was chasing through the orchard gobbling up every bit of fruit that stood in my path. I was going to write great language such as that, and I was going to write for the theater, and that was that.

It never occurred to me join a theater group, or even to attend a play on campus. I went to the movies, of course, but that was strictly for pleasure. I also discovered the Howard Theatre, not far from the campus, but that was vaudeville—music, singing and dancing, with lots of blackface comedy in between—where I first saw Ethel Waters, Fats Waller, Duke Ellington, Billie Holiday, Cab Calloway, and the Nicholas Brothers. I never thought of it as preparation for the life ahead.

In the end, it was not in the classroom that I did most of my learning; but rather in the bull sessions that took place on an almost continuous basis in the rec hall in the men's dormitory, or in the study hall. Those places were constantly abuzz with discussions that sometimes boiled over, but never erupted into fistfights, though often they came dangerously close.

Women, sex, and manly conquests were topics of continual discussion. Down home, we, too, had had these sessions among ourselves as we boys tried to fathom the proper way to deal with women and with sex. Our conversation had usually been secretive, with slightly pornographic overtones and an overriding sense of danger. But here, in these Howard bull sessions, women and sex were treated far more casually. The thought of sex outside of wedlock, on the one hand, and without the stigma of sin and damnation, on the other, was totally new and liberating to me. It enabled me to look at women in a new light. Sex might be indulged in in an offhanded manner, without so many complicated consequences.

Politics and social injustice would also come up for discussion: a lynching in the South, some outrageous act of segregation in D.C., or even what was happening overseas with Hitler and Mussolini were especially fertile topics of discussion. Somebody might show up with a petition for us to sign, or a manifesto for us to ponder. I was a good listener but seldom took part in these conversations. People who knew me tended to like me, to find me amusing. Not only were these verbal brawls a stimulating challenge, they also stretched my horizons.

In the South, we mumbled our discontent to one another, clucked our teeth, and went on about our business. We tended to end such discussions in prayer, leaving the dirty work to be done by the Lord, but here the appeal was to our unaided intelligence. Were we not men, like everybody else, and shouldn't we use our minds, our dollars, and our votes to change those things in our environment that we didn't like? Howard University students not only took themselves quite seriously but Washington, D.C., with its Jim Crow laws and arrangements, was a particular insult to them. They were angry, hostile, and openly contemptuous of their "racist oppressors." They not only spoke out quite loudly, but also seemed prepared—never mind Jesus—for a coming vengeance of their own!

There was a new movement unfolding right before my eyes, and I couldn't get enough of this new way of looking at myself, and at my people. It was mostly in these bull sessions that the Struggle into which I was irrevocably born began to define itself, dragging me toward self-consciousness in the process.

Another group of students who touched my life profoundly were the West Indians. They were mostly young men who had come to Howard from their islands feeling very good about themselves and their obvious superiority to the American Negro. Most of their parents were rich, and they seemed much more at ease with their wealth and family backgrounds than we Americans did. Each one had come to Howard with the purpose of getting a degree in some respected discipline such as medicine, dentistry, or education, and each one had a position waiting to be filled when they got back home. At any rate, they were not the social equals of the American students and formed a clannish group of their own on campus. Somehow I gravitated toward them and they were glad to take me, and a few others like me, into their circle.

The West Indian bull session was nowhere near as sex-obsessed as ours was and the subject of politics back home was one of its constants. Women were discussed, but girlfriends, mothers, sisters, and prospective wives were all expected to find their places somewhere near the bottom of a man's list of interests, and to stay there. The men expected to marry, and to marry well, to have children and also to have a mistress, almost as a matter of course. Sex and women were seldom subjects worthy of serious discussion among gentlemen. That seemed to be the West Indian attitude.

Whereas the regular bull sessions quickly deserted logic and conversational fair play, and wound up as shouting matches, with one opinion trying almost by physical force to out-shout, and hence overpower, the other, among the West Indians it was entirely different. Their bull sessions, in form, were modeled on the British Parliament. One speaker, for instance, might make a point to overwhelm his opponent, who would, by way of concession, express himself in legalese: "Nolo contendere," which means "I do not argue the point," to which another speaker might rejoin, "No, no, bolo contendere, milord, You must argue the point!"

I used to sit absolutely fascinated, watching their studied behavior, listening as the arguments wheeled and turned, leaping back and forth, point-counterpoint.

In many ways I became very much like the West Indians. I had a good ear, and could easily distinguish the Jamaican accent from the Barbadian accent, which differed of course from the Trinidadian and the Guyanese. Sometimes one of them in the discussion would turn and ask my vote on his opinion, and I would be flattered beyond measure, to chime in, often slipping thoughtlessly and effortlessly into my own version of West Indian dialect.

The undeclared leader of this group, the most West Indian of them all, was my good friend Eldon Stuart Medas. Of all the people I met while I was at Howard, Medas was the most influential one. I was studying English literature and enjoying every page, but Eldon had made English lit the basis of his lifestyle. It was from him I first heard of Oscar Wilde, from whose wit Medas would not hesitate to borrow. Eldon was also fond of Byron, mostly because of his decadent ways. He had adapted all the affectations of an English aristocrat, a perfect snob both in language and manners.

I was so fascinated by Eldon's ornate manners and amused sense of superiority, his wit and *savoir-faire*, that I became his most devoted and his most ardent disciple. For all his outrageous behavior, Eldon was a serious student and took it upon himself to further my education. He also respected me, never took advantage of me, or made me appear foolish. He never missed a chance to quote his favorite English poets, including Shakespeare, and made a habit of threading such passages into normal conversation. One quip from Eldon would send me scurrying to the source. In short order, I had read everything that Oscar Wilde had written, while Eldon lived out Wilde's lavish lifestyle. He carried the critical principles of Oscar Wilde not only into the classroom, but also onto the campus. He could quote Wilde by the ream, and before long, so could I.

My closest friend in all of this was James Fuller from Newcastle, Pennsylvania. He also associated with the West Indians. Our joshing and our patter carried over from the bull sessions into the classroom, where I was always a heavy contender.

I managed to land a job working in a laundry that operated just down the hill from the campus on Georgia Avenue, and moved away from my aunts to a room on W Street, which was within walking distance of the campus. I discovered Chinese food, and pineapple pie. Also, radio was burgeoning and there was plenty to listen to, even if little of it was black.

I was a student, but I was a boy still, and in many ways, a child. I don't remember anybody taking me in hand, helping me make choices, and guiding me to toward a specific degree. Academically speaking, I was on my own. Howard, for me, was an orgy of academic self-indulgence. I only took courses that appealed to me, with no compulsion to fashion my selections toward a degree.

I knew, for example, that ROTC was a subject required of all male students before they could graduate. Yet I had no intention of taking it, simply because it didn't appeal to me. Though I had been a crack student in chemistry and math at Center High, I didn't go near the sciences, concentrating instead on literature, psychology, philosophy, history, and, of all things, German. This was simply because I was captivated by a novel about German spies that I'd come across back home. Though I was having the time of my intellectual life, and made very good marks in those classes that interested me, l paid not the slightest attention to those that didn't.

There was no way whatsoever I could ever have graduated being as eclectic as I was, but that didn't seem to bother me at all. I knew I was destined to be a writer, but I made very little effort to write. Obviously, as I look back now, I was in serious trouble, but I didn't know it at the time.

All was not peaches and cream. I missed my family, especially my father, but I didn't know that I missed them. Even more, I missed the warm, intimate neighborly relationships that were the norm for life in Waycross and Valdosta—those personal interventions that were always there to feed you, to reassure you, and to sustain you. In a peculiar sort of way, Howard made me an orphan for the first time in my life. The family disappeared. I was not much for writing and keeping in contact with the family. It was as if I was completely cut off from my past.

Except for the West Indians, whom I'm afraid I followed around like a puppy, the students in my class acknowledged my presence only in the classroom. Out on the campus, we might as well have been strangers. I wasn't used to that impersonality. I thought being in the same class gave us a special kind of bond just like it had in Waycross. But such was not the case. So, in many ways, I was almost an absolute stranger up on campus. Many a time I felt completely isolated and abandoned. I remember in my second or third year, walking around the reservoir and seriously thinking about jumping in and drowning myself.

Long seasons of laughter is my natural state, but every once in a while the laughter runs out and I am plunged into the deepest pits of darkness and despair, which, with my natural leaning toward self-pity, soon become ridiculous. So ridiculous, in fact, I have to laugh. And once I start to laugh, the spell is broken and I am quickly safe and sound again.

When I first read Gray's "Elegy Written in a Country Church-yard," I knew I had found a brother. And there were other English poets who always made me feel consumptive, as though suffering and dying, when I read them. My imagination was crowded from time to time with images of my own death. I saw myself pining away, a sacrifice to some fickle-hearted maiden who had rejected my passionate plea. And I probably wrote some sonnets steeped in my own gloom and doom. Still, even these high moments of melancholia did not entirely escape my desire to laugh and make serious fun of my own imagined disabilities.

There were plenty of beautiful young girls on campus looking for a dying poet to be madly in love with, and I had but to see them to be head over heels in love. But it never occurred to me to invite one of them to the Howard Inn for a hamburger and a Coke.

The girls were sequestered, locked away at night in their dormitories. You might arrange to see one of them, but getting into the dormitory was a tedious matter. I remember one girl to whom I was attracted. She was studying to be a nurse. I called on her a time or two, but that was it. Whatever sex life I had during those years never involved a student.

Part of this reluctance to go to the limit with a student was due to Mordecai Johnson, president and father figure to all on the campus. Something about his courtly, kindly treatment of the ladies rubbed off on us. On Sundays, Mordecai would preach at Rankins Memorial Chapel, where I was an usher. I never had occasion to meet with Mordecai beyond that. But that was enough.

As far as faculty was concerned, we had the best. They were brilliant men and women—geniuses—who, because they were black, found little or no acceptance on white campuses. Howard was the premiere black educational institution and had its pick of the best black minds in the country. And so, in response to Mordecai Johnson's invitation, they flocked to Howard. Among them were Thurgood Marshall, Ralph Bunche, E. Franklin Frazier, Ernest Just, Kelly Miller, and the two who touched me most—Sterling A. Brown and Alain LeRoy Locke. For me, as they walked across the campus, they were an added set of heroes, altogether different from my daddy.

Sterling was open and familiar in his demeanor with a down-to-earth sense of humor that made him very easy to know. I took his class not only for the instruction, and God knows that was rich and filling enough, but also for the entertainment. He was a first-class raconteur with a pipe in his mouth, a twinkle in his eye, and laughter in his voice. There was a sauciness about him, and though he was never abrasive, he could sting. There was much about Sterling that reminded me of Daddy, so naturally I took to him.

Sterling knew all about John Henry, Br'er Rabbit, and High John the Conqueror. And there was also his poetry, which many of us could quote. His take on the black experience was priceless, and his criticism helped many of us to begin to form our own opinions. He was against cant, false pretense, and Uncle Tomism in places high and low. His laughter encouraged us to laugh, but also taught us how to be selective in our laughter.

Once in a while, some few of us students would be invited over to Sterling's house, where we would sit around in the basement and listen to his record collection. Often we had fruit juice and cookies, but no beer or hard liquor. Sterling liked to talk about his bouts with Wild Turkey, giving off the impression that he was a two-fisted drinking man, but I never saw him even take a drink. His conversation was a part of his rough-and-ready persona, something he borrowed from a hobo or a murderer on the chain gang—an unlikely image for a professor who had taught at Harvard.

Sterling was always approachable and a few of the students took advantage. In any dispute between the faculty and the student body, his sympathies always seemed to lie with the students. Easygoing, casual, even careless, he appeared, but something about Sterling, something quite deliberate, was always teaching. He seemed to know the ways of the world, and particularly the white folks in it, better than anybody, and he was always, through his questions and his explanations, leading us toward a greater understanding of the way the world wagged. It was Sterling who taught me that the blues were poetry, and that the stories I knew so well from my own childhood were first-class literature.

Then there was Alain Locke, who had received his Ph.D. from Harvard. It was Locke who formally introduced me to the theater, to the world of black drama, and hence, ultimately to myself. He supplied the one bit of information I had come to college to find, although I had no idea what I was seeking.

Dr. Locke had a shy and reticent personality with a little melancholy on the side. He was not just a scholar, but a Rhodes scholar, the first Negro ever. He was head of the department of philosophy and an art critic whose works on the aesthetics of African art and sculpture had appeared in the *Encyclopaedia Britannica.* All of this he took quite seriously, but he was by no means puffed up or egotistical. Rather, he tried to be fair in his judgment of all things, including his own worth, and he stood by his opinions to the death.

A bachelor who lived alone, Dr. Locke owned a four-story brownstone on T Street to which a few of his students would be invited on a Saturday afternoon, if they were lucky. I was happy on the few occasions I found myself among the chosen few. His house, in contradistinction to Sterling's basement, was a world of deep artistic law and order. The place was immaculate, the colors properly subdued but vibrant. Pieces of sculpture, mostly African, lay about in orderly profusion. Paintings, drawings, and sketches were on the wall. Books were everywhere, including a big dictionary that stood alone on its own pedestal, and large picture books on the coffee table. A diffident circumspection was in order for those of us who came in as his guests. We tiptoed around, oohing and aahing, instinctively speaking in awed whispers, trying to reach the same depth of communion with his treasured masterpieces as he did, always to no avail.

There would be cookies and punch, milk and crackers, and little cubes of cheese for us to nibble on while waiting for that precious moment to arrive—the moment that made Saturday afternoon so very special to Dr. Locke. NBC Radio Network had lured Arturo Toscanini, the great Italian conductor, to conduct the NBC Symphony Orchestra. Every Saturday at 4:00 P.M., a concert conducted by Toscanini would be broadcast over the radio, and these broadcasts had become the cultural centerpiece of Dr. Locke's off-campus life. On the ground floor, we students would gather around the big cabinet that housed the radio and listen to the concert, while he would go to the fourth floor where he had another radio console in his private quarters. And there, completely alone, he would listen to the concert.

One day, after a test in his philosophy class, Dr. Locke summoned me to his office, offered me a seat, closed the door, and asked me a question. I gave him my answer, in response to which he, in turn, gave me a life. He asked, "What do you plan to become?"

"A playwright," I answered, which surprised him. He wouldn't have been surprised if he'd known me better. I was so sure of what I wanted to do that I had never taken the time to describe it to myself, let alone name it. All I knew about plays was the fact that I had already written one in high school. About the theater—acting, singing, dancing, the craft of play production—I knew absolutely nothing. As a matter of fact, I had never seen a professional play. Still, I answered with every confidence in the world, "I want to write plays."

"You mean plays for the theater?"

"Yes," I said, emboldened by my ignorance.

He looked at me and a furrow wrinkled his brow. "Where are you from, Davis?"

"Waycross, sir. I am from Waycross, a little town in Georgia."

"I thought so. I doubt very much you've ever been in a theater."

"Oh, yes, sir. Every Saturday afternoon, me and some of the boys, we go to see the cowboy pictures."

"I don't mean moving pictures," he said. "I mean live theater with live human beings up on the stage, acting out parts."

"No, sir, I've never seen anything like that," I confessed. It wasn't such startling news. Live theater was not a regular part of the black experience at that time, anywhere, even in larger cities of the North.

"Well, if you are serious, if you really think you want to write plays, I have this suggestion. Go to Harlem as soon as you graduate and find a Dick Campbell and a Muriel Rahn. They've just started a little theater group. Tell them I sent you, and ask them if you can join. I'm sure they'll let you in, but that's where the work begins. You'll be writing, of course, but don't stop there. Try your hand at singing, dancing, building scenery, painting sets, directing, passing out playbills, being a stage manager—anything and everything. You'll know in pretty short order whether you've got what it takes to write plays or not."

This was destiny talking. I knew it was time to go. And I was determined to go, but I wanted somebody's approval beside my own. I told several people, including Dr. Kenneth Clark, of my decision. He responded, "How are you going to feed yourself? Pay your rent? Do you have a job waiting for you in Harlem?"

"No," I told him. I hadn't really thought about it. He warned me of the dangers of becoming a literary bum. No one except James Fuller thought it was a brilliant idea; he was so impressed he decided to quit when I did and go with me.

While I was stumbling around in my own mind trying to reach a decision, something happened that sealed my fate. I happened upon a section of the library where it was possible to play records, and I heard some music, the likes of which I had never heard before. I later found it was Mozart's "Concerto for Piano in D Major." I found a chair, sat down, and listened, absolutely stunned! After the student was finished with the record, I pulled it myself and played it again. The next day, instead of going to class, I went back to the music section, took out the same Mozart concerto, and played it again.

I knew about classical music. I had heard Toscanini, but this was different. This almost drove me crazy. I couldn't get it out of my mind. Soon Peter Ilich Tchaikovsky joined Mozart, and I found myself deep under the spell of their tragic melancholia, head over heels in a spiritual malaise that fitted exactly with Mozart's sad and magic music. These two great artists became my confidants. Something in the sadness of their music kept assuring me that Howard was no longer the place my yearning soul should be. I never went back to a single class again, but spent some part of every day listening to that concerto, and to others. Classical European music suddenly became an obsession with me.

Meanwhile, Fuller had told the West Indian contingent about my plans to quit Howard and go to Harlem. They were ecstatic, and proceeded at once to join us in the great conspiracy, instructing Fuller and me on the finer points of making it in New York—a craft at which they were masters. Every summer when school was out, most of the West Indians did not go back to the Caribbean, or if they did, they did not stay too long. Rather they gathered in New York, spending as much of the summer vacation as they could with friends and relatives in Harlem.

Medas was especially intrigued and took over planning our escape as if it were a major military campaign. It was easy enough for Fuller and me to get to Harlem. The railroad fare was cheap enough; the real question was how were we going to manage to survive once we got there? They decided, as Medas insisted, that we should throw ourselves on the mercy of the large network of West Indians there. Medas gave us the address and a letter of introduction to the Camerons, a wealthy family who lived on 133rd Street, who ran an employment agency. They could see to it that we got cheap accommodations, and more important, send us out on jobs.

The West Indians could be somewhat cool to outsiders, but they took a special interest in their own kinsmen, especially the students who went to Howard. It was decided, partly as a joke, but only partly, that it would be better if I passed myself off as a West Indian. I had the facial features to play the role. Also, I was quite facile with the language—the idiom and the lilt—I loved the way it rolled around on the tongue. So it was decided that once I got to New York, I was to announce that I was from Demerara, a small place I could claim as my birthplace since very few people knew of its existence.

We would save up thirty dollars apiece and take the train to New York on April 16, 1939. But history intervened, and we delayed our departure by one full week.

Marian Anderson had been booked to give a concert on Easter at a church not too far from the campus, but the church caught fire and burned down. It was then thought that the concert should be moved to Constitution Hall. After all, Marian Anderson was a singer of international reputation, as well known to the world as Arturo Toscanini. But Constitution Hall was owned and operated by the Daughters of the American Revolution, under whose policy of strict segregation no Negroes were allowed.

Once again, the campus came together around a cause. Eleanor Roosevelt resigned from the Daughters and used her influence to get Marian Anderson a permit to give a concert on the steps of the Lincoln Memorial. April 16 was gray and chilly. Marian Anderson had to sing in her winter coat, but sing she did. Among the seventy-five thousand people gathered at the Memorial to hear her sing was a large segment of students from Howard University, among them James Fuller and me.

I remember most that voice, that indescribable voice that held seventy-five thousand people in its arms and rocked us like a baby. It inspired us, calmed our fears, and carried us up to the mountaintop, the same one Martin Luther King climbed in Memphis, the night before he died. It was what Abraham Lincoln would have said, with just such grace and gravity, had he sung the Gettysburg Address instead of saying it. Tears, not of sorrow, but of exaltation flowed down many a face, black and white, my own included. It was for me an act of definition as well as of defiance, with its own salute to the black Struggle. It married in my mind forever the performing arts as a weapon in the struggle for freedom. It made a connection that, for me and for thousands of other artists, has never been severed. It was a proclamation and a commitment. I have been in love with Marian Anderson ever since.

Art among us blacks has always been a statement about our condition, and therefore it has always been political. The concert didn't change me, but it did seal my calling and bless the effort upon which I was about to embark. I was already who I was supposed to be and would soon be on my way to the New York theater to prove it. That voice focused me and gave me my marching orders. It reminded me that whatever I said and whatever I did as an artist was an integral part of my people's struggle to be free.

The very next Sunday, Fuller and I, with all of thirty dollars in our pockets, said our good-bye to Howard University, went to Union Station, and took the train to New York.

CHAPTER 9

Steps Along the Way

My Aunt Cassie and Uncle Walter lived in Washington, D. C., and we thought they were very rich. Every year at Christmas, Aunt Cassie would send us a generous check and one of her homemade fruitcakes. Uncle Walter was a bail bondsman, and they lived on T Street NW in a beautiful new brick house that they'd had built to order. They didn't have any children and whenever Mother took us to visit, it was truly a special time. We would have dinner in their formal dining room where Uncle Walter, a jolly man with freckles, presided from the head of the table. Aunt Cassie, a nut-brown colored woman, taller than mother, stood very erect, as if she had been a teacher for many years; but I don't recall that she ever worked outside of the home.

I was always one of Aunt Cassie's favorite nieces, and when I came of age, she wanted to have a sweet sixteen party for me. That summer, she persuaded Mother to let me visit by myself and sent for me. One day when I was there, a box was delivered to her house from a big department store. Inside the box was a long, peach-colored, silk organza eyelet-embroidered dress with a matching slip. It was a gift for me! She admonished me not to tell Uncle Walter she had bought it. I wondered at this because I couldn't understand why he wasn't as excited as I was. It was my first long dress and it was beautiful. I couldn't wait to get back home and show it to LaVerne.

A few days later, I felt very sophisticated dressed in it for my party, which was attended by some of Aunt Cassie's friends' children. They were an assembly of very attractive, fair-complexioned young people with beautiful hair, bobbed or in long curls. The boys, too, looked almost white except for one who was very dark. He and I were the darkest people there. It was my first encounter with class-consciousness based on color.

Before the end of the affair, one of the girls took me aside to explain that the very dark boy was invited because he was really smart and got along so well with everyone. The excitement of the day robbed me of sleep that night until almost morning. Lying in the fairy-princesslike guest room, I felt so lucky. All those beautiful people, speaking in such a mannered way, laughing, dancing, and having a good time—and all of them liked me. Even though I was brown and my hair had fuzzed up in the heat, they liked me.

Before my eyelids closed, however, I told myself that were it not for the fact that the wealthy Mrs. Cassandra Stewart was throwing an elegant garden party for her niece from the lawn of a gorgeous brand-new house, they probably wouldn't even speak to me. I convinced myself that they really didn't like me. Even though, years later, many people I would come to admire and respect would come from such "almost white" ranks, at that time, I concluded I didn't like them very much either. Why had I let such people think that I felt somehow privileged to be among them?

Though I was unaware of it at the time, this experience with "high society" was another manifestation of the divide-and-conquer mentality that racism encourages and foments. So many details of that day paralleled the world of the play that brought me to my first role in the theater a few years later—as a debutante in love with a poor but worthy young man. That party was a sweet and sour event that stayed with me a long, long time.

High school felt like a time when my life was shifting gears and moving me toward contemplation of the world and black people. Also, it was a time to witness and experience the disintegration of my family and to try to get to know some boys.

My first beau was the son of a friend of Mother's. I liked him enormously but at first I thought he was coming to see my sister. I couldn't imagine that this handsome man with the big, clear brown eyes and curly lashes had a heart that was lub-dubbing for me. Didn't all the boys pant after Angelina and LaVerne? He and his mother, a nurse who knew our mother very well, were frequent visitors. Sometimes he would take me to his house, where his mother welcomed me and served us cookies and lemonade. Soon we were holding hands and going for walks. My sisters started teasing me about him, calling him my boyfriend, and I really did like him, too.

One day, we walked to his house, but his mother wasn't home. We started in kissing and groping. Part of me wanted to leave, but my curiosity and excitement dictated otherwise. It was then and there that he harvested the cherry berry. "Whoever plucks the cherry berry," it was said, "wins your heart forever. You can never forget him, no matter what." (Now, what was that boy's name?)

There had to be more to it all than this. It's supposed to be mesmerizing, a bell ringer, a beautiful time in a young woman's life. All I had truly felt was some pain, a raging indifference, and great disappointment with the whole business, which I tried not to show. Although he still came to the house, my main ambition now, it seemed, was not to hurt his feelings. I concluded that Mother was right when she said, "A girl doesn't need to spread her legs until she's married, except to wash or to pee."

Relationships are not always something you learn about in school. I couldn't even imagine talking about sex, or about love, with my "get out of my face, men are just dogs" Mother. Daddy, I believe, could have given me some pointers, but I couldn't imagine talking about such things with him. He tried talking to LaVerne and me about boys and other doggy matters soon after she started to menstruate, but he caught the glance between us just as we turned our eyes heavenward. The talk faded, petered out with "I'm telling you, you have to be careful out here."

Having attended all-girl schools, I didn't know how to relate to boys. I was busy bragging about the heavy objects I could move and showing off my huge arm muscles every chance I got to prove how strong I was. One of my male friends told me that fellas didn't want to hang out with me because I was a Hunter girl, and they had a reputation. They were considered too smart. They weren't boy bait. My first significant movement outside the all-girl cocoon, besides the cherry berry breaker and Stanley Ford, would come with my discovery of the American Negro Theatre and the beginning of my career as an actor.

I had thought about theater when I was in high school because Mother's niece, my cousin, Frances Benson, belonged to the drama club, which she wanted me to join. Although I took every opportunity to read aloud, and I felt my classmates and my teachers respected my ability in this area of reading and interpreting, I didn't join the club. I didn't tell Frances that once I had asked the person who headed the group if I could get a part in whatever play was being done, and that she had replied, "But, Ruby, there are no maids in this play." I never inquired again, and I never went to see any plays there, either.

I graduated from Hunter High School in June 1939, and in September, entered Hunter College, which was indeed a continuation of Hunter High School, only more demanding. There were no entrance exams required if you had attended Hunter High School, but to be admitted to the college, you had to have a certain grade point average, depending on how many girls from all the other high schools were applying. So fierce was the competition that any student whose grade point average fell below a certain mark for the term would be asked to leave. Four was the highest grade. The year I graduated from the high school I believe the passing grade was 3.6 and I had made 3.8.

I wanted to be an actor but the chances for success did not look promising. Most blacks in film or on stage played servants, exotics, criminals, or comics. Concentrating on studying theater and related topics just didn't seem practical or important enough. What about becoming a speech therapist? Mr. Spadino, who taught phonetics, arranged for some of his students to visit a rehab center where people who had been wounded in ways that impaired their speech were learning to speak again. Most were soldiers. It was a shattering encounter. I knew right away that the objectivity required to be helpful was not a part of me. I couldn't be a therapist.

I enjoyed learning languages so I changed my major from speech and drama to languages—French and Spanish. "In case you don't make it as an actor, you'll have something to fall back on," was the general advice from those, including myself, with little faith in "this acting business." I'll be a translator, I thought, or a court stenographer with a capacity in French and Spanish. To that end, I also began studying Chinese and Portuguese, and took classes in shorthand, typing, and stenography.

In 1940, Abram Hill and Fred O'Neal had just started the American Negro Theatre in the basement of the public library on 135th Street, where the Schomburg Center for Research in Black Culture is now headquartered. There I auditioned for my first role in a play.

I had heard about the American Negro Theatre from Stanley Ford, one of the boys who met with Mother's approval and who often came to call on Sunday afternoons when we girls were allowed to have company. His sister, Ruth, was a member of the group and knew of plans to mount the first production, a new comedy by Abram Hill called *On Strivers Row*. She told Stanley, who suggested that I audition for Cobina, the debutante and leading love interest. Mother and Daddy thought it was a good idea, so I took the chance.

I had been in the library many times, but I didn't remember a theater there. There was one just up the street near Seventh Avenue in the YMCA, but Ruth had said that this was in the library. There were no signs to indicate American Negro Theatre, so I mounted the steps, went inside, and asked one of the librarians, who told me where the theater was.

As I descended the steps to the street, I looked to the right, as she had instructed me. There was no sign, only a gate that opened onto a steep flight of cement steps that led down to a dismal alley below the street. With some hesitation and trepidation, I turned and there to my right was a double metal door, which I pushed open. The idea of turning back flashed through my mind, but a not too friendly voice said sharply, "Come in, come in."

"My friend, Stanley Ford," I said, "his sister is-is—and he said you were putting on a play that I could, could—"

"Yes, yes, we're about to do a play called *On Strivers Row*. Do you know anything about Strivers Row? How it got that name or where it is?"

"I believe it's what 139th Street is called. That's Strivers Row."

"That's right. Some of the most accomplished, wealthiest Negroes live on Strivers Row. You may sit back here—this is backstage—and read over these pages. Just come out on stage when you're ready. The character I'd like you to read is called Cobina. One of the main events of the play is a coming-out party for her, an elaborate debutantes ball." He showed me the passage that he wanted me to look over, disappeared into the darkness of the room, and called, "This is Howard Augusta, our stage manager. He'll read the scene with you." A very skinny man with a gentle smile popped his head in and we exchanged hellos. He said, "I'll be sitting on stage when you're ready."

After I don't remember how long, I came out of the backstage area, which I discovered later, was to become the dressing room. I felt cold. One knee trembled. My throat didn't belong to me. Howard began to read. Although breathing is considered a very natural and ordinary activity, there are times when you can forget how. No matter that I'd recited, read, played the piano and violin, and even danced in front of people, the emotional attack was severe.

"Speak up. Speak up. We can't hear you." The command sounded impatient, harsh, and I felt tears threatening, but I persevered. Finally the audition was over and a woman's voice, coming out of the huge darkness of the acting space, said, "That was very good. Thank you for coming." I couldn't see who was speaking. Howard shook my hand. As I left, they were talking as if I had never been there. I ran into this below-ground alley, mounted the steps, ran up 135th Street all the way to 137th and Seventh, apartment 52, plunked down on the couch, and pretended I hadn't even gone out.

It was Saturday, so gratefully I had housework to do. Mother was cooking. I found myself babbling about what had happened and how scared I was.

"I don't see why," she said. "You've been talking about being on the stage, so now's your chance."

After a few days, I was informed that I got the part. The American Negro Theatre wanted me to play Cobina in *On Strivers Row*. This event was the beginning of one of the most significant times in my life. Through my association with ANT, I took one giant step along the journey to myself as a human being and as a performer.

In addition to all this, LaVerne and I took dancing lessons in an upstairs studio that overlooked 125th Street. Mary Bruce was our teacher. With metal plates on the soles of black patent leather shoes held on to our feet with black grosgrain ribbon bows, we were neat, petite, and oh so sweet. Smiling, sparkling from our heads right on down to our little hoofing feet. Once we got good enough, with routines down pat, we were called the Brucettes—even the boys—a one-of-a-kind chorus line. Mary Bruce presented us on many community occasions, outfitted in snappy costumes, tails, canes, and top hats. Oooh-weee, we were truly something.

A regular visitor to the rehearsals was a friend of Mary's, a little man named Frankie Dee Brown. Mary was a little person; we Brucettes, except for some of the boys, were mostly small people; but Frankie Dee Brown was smaller still. He was a midget; not a dwarf, a midget. A well-proportioned medium brown man with hazel eyes, a ready smile, and a good sense of humor. He would sit to the side, where he seemed to enjoy watching Mary Bruce put us through our paces.

One day during a break, I sat beside him and we introduced ourselves. Weeks later, he mentioned jokingly that he was looking for a wife. I spoke very encouragingly about the prospect. "You seem to be a very good person, and I'm sure there is somebody out there who'll make you a good wife. I have seen small people who were married."

"I have, too," he said, "in a damned sideshow. Aw, come on," he asked, with a tinge of self-disgust. "Who would want somebody like me? Would you go out with me?"

The break was over, and it was time to get back to the rehearsal.

"Of course, of course, I would," I answered with more enthusiasm than I felt.

In addition to taking dance lessons, I also belonged to the Interracial Baptist Youth Fellowship, and did the artwork for its programs, continued with the piano lessons, and studied hard to keep my grades in good order. They had not been as high as I would have liked, but I felt in no danger of failing anything. Little did I know.

One morning toward the end of June of my first year at Hunter, Mother came in from the mailbox and handed me a letter. Some annoyance came over me. Couldn't she see that I was on my knees scrubbing the linoleum in the long hallway? "Be careful, please, Mother, you are walking too fast; the floor is not yet dry. I have only two hands, please put the letter aside for now, I'll soon be finished." These thoughts ran through my mind as I put the scrub brush aside, wiped my hand on my clothes, and reached for the letter. It was from Hunter.

My heart thumped against my chest. "We regret to inform you . . ." My grade point average had fallen below the requirements to remain a matriculated student in the daytime program, and I had been dropped. Fear overtook my desperation and shame. What a spirit-killing word: Dropped! Were I a dog, I'd grab my tail and bite it off, or become a ball and smash myself into a wall.

Mother mercifully continued up the hall but she heard me howl, so she came back, took the letter from me, read it, and put it in her pocket. I don't recall her saying anything. I picked up the brush and started scrubbing again. Kicked out. Smart Ruby, Mother's darling, teacher's pet. Expelled. Messy tears fell on the linoleum.

Daddy came to the apartment later that night, and when I opened the door, he passed me without a word. After all, I was living in the ene camp. He went to the living room where Mother was. Maybe he u n another threat that his pay would be garnisheed for child support. I dn't hear what they talked about; after a few angry words, they began to whisper.

I was sitting in the kitchen as he was heading out. He stopped in the doorway, and when I looked up at him, his belligerence had shifted to something much warmer, to sadness, I think. I thought about jumping up, putting my arms around him, and sobbing on his shoulder. I didn't, though.

"Your mother told me what happened," he said. "Leave it to Emma. You'll be all right." He clapped his big hand once on my shoulder and left.

Over the next two weeks, Mother helped me pull myself together. She talked to me about summer school and night school. I registered for the necessary remedial courses, and two semesters later, I was reinstated.

Although my friend Carlotta and I have seen little of each other in our adult years, she recently sent me a letter I had written to her, dated August 1940. I had been in college one year. I share some of that letter here partly as an explanation, I suppose, for having been expelled. It is an indication, at any rate, of the many activities that claimed my attention that first year at Hunter College.

Hello, Ginger Honey [my nickname was "Boots"],

My summer so far has been marked with advancement as far as my career is concerned, mainly because I have concentrated in that direction. I think I've been to all the broadcasting studios in New York, and RCA has offered me a job this fall if I meet the requirements. That however has not stopped me from working with Columbia's workshop theatre under NYA [National Youth Administration] supervision, which trains prospective radio performers. I had a part in a skit last Thursday at 5, over WNYC, and l hope to get one every Thursday, so try to listen. I've also gotten hitched to the American Negro Theatre, a semiprofessional group, and I mean progressive.

I have a part in *Strivers Row* as the debutante around whose debut the comedy is based. It opens September 11, so l know you will get a chance to see it. Mary Bruce, you remember my dancing teacher, has girls at Michael Todd's Gay New Orleans at the Fair and on Broadway. An agent wants her to put some more on Broadway in a few days. We're rehearsing like mad for a neat and nifty li'l routine in which we'll wear sport outfits. It's really a killer. So now I only spend about 1½ hours at home to change my clothes or eat. But I really (so far) enjoy it.

Boys, well they have been playing such a minor role in my life except on Saturdays and Sundays. I've met a few more boys who are quite exciting. Vertner Tandy, son of Mrs. Tandy, our fourth grade teacher, has been giving me the rush (in many ways). By the way he is 6 ft. 4 in. To the other extreme is a 23-year-old midget. He's perfectly normal, extremely popular among Broadway celebs and in Harlem; in fact, everybody knows him. He has offers from four Broadway producers, makes plenty now with a liquor company, and drives a little Bantam that stops traffic on corners like 42nd and 5th whenever there is a red light. I feel queer walking with him but he claims he wants to marry me and he now wants me to accept a Packard from him as an engagement present. In riding with him I feel thoroughly embarrassed as he and his little car attract so much attention. He insists that I allow him to open the door of the car, and honestly, it tickles me so; for I could so easily step over the door I think, without even opening it. I'm so afraid that I more than like him.

By the way, I'm going to night school at Hunter as I am really embarking on my road right now. I feel I am doing the right thing, huh? Did you get my card from Nassau where I spent a whoopin' good time with Stanley under the guard and guidance of his whole family. Had to write this letter between lessons and rehearsals at the studio, so excuse lack of continuity and all of anything that makes you unhappy.

Love,
Boots.

When Carlotta came to see me in *On Strivers Row*, she was so enthusiastic in her appraisal. She certainly helped strengthen my resolve to become an actor.

The college years continued to be busy and unsettling. Mother and Daddy finally separated in bitterness and frustration. I continued my studies at Hunter, along with all the other things in which I was involved. Finally, after five years, I graduated.

I am deeply indebted to the New York public school system. Had there been no Hunter College, perhaps I might not have attended college. I believe the public school system is one of the most valuable, intelligent, and farsighted institutions in the world, and to the extent that we devalue it, and those who serve it, we devalue ourselves, our times, and our future. All children, I believe, should have access to free, quality education.

Especially do I believe that those of us who have benefited must be concerned, must make some effort to help sustain this priceless resource. I have made contributions and written some letters over the years but I say here, it is not nearly enough, and I pledge to make amends.

My life today is centered on words and ideas. Although the literature courses I took did not emphasize African-American contributions, they gave me a greater general appreciation of the spoken and written word. Courses in speech, phonetics, diction, and delivery helped open me to inherent gifts and led me to a special appreciation of the nature of words, and how speech enhances them.

A familiarity with languages other than English has been extremely valuable in my life, in travels abroad, as well as here in the United States. Hunter College increased my capacity to appreciate the richness of the human experience. Above all, my college education broke the seal on the door to myself, and keeps on beckoning and leading me to explore infinite inner space.

CHAPTER 10

Ossie's Harlem

Fuller and I arrived at Penn Station in New York in the middle of the afternoon. We didn't stop to gawk and look around—that would have given us away. We didn't go outside; rather, we found our way to the Eighth Avenue subway, just as Medas had instructed, and caught the A train, thinking about Duke Ellington and the music, as we rode uptown at a rapid rate of speed.

We got off at 116th Street, walked across Eighth Avenue, turned north, went to West 133rd Street, and found Mr. Cameron, a West Indian from Jamaica, waiting to welcome us. His family lived upstairs in the three-story brownstone, which he owned, and in the basement was a well-furnished office from which he ran the Cameron Employment Agency. We sat down to the meal that was waiting, after which we got down to the business of planning our new life in Harlem under Mr. Cameron's supervision.

He asked how Eldon and the other West Indian students were doing and laughed when we told him Eldon's plot to pass me off as a student from Demerara. He talked awhile about Eldon, whom he obviously liked, then said to consider ourselves like family and to let him know if there was anything we needed. We were to come back tomorrow for dinner with the rest of the family and some other West Indians he wanted us to meet. He suggested we take a week or two to get to know Harlem. Then, when we were ready, he'd find us both jobs.

He already had a room for us, cheap but clean and friendly. He suggested we go now, and get ourselves settled in. He handed us over to one of his cronies, who walked us to Morningside Avenue and 120th Street, and turned us over to Mrs. Sealy, a motherly Barbadian woman. She seemed very glad to see us. We quickly settled on the rent, paid her ten dollars apiece for the first month, then followed her up to the room, which seemed warm and cozy—just right for the two of us. She asked if we were hungry; we told her no, but she fed us "a little something" anyway.

Next morning, I got directions from Mrs. Sealy and quickly made my way to the 124th Street library in search of Dick Campbell and the Rose McClendon Players.

Dick was on stage kneeling down in the semidarkness, building a set for a forthcoming production. I couldn't see his face, only his back. I told him that Alain Locke had sent me to see him. His mouth sounded full of nails, but he did grunt—and went on hammering.

I told him the only reason I had come to Harlem was to meet him, and to join his company if he would let me, so I could learn enough about the theater—about acting and all the rest of it—to become a playwright, which was my life's ambition.

He grunted again, turned around, and looked me over. He took the nails out of his mouth, and asked, "Would you please pass me the saw? And then hold this piece of molding while I cut it."

Dick was always a great one for talking while he was busy doing something else. He told me about the Rose McClendon Players, which he had modeled somewhat after the Lafayette Players—a group of Negro actors who had made a name for themselves all over the country. He explained that the company was supported by subscription; people bought season tickets, which entitled them to free entrance to the four productions a year that were being offered.

He told me about Muriel, his wife and partner, who was a singer with an operatic voice, with nowhere to practice her craft. Dick was an actor, and a vaudevillian, a song-and-dance man, when he could get work. But there were so few jobs for black actors anyway, and Dick, being very fair, was not nearly Negro-looking enough to get any of the few jobs available every once in a while on Broadway, and certainly not in Hollywood. But not to worry. They satisfied their deep, creative need by creating the Rose McClendon Players which, *with no state or city funds* on which to draw, depended entirely on what they could provide themselves or scrounge from the community.

Dick Campbell and Muriel Rahn—as I would soon find out— were dedicated people, always involved in something for the good of somebody or other—staging pageants for the NAACP or emceeing the Beaux Arts Ball for the Urban League, but essentially, they were people of the theater, which was indeed their whole preoccupation. Dick Campbell and the Rose McClendon Players—as if they were a theatrical graduate school—supplied me with the last of the missing pieces.

"Why wait? Come back tomorrow," he said. "I've got just the part for a heavy voice like yours and we're just beginning rehearsals. I'll introduce you to Muriel and the rest of the company." Tomorrow, I would be on my way to being a playwright, and as a bonus, an actor, too.

They had only one rule: Everything had to be Negro. He would only produce plays written by us, about us, and for us—that was their credo. I couldn't wait to get myself in gear and start turning out the masterpieces that were already beginning to crowd my head.

Dick was an activist entertainer, a song-and-dance man, yes, but with something else on his mind. Theater for him was not only artistic, but was also promotional, designed to build black self-confidence and morale. Harlem was world enough for him and that's what he expected from the rest of us. Harlem was where we could build our own nation, our own civilization, certainly our own black theater.

"Rehearsals begin promptly at seven P.M.," he warned me, and then he let me go. And I went out to meet this Harlem he was so enthusiastic about.

Fuller and I hit the streets as if they were familiar, etched onto the landscape of our instinct, feeling not like strangers, but like absentee landlords come to collect the rent. A man, in our opinion, should know his Harlem before he got there. We certainly did. We knew Harlem—thanks to Medas—better than we knew heaven, though we hadn't seen either.

Harlem was—in ugly fact—a *ghetto;* a teeming black pressure-cooker surrounded by two rivers, jammed in between the devil and the deep blue sea, encircled by white power at every turn. But when we set out to see what we could see, we didn't see prison, we saw paradise.

Harlem, barely thirty years old, was the new black Rome of the African Diaspora; it was a showcase for the talents that made us powerful. The Struggle that embraced us all made it home and head-quarters—at the very center of which was Micheaux's legendary bookstore on the corner of 125th Street and Seventh Avenue. It was said to house every book ever written by and about black folks. To enter it was to be automatically subjected to a lecture by old Louis Micheaux himself, master of black history as a spoken art form, who used to say, "If you want to hide something from black folks, put it in a book."

On afternoons, especially on weekends, the street corner speakers would bring their ladders with their little American flags, and set them up right in front of Micheaux's—safe haven and sanctuary—and launch into vociferous disquisition, mostly attacking the white man for being mean and greedy and racist, and the black man for *not* being mean and greedy and racist, in return. They covered everything black from A to Z, but mostly they railed against white merchants along 125th Street, the heart of the black community, who wouldn't hire any Negroes to work in the stores. Hot boiling rhetoric, raw and raucous, all meant to free the lazy black man, and set him in motion.

Still, to those who were madly in love with her, our souls grown fat with ethnic satisfactions, Harlem was black culture at its best. Harlem, where, for me, slavery had finally been brought to an end—no more running, where Negroes had decided to stop and make a stand.

Our first objective, according to Marcus Garvey, was to take Africa back from the white man—reclaim our civilization, establish a new black nation, our own civilization, our own separate but equal manifest destiny, just like the white man's.

Such self-assertive doctrines drew black people toward self-definition. The thought of not having to answer to the white man for everything we said, or thought or did, was intoxicating. We remembered the motherland in our prayers, but now, Harlem, not Africa, was where we wanted God's kingdom to come. Garvey at least had freed us from the bondage of the white man's opinion. Whether we would settle in America, or whether we would go, was entirely up to us, and to black power—power that would spring to life automatically, if only we could find another Garvey, another black messiah, to stick us back together again.

One such potential black messiah was Father Divine. He had a great big Heaven, as he called his establishments, on 126th Street where a man could get a good meal for twenty-five cents. That's where we went first.

Father Divine was, in many ways, the exact opposite of Marcus Garvey. He was strictly nonmilitant, not deigning to confront the white man or anybody else. Rumor had it that Father Divine was God. Father refused to affirm or deny it. He was not come into the world to ask the question, but to provide the answer. And the answer was peace. He brought redemption to the sinner by completely ignoring the sin, but without all the sweat and frenzy.

There were several of Father's Heavens all over Harlem. They were clean, warm, neat, and full of angels proudly but quietly scurrying about their Father's business. The one on 126th Street was the second-largest one. We made it our business to have dinner at one of the Heavens, not only because of the food, but even more so because of the pageantry.

In the midst of the Depression, when the U.S. government was trying to minister to the basic needs of the people, Father Divine proved a shining example of how to do it. He managed to feed the people and provide them with a clean, safe place to stay, but also he changed their lives, inside and out, for the better. His cult was not mysterious or mumbo jumbo; it was open for everyone's inspection. Loving Father Divine was about as easy as pie. Everybody in Harlem dropped in once in a while. Fiorello La Guardia, the mayor of the city of New York, was glad to visit with Father, and so was Eleanor Roosevelt.

The faithful would begin to pour into the restaurant in the late afternoon to wait for the arrival of Father, which was sure to take place before midnight. Also present were the curious, the voyeurs, like Fuller and me.

There was usually a piano, and most every evening, a different somebody would be there plunking on the keys. Sometimes, a second talent would come in, have dinner, then join the piano player with his clarinet, trumpet, or sax. He'd play for a while and then be on his way to his gig. Men and women were forbidden to dance together, but nobody stopped you if you felt like taking the floor by yourself.

Often by ten o'clock at night, the place would be jammed. Then suddenly a tremor would run from corner to corner, signaling that Father was close by. Everything and everybody would stop in their tracks. The restaurant would be closed and all attention shifted to the main dining room, centered with a long table upon which twenty to thirty settings—plates with their gleaming crystal, linen, and silverware—were already in place. Officers, members, dignitaries, and staff, fluttering like nervous pigeons, would hurry themselves to the doorway. A few minutes more, then a furious joy would find tongue. People would be asked to kindly make way, and Father Divine, accompanied by Mother Divine, a young white woman from Canada whom Father had made his bride, would enter the room. Father would swiftly move to the head of the table, take his seat, and that was the signal for bedlam.

One serving plate after another—chicken, lamb, pork, beef, followed by rice, white potatoes, sweet potatoes, greens, peas, beans, and more—would be set in front of Father. He'd put a little, a very little, from each plate on his dish then pass the plate to his left, and thus it would move around the table until its contents were gone.

Father Divine was not the only God for poor folk regnant in Harlem. The options were plentiful, and easily accessed. It's often said that if you put a bunch of black folks between a rock and a hard place, they will build a church. And Harlem had many churches, to be sure; but our most important religious institution, in my opinion, wasn't called a church—it was called the Apollo Theatre.

The Apollo Theatre was a solid, irrefutable display of Negro expertise, authority, and power. It was not like the real black church, where we were supplicants, throwing our miserable selves at the feet of the cross, on the mercy of Jesus Christ, begging His forgiveness with sorrow in our hearts and tears in our eyes. No. At the Apollo, we weren't praying to anybody. Power doesn't pray. It doesn't need to. Power is sassy and impudent and doesn't give a damn about white folks. In the Apollo, it was us, black folks, calling all the shots, not Jesus.

The Apollo was our conjure, our mojo, our voodoo, our Negro empowerment zone . . . our black magic, in whose hallowed confines we could overcome all enemies, even white folks. Where every week, we proved to ourselves and to the world that we had something the rest of the world didn't have, and was not only hungry for, but desperately in need of—our music! Jazz, blues, boogie-woogie, a new way of flouncing the secondhand culture we were wearing, and a brand-new dance for every change of mood we happened to feel. It was something God-given, which only Negroes could produce—something that gave us power. And power was where we were headed, so help us God!

Feasting at the Camerons was always a minor affair of state. No telling who might be there from Africa, Asia, or back from the islands. The meals were strictly West Indian, and always sumptuous, the atmosphere open, easy, and convivial, and any West Indian student was always heartily welcomed. Fuller and I, on Medas's recommendation, were immediately accepted into this family ritual as if we were the real thing. Nobody was fooled, of course, and deception was not our intention. It was all a part of the playful pageantry with which the West Indians liked to amuse themselves. Fuller and I fitted into the charade with a vengeance.

The Camerons, of course, were careful also not to seem too presumptuous, or insistent. In addition to all this food, drink, and imported Caribbean comfort, they also offered jobs, but we hadn't completed our formal introduction to Harlem.

Meanwhile, my other life—in the theater—was beginning to take root. The Rose McClendon Players became my real family now, the center of my being. And I soon found myself caught up in rehearsals. Every night, Dick would put us through our paces. Not only did I learn the lines and movements of the Reverend Stokes in a play called *Joy Exceeding Glory,* but under Dick's direction, I was learning about myself. I discovered that, with my elongated height, my very thin build, my long, stringy arms, my country ways and deep and resonant voice with the southern accent, I wasn't such a bad actor. They all seemed to like whatever it was I was doing and that made me happy.

After rehearsal, we'd sit around, laughing and hating to leave one another, finding something increasingly nice about being on stage together and not wanting to let it go—talking theater and show business, which to me was somewhat like a foreign language, but I soon got the hang of it. Or we would go to a neighborhood bar where you could get cold, fresh hard apple cider that could put your head in a spin if you weren't careful, and sit there talking trash till they closed the place. Freddy Carter, a chiropodist, had a practice of his own, so he could afford to pay for the cider when the rest of us couldn't. These magic people existed in a world for which I, too, had been born, to which I would always belong, forever and ever. Amen.

And that produced in me an obligation. I had to get busy. I couldn't wait any longer. I confessed to them that I was a playwright, but was way behind schedule, and in order to merit their trust and confidence, I had to catch up right away, which I promised to do. That was the kind of Rose McClendon Player I intended to be.

And to that hurried end, I did a lot of dreaming, and scheming, and planning, and plotting, and writing—but most of all, reading. There were three libraries in Harlem, one on 135th Street, another on 124th Street, which housed the Rose McClendon Players, and one on 115th Street. Fuller and I would sometimes visit all three on the same day just to stretch our legs, and to try our luck. And surely, to feed our souls. But other parts required feeding too, and money was running low. A meal at Father Divine's didn't cost but a quarter, but seldom now did we have that kind of money to spare. The time had come for us to get a job. The Cameron Employment Agency was glad to oblige.

My first job was to carry a big suitcase full of patriotic notions— little flags, and campaign buttons and badges—for a man who lived on Central Park West who had, in addition to a hernia, a case of hemor- rhoids and a smelly stool. His morning trip to the toilet was loud and confrontational, full of groans and grunts, and curses in some heavy, foreign language. As we walked along later toward Columbus Circle, he filled my ear with the sorrows of his life, which were endless. I found myself being glad that he had hemorrhoids and that "he trips to toilet hurt." It seemed an appropriate response to all his whining. I quit after the first day.

My next job was with a man who sold flowers in Harlem on the weekends. Early Friday morning, we would drive down to the flower market on 21st Street and buy a carful of roses, gladiolas, ferns, and other greenery. We'd spend the day cutting and making up bouquets wrapped at the bottom with green paper. Later that evening, I'd load up my basket with bouquets and hit the streets.

Weekends were always a special time in Harlem, the time when whatever indignity we had had to endure to make it through the week paid off; a time to fully enjoy the fruits of our labor and to make sure our neighbors saw us do it. This ripening excitement that would bear fruit in an explosion of sounds, smells, and color on Sunday began Friday night and Saturday, which was the day to shop and haggle and buy for the weekend carnival that was slowly coming to life, which swirled like the wind through Harlem's throbbing veins. The stores along 125th Street would be crowded with consumers, even though no black people were allowed to work there.

But we had our traders, too, street merchants who shouted their wares and their prices from tables set up on the sidewalk especially to catch the Negro eye. Street hawkers, such as I, were out in such profusion, we literally bumped into each other. Business was always brisk; and I always sold out and had to go back for more.

It was easy work and I got a percentage of every sale I made. You only worked on weekends and that suited me fine. Everybody hustled, joining the joyous community tension that was building up. Then Sunday would finally come.

It started with a deep, respectful pause—religion time for those who were believers. Street life subsided on Sunday morning as Harlem put on its best and went to church. Paydirt only came in the afternoon, and that meant Strolling. Men and women, boys and girls, dressed in fashions they themselves might have created, took to the streets in droves, and walked along 125th Street to Lenox Avenue, where you would turn left, then stroll for ten blocks to 135th Street, turn left again, which brought you to Seventh Avenue, then left again, and back to 125th Street where you started.

Flirting, laughing, styling, strutting your stuff, calling aloud to your friends, and waving, too, making sure that everybody else took notice as you and your date passed by. And you keeping it up till, finally, the sun went down.

I liked selling flowers. It put me into the very thick of Harlem, and suddenly I, too, was on the inside, a living, breathing part of the golden hustle. Suddenly, I, too, acquired my share of territorial authority. I was no longer a "lame"; I was a "homeboy." Harlem had called my bluff, but I didn't fade. Well, not at first.

On one occasion, I ran into the assistant dean of men from Howard, who remembered my face, but had to ask me my name. He looked at my basket of flowers, awkwardly shook my hand, and wished me well.

As if that wasn't embarrassment enough, one Saturday afternoon, as I worked my way along 135th Street, right in front of the YMCA, I ran smack into Kenneth Clark and Mamie Phipps, who by now were married. I was more than embarrassed. This was the last man in all this world that I wanted to see. The professor who had warned that I was bound to wind up nothing but a literary bum. They recognized me, so

I had no choice but to mumble some kind of weak hello; then I got the hell out of there.

The garment center, where the Cameron Employment Agency sent me next, was in downtown New York, but easy to get to by subway. Just take the A train and get off at 34th Street. I was a little short that first day out, so I asked a policeman for a nickel to pay my fare.

My job was to help Henry, the general handyman, who was a genius at making repairs, and George, one of the shipping clerks, both of whom were black; there were also about ten or fifteen black women who worked at the steampresses. At the sewing machines were Puerto Rican and Jewish girls. The blacks were warm and friendly, and immediately protective, making me feel right at home from the very first day. But it was the Jews from whom I was destined to learn the most about the Struggle.

Handcraft Blouse gave me work—the very first step to my manhood, because in America, work defines the man. But for a brief moment, right there at the beginning, I wasn't going to work, I was going to prison!

It was the first week of August. Neither Fuller nor I had the money to pay the rent, so for the last few days, I had been sleeping in the park. I didn't have to. Mrs. Sealy would have been the last person in the world not to understand. She might have talked to us a little sternly, laid down the law again, but she was too much of a mother to have turned us out.

No, it was summertime in Harlem, and a breeze of any kind was hard to come by. That little room of ours, with only one window facing a bricked-in alley could get quite stuffy—sometimes unbearable.

Fuller and I, adventurers still, had already tried the city shelter for homeless men, where they fed you, gave you hospital pajamas, old but clean, and a bunk bed that was free of chinches, which was nice. The sheets on the bed were clean, but rough and grainy—I think they were made of canvas. The place was bright and orderly enough, I suppose, but it was filled with our fellow homeless, many of whom snored, and talked aloud in their sleep. But mostly they farted—long, loud, and endlessly, all through the night; growling stomachs, with all the winds they prisoned in by day, glad at last to be free. One night was about as much as even a writer could stomach. No, no, sleeping in the park was much better.

Mount Morris Park was right across the street from the library where we were rehearsing. It was about midnight when, deciding to retire, I went into the park, selected a bench, took off my shoes, put them under my head for safekeeping, and soon was fast asleep. I had sweet dreams, such as only the recently employed might have—until about two o'clock in the morning when a furious pounding on my feet brought me awake.

The cop was apologetic—and also Irish in his mockery. "Sorry for the disturbing of your slumbers, sir, but His Honor, Mayor Fiorello La Guardia, has a brand-new World's Fair coming to the city, to accommodate the which I have been instructed to cleanse Mount Morris and these immediate environs of all who may be bums and vagrants."

I vigorously protested that I was neither, but rather a brand-new member of the working class, temporarily disadvantaged—

"Perfectly understandable, sir," he told me. "But the World's Fair is coming, so we must clean up the parks. But not to worry. His Honor is providing alternate accommodations—step right this way, and a police van is waiting." I spent the rest of the night in the 127th Street precinct jail.

Next morning, at nine o'clock sharp, I found myself standing before the seat of judgment. His Honor seemed very annoyed, so I was properly respectful of the bench, deferential in my demeanor, and absolutely contrite, wearing that certain look on my face that I had learned in Georgia, meant just for throwing yourself upon the white man's mercy. His Honor was not impressed. He slammed the case file shut, and was getting ready to throw the book at me, when suddenly I added to my piteous plea this one important fact:

"I'm not a vagrant, Your Honor. No, sir, I have a job. Just yesterday, I started work down in the garment center"—and with that, I produced the transfer slip that the Cameron Employment Agency had given me, which had the address and telephone number of Handcraft Blouse, Inc.

"Bailiff, call this number, and see if this boy is lying to this court." The bailiff made the call that set me free. I think the judge, from his looks, would still like to have climbed down off the bench and kicked me. I got the hell out, and fast, as the bailiff advised. I was two hours late to work, but everybody still seemed glad to see me.

Among the workers, the cutters and the designers seemed a class apart from all the rest. They were Jews but slightly aristocratic, even temperamental, artists, not workers like the rest of us; they had mastered their craft and made their reputations in Europe. But also they were refugees from Hitler; some had barely escaped with their lives. It was history more than anything else that set them slightly apart and made them special. They spoke to each other in Yiddish, or in heavy German accents, and kept mostly to themselves.

Part of my job was to bring in sandwiches from a nearby delicatessen at lunchtime. Corned beef, pastrami, herring in sour cream, pickles, knishes, and apple strudel, together of course with bottles of cream soda. The designers and cutters had their own department, where they ate, and where they talked. Often music from WQXR, which only played the classics, would be on in the background. Their favorite composer seemed to be Beethoven.

They would talk, talk, talk, mostly in English, which they were determined to master as a second language, and I, having lunch nearby, would sit and listen. Most often, the subject was Hitler. Even though I couldn't understand what they were saying, their passion was clear to me. Listening, trying to learn, and, in my own way, identifying, I began to share their passion and to see a new, international dimension to the struggles of my own people.

Anti-Semitism and racism were one and the same. I began to read *The Daily Worker,* especially the black writers in it like Abner Berry, and others, who pointed out how the struggles of the Jewish people in Germany, the colonization of the people of Africa, and the persecution of Negroes in America all overlapped. I was profoundly impressed with this growing insight. My attention began to expand, to observe events occurring overseas as well as here at home. It was all the same fight, fought with the same passion that even now was burning the lips of the flag-and-ladder men speaking up in Harlem—Garvey's remnant, who continuted to protest against the merchants on 125th Street: "Don't buy where you can't work."

Now the message was being carried in the voice and in the eyes of Adam Clayton Powell, who flung out his arms and pointed his deadly, accusatory finger at La Guardia for excluding colored workers from the World's Fair. He led his congregation and anybody else who would follow on charges up and down 125th Street, preaching the same gospel: "Don't buy where you can't work." I listened and I marched, too. I read, I pondered, I listened, and then I read some more.

The superintendents of the Struggle, and the applicants for leadership, were all living in Harlem when I got there: A. Philip Randolph, James Weldon Johnson, Walter White, Father Divine, Adam Clayton Powell, Jr., W.E.B. Du Bois. I, too, felt the call to leadership, but only as an artist. Like Paul Robeson, and Sterling Brown, and Langston Hughes, and Alain Locke, and Richard Wright—and like Marion Anderson—I wanted to sing my service to my people. But only as a playwright. That was what I had come to Harlem for. The Communists were waiting there to help me.

The Communists I knew seemed not only to be clear thinkers and patient teachers, but also were action-prone. They didn't seem afraid to go into harm's way to make their point, reminding me much of Saint Paul of the early Christian church. They could without stopping for breath show me the basic relation between what Hitler was doing against the Jews, what Mussolini was doing against the Ethiopians, and what Alabama was doing against the Scottsboro Boys.

The Marxists wanted to be our allies, but in return they insisted that we expand our thinking. They divided the world into workers and exploiters, natural enemies, locked in a war—a class war—with each other. For them, the coming war in Europe could have only one outcome—resounding victory for the working class, which, when it came to power, would establish a society where all the wealth belonged to all the people, people whose labor created wealth in the first place, and not to the fat-cat thieves and exploiters, bosses and bankers, who—

but for the labor unions—would treat their workers just like the old white slave master treated his black slaves, or even worse. A workers' society based on the equality of all people who worked, regardless of race, color, or creed.

It was obvious when one listened to them that the Communists were dreamers, maybe also fools. But I was a dreamer, too.

My heart was flying, my head full of plots, plans, story ideas, characters, incidents from random episodes to fully developed ideas for full-length plays, bubbling up out of my restless daydreams, jostling each other, clamoring to get my attention, hogging the stage, sometimes driving me to distraction. But that was good. All I needed to do, I thought, was to choose the most likely idea, the one most pertinent to the Struggle, the most urgent, wrestle it down onto paper, and presto, I too, would take my place in the pantheon of heroes, along with Paul, and Langston, and Marian.

Dreaming is, of course, the simplest, most instinctive, and most immediate form of creation, but trying to write it all down—something I had never done before—was something else again. Writing must be active, imperious, even dictatorial—the creative ego making choices and taking control. My ideas came, not in bits and pieces, but like a sudden flood, bright flashes in a place too dark too long, new ways to see the world. There were new gods to worship, like labor and the working class; new devils to fight, like capitalism, colonialism, and, certainly, racism. Feeding my greedy imagination was this further excitement: The rampant indiscipline—the lack of creative focus from which I suffered—did not affect me alone; it affected the very culture that defined me. Drastic change was needed in a hurry, not only from me but from all other playwrights—from drama itself.

What was called for now, as I began to see it, was a *new* kind of drama (exactly like the plays I had in mind!), with a *new* cast of characters: workers, not aristocrats; and black folks, to replace the kings and queens and emperors. We needed a drama suited to our own day and age and temperament—exactly the kind of thing I had in mind for the play I was working on now. It already had a title: *Leonidas Is Fallen*. It was a play in which a noble slave is pitted against his masters in a struggle to be free that ends in his death.

But to be tragic, as I saw it, Leonidas had to speak, act, and carry himself with all the grandeur that Shakespeare's heroes did. I wrote like a furious demon, but when I read back what I wrote—Leonidas wasn't happening at all.

All Struggle is between the power to oppress and the power to resist—in Leonidas's case, white power versus black power. But black people had no power. On the contrary, we were power*less*—just like the white folks wanted us to be—a condition conducive to the production of niggers, but not of heroes.

But nigger was not what I saw when I looked at my dreaming fancy—me, black me, with my poet's hunger, and my ardent eye. That's not what I saw when I saw Leonidas. Rather, I saw him—and the rest of my people—as strong, noble, self-sufficient, authoritative, and powerful. Like Marian Anderson saw us when she sang.

I, too, though young, was ambitious and inspired, following my own artistic instincts, trying by blood, sweat, and callow artistic genius to create—as Shakespeare would, or King David—a world inhabited by a people who hadn't come into being yet, let alone into power. My job was to make it happen anyway.

No, in my daydreams, black people did not only suffer. They lived! They walked abroad, and ruled, deploying their ambient power far and wide upon an earth that trembled as they spoke. Why? Because they spoke the language power speaks. They carried themselves the way power carries itself—like Gabriel Prosser, who led a slave rebellion in 1800; or Denmark Vesey, who did likewise in Charleston, South Carolina, in 1822; and Nat Turner in Virginia, in 1839. Why were there no great dramas about these giants, these authentic heroes who truly defined black people? Well, I would change all that. These were the giants my Leonidas would be modeled after!

Once again, easier said than done. Try as I might, I couldn't make it happen. The more I tried to wrestle my characters into strict dramatic order, give them my spine and my purpose, the more they wrestled back or simply dissolved like quicksilver, slipping through my fingers.

Days became weeks, weeks became months, and months became a year. I was at the library every chance I got, writing, reading, rewriting. There I was with my notes, filling pads and notebooks of all sizes, as well as scrapbooks, loose sheaves of paper, practically anything that would hold ink—and containing everything from random, isolated sentences to full-blown paragraphs to episodes complete with dialogue, all spilling, spewing, cluttering. For months I had been scribbling like mad, but all the time getting further away from what I wanted to say, and how I wanted to say it.

Slowly I learned to curse the day that I was born a dreamer. Instead of harnessing my imagination, my imagination harnessed me. I was forced to finally admit—and it came to me as a shock—that the great playwright who had come to take Harlem by storm was nowhere to be found!

Having sworn to myself that I would hit the ground running, and have a finished product for Dick and my fellow actors in time for next season, I was considerably annoyed when it didn't happen. Annoyed, but not worried. "These things take time; it's only your first time out," I reassured myself. I decided to abandon the reading room for a while, put my writing aside, and went back to the streets and the Struggle for further instructions.

My flirtation with the Young Communist League was partially an effort to solve a literary problem by nonliterary means: I had been reading too much, choking myself up with books. Some form of agitation might be just the thing to tie me down to one dramatic idea and keep me there.

I went to my first meeting with great expectations, and at first it sounded promising. The issue being debated was whether or not Negroes constituted a nation in captivity and should, therefore, by revolutionary right, be granted autonomy, if not independence. I thought of Medas and of those old Howard University bull sessions, and leapt gleefully headfirst into the conversation.

Suddenly, another group of young Communists, mostly white, loud, boisterous, bubbling with enthusiasm, burst into the session, yelling, "Hey, there's a bunch of Trotskyites trying to hold a rally over in the park. Let's dash over there and break their fucking heads!" That broke up the discussion and soon everyone was arguing hot and heavy how such an action might advance the class struggle, and benefit the Revolution, while the lecturer tried valiantly to restore both order and perspective. I had no quarrel with the Trotskyites or anybody else, and I knew my own way out.

Blind action motivated by an even blinder passion made it impossible to tell the revolutionists from the rednecks. That was action all right, but not the kind my mind was looking for. I felt a burning need to hit the books again, still looking for directions that might lead me to the play—but this time under guidance. For that, I went down to the Workers School, on East 13th Street, to study Marx, and the other giants of socialism.

The classes were held at night, and there were professors who recommended books and gave assignments—which included the writing of Du Bois, Frederick Douglass, and of course, Karl Marx. Also, I went back to the library and to Leonidas. Once again, the language gave me problems. When Leonidas summoned his people to meet him in secret to plot the great rebellion, I had him speaking in iambic pentameter, the language both of poetry and power. But something just the opposite seemed to happen: my words in Leonidas's mouth didn't sound like Shakespeare, didn't ring like David's; rather, my character sounded wooden and ridiculous. I was not inspired as I thought I'd be when I read them over; I was embarrassed. Once again I had run smack into a creative wall of stone!

I began to sense that the problem was more than language; the problem was power. People who have no power have no heroes. But that could not be true. And anyway, we black folks *did* have power. What else was it that I felt that April day, at the Lincoln Memorial, when Marian had done that strange and wonderful thing—had taken us blacks from being clowns and victims, and by the sheer force and authority of her mighty art, empowered us on the spot? If Marian could do it, why couldn't I?

That was my determination. That was what I wanted to do. I kept on haunting the reading rooms, trying to write, going through the motions, again and again and again, but to no avail. I tried. I tried like hell. I failed.

I began now to lose my confidence, to entertain great doubts about myself, to be haunted and harried by the great and passing events going down in the outside world: first by Franco's victory over the Republican forces in Spain; the deteriorating situation in Ethiopia; the naked, war-like aggressions of Hitler and his Nazis; and finally, the invasion of Poland and the coming of war to Europe. These great defeats paralleled my own. The fate of the African colonies was suddenly in play. The USSR, a socialist country, the workers' last hope of victory, was reeling toward defeat—or so it seemed. I knew in my heart of hearts that I was failing, but had nowhere to turn.

Perhaps if I had spoken to Dick or talked with Langston, or even Richard Wright, they could have helped me. But somehow it seemed too presumptuous; I didn't dare. My bouts of melancholy, deep alienation, and isolation increased. No need to look to God; He wasn't there.

I had started out a true believer, but not a zealot, accepting the fact that God and His relation to me and to the world were clouded in mystery, and that the only approach to the substance of Him was through faith. You had to believe in order for God to exist. And up to now, I had been able to live with that. But when I saw what was happening to the Jews in Europe, God's Chosen People dragged off to concentration camps and slaughtered by the millions, I rebelled. I slammed the door of the tabernacle in His face and went in search of another God. Someone to help me in my fight with Adolf Hitler—someone like Karl Marx.

Hitler frightened me in a special way, put me on the defensive; it had something to do with whether I and my people would be next. I could laugh at Mussolini, even in spite of Ethiopia; he was in my opinion basically a clown and a buffoon. But I never, ever learned to laugh at Hitler. I still can't. I feel him out there sometimes, even now, still working the crowd, and looking dead at me.

I was never a Communist, but I was a fellow traveler. Though layered, my loyalty was never split; always at the bottom, even if I did have to constantly shuffle my tactics, was black itself. I was "red" only when I thought it a smarter way of being "black."

I had read all about the exploits of the Lincoln Brigade, those three thousand American volunteers who had gone to Spain, and I was personally proud that some of them were black. I cheered them on and thought of them as heroes in the Struggle. Soldiers fighting in my place. I envied them and the clarity of their statement. No hassle, no sweating it out in the library. All such wavering and indecision over and done with. The Struggle called for all they had to offer, even their lives, and they had answered. Why couldn't I answer, too?

Day after day, I wrestled with my angel, always coming up empty. I had read every book relative to the subject of power. I knew that was the hang-up; but the more I read, the less capable I was of using what I read to make my point. I tried to give up reading but I couldn't. But the books I read turned bitter in my mouth.

Failure and frustration began to take their toll, and finally, I hit rock bottom, down in the hell that lives in every black man—one base suspicion explaining all the rest. The question gnawing at the edges of his ego, put there by white America before he was born: Am I, in spite of myself, my home, my church, and my teachers, Negro History Week, Karl Marx, and Dr. Du Bois . . . am I, in spite of them all, am I a nigger? How much was my inability to finish *Leonidas Is Fallen*—or anything else—due to a negative cultural imperative, planted in my mind by racist paternalism, like the syrup poured on my head by kind and smiling policemen? Was something Southern and unfathomable withering my will and crippling my capacity to think and to stand behind my thought as a man is supposed to do? If Dick Campbell, or some other mentor, had been a white man, giving me a white man's permission, would I then have become a great American playwright, instead of remaining a boy with great, unfinished daydreams on my conscience?

In the past, such bitter musings—watching myself sink deeper and deeper—would always leave me laughing at such foolishness. But not this time. Now humor became punishment, and laughter, bored with my puerile whining, stopped being amused.

Encouraged by this blind and eyeless moment, I even considered suicide, which actors, and other adolescents rehearse before the mirror to keep in practice. I'd put a bullet through my stinking brains, I said to myself, if by my dying, Leonidas would live! This time, there was no Alain LeRoy Locke. No Eldon Stuart Medas to show me another clever stratagem. No, it was the Japanese—bearing war—who came to my rescue.

Now was the time to act, and not to think! So, on Monday morning, even before President Roosevelt called the rest of the nation together, I went to my draft board and made a deal: If they'd let me go home—spend Christmas with the family—I'd enlist while I was in Georgia, under my own steam. They agreed. I said good-bye to Dick and Muriel; to Fuller; to Mrs. Sealy, my kind West Indian landlady; and, of course, to Leonidas. And to Harlem, black city of dreams which I had come to conquer, thinking of how Caesar himself might describe my bitter predicament: I came, I saw, I went . . . down to Penn Station and caught the first train South.

CHAPTER 11

Some Men in My Life

Frankie Dee Brown talked a lot about having babies, raising a family, and buying me a house. He'd wanted me to visit his folks in Oklahoma. I felt that he did love me. One day, he asked me to marry him. He was trying to smile, to make a joke even, but I could see he wasn't joking. My insides were screaming, "No, no, no," but I didn't say it. I didn't want to hurt his feelings.

I said, "Mother doesn't want us to marry until we get out of school."

"You can still go to school. You don't have to have a baby until you get out of school. I'll talk to her," he said.

Daddy and Mother remained apart. Then Mother became quite ill and had to have an operation—a hysterectomy. The idea of me marrying Frankie Dee Brown appealed to her. "He's a decent man with a good job," she said. "He can take care of you while you finish school. Do what you want. You've asked for my opinion; I'm giving it to you."

Daddy seemed nervous for me. He asked, "What did your mother say?" I told him.

"I don't know what to tell you, Ruby. I just don't know," he hedged. "He's mighty little. Doesn't mean he can't be a good husband. If I could be a fly on the wall and watch you two together sometime—"

Right then, I tuned Daddy out. Turned him off.

Frankie and I were married on August 31, 1941, in Mother Zion AME Church by Reverend Benjamin Robeson, Paul's oldest brother. I wore a dress I'd made. It had a black velvet bodice, with a red plaid skirt and sleeves. The weather was too warm for such a dress.

Frankie bought a two-family corner brownstone house on West 141st Street in Harlem. Next door lived Noble Sissle and Eubie Blake, well-known musicians and composers who made history as collaborators on Broadway musicals. The row of houses faced the St. Nicholas Park, and around the corner and up the street was the Alexander Hamilton Museum and a row of houses named in his honor.

I felt so lucky to be in my own lovely house with a backyard, kitchen, laundry area, two bathrooms, and great neighbors. Tenants, yes, but they had their own separate entrance and living space. I couldn't imagine how I could ever leave it. Mother was right; he could take care of me.

From the beginning, however, soon after we married, I insisted that he drop "Brown" as a last name. I didn't want to be Mrs. Brown. Mrs. Dee sounded better. In short order, he made the necessary arrangements and had the name changed.

Frankie traveled a great deal with his job at Schenley Distillers, where he worked in promotion. But in the first weeks and months of our marriage, he took me many places—to the movies, the theater, and especially to the finest hotels and restaurants in New York City. On the occasions when he took me to dinner where he was working, I dined alone because his job required him to be dressed much like Johnny, the small man who worked for Phillip Morris, to approach the guests at an appropriate time in the meal and offer drinks, courtesy of Schenley. There was an elegance about him. When I could see him, I noticed that the initial amusement of the guests gave way to respect.

He was pleasant, witty, and very relaxed. He withdrew quickly and gracefully from the disinterested.

Mother was taken with him. They seemed very comfortable with each other and would talk and laugh together, as if they constantly shared some inside joke. I enjoyed the fact that he seemed to please her. He took her to baseball games, they talked horses and numbers, and he frequently bought her gifts.

We had shared some intimate, well-planned moments in exquisite hotels. It was the first time I'd been exposed to such beautiful surroundings. Had Frankie been a normal-sized man, he might have been an irresistible lover, I imagine, but nothing occurred that could change the reality of the matter. I truly don't remember the details, except for the fact that he seemed pleased.

Everything seemed to be happening to me and in the world around me at once. Frankie was rarely home, I was in college, and I also had a job at Westinghouse in New Jersey, balancing gyroscopes and wiring radio panels to blueprints.

Through it all, I managed to become more involved with the American Negro Theatre, appearing in one production annually: *Starlight* in 1942 and *Three's a Family* in 1943. That was the year I got my first job on Broadway, playing a young native girl in a drama called *South Pacific* (no relation to the later musical of the same name). In this production, I also understudied Winifred Johnson, who played the lead opposite Canada Lee.

In 1944, I graduated from Hunter College and took a job as a translator for an import-export company. It only lasted a few weeks before I was offered a role in another ANT production, *Walk Hard*. During this time, ANT was leaping into citywide, then nationwide, prominence with its production of *Anna Lucasta*. Men whom I'd known just a few years earlier began to show interest in me. I felt like a different person. I was changing from a girl to a woman.

What a marvelous feeling to be mistress in my own house! Frankie was on the road a great deal and I began to give impromptu parties, especially after rehearsals. They were warm and joyous times with people who felt like family, who felt like my first real friends—Betty Haynes, Clarice Taylor, Jimmie Jackson, George Lewis, Harry Belafonte, Olive Tucker, Kenneth Manigault, Claude Sloan, Chickie Evans, and several others who are gone now. We were all struggling actors, and we spent long hours laughing and joking together, enjoying one another's company, and savoring the possibilities that lay before us.

Occasionally during these evenings, Harry would get up and sing along with the music playing on the radio, and some of us would tease him, "Harry, puh-leeze! Do you have to?" Or we'd look at each other in mock despair. It didn't faze him, though. He'd strike his singer's pose, laugh along with us, and keep on singing.

One New Year's Eve, Frankie wasn't home, as usual. That was the night, I suppose, that I fell in love—again. And Elwood Smith fell in love with me.

A group of us had been out earlier that evening and come back with food and drinks. There was no furniture, as I recall; we'd not yet bought any, so we sat on boxes. Elwood and I were inseparable, and we were all over the place. Everybody was noticing how we couldn't keep our hands off each other. I just exploded into a kind of craziness with this man, but not to any degree of intimacy; there was just a lot of groping, panting, huffing and puffing, and kissing.

Elwood was a singer and he took me to hear him sing. There were other women there who liked him, but he always came over to me. He treated me so well—he was princely. But looking back at it now, there was a deep yearning in him for something he wasn't getting.

It lasted a few good weeks. I don't even recall how it ended, but I remember that mad New Year's Eve. This thing with a man. That was the beginning of the end between Frankie and me.

If Mother had told me, "No, you should not marry him," I wouldn't have married him. Until that time, Mother had been the strongest influence in my life, but now, sensing myself as a woman, I became aware of other influences, and began to receive a new kind of attention, not only from men, but also in the press. At the American Negro Theatre, people wrote about me. I began to be noticed as an actor.

CHAPTER 12

World War Two, 1942–1945

My Army draft board was understanding, but admonishing. They gave me permission to go home for Christmas, as I requested, but warned me to volunteer right after the holiday, as I had promised, or they would hunt me down like a dog. Christmas with the family in Valdosta was totally unremarkable. It was both homecoming and leave-taking, but I don't remember it at all.

On January 5, 1942, the family drove me over to Waycross and I enlisted, and before sundown, was on my way to Fort Benning, Georgia. I was assigned to the Medical Corps, and put on a train for Camp Lee, Virginia, where I was sent along with a lot of other black raw recruits to complete my basic training. Two or three weeks of drill and drill and drill some more; then I was told that because of my college background, I didn't have to drill anymore. I had been selected for something special. Nobody could tell me exactly what it was, but in short order, I found myself—of all places—back in Washington, D.C., at the Army Medical Center, attached to Walter Reed Hospital. About thirty other young black men had been assigned to the same secret mission.

We were under the supervision of a master sergeant who had made the Army his career. He hinted at how lucky we dumb, black, country sons of bitches were, but went no further. We were being trained, not as medics to work in the field, but rather to work in a military hospital, but that was all we knew.

No choice was allowed. I was told what they had in mind for me to do: I would be a surgical technician, which was the equivalent of a scrub nurse in a regular hospital. My job would be to assist the "medical officer." There were no doctors or surgeons in the Army's operating room.

It was springtime in Washington, D.C., in a way that I hadn't noticed when I was there seven years earlier as a student at Howard. For the first time, I think, I saw what the tourists saw. And I was impressed. It was still a segregated city, but wearing the uniform did make a difference on the streets. I was still thin as a rail, gaunt in the face as a billy goat, and I thought I looked rather sexy in my uniform. And so thought some of the ladies. I still equated sex with sin and was determined, as my father would have it, not to live a loose and profligate life. But neither was I a celibate.

There was one girl I happened to meet on the bus, and I, remembering Medas, thought she might be responsive to a black soldier on his way overseas in the service of his country, whence he might never return. I thought she was shy—and she was—but most kind and empathetic. I kept my end of the conversation a little above her head, and that impressed her. Questions of intentions that we may well have asked each other were made moot by the fact that this was war. I saw her last when she came down to the train station to see me off as we were being transferred south at the end of our training. She wrote me many times when I was overseas, and sometimes, I wrote back. Then it trickled off and finally her letters stopped coming altogether.

I am profoundly embarrassed, but I can't even remember her name. All selfish people are not mean, or petty and small-minded. Some are quite noble in outlook, even if totally self-absorbed, as I was. It has been one of my most distinguishing characteristics never to look back.

She joins a whole list of people—Mrs. Sealy, Medas, Chappie, Ilonka Lovinger, Ann Jackson, Gladys Jackson, and my two aunts, Effie and Florence—people who loved me dearly, and I know it—to whom I never took the time to stop and say thanks.

In May, when our three-month training period was up, the lot of us were sent to Fort Bragg, North Carolina, preparatory to being shipped somewhere overseas, but nobody could tell us where. They gave us a refresher course in basic training: close-order drill, rifle marksmanship, hiking, bivouacking (temporary encampment with tents). A week or two of that, and then we were loaded onto a Liberty Ship in Charleston Harbor, along with ten or fifteen black medical officers—all of which increased our growing excitement.

Then, on the first day at sea, we were assembled on deck to hear our orders. We were now the medical officers and staff of the 25th Station Hospital, the first black Station Hospital ever commissioned by the U.S. Army! Already, by just being formed, we had made military history, joining the all-black 24th and 25th infantry regiments, which had distinguished themselves in pursuit of Pancho Villa in 1915, and later in World War I. We knew about the 9th and 10th cavalries, which had fought as buffalo soldiers against the Indians. Those units had already made names for themselves, and we were to be next in line.

Now add to that another piece of unbelievably good news— especially to me. The 25th Station Hospital was to be permanently stationed in Liberia, West Africa, in a facility that was being built just for us. The U.S. Army was sending me back to my ancestral home— Africa! That was almost more than I could bear.

I already knew a great deal about Liberia. It and Ethiopia were the only two independent countries on the African continent. Liberia, a free country since 1827, had been built by freed American slaves, and set up by the African Colonization Society as a showcase. The country, though ostensibly free, had leased much of its land to the Firestone Tire Company, an American corporation, for the cultivation of rubber. There were some people, mostly Marxists, who said that Firestone literally ran the country and that Liberia was, in many respects, as much a colony as the other African countries. I couldn't wait to get over there and see for myself.

Liberty Ships were small and independent. Their job was to ferry troops, cargo, supplies—whatever—to wherever they were needed, sometimes traveling in convoys, and sometimes, as with us, sailing alone. The Atlantic was alive with German U-boats, and either way could be dangerous. So we didn't sail directly to Africa as the crow flies. After stopping first for fuel in Trinidad, we zigzagged all over the ocean, ducking those submarines. It took about fifteen days for us to complete the trip.

Meanwhile, on board, we got to know our officers. These men were lately doctors, dentists, pharmacists, lab men, who had been highly successful in their professions—the very best the Negro had to offer, at least in our opinion. This was getting better by the day. From them, we got our assignments. I, by now a full-fledged surgical technician, was trained as a scrub nurse, assistant to the operating physician. I was put in charge of the surgical ward and introduced to my superior officer, Captain Washington, a surgeon from Evanston, Illinois. The rest of the men were set up in pretty much the same kind of situation.

We were also introduced to Colonel Berardinelli, head of the 25th, and Major Weigel, his second-in-command, both of whom were white. As soon as we were firmly established and up and running, they were to be replaced by John West, a colonel from New York City, who was black. Then we would indeed be an all-black outfit.

It was impossible for us not to be proud, highly motivated, and determined. Everybody in the whole damn Army would be watching us because we were black, expecting us to fail. But we said we would swear and be damned if we would give the sons of bitches the pleasure. We'd be the best damned station hospital in the world—so help us, God!

They also told us how important we were going to be as a key part of Allied grand military strategy: America had been at war less than six months; her military had not yet engaged the Germans anywhere. France had collapsed, and Britain had been kicked off the European continent, leaving Hitler and his Nazis in complete control. Russia was expected to collapse at any moment. At the time of Pearl Harbor, the Wehrmacht was less than fifty miles away from Moscow. Winter had halted them then, but now they would surely complete the job. Only in Africa was Hitler's march to total victory being contested.

It was in North Africa, therefore, that Eisenhower was going to throw the first American troops against Field Marshal Erwin Rommel, in a battle the whole world would be watching. Hitler had to be stopped or he would hold all the cards. And the 25th Station Hospital was assigned a very important part of the battle plan. Our job was to receive Eisenhower's wounded from North Africa, stabilize them, and put them on planes at Roberts Field in Liberia, which the 44th Engineers—another newly commissioned Negro outfit—had just finished building. From there, they flew across the Atlantic to Natal, Brazil, the closest point between the two continents, then back to the U.S.A. We at the 25th knew very well what was at stake; we had been briefed, the whole operation explained to us more than once. And we were ready. But warfare chanced to take another path.

Montgomery's campaign eventually forced Rommel out of North Africa, and helped to establish America's military presence in the war. That was the beginning of Hitler's long retreat. The war rapidly moved north, away from us, into Sicily, then northern Italy; so more and more we turned our attention to other things.

This shift completely changed the nature of our mission. The 25th Station Hospital now had a different assignment: We were to service, instead, the airfield at Roberts Field, which now became a rest and refueling station for U.S. Army cargo planes flying over from Natal loaded with military goods and supplies headed for the China-Burma-India theater of operations. In addition, we were to specialize in tropical medicine aimed at reducing sickness and disease among the native population. Malaria, yaws, filariasis, and a disease I had never heard of before, sickle-cell anemia—not Hitler, the Nazis, and the Wehrmacht—became our target.

The wards were open now to the Liberians as well as to the personnel at Roberts Field. The 25th was made up of three wards: the surgical ward (of which I was the head), the medical ward, and the officers ward. Army regulations forbade fraternization between officers and enlisted personnel, so all patients who were officers were assigned to the officers ward. That part of it was all right. That was the way the

Army wanted things to be. But it was not quite that simple. The law of segregation, which forbade the fraternization of white and black soldiers, also had to be honored, and that meant that whenever a white enlisted man was admitted to the hospital, he was assigned to the officers ward.

The same segregation that applied to sickness applied to sex. There were several villages set up near the military base where Liberian women who passed a physical examination would come to service the sexual needs of the soldiers. These visits, too, were strictly segregated; there were villages expressly set up for the white soldiers, and several set up expressly for black soldiers, and never the twain were supposed to meet. In every instance, the black soldiers were made to understand that we were inferior in every way to the whites. That galled us. And, as time went on, it bred in us a growing sense of alienation and rebellion.

Here we were, in Africa, of all places, fighting against racism, of all things, and the American Army was practicing racism itself. It might have been bearable had we all been in the thick of the fighting, but the front was far away, and getting farther. As busy as we were, there was still a lot of time to sit and yak and think and gripe and grumble. Something had to give. And something did: Big John Williams, a warm, friendly, even-tempered man from Baltimore, went on a rampage and wound up killing four men and then himself. It put an end to segregation immediately.

I am not a sentimentalist. I don't know what I was expecting, if anything, but I do know it did my heart, my soul, my whole purpose in life a lot of good to find myself in Africa, especially Liberia. The people were open and friendly, and made us feel more than welcome.

The Americo-Liberians were descendants of the repatriated slaves, and though they spoke with a lilt that sounded like West Indian calypso, they looked so much like us, it was amazing. They were now the ruling class, and that was disconcerting. They had nice homes and were wealthy but their servants, drawn mostly from the other indigenous tribes, were by and large poor and could not vote. The Americo-Liberians behaved toward them as any other ruling class, obviously forgetting what it had meant to be a slave. That bothered me a great deal. I felt proud to be there among my people, in a double sense of the word, but I also felt ashamed.

The brotherhood based on race, which I had fully expected, was nowhere to be found. Rather, the oppression of one class of people, the native tribes, by another class, the Americo-Liberians, was everywhere in evidence. Had Marx been right—that people, as a whole, were much more loyal to their class than to their race?

Still, class oppression was not all I found in Liberia. The twenty-four indigenous tribes could speak little English, which was the language of the Americo-Liberians; quite a few of the tribes couldn't even speak each other's language. Ah, but their music could speak, and whatever they spoke through the music, they made it sound like welcome. They truly were glad to see us and made no effort to hide it.

They were as curious about us as we were about them. We must have seemed like children swapping toys. They invited us to their villages, fed us kola nuts and dumbo, a delicacy made from pounded cassava to be dipped in gravy. They entertained us with their music, their drumming, their singing, their dancing, and introduced us to their families. They gave us their palm wine and their cane juice, which must have been 100 proof and was highly appreciated instead of the 3.2 beer the Army officially allowed us in the PX.

Some miles from the base was the Firestone rubber plantation. Firestone had a ninety-nine-year lease granting the right to grow rubber trees on their plantation and to process them for latex, which was later turned into rubber from which automobile tires were made. Firestone, by virtue of this operation, was in control of the economy.

We were reminded of this fact when we tried to establish a fair wage to be paid to the Liberians who worked for the United States on the camp. Firestone's policy was to pay its workers one shilling per day, and they wanted us to do the same, but we refused. This made Firestone—though it was only a corporation, not a country, like England and France—a colonialist exploiter just as they were. We discussed this issue in the barracks, along with the other things that were beginning to bother us, which we thought constituted racism on the part of the Army as well.

But none of this meant we couldn't enjoy ourselves, getting to know the people and their customs. One day, the first sergeant had us out for a march of a mile or two, to stretch our legs after our long sea voyage. We came to a bridge that crossed a running stream, and in that stream were several ladies with their children, completely nude, taking a bath after the long walk back from the plantation, where they went to shop at the company store. They saw us coming but went on with their bathing.

Not so with us. The platoon broke step, came to halt on the bridge, and stood staring down at the buck-naked ladies, some of whom were young and delightfully endowed. They looked up at us and began to ask us questions: "You never saw your sister without her clothes? You never saw your mother?" Well, the truth of the matter was that most of us hadn't. We were puritans, and nudity in the female was an evil, not to be stared at, but to be avoided. We stood there looking foolish; the ladies with no embarrassment whatsoever finished bathing, put on their robes and turbans, lifted their baskets laden with supplies, and went their way, still laughing as we gawked.

I looked and learned and loved it all, especially the music. I could listen to a song—hear it one time—and weeks later, when I came back to the village, I could sing along with the native singers.

The songs were sprightly stories told in fun. They dealt with what was happening in the villages and at the base. Listening to them was almost like reading the gossip column in a racy newspaper:

> *Airport soldier drowned in the river,*
> *No more jigjig, no more money,*
> *Sister Taylor, why do you cry?*
> *'Cause your darling boy is dead and*
> *Gone to hell.*

Song after song, I learned them as soon as I heard them—and sang them all over the place. They were topical, funny, and satirical, just like the calypso I had heard and loved back in Harlem. These songs were as popular as they were funny, and every time we visited a village, the people would sing them as a part of the evening's festivities—their way of entertaining us. And after a few drinks of cane juice to warm me up, I would join in.

The villagers were flattered that a black GI could sing their songs—word for word, accent for accent, and gesture for gesture— almost as if I were a native. Soon the word about me and my singing spread and every time I showed up, I would be lionized, plied with plenty to eat—and to drink—and expected to join in the singing; and I would be glad to oblige. Sometimes, on special occasions, like the visit of the paramount chief of the tribe, I would be sent for. When local dignitaries came to visit the post, they'd point me out, and some-times invite me to participate in the conversation. One visitor in par-ticular was deeply interested and impressed.

Her name was Eva Morris, and the Morrises were Americo-Liberians. They were rich, powerful, and personal friends with Robert Barclay, the president of Liberia. Eva was sensitive and intelligent, and possibly lonely. Her father, a man of great social and political impor-tance, loved her and gave her everything she could possibly want. But Eva was a love child, not part of the regular Morris family.

I loved to talk to Eva. She was stimulating and curious; wealthy, but not a snob. Though her own mother had come from the village, Eva was less knowledgeable about the tribes and the villages than I was. I liked her very much, but never felt totally at ease in her presence. I felt more like a traitor to the working class.

One friendly young man, a graduate of Howard University, of-fered to intercede. He pointed out that Eva already owned acres and acres of young rubber trees, the chief source of wealth in Liberia, which would begin to produce latex when they were fifteen years old—latex for which Firestone would provide a hungry and waiting market. If I married Eva, all of that would be mine. I would be a rich man, fixed for life.

Yes, I said, but I didn't come to Liberia looking for a wife. Eva and I remained friends, but always with this distance between her way of life and mine. Eva was always a lady, and I was always a gentleman. And that was all there ever was between us.

The Americo-Liberians, black though they were, tended to live like Europeans or Americans, and that surprised me. They had new cars; they regularly sent their children off to Europe or America to college, and they fraternized with their peers at Firestone. They seldom mixed with the natives, with whom I had already bonded, who were authentic Africans and much more fun. I was not only uneasy with the class conflict I felt was brewing in Liberia, I was disturbed by it. But most of the soldiers on the post were not. They, too, quite easily, took to treating all the natives, not as brothers and comrades, but like servants, in much the same way white folks treated black folks down in Georgia.

This arrogance disturbed me, too, and I began to entertain a horrible suspicion. For most of my life, I had believed that black folks were in many ways morally superior to white folks, especially in our dealings with each other. I was profoundly disappointed that the Americo-Liberians, the children of slaves themselves, would come to Africa and behave as if they themselves were the slaveholders now.

I was even more disappointed in much of our behavior, at how easily we became racist and exploiters, treating the natives with that very same superior disdain and disrespect about which we ourselves were constantly complaining to the company commander. Calling the natives zigaboos and burrheads, some of the soldiers were patronizing, and condescending, treating them, in many instances, as if we were white, and they were niggers. I listened, appalled, as soldiers in my own barracks would sometimes brag about how they had tricked some dumb and stupid Liberian out of his money.

The natives were neither as naive nor as stupid as some of us thought. One soldier, a bit of a lady's man and a city slicker, established a sexual line of credit with a young lady, promising that come payday, he would come to the village and pay up. Payday came, but the soldier didn't show. The woman came to the camp with her father, the local paramount chief, pointed the soldier out, and neither would leave until that soldier, under orders from the company commander, paid his obligation.

Then there was Jackson, the man who bragged of knowing exactly how to handle women. There was a village of several thatched huts set up in a couple of neat rows, where the girls would come mostly on weekends to conduct their business—first come, first served.

But Jackson had made his own arrangements. His woman had her own individual hut, open only to Jackson. All he had to do was pay the monthly expenses. He had it made, until one payday he lost all his money gambling. Jackson was in trouble. But after a few drinks of cane juice, he didn't see it that way. He got boisterous and belligerent, and finally decided the time had come to show his woman who was boss. A few of us, sharing the bottle with Jackson, went along to the village to see how the master would handle this situation.

He started cussing and shouting even before he stormed into the hut, loudmouthing the woman from one end of the little street to the other. The woman begged him to quiet down, asking, "Please, Jackson, tell me, man, what is the matter with you?" Something about the question must have insulted Jackson, and he decided to whip the woman for her insolence. There were sounds of a face being slapped, just like he said there would be, a gasp of surprise from the woman, followed by a thud, then a grunt and a scream, but not from the woman—from Jackson. Then there was the sound of mighty fumblin' going on inside the little hut, bodies heaving and twisting and crashing into things . . . the sound of Jackson begging, "Woman, don't make me have to hurt you!"

"Hurt me? Jackson, man, you fucking with your own death." Then—according to Jackson when he could talk again—she butted him on the jaw with such force that his flying body crashed through the walls of the hut, crumpling it to the ground. The woman came bounding out, but luckily some of the soldiers were able to restrain her, until we could get the semiconscious Jackson out of the village, which we did as fast as we possibly could.

In February of 1945, I was returned to the States, to Fort Dix, New Jersey, right across the river from Harlem. Before I left on my furlough, I was given an evaluation by an Army psychologist. I told him that I was drinking a fifth of whiskey a day, about my vivid nightmares, my feeling of being lost and at my wits' end. The drift of his questions, his attitude, seemed very sympathetic. After all, I had spent thirty-two months overseas, all in one spot, doing my duty, and serving my time, and I fully expected to be discharged, that the war for me was over. I thought he understood the anguish I was feeling. I told him I wanted to spend my first few days home in Harlem. He said, "Go right ahead."

Harlem hadn't changed and acted glad to see me. There were the old hangouts—the Apollo Theatre and Father Divine's. Dick Campbell was now the head of Camp Shows, Inc. His job was to recruit talent and send them to entertain the troops overseas. He and Muriel treated me as if I were their own son, home at last from the war. They wined and dined me, putting me up in their new apartment, way up on Sugar Hill. They took me downtown to see *Cabin in the Sky,* then backstage to meet Ethel Waters.

My final session with the psychologist hit like a bombshell. I was healthy as an ox, he said, in superb condition, and eminently fit for duty. My drinking didn't matter. I was not going to be discharged; rather, I was being reassigned. I was allowed to go south and spend the rest of my furlough with my family. After that, I was to report to Lake Placid, New York, whence I would go to Fort Leonard Wood, Missouri, to be retrained, and after that—off to the South Pacific.

I made a quick trip home to Valdosta to see the family. Then I reported, already depressed, but as ordered, to Fort Leonard Wood, Missouri.

Leonard Wood confirmed what I had already begun to suspect: Conditions for blacks, in the service and out, had not improved at all, but maybe had gotten worse. On my very first night, the lights in the barracks were suddenly turned on at about two o'clock in the morning, and we were ordered to fall out into the company street. Outside, we were lined up, stiff and grumpy, and a local sheriff, walking along with a crying white girl, shined a big flashlight in each soldier's face, trying to identify the one the weeping girl said had raped her. She didn't find him.

I was assigned to the dispensary, along with two other medics and two German prisoners of war whose job was to do whatever we told them to do. Usually they cleaned up the place, which didn't take very long. Traffic was seldom heavy—an upset stomach, a few headaches or toothaches, boils and blisters, which were soon disposed of. Nothing to do then but sit around and talk—sometimes with the prisoners. I knew a little German, they knew a little English, enough on both sides to maintain conversation. They had been captured on the Russian front in the dead of winter, and were very glad that they had wound up in America. They showed us pictures from home they carried in their wallets, and the sergeant in charge reciprocated. I didn't. I'm not sure I even had a wallet, and if I had, it certainly didn't have anybody's picture in it.

There were no classes, no drills, no planned recreation. Soldiers we were with plenty of time on our hands, not much freer than the German POWs who did the dirty work. I personally could make no sense of what was happening. I was lost, totally without personal aim or purpose, involved in a war in which I did not believe. Hitler was dead. I had fulfilled my commitment to that part of the Struggle.

Most black soldiers had little animosity toward Japan. Rather, it almost did our hearts good to see the white man—the British, the French, the Dutch, the black man's traditional masters—in Southeast Asia, getting their asses kicked by the Japanese who, after all, were colored people, too.

It was natural that I'd find the post library and become reacquainted with books. The librarian was a young lady named Elsie Herald, quiet, well dressed, and very attractive. We hit it off immediately. Friendly but not forward, she was a perfect reminder of the sister many of us had left behind.

All of this should have put me right at home, but it didn't. The books were more frivolous than serious—novels, detective stories, stuff like that. I had enough Harlem in my manners to captivate Elsie, who had never been to any place bigger than St. Louis. I believe she enjoyed the times when I came in and talked with her—I could tell. I had my own standards of masculine behavior, however, my own code: Elsie was much too nice for me to fool around with. Like the rest of the soldiers, I went to St. Louis on a weekend pass to go to the dance hall, catch whatever was playing at the movies, get drunk, buy a good meal, and to visit with the whores; but that was only once or twice.

No, I was in no mood for books, or for nice young ladies like Elsie Herald. I, who was born to laugh and could hold my own with all of the GI lover boys and jokesters, found little to laugh about at Fort Leonard Wood. I was looking desperately for a sense of direction, somebody to tell me what the hell I was fighting for.

So there I was, with all this pressure building up, all this alienation rambling around inside of me, with no connection at all to the Struggle. The easy camaraderie that had been so much a part of those first days in Liberia, when everything was clear and relevant, when hell or heaven could be easily described in terms of how they served the needs of that Struggle, was nowhere in sight. Even laughter had abandoned ship. Nothing was funny now. Seizing property, throwing the Japanese into camps, and whipping Japan had nothing to offer black people, in my opinion. Here was something that even Br'er Rabbit couldn't weave into the black experience. No High John the Conqueror could tell me what was in it for us! Nothing here that I could be colored about. I was determined not to be sent to the Far East, but did absolutely nothing at all to prevent it.

V-E Day in Europe was anticlimactic—didn't affect me at all. The death of Franklin Delano Roosevelt, however, did. It came to me as a private piece of sorrow with nobody there to share it. I remember sitting under a tree on the grass staring at the knowledge that something intimately related to the Struggle was over and done with, and he who had been so long the guiding light, the magnificent explainer, was available no more.

It seems to me, I was under that same tree on August 7, 1945, when I got the news about the atomic bomb being dropped on Hiroshima, and my long season of mourning came to a head. It seemed that a whole matched set of assurances about civilization had just been wiped out—that something humanly precious had been thrown away forever. That was the last coherent thing I remember about Fort Leonard Wood.

I ended up involved in the commandeering of an Army truck and roaring around the post with a bunch of drunken soldiers. I, along with the rest of the men, was arrested and brought up on charges. But the war was finally over and the Army was anxious to rid itself of excess baggage. The charges were dropped, and I was given an Honorable Discharge on October 11, 1945.

CHAPTER 13

Ruby Turning Corners

Four events of great personal importance happened to me in 1945. All efforts to maintain the marriage with Frankie Dee Brown came to an end. I came to a new level of myself as a woman. Franklin Delano Roosevelt died. And I worked with an actor I had never heard of before—Ossie Davis.

Frankie was a sincere and decent person, and a good provider, but marriage to him was becoming more and more unsatisfactory. During this time, he would occasionally stalk me. At rehearsal, people would tell me they had run into him and that he was not friendly, that he was angry and waiting for me outside. I began to be afraid of him.

Early in 1945, I asked him for a divorce, and finally, he agreed, saying he would attend to the legalities. I still stayed at the house, however, when he was away, but I went to Mother's when he was due back in town.

Back and forth between Frank's house and my mother's apartment, I was uncertain of how to go about initiating the divorce. He'd done nothing about it. I suppose I should have just made a clean break, but I liked being in the old brownstone when he wasn't there—the privacy of living alone, despite Frankie's father who stayed on the ground floor. Besides we hadn't yet made arrangements, or discussed who would take care of the house, handle the expenses, the bills, and so forth. I couldn't just turn my back and walk away.

When it was known that we were separated, men began to look at me differently and I even received two marriage proposals. I guess I exuded an air of availability. It was a heady, scary time. I had never experienced this kind of attention before and I welcomed it.

I began to date a Harlem businessman, who soon had me spinning like a top. He seemed so knowledgeable and self-confident, and gave me a sense of security and strength. He had broad, comfortable shoulders, was gentle and reassuring, and made me feel as if I were the only woman in the world possible for him. He had taken me many places, including two business meetings, at one of which I waited two hours for him. He spoke affectionately, but for a long time he had not even tried to kiss me. All that was to change.

One beautiful day, we sailed up the Hudson River. I'd never been on a yacht before. After a light meal, he took me to the quarters below deck, and after a while, he proceeded to undress me, to kiss me, and to tell me of his love. He then carried me to a small but elegant bathroom, put me in a bubble bath he'd prepared, washed, dried, then wrapped me in a towel that looked like clouds, and carried me to an exquisitely dressed bed.

Before he returned from his bath, I looked around at the luxurious, cozy setting, felt the motion of the boat, and listened to the soft music as it accompanied the sound of the water. Paradise, I thought, must be something like this. With my friend that day, I experienced more about the physical aspects of love, about suspense, sensuality, and excitement than I'd even imagined. What a marvelous lover! Could anything on earth or in heaven compare with the joy of this experience?

He had "located all the bells and blown all the whistles," was how my sister LaVerne expressed it after he dropped me at her apartment on 150th Street, where I spent the night. I told her what had happened. We both concluded that I must be in love.

We met frequently at his apartment, and after about a month, he gave me the keys. I don't remember discussing love, marriage, or relationship issues. I felt I was on a roller coaster in an adult amusement park. His attention was constant and almost overwhelming. He made me feel that I belonged to him completely, like an obsession.

One day, we had arranged to meet at his place, but I was early and intended to let myself in as usual and wait. The keys, to my consternation, didn't work, because the door was bolted from the inside. A kind of panic began as I called for him to let me in. It seemed to start from the base of my spine and work itself up to my head and through my mouth as I continued to call and bang on the door. He was inside with someone! I could hear voices, muffled voices, women's voices, whispering, scuffling, and scurrying around. What was going on in there?

How dare he invite me to his house and lock the door against me? Who the hell did he—? What the hell—? "Let me in before I break down this door!" I screamed, pounded, and kicked the door. Never had I felt such fury. I knew they heard me. The world probably heard me.

Dogs. Dogs. Men are just dogs! My mother is right. You are all dogs! With shoulders, hips, fists, I tried to break the very substantial door. I had to get in. All hell was not going to keep me out!

Finally, I heard the floor bolt being moved. Locks unlocked, and a sheepish-looking man, my friend's driver, opened the door. My anger blazed past him to two women who seemed in shock as I slammed my way into the apartment, feeling blood and fire pumping from every aperture in my body. *He* wasn't there!

The driver then explained that he had been instructed to call and inform me that a sudden trip out of town had been necessary and that my friend could not keep our date—but he had completely forgotten to tell me. As the two young women who seemed to have dressed hurriedly sat in the living room looking embarrassed, the driver apologized profusely and asked if I would see fit not to report the incident.

I fled the scene, trembling, a cold escape in a sweaty body, trying to recover from a sickening, jealous rage. My hand hurt from all the pounding, and my mind hurt to think that this angry, irrational, dangerous person of a few minutes ago could be me!

Through that experience, I discovered dimensions of myself I had never known. The bursting forth from girlhood into womanhood was painful, but in retrospect, it was beautiful, too. It taught me how little and how much it means to be a sexually fulfilled woman. I was no longer spinning like a top. I had reclaimed myself and was standing on my own two feet.

My friend continued to travel a great deal, but it didn't matter now. When I looked at him, he was the same man—confident, charming, debonair—but something in me had changed. With so much happening in my personal life and in the political life of this country, before I could take stock, he had traveled out of my mind.

Franklin Delano Roosevelt, FDR, had been President as long as I remembered. He was the only one I'd heard talked about in our house. Everywhere, during four elections, black people would speak of him, his wife, Eleanor, and Mary McLeod Bethune, with affection and hope. Ms. Bethune had been appointed to FDR's "Black Cabinet" as the director of Negro affairs of the National Youth Administration. In programs like the WPA, where Mother got a job teaching adults to read, FDR had taken people off home relief and put them back to work. There were programs—and jobs—for builders and artists, actors, and writers, and many more. I received training in radio theater as part of the National Youth Administration. All of this, thanks to FDR.

FDR was a politician, however. It took Eleanor and Mary McLeod Bethune to keep Franklin on course, it was believed. These two women helped put a human and feminine face on the New Deal. Roosevelt, an aristocrat, encouraged the wealthy to accept the responsibility of privilege, and injected capitalism with compassion and common sense, as I reason today. With Eleanor and Franklin, ordinary folks knew they had caring friends in the White House. His sudden death in April of 1945 stunned the country. A feeling of spiritual devastation unexpectedly overtook me, and joined me to millions of others all over the world.

Around the time of his funeral, I found myself alone in Frankie's house wearing a black dress, standing at a window, tracing raindrops with my fingers as they scurried down the windowpane, like I'd done as a child. Why wasn't it storming? I became the thunder, the lightning, the flash flood, and the wind, howling in an effort to rouse the elements to join in the distress that came unannounced, as I slumped down on the piano bench, with head in hand, and elbows sounding a discord, insulting the piano keys. Good-bye, FDR.

Later that year, I got a call from the Broadway producers of a new play called *Jeb,* starring Ossie Davis. Would I come in for an audition? I said yes.

CHAPTER 14

Home Is the Soldier

In the fall of 1945, my return home to Valdosta, what I remember of it, provided me with no sense of joy at all, and did nothing to relieve my sense of solitary confinement. I was sullen, moody, hostile, filled to the brim with self-pity and despair, and wanted only to be left severely alone. The family obliged. I don't remember much of anything about my return, except that it was very brief. I was often drunk and smoked a lot, a habit I had acquired from Special Services when I was in Liberia. I remember that Mama was very concerned about me, but said nothing. I remember Daddy, sensing my need for silence and for privacy, also said nothing. I don't remember the rest of the family at all.

What I do remember is that one day, a telegram came to me from Dick Campbell. He said that a new play about a black veteran returning from the war was being produced by Herman Shumlin, who was looking for someone just like me to play the lead. Dick suggested I get back to New York as fast as I could. A couple of days later, I was on my way to catch up with the rest of my life. And that of course meant meeting Ruby Dee.

The melancholia that had followed me to Valdosta, hanging over me like a death sentence, faded away with the miles. I had been reprieved and I was free. Going north this time had all of the elements of a great escape on the Underground Railroad.

Back in Harlem again, I at last felt a sense of safety and security. The long and endless burden of fighting, killing, and dying had suddenly lifted; people belonged to themselves once again, and not to the war. The feeling of carnival, to which the whole world was invited, waited for returning soldiers at Penn Station, a general intoxication, a welcome home, where joy was mandatory, and sleep against the law.

Dick and Muriel moved me in with them; then Dick took me, uniform and all, downtown to see Herman Shumlin, who was the producer and the director of the play *Jeb.* In those days, Broadway had a conscience and Shumlin was one of its most liberal voices. The war against racism in Europe was over; the good guys had won by the skin of their teeth, and were determined that now was the time to attack racism in America, head on.

Several plays on the subject of America's continuing shameful behavior toward African Americans hit Broadway that season: *Deep Are the Roots,* which was a smash hit, followed by *On Whitman Avenue* and *Strange Fruit.*

Then came *Jeb,* which was about a black soldier returning from the South Pacific where he had lost his leg, making it impossible for him to return to work in the cane fields of his native Louisiana. While in the service, however, Jeb had picked up several clerical skills, including how to operate an adding machine. It so happens that the old bookkeeper, white of course, is retiring, which leads Jeb to ask if he might not now have the job. The plantation owner, who has known Jeb and his family all Jeb's life, tries to explain to him that a black man working in the office instead of out in the cane fields was out of the question. He offers other jobs but Jeb, superconfident of his skills with the adding machine, insists on being given a chance. This leads to a confrontation with the Ku Klux Klan, the cane fields are set afire, and Jeb barely escapes the city with his life. In the end he decides to return to his home, to his family, and especially to Libby, his beloved, and to take his stand like a man, even if they kill him for it.

I read for the part and got it.

CHAPTER 15

We Meet

Ossie Davis? Humph! In the newspapers, there was this picture of the man who was to play the lead, a veteran of the war, still in uniform. I said to myself, and to some other actors, that the casting people probably snatched this man from behind a mule, stuck him in a uniform, and cast him because "all colored people can act, can't they?"

None of us had ever heard of this Ossie Davis person. Why couldn't somebody from the American Negro Theatre get the role? I auditioned for the part of Libby, Jeb's girlfriend. I didn't get it. I was later called to understudy, however, which made me feel somewhat better. At least it was a job in the theater and on Broadway.

PART TWO

CHAPTER 16

Jeb: The Play Is the Thing

RUBY: The rehearsals for *Jeb* began the last week in December 1945 at the New Amsterdam Theater. As an understudy, I may not have been present during the first week. At any rate, I don't recall ever being formally introduced to Ossie Davis.

That first week or two, I see myself sitting in a darkened theater watching the director, Herman Shumlin, discussing the Robert Ardrey text with the actors, or staging and reworking the action. I was covering the role of Libby for Geraldine Prillerman. William Marshall was the understudy for Ossie as Jeb and some of the other male characters. Marshall, a tall, regal-looking actor, had quite a sense of humor. Often we would sit together, and from time to time, we would talk about Ossie. We agreed that, surprisingly, he was a good actor. He was probably hired, though, because he looked like a country bumpkin—innocent, good-natured, and not too intelligent, perhaps—and just the kind of person with whom white folks felt comfortable.

In the first place, he was tall and gaunt, with a pronounced and very active Adam's apple when he spoke. Second, his clothes seemed decidedly to belong to somebody else. The jackets and shirts he wore were too big and the sleeves seemed to land in the middle of his fore-arm. Pants came nowhere near his ankles—a tall, skinny man dressed in the well-worn apparel of a short, fat man. Perhaps he had shopped at the Salvation Army stores, Goodwill, or rubbish bins—with his eyes shut, we concluded gleefully.

OSSIE: I remember one day I was rehearsing on stage, and I was wearing this secondhand houndstooth coat, with the zooty pants—I think they were secondhand, too. The sleeves on the coat were too short; I knew it and I didn't give much of a damn. I was aware, as we rehearsed, that sitting in the auditorium were the understudies. There was Bill Marshall, a tall, imposing-looking guy. Sitting next to him was a little girl who looked like a teenager with long, plaited hair that came down her back, and big eyes—a very nice-looking young lady who turned out to be Ruby Dee.

Geraldine Prillerman was pretty and one of the nicest people in the world, but her interpretation of the role of Libby was less than pleasing to Shumlin. Not nearly southern enough. After a week or so, the decision was made to let Geraldine go and find another actor. Meanwhile, in order that the rehearsal schedule not be interrupted, Ruby Dee was called on to do what understudies do—fill in till a suitable replacement could be found. But when "the Dee" hit the stage, the search for a replacement was immediately called off. Ruby had landed the job.

Ruby was a professional. She knew exactly how to handle herself, which surprised everybody because she looked so young and immature. She knew the character, she knew the lines, and she knew the blocking. The rehearsal didn't miss a beat because of her. And she was very easy to know—in no way standoffish, or self-centered, and certainly not temperamental. Friendly, but not familiar. I liked her right away. So did the rest of the company. She belonged.

Ruby impressed me as somebody that I had known all my life.

RUBY: I got the role, but I don't remember feeling ecstatic or vic-torious, because I liked Geraldine and thought she was doing okay with lines that were not the greatest in the world. I still came out into the house when not on stage, but as a part of the company now; I didn't sit with Bill Marshall and the other understudies anymore.

Our lines in the play were written in dialect, and though well intentioned, they were sometimes quaint and a little sticky. One that has stuck in my mind through the years is when Libby, realizing that Jeb has to wear an aluminum leg, exclaims, "Oh, Jeb, yo' laig, yo' laig, yo' po' laig!"

Ossie was gentle, almost shy, I thought, when we began working together in our few but important scenes. We were not quite friends, but at least, I felt more civil toward him.

There were two unusual occurrences in January 1946, however, that were harbingers of deeper things to come. We were perhaps in the last week of the four-week rehearsal. I was sitting in the front row of the theater when we came to the part in the play where Jeb's boss is questioning him about a misdeed of which he's been accused, and part of Jeb's defense is "You know me, you know Libby!" My heart leaped when I heard him say instead, "You know me, you know Ruby!" Even after the director finally corrected him, "Libby, Libby, Ossie," he seemed oblivious to the fact that he was substituting my name. He looked surprised, unbelieving, that he was making such an error.

A few days earlier, something much more unsettling occurred. I was sitting watching a scene. At one point, Ossie stood up on stage and silently, slowly began tying his tie. At that moment, I distinctly remember feeling something like a bolt of lightning, an electrical charge, flash between us. Although I didn't move, I felt a physical jolt. Other than paying attention to the scene, I had not been thinking about him in any particular way.

The whole thing made me think of the classical Cupid with his bow and arrow. It was an odd sensation, as I had no romantic notions about him personally. Only Libby loved Jeb and vice versa. For many years after, I could recall the sensation of that marvelous moment. Now only the memory of the fact remains.

This last incident leads me to believe that maybe Ossie and I had known each other in some previous existence.

Jeb began its pre-Broadway run in New Haven, then went to Boston and on to Philadelphia. At that time, black people could not stay in hotels owned and operated by whites. However, in Philadelphia, I think Shumlin used his influence to permit me to stay in a lovely hotel near the theater.

As vanity would have it, I caught a severe cold with fever two days before the opening. In preparing for the trip, I decided not to wear or to pack my snuggies, those very warm undergarments that come to the knees. All my life, it seemed, I had worn them in winter along with the matching undershirts. Although Ossie had given me no indication that he entertained the idea of viewing me in my underwear, the idea had lodged itself in some remote part of my brain and dictated that for this set of ugly drawers I substitute some frivolous, delicate, and male-pleasing lingerie. Well, that decision cost me dearly.

Mr. Shumlin sent a physician to ascertain my ability to open in the play. Medicines were prescribed and administered. It was determined that I must miss the final rehearsals and remain in bed. Mr. Shumlin was confident that medication and a day's rest would leave me fit enough for the opening in the next two days. He seemed not at all worried when he came to check on me.

Later that day, Ossie also visited me. I was very glad to see him, but I felt somewhat foolish, knowing that all this concern may have been avoided were it not for stupidity, vanity, and lust. Ossie was sitting in a chair, reassuring me that he would rehearse with me anytime it could be arranged, should I feel it necessary.

Suddenly there was a loud and insistent knocking at the door, which startled us both. "Yes," I inquired, "who's there?"

"Security" was the unpleasant and authoritative answer. "It is against hotel regulations for an unmarried guest to entertain men in the room. You will have to leave," he called out to Ossie.

Ossie opened the door to reassure the man that he had come to visit a sick friend. Racism, my guilt about the reasons for being sick, embarrassment for Ossie, and just the fact that I was in bed unnerved me. I didn't know enough about hotels to have called the front desk to inquire about the intrusion.

Headlined in my mind was "Negro Man in Room with Negro Whore!" Ossie and the intruder talked at the door; then he came back to the bed, kissed me on the forehead, promised to return, and left. As the door closed behind him, a feeling of shame came over me, I plunged my face in the pillow, and cried.

On February 7, 1946, *Jeb* opened to constructive and generally good out-of-town reviews. One reviewer, R.E.P. Sensenderfer, of the *Evening Bulletin,* said of me, "But it is Ruby Dee as Libby, his sweetheart, who calls for greatest praise." That should have made me feel proud, but my mind turned to Ossie. I wanted the reviewer to have written more appreciatively of *his* performance. As a man and as an actor, he was warm, intelligent, and enormously appealing.

Sensenderfer went on, "Negroes . . . as usual demonstrate the natural and remarkable histrionic talents of this race upon the stage. They seem instinctively to grasp the meaning of their part and give it an uninhibited projection. That the emotions called for are primary, need not detract from the performance." That comment gave us all good reason to discredit him. How dare he imply that Negro performers didn't need to study technique and craft!

By the time *Jeb* opened in New York, Ossie and I had become good and intimate friends. Neither of us had had extensive sexual experience, to say the least, but I think I knew a little more than he. After all, I'd seen two pornographic films, which taught me a lot. Then there was his discomfort with the fact of my previous union because his father—who didn't believe in divorce—could never approve of me.

Jeb opened in New York at the Martin Beck Theatre on February 20, 1946, and closed after nine performances. Ossie came to see me the day after the opening. True, unlike Philadelphia, the notices were fair to awful; it was obvious the play would have to close. A little regret was in order, but not this depression. He seemed vulnerable, helpless, and distracted. I asked him what was the matter. He wouldn't tell me, so I began to worry.

OSSIE: The postwar flow of adrenaline had suddenly stopped. After the flowers, the "Break a legs," the wires of congratulations and best wishes, the cheering of the audience at final curtain call, the opening night party for the cast and crew at Sardi's, that old depression—which I hadn't felt since stepping out of uniform and into the theater—had come to visit again, bringing with it a deep sense of guilt and self-betrayal. It was like being on a speeding train to heaven, when heaven is not the place you want to go.

Success as an actor was not what I had been waiting for. I loved the theater; maybe I loved it too much—the nonspecific camaraderie, the easy passions, the sensuous atmosphere, the self-kissing indulgence almost demanded by an audience whose applause was like a shot of heady wine, intoxicating to the point of subaddiction—I loved it all. But I didn't come into the world to be an actor. No, it was *writing* to which my soul was committed. Suppose I became a star, with role after role taking all my time and all my effort. What about my writing then?

Ruby was the only sympathetic ear, the one person, I knew instinctively, to whom I could turn for aid and comfort. But when she questioned me, I couldn't answer.

"I know you wrote for the Army newspaper," she said, "but have you ever had anything published?" Which was none of her business.

RUBY: The show was bound to close, but I needn't have worried. Almost before the closing notices were posted, some people from the production of *Anna Lucasta,* one of the biggest hits on Broadway, came backstage to see us, and Ossie and I were hired on the spot.

CHAPTER 17

The American Negro Theatre: Anna Lucasta

RUBY: *Anna Lucasta* had originally opened uptown at the American Negro Theatre in 1944. It had been adapted from a Polish play, *Anna Lukaska,* written by Phillip Yordan, but Harry Wagstaf Gribble, one of Broadway's premiere white directors, brought it to Abe Hill and Fred O'Neal, the founders of ANT, because he thought it might do better with an all-Negro cast. They agreed. *Anna* was then showcased at ANT, where the process of adapting the play had begun.

I remember watching Harry Gribble and some of the actors during rehearsal as they improvised on the script—making up dialogue on the spot, throwing out scenes, and creating new ones. There was much writing, rewriting, then hopping up on stage to try it all out. I was deeply interested, but hardly involved, in all this activity. Finishing college, working at Westinghouse, managing a house, and carrying on with the rest of my life, left me with little time for ANT projects, but whenever I could be, I was there.

Anna Lucasta was a comedy-drama. True, the central character was a streetwalker, and in that respect, the play was in no way groundbreaking, but it was original; it was a fresh look at Negro life, without apology, from a bright, almost sassy perspective. The original cast included Hilda Simms, Fred O'Neal, Earle Hyman, Alice Childress, her husband, Alvin, and others. It was a hit in Harlem and immediately attracted Broadway's attention, which I'm sure is what Gribble had in mind all along. It wasn't long before John Wildeberg, a businessman, bought the entire production and moved it straight downtown to the Mansfield Theatre on 47th Street (no out-of-town tryout expense).

It was July 1944, Broadway needed a lift, needed a laugh, needed to try to forget the war in Europe. *Anna Lucasta* was just the ticket. It opened to rave reviews, and two years later, the show was still playing to full houses. At times, as many as six companies were playing somewhere in the country.

The producers thought it was time to send the show to Europe, where a London production was to be mounted. They also planned a national tour. Ossie was hired to play Rudolph, but it was not certain that I could play Anna.

Walter Ashe, assistant to Harry Gribble, was in charge of casting. He considered me too gentle and naive to play Anna, a street-smart hooker with a sensitive inner core. He could see me as understudy, but as little else. After several weeks of intensive rehearsals, I was given a chance to play a Wednesday matinee. To everyone's surprise, including the producer John Wildeberg, Walter immediately offered me the part. The leading role in *Anna Lucasta* was the first such assignment during my time with ANT. It was one of the few major roles I would play in my career.

Meanwhile, Ossie had been sent to join the Chicago company to ready himself for the September tour.

OSSIE: Chicago, at that time always in short supply of theater, took its theater much more seriously than New York. The black community had pounced on *Anna* like a leopard from ambush, hungry to make a kill. Actors were treated like demigods—we could do no wrong.

We were at the Civic Theatre. At the same time, there was a Bernard Shaw play in town that had Katharine Cornell and Marlon Brando in the cast. John Bowie, a member of our cast, and Marlon were close friends. Every night, as if it were a running competition, somebody would put on an after-theater extravaganza, complete with wine, women, and song—and some of Chicago's best eating. All of this required a lot of serious drinking, but I never muffed a cue or missed a performance.

By day, I rehearsed with Janice Kingslow, a beautiful, versatile young actress being groomed to replace Hilda Simms, who would soon be going to London to star in *Romeo and Juliet*. I also got to know Harry Gribble, who seemed intrigued by the fact that I was a slightly different cut from most of the other Rudolphs he had trained over the years. My hangovers, which were as sizable and constant as his, were verbalized with just a touch of the old iambic pentameter. Sometimes we'd spout between us from Keats, Shelley, Omar Khayyám, Shakespeare's sonnets, and other exemplars of England's "poetic melancholy." I learned that he, like me, was a writer who didn't write. He insisted, though, on getting first crack at anything theatrical that I might chance to write. That was the beginning of a warm and longstanding personal friendship that later included his generous gifts of books, ballet tickets, and holiday parties for our children.

RUBY: Many things were happening to me in Ossie's absence. I had already made one motion picture short for the U.S. Army Morale Division in which I played an innocent-looking girl who had venereal disease. Thanks to all the recent publicity from my outings in *Jeb,* and now in *Anna,* the calls started coming in from independent filmmakers, like Toddy Productions, and later, the Smith twins from Harlem, Morgan and Marvin.

These films were short and very cheaply produced, but they did pay, and a string of Negro theaters all over the country distributed them. This operation grew to be so large and so lucrative that Hollywood finally took notice, and began making films like *Hallelujah* and

Sing, You Sinners, specifically designed to compete for these black dollars at the mainstream box office.

On one independent job, I remember working without a script. The director, who was also the producer, would lay out the story and break out the specifics as we went along. The entire film was shot in a room about twenty-five by thirty feet, and it starred Lawrence Criner. He gave me pointers on improvisation as well as telling me exactly what to do and say.

In one story, he played a man who had just been released from prison, and he was looking forward to his first meal as a free man. He was sending me, his daughter, to get him a steak, some greens, some cornbread, some pie, and a good bottle of booze. And as he gave me the money to pay for it all, he said—and this was the punch line— "And what kind of sandwich you want?"

OSSIE: After the war, I was eager to get back to writing, and while I was in Chicago, I started a new play, *Nineteen for Nothing,* that included some Army experiences. A Negro sergeant is cut off from his company in a fierce battle. After the battle is over, in trying to make his way back to his own outfit, he stumbles upon a group of white American soldiers—leaderless, scared, trapped, as he is, behind enemy lines. They quarrel among themselves, first over accepting a black man among them, then over whether to allow that black man to lead them out of the trap. A rabid racist in the group opens fire on some of his own comrades who want to forget about color, thereby revealing their hiding place to the encircling Germans, who rake them with a withering fire. All nineteen men are killed. My thesis was that white America, rather than accept black leadership, would rather die.

I wrestled with the play whenever I could, but the iambic pentameter verse I put into my sergeant hero's mouth—as if under compulsion—was much too grandiose to be believable. I tried to fix it, but I didn't know how. I was finally forced to abandon it.

What I needed, in my opinion, was some formal nonmatriculating courses in playwriting, such as I heard were being offered at Columbia University. I welcomed the chance to go on the road because I'd be able to save money for tuition.

RUBY: Upon the realization that Ossie was an aspiring author, my antennae lit up and tingled. I remember one evening at a gathering in someone's home when we were discussing our ambitions, and he told me that he was a writer.

"Shouldn't you have something published by now?" I asked with less than great tact. I felt impatient to read some of his work. After all, he was a genius. He'd told me so himself—that he'd been classified as such—and I could believe he was. Not long afterward, he gave me a pile of his poetry to read. Although I was no judge of genius, I'd had some grounding in literature at Hunter College, and in my opinion, the man had been underestimated.

Immediately I set about putting his poems in presentation form and submitting them to every magazine I thought worthy of this great work. Some of the poems had a formal ring, like those of the English classicists; some were witty, wicked, or naughty; and others were compassionate and deeply perceptive. Oh, my God, this marvelous man had a beautiful soul, I thought, as I furiously typed and packaged these jewels for wider dissemination. The rejections came in a steady stream, but I was undaunted. Someday, somebody will appreciate this great mind, and my faith will be vindicated.

The need to personalize my deep admiration for Ossie, this person who was also stunning in other ways, began to take form. As a child, my father had interrupted the needlework lessons that Mother had arranged for me to take from a lady in our building because he knew for a fact that she was a "bull dagger," I heard him say—and he didn't want me going to her apartment anymore. Years later, I reached back in my memory for what she had taught me, and now, with craft book open, I finished teaching myself how to knit.

It was the poetry that led to the adult onset of knitting socks with reinforced heels and toes. The wielding of needles resulted, I reason, from some primal urge to serve genius.

Years into the marriage, even when the genius halo got rusty and bent, I continued to crochet, knit, and sew—scarves, ties, socks, sweaters, shirts, shorts, a hat, and robes. I don't know what I thought I was doing. Although he seemed appreciative, this activity was not the path to greater attention or affection. He really didn't, and doesn't now, give much of a hoot about such offerings. I must confess here, however, that most times, when he goes walking, he wears the hat I made for him.

OSSIE: When Broadway producers saw how much money they could make showing this brand-new, broad, uproarious version of Negro life in America—something that appealed to both white and black audiences—they quickly let down the barriers. Racial segregation as a policy in hiring—and in seating—on Broadway was officially over. Nearly fifty years after they had chased us away with the riots of 1900, Broadway seemed anxious to welcome us back, both on stage and in the audience.

Though we didn't know it, being able to leave Harlem was a mixed blessing.

RUBY: Abram Hill and Fred O'Neal followed in the tradition of others to whom communities owe a profound debt of gratitude. Pioneers like them, who recognize the importance of the survival of black theater, have made and still make enormous sacrifices to establish and sustain spaces to support their vision. Some work at regular jobs, some work part-time without social security, pensions, and other benefits that might ensure a comfortable old age. Few, however, can afford the full-time attention that such theaters need. Occasionally, in spite of all they do, there comes a time when such passion and dedication are not enough.

The American Negro Theatre had not been prepared for the enormous success of *Anna Lucasta*. When Fred O'Neal went with the Broadway company, Abe Hill essentially managed the affairs of the theater by himself.

Anna had been, in many ways, a dream come true, beyond ANT's wildest expectations. In the first place, the new sources of revenue—the royalties, which came in unprecedented amounts from Broadway, from Chicago, from London, and from other touring companies all over the country—should have made things better, but didn't. The handling of the increasingly complex affairs required skill, time, and expertise far beyond the managerial capacities of Abe or of Fred.

Aspiring actors who had never heard of us before now flocked to our tiny theater in the library basement. Our facilities were quickly overburdened. We became integrated. We became a new hope for authors, directors, and technicians who admired what had been achieved. We began to be perceived as a stepping-stone to Broadway and possibly Hollywood. The casting demands quickly exhausted our older membership talent pool.

Too much was happening all at once, leaving ANT vulnerable to confusion, despite the written principles on which the group was founded. Abram Hill tried desperately to hold it all together. A lawyer was hired; however, the basic need was for a full-time, salaried administrator with a competent staff to handle the new rush of business and attention.

The aim of the theater now seemed to be to find another *Anna*—some vehicle that could feed the momentum and enable the company to steady itself during the onslaught of success. Abe, and some of those actors who remained, like George Lewis, Claire Leyba, Howard Augusta, Chickie Evans, Claude Sloan, and Clarice Taylor, tried to balance the conflicting challenges and bring some order to the chaotic enthusiasms of the well intentioned. In the end, it proved overwhelming. We didn't see it then, but this was the beginning of the end.

The American Negro Theatre was as significant in its time to Harlem, the black community, and the arts in general as was the Group Theatre to the rest of the country. Springing from its creative loins, following in the mighty footsteps of Abe Hill and Fred O'Neal, came other builders and tenders of the cultural spaces that nurture new talent. We think of such producers, past and present: Roger Furman, Betty Allen, Gertrude Jeannette, Voza Rivers, Barbara Ann Teer, Woodie King, Hazel Bryant, and Garland Thompson, to name a few who have kept black theater alive in Harlem.

Elsewhere in the country, we think of Rick Khan, Tina Sattin, Frank Silvera, Marla Gibbs, and many others whose theaters we've heard about, or visited. I wrote a poem to Abram Hill after he died, later expanded it at Fred O'Neal's death, and now I dedicate it to all founders. I salute them here with this excerpt:

> *Like a first love, we remember vividly*
> *A first affirmation of our particular gifts*
> *A first opened door where someone says yes,*
> *Come in, you belong here among us.*

OSSIE: Ruby and I finally came together as Anna and Rudolph at the Mansfield Theatre on Broadway sometime in late July, taking over the roles from Yvonne Machen and Earle Hyman in preparation for the coming tour. Rehearsals were important, but only a small portion of the action in which we found ourselves caught up. A new kind of show business was coming into being, and we were a part of it.

That *Anna,* now a play about black people that got its start in the heart of Harlem could be such a resounding hit, artistically and financially, was a source of tremendous pride. We became the new pioneers, aware that we were being watched, measured, and compared, aware that everything we did reflected credit or discredit on the black community. Not heroes or leaders, perhaps, like Paul Robeson, Canada Lee, and Lena Horne, but foot soldiers, ready, willing, and able to do our part in the Struggle. Nothing mattered to us more than that.

The year 1946 was one of agonizing decisions. The war had come and gone, leaving everything changed in its wake. This applied to black people in its own peculiar way. We had followed Roosevelt into this war, expecting that when it was over, race relations would be changed at home and abroad. But Roosevelt was dead. And Truman was a southerner. We didn't know how far we could trust him to deal fairly with black concerns. And there was much to be concerned about.

Maceo Snipes, a returning veteran, had been killed in Georgia for trying to vote. Nazi prisoners of war who were being transported for shipment back to Germany could ride in the rear of the train with the white folks, while black veterans on that same train were forced to ride up front in the segregated, Jim Crow section. Two veterans and their wives were gunned down in Monroe, Georgia, for no apparent reason. It was obvious to any observer that the war hadn't made things better for black folks in America; it had made them worse.

Rosetta LeNoire, a member of the *Anna* cast, organized a benefit for the families of the four people killed in Monroe. That performance brought me back, full circle, to the Struggle. As cast members of *Anna,* and as individuals, we helped raise money, attended rallies, and lent our names to many functions, the aims of which were to raise consciousness, alleviate suffering, or secure justice.

Shortly after that, in September, the national company of *Anna Lucasta,* starring Ruby Dee and Ossie Davis, as well as Laura Bowman, Frank Wilson, Warren Coleman, Alice and Alvin Childress, Lance Taylor, and Yvonne Machen, began its cross-country tour in Bridgeport, Connecticut.

The company had a Pullman sleeping car, just for us, and each actor had a berth in the sleeping car. When we moved from one city to the next, that Pullman would be hitched up to a train that happened to be going in that direction. Some of us had trunks as well as suitcases, all of which were carried along with the set and physical properties for the production.

RUBY: The road provides little opportunity for social life except with the members of the company, especially for the women. Being on tour with a show is like no other experience for an actor. To be cut off from familiar circumstances, especially from family, can be traumatic as well as gloriously exciting. The company of players, the manager, and the crew form a new family and become a community, with its own church, teachers, and hopefully, the preacher, and friends.

OSSIE: As I think back on it, the 1946–47 tour of *Anna* had a profound effect on Ruby and me. Thrown together, under all kinds of conditions, for more than nine months, it became a chance to rehearse our coming married life. It was haphazard—we certainly hadn't planned it—but it was absolutely invaluable.

It was love at first sight, without my knowing it. What I did know, intuitively, beyond any conscious reckoning, was that the two of us belonged together: blood of one blood, flesh of one flesh, until death do us part. That's what I knew when, for the first time, I really took a prolonged look at this woman.

I was not jealous, and am not to this day. Such rock-ribbed certainty right at the beginning had that effect on me. I knew, my heart knew, my soul knew that we were in this thing together, and that was that. My absolute conviction called for no further action or validation on my part. I don't think I even discussed it with Ruby. Somehow, we had always been married. Leave it to God, and time, to handle the details. I knew that and I was sure Ruby did, too.

But we couldn't keep it from the world forever. The ceremony that really made us one was spontaneous and it took place in the middle of the tour.

It was Christmas Eve, and Ruby and I had gone with some of the others in the cast to an after-theater party at a restaurant in St. Paul, Minnesota. Nat King Cole had just released his recording of Mel Tormé's "The Christmas Song," and was singing "Chestnuts Roasting on an Open Fire." It was the hottest thing on the jukebox and was on its way to becoming a smash hit. Ruby and I drank, toasting each other, sang carols with cast members and other customers in the place, and—most of all—we danced. Even when it got late, and the party was starting to break up, and all the people, including the cast, went home, we danced. When the sun came up on a brand-new, snow-white Minnesota Christmas Day, Rube and I were still dancing. Only a little slower now.

And I remember, through it all, knowing—neither of us speaking a word, just knowing—that we were in love, head over heels, and stuck with each other forever! It didn't at all seem extraordinary. There we were, principals in one of the great love stories of the twentieth century. And nobody even told us!

It took us from Christmas till April to complete our journey to California. This was certainly the most scenic part. There were long stretches of open country, seen through warm and toasty Pullman windows as we climbed through Utah, Wyoming, Colorado, stopping to play for one week, or for a one-night stand. We traveled on, up to and over the Rocky Mountains, down to Albuquerque, New Mexico, one night in Reno, Nevada, then across the desert and on to Los Angeles—to Hollywood.

In Hollywood, the opening is all: gaudy lights raking across the sky, and limousines crawling to the entrance, disgorging celebrities who immediately find the nearest camera and smile. So it was with *Anna.* For twenty-four hours, we, too, would be the toast of the town. After that, we became strangers and tourists again, like everybody else. It was nothing personal, just a routine parade catered at the entrance by Public Relations. Tomorrow, of course, it would be completely forgotten. But we didn't care. Inside, we were primed and ready—opening night in Hollywood—everybody rise and shine. And shine we did.

Almost before the curtains fell, the gods descended upon us, bearing our victors' crowns: Charlie Chaplin, Sydney Greenstreet, Thomas Gomes, hugging us, pumping our hands, arms around our shoulders, treating us as equals, especially in front of the cameras. The long travail was over. We had made it. This was as good as it got.

Chaplin was particularly exuberant. *Anna Lucasta* was perfect for the movies! He was not alone in his enthusiasm. To be made into a movie was the highest blessing America could bestow on a play or a novel. It sounded to us like a foregone conclusion: *Anna,* with its all-black cast, was going to be made into a movie—God be praised!

The dream came true. Chaplin did make *Anna* into a movie—but with an all-white cast. Opportunity's golden door, which was to have led us all to fame, glory, and stardom, had closed before it opened.

Hollywood's lavish opening-night welcome did not extend to hotel accommodations. Some members of the cast were from Los Angeles and they had no problem. The rest of us were parceled out among various black families, who were glad to rent their guest rooms to entertainers on the road. I wound up on San Pedro Street, down near the railroad station, where there was lodging for railroad sleeping car porters.

In L.A., there were few buildings that stood over five floors tall, for fear of earthquakes. The freeways hadn't been built yet. Public transportation was provided by a fleet of spic-and-span red streetcars that went all over the city. The area at Adams and Western, dominated by the Golden State Insurance building, was the hot spot by day, where the black community conducted much of its business. There was even a small black hotel, which didn't quite merit our trade, but after dark, the action shifted to gaudy, steaming Central Avenue, where the nightlife flourished. It was not far from the theater, and almost every night, the cast would drop in and catch whatever attractions were being offered. And there was plenty—good food, good music, good whatever you might want to smoke or drink. For me, it was always the drink.

I was tough, young, resilient, and could easily bounce back. But slowly, behind a smoke screen of laughing, singing calypso, and spouting everything from dirty jokes to high iambic pentameter, I was becoming a drunk. I never stumbled around or became obnoxious. It wasn't so much a love of whiskey to which I was responding; it was rather my way of finding a deeper place within myself to hide. A slow, long withdrawal from the world outside—so smooth, so slick, that nobody knew that Ossie had disappeared. Seeking the bottom of the bottle, but finding none. Still, I was an amiable, even a charming drunk, and was known as a man who could hold his liquor pretty good. It was liquor that finally brought an end to my long period of postwar grief and mourning. As usual, Ruby was there to help me.

It was late Sunday morning. I was with Ruby, waiting for her to rescue me from my usual Saturday night hangover. Like most theatrical drunks, I laughed by night, but the next morning usually found me somewhere crying. Being a veteran recently returned with wounded spirit, if not limbs, I had much to cry about—or so I thought. Such lachrymosity, though self-contained, desperately begs an audience—a woman, by herself, if you can manage it. Ruby, of course, was perfect.

I sat there slumped over on the bed in my underwear, tears streaming down my swollen face, telling Ruby perhaps for the thousandth time what it was like for us poor GIs in the war. Like all returning soldiers, I felt bound to take revenge on the rest of the world for the injuries my soul had suffered during the war. I saw myself as victim, beyond the reach of anybody else's pity but my own. And thus each soldier carries around for all the world to see his own little catalog of horrors, growing more bloody and disgusting with each recital. I sobbed aloud, burying my head in her shoulder, wondering if I was going to be punished with this bloody pain and these unspeakable memories for the rest of my life.

"Oh, I don't think so," Ruby spoke up, interrupting my story—something she had never done before. "The fact is," she continued, "one day, you're going to get as sick of all this puking and whining, this po'-colored-soldier-begging-for-pity shit as I am. And that will be the end of that. Here, drink this coffee. We've got to sober you up."

RUBY: Ossie and I were recognized as being very close friends. It was as if the company had accepted that what was between us was permanent, and had given us its blessings. There were always women who were attracted to him, though, in the various cities we played, and one particular woman in the company.

At first, she and I were good friends, sharing experiences and talking about many things, sometimes about Ossie, on the long ride. Then she and Ossie seemed to be deepening their relationship. Ossie assured me that my mind was carrying me in the wrong direction. The ugly green monster in me tried to escape, and thank God, prayer nestled in common sense kept me cool.

Nevertheless, I felt he was attracted to her and I wanted to flee—to put distance between us, to give him a chance to take a breath without a witness. After all, he was still single. He should be free to have whomever he wanted, I lied to myself.

These thoughts, of course, were the musings of a jealous woman. What really drew me back to New York was love in another form. The prospect of being involved in a film production drew me like a magnet.

Therefore, in June of 1947, when the time came to renew the road contract, I said no—to everyone's surprise. The film about to go into production was *The Fight Never Ends,* starring Joe Louis, one of the greatest boxers of our time, and they wanted me to play the female lead. Adding to my excitement was the fact that a black man, William Alexander, was the producer. It was hard to leave the company, especially Ossie, but I said good-bye and took the train back home.

OSSIE: It was many years later that I learned the part that Miss X played in Ruby's leaving us in Los Angeles. Now X was nice enough, a virgin in her mind, as well as in her body, I understand. I never found out.

I liked her in the general, warm, and ebullient way I liked everybody, especially after the performance, when I was in my cups and full of poetry, song, and witticisms. I knew she liked me more than somewhat, but that was the price she paid for knowing me. I have never been a shy, retiring man, and I knew about women from my mentor, Medas. Whatever eyes I had were not for her. Of course, I was in love, not only with her; everybody else was welcomed, too. Love, but nothing personal.

In matters like these, I have always been more of a poet than a predator, with my own sense of honor, my own code of conduct. It was love—love, not sex—that was ever my objective, and in my purview. That gave me plenty of room to maneuver, but kept me safe. And most of all, it was what I owed to Ruby. X was Ruby's friend. Touching her would have been like touching one of the family. And that was a form of incest.

I read her feelings precisely and saw her intentions coming a mile away. She arranged one night after the show to take me somewhere up in the Hollywood Hills to meet a young, white married couple, friends of hers.

I remember drinking, laughing, and singing calypso, as was my wont, all through dinner. Then, when we all retired to the living room, I took over the sofa and launched into my best Ossie the Clown routine, which consisted of the latest, dirtiest jokes I knew. It was not my intention to be offensive, only amusing. But, of course, I had the wrong audience. X, already knowing the punch line, couldn't bear what she knew was about to happen. She jumped up and ran from the room, leaving the two young hosts to hear me out.

I don't remember the buildup, but the climax to the story was a man losing control of his bowels, in a rather explosive manner, which

I, at the top of my game, proceeded to illustrate with accompanying grunts and groans. The joke was so funny to me that I fell off the sofa, onto the floor, and laughed, and laughed, and laughed.

But I laughed alone. The white couple, helpless, completely at a loss, just sat there, staring. Poor X, she managed to get me home all right, but we were never quite as friendly after that.

CHAPTER 18

The Fight Never Ends

RUBY: Almost the moment I got back to New York, I went to see Bill Alexander, the producer of *The Fight Never Ends*. He was a gracious and forceful-looking man who seemed knowledgeable about actors, about entertainers in general, and about the movie business. All the pieces were in place, he had said. Although I felt the script needed work, and told him so, I liked it. I was delighted that he wanted me to be a part of it. Despite the distance between Ossie and me, I felt a great excitement. This chance was one that I couldn't afford to miss. I put him and *Anna Lucasta* at the back of my mind, and eagerly plunged into the new adventure.

   In my next meeting with Mr. Alexander, he agreed to the story changes I'd suggested and he introduced me to his partner, Ted Parisi. It was reassuring to learn that he was to help Mr. Alexander get over some financial difficulties and back on track. I liked Parisi. He was a no-nonsense, yet gentle man who seemed to understand and appreciate what Alexander was trying to do. I did, too, and told him so.

Getting the film completed, however, took its toll on those closest to the operation, including me. It was a tightrope walk, with creditors, unions, and labs pulling on the ends of the rope because they had not been paid. I could sense Parisi's concern, but Alexander, ever the optimist, went from one narrow squeak to another. I can't say I was totally surprised, but finally one afternoon, he asked if I could possibly lend him $7,000 or help him raise it. An emergency had arisen, but he could return the money the following week.

I had saved money while on the road with *Anna* and I agreed to lend him $5,000. Affairs seemed to move more smoothly after that, but he did not return the money. He suggested that I turn the loan into an investment—an arrangement that I had fleetingly considered when he had first approached me. I'd had intimations of becoming a producer myself.

Matters went from bad to worse, however, with the lawsuits, the cessation of filming, and the seizure of footage. Alexander and Parisi were in a frenzy. The three of us tried to maintain an air of normalcy with the cast and crew.

OSSIE: I understood Ruby's appetite for working in black films, but for me, there was no temptation to leave for New York when she did. My plan was to stay with *Anna* to the bitter end, saving all I could so that I could register at Columbia come September, which was only a couple of months away.

The company spent another two weeks in San Francisco, one week in Portland, Oregon, another week in Seattle, and then we disbanded. It was time. Eleven months on the road was enough for me. I had seen all the mountains, crossed all the rivers, talked with all the reporters, visited all the schools and hospitals, smiled for all the cameras, and signed all the autographs—enough to last me for a lifetime and a half. I never wanted to pack and unpack another suitcase or see another Pullman car again.

For me, the trip had long been over. The excitement had long ago begun to ring false. The smile was a part of an act that, little by little, began to bore me. I was sicker than I knew of drunken sprees, spouting poetry, telling off-color jokes, and singing calypso at some party. I was sick to death of being Ossie Davis, and the people in the cast, who had heard it all and seen it all before, began to yawn when I approached. I was thirty years old, and being young and giddy had lost all its former attraction. I knew it was time to straighten up and settle down. That, for me, meant getting seriously down to the business of writing. Five railroad days, from one side of this country to the other, and I was home.

I confess, few things in my life have been so beautiful as looking up in Grand Central Station and seeing Ruby Dee standing there waiting. I was flattered with the thought that she was glad to see me. Ruby, however, had something more than my being home on her mind.

RUBY: I met Ossie at Grand Central Station the day he arrived. He was happy to see me. In a rush of relief, I realized how overjoyed I was to see him. He sensed, in no time, however, that something was wrong. I told him about the film, that the work was very good, but that the production was in trouble.

"Would you . . ." I said. "Could you . . . I know you've been saving to go to Columbia. . . . Could you, though, in light of all we've said about the exclusion of our people in the kinds of films we envision. . . . Well, we've got to begin to make the films ourselves. This man, Alexander, is trying to do right. We've got to begin to control, to have some input into the kind of images that govern us—"

"Hold on, hold on a minute, just calm down," Ossie interjected. "You mentioned something in your letter about becoming an investor. I haven't saved that kind of money."

I said, "There's to be a substantial investment in about ten days— the footage looks really good. The main action takes place in the boys' recreation center, and Joe Louis—never mind the story for now— there's great concern about payroll this weekend."

"Ruby, Ruby, listen to me," Ossie said, "all I've got is three thousand dollars. Now if that can help. . . ."

"I really can't ask you to—if that's all you've saved, you can't . . ."

"Take it. It's yours. We'll get it in the morning."

"As I said, in about ten days, I'll see to it that—"

"Call it a loan. Okay? Okay. Let's get out of here. I need to talk to you about another matter. When you left, you weren't trying to walk out on me, by any chance?" Ossie asked, as he struggled his luggage to the street.

Although making *The Fight Never Ends* was a nerve-wracking hassle, I was proud of my involvement. Ossie, too, felt it was the best independent film of that kind that he'd ever seen.

Months after the film was finished, I heard that the unions were dissatisfied, that the picture had been seized by creditors, and that Bill Alexander could only come to New York on weekends if he wanted to avoid arrest. Ossie and I tried to reach him over the years, and also to locate the film and Ted Parisi, without success. William Alexander died in 1971.

I hadn't expected to recover the money I invested, but I had hoped to recoup Ossie's money. Here's the almost lie he likes to tell about how he recouped his $3,000 anyway.

OSSIE: Beauty always takes me by surprise. There stood Ruby, whom I thought I knew as well as I knew the back of my hand, spankingly brand-new. I swallowed my tongue completely. She, of course, was exactly whom I expected to meet me. The long, crawling trip back to Grand Central was made with Ruby in mind. Yet seeing her, all of a sudden like—I wasn't prepared at all! And in less than thirty minutes, she had my $3,000 and was gone.

She told me all the details, glowing from the inside as she did— the picture, the people, the problems, the immediate need of funds to finish it up. She would arrange for me to see a screening, and my money would be repaid in a matter of weeks. It was a sound investment in the future of black filmmaking, with profits guaranteed. But she didn't need to talk, just graciously smile upon me, like she did, and hold out her hands—the money was hers.

Sure enough, about three weeks later, I opened the door to her knocking, and there she stood—petite, demure, totally irresistible— except for her eyes, the saddest I'd ever seen in a woman's face.

"Can I come in?" she asked.

"Of course you can. . . . Just let me take this nonsense off the chair. Won't you sit down?"

"No, Ossie," she said, "maybe you'd better sit down." I chose to stand. And then Ruby told me a story that broke both her heart and mine. The money she had borrowed, my $3,000, was gone beyond all hope of retrieval, and she herself was broke. There was nothing she could do to pay it back. She softly said she was sorry, then started toward the door.

"Hold on dere, Sista Ruby," I heard myself saying, sounding just like Kingfish from *Amos and Andy.* "Sit down; come join me here on the sofa. I'm sure that, between us, we can come up with a solution to this problem." We sat. We talked, and ultimately, we married. A man is duty-bound to protect his investment.

No matter how fast you move, New York is always a step or two ahead. After eleven months on the road, my only choice was to close my eyes, jump right in, and come up trying to swim. In 1947, the air was heavy with conflict, Struggle was of the essence, and the only way to participate was to be everywhere at once. Only the very young are capable of this, and Ruby and Ossie, in many ways, were very young indeed.

What to do about the atom bomb was the basic question World War II had left behind, preventing closure. Some Americans, with whom I agreed, said the only way to peace is sharing the bomb with the Russians, our new ally. Others said, Hell no! Russia is now the enemy—let's keep the bomb for ourselves. Back and forth it went, crescendo rising.

Winston Churchill, in Fulton, Missouri, in 1946, had already drawn the line and thrown down the gauntlet. He spoke, not of a world united, but of an iron curtain, which now divided the whole of existence into two opposing camps. A call to a brand-new battle was blaring from new trumpets, and we young had to hurry up and take sides.

Ruby busied herself with trying desperately to rescue *The Fight Never Ends.* I applied for unemployment insurance and went up to Columbia University to register for a class in playwriting. Our lives ran now on parallel tracks, intersecting at various times and places, but gone was the intimacy we had known on tour, when we literally lived out of each other's pockets. She had her own career and I had mine. She went back to Sugar Hill, where she had a room with her mother.

I went back to the Bronx, where I still had my rooms, my books, and my papers.

The winter of 1946–47, one of the worst in Europe's history, forced Britain to the edge of collapse. Harry Truman stepped in to pick up the pieces, molded American policy to fit America's new role as leader of the free world in the growing quarrel with Russian communism, and the cold war was on.

Traditional black leadership always treated foreign affairs as the province of White Folks Only. Greece? China? The atom bomb? The Marshall Plan? The United Nations painfully coming to birth out in San Francisco? Leave that up to the white folks. . . . Never mind what Truman was doing overseas; our only concern was how he affected us. The rest was none of our business.

There were other blacks, however, who argued differently. To them, our Struggle here at home was part and parcel of the worldwide struggle against capitalist exploitation, which they saw as driving toward another war—this time with Russia. They vowed this must not happen and we felt ourselves included in that vow.

We young ones in the theater, trying to fathom even as we followed, were pulled this way and that, by the swirling currents of these new dimensions of the Struggle, which split us down the middle. Black revolutionaries fighting, just like the Russians, to liberate the workers and save the world, against the black bourgeoisie fighting, at the behest of rich white folks, to defeat the Communist menace and save the world.

I, for one, had no trouble identifying which side I was on. I was on the side with Paul Robeson and W.E.B. Du Bois. Following them became my assignment. More than ideology was at stake in the black community.

In 1947, Isaac Woodard, a soldier in uniform, was arrested on a bus in North Carolina, put in jail, beaten, and had his eyes gouged out. It was obvious to many of us young folks that whoever had won the war, black folks hadn't. And we were angry. Traditional black leadership counseled patience. Give Truman and his policies time, they said. We no longer trusted Truman. We no longer trusted traditional black leadership. We wanted action and we wanted it now.

We wanted leaders who knew about revolution, the class war, and the dictatorship of the proletariat to take charge of the Struggle. We wanted Du Bois, Alphaeus Hunton, Ben Davis, and William L. Patterson. They were our heroes, our role models, our avatars. And most of all, we wanted Robeson.

Paul was at the height of his popularity, and to us that popularity meant power. He had been given black America's highest award, the Spingarn Medal of Honor, by the NAACP in 1946. I remember standing outside the old Madison Square Garden. A big rally was being held inside for some momentous occasion, when Harry Belafonte, whom I scarcely knew, came along and put a ticket in my hand, enabling me to go inside. I eventually met Paul and eagerly became one of the numerous young people—mostly black actors, singers, and dancers—who followed in his wake whenever we could. A semicadre who saw ourselves as revolutionaries, too, whose greatest joy was to just be in his presence.

Paul, no matter how busy, was always accessible. Sometimes we met at his home, where we could talk, and watch the Red Buttons television show, which he seemed to like. Paul would listen to our proposals, no matter how off-the-wall or bizarre, then make his pronouncements. A Socialist, as far as we understood it, Paul believed that black people would never get their freedom under capitalism. He felt that Churchill and Truman, with the bomb in their sole possession, were trying to force the genie of socialism, unleashed by the war, back into the bottle of the status quo.

There were many things we wanted to know about this socialism and how it would work to free black people, not only in America, but all over the world. Paul never proselytized; however, he was always ready to share his beliefs, one of which was that the workers of the world, not the bourgeoisie, deserved to rule the world.

He was particularly proud of the heroic struggle of the Soviet people, who had sustained the death of millions—soldiers and civilians—in World War II. They had contributed as much as the Allies to the final victory over Hitler, and now were being squeezed out of their victor's share by Churchill and Truman, who seemed anxious to bait the Soviets into a war in which they could annihilate them with the newly acquired terror, the atom bomb.

Paul was by no means alone in this opinion. Henry Agard Wallace, Roosevelt's Vice President who became the secretary of agriculture under Truman, was outspoken in his opposition to Churchill and to Truman, and ultimately was forced to resign from the Cabinet. When Wallace decided to run for the presidency against Truman, Paul was quick to offer his full support to Wallace. We, of course, offered our full support to Paul.

No single one of us remained untouched by what was happening to Paul, situated as he was, in the middle of the whirlwind spinning around his head and shoulders, the colliding worlds that shook the final days of our youth.

Nineteen forty-eight was an election year like none other, with Wallace on the left, Harry Truman in the center, and Strom Thurmond on the right. This election, in our opinion, could determine the issue of war or peace between the Western powers and the Soviet Union. I did whatever work came my way from Wallace's campaign headquarters, especially by night, since most of my day was spent in class up at Columbia.

My classes, which were taught by theater critics, were general in their focus. We were assigned various plays to read, and then to write a review of the subject matter. One of my assignments was *Green Pastures*.

I had seen the film with Rex Ingram playing De Lawd. Reading the script didn't temper my scorn. *Green Pastures,* by Marc Connelly and Roark Bradford, had been a huge moneymaking success both on Broadway and in Hollywood. It was a classic example of the kind of plays about black people that I was in a great hurry to get away from. I objected to its patronizing view of black religion.

In *Green Pastures,* the people are simple and childlike, walking around heaven all day, having a singing good time. Their constant life of devotion was focused on De Lawd, a benign father figure who addressed them, one and all, as children. Heaven in their view was one vast fish-fry celebration, presided over by De Lawd. All this was further filtered through the magnificent singing of the Hall Johnson Choir—so sweet, so syrupy, so overflowing with southern-fried milk and honey, fried catfish, fried chicken, and the fun of just being colored in the presence of the good white folks.

There were among us actors always critics, skeptics, and jokers—talented people who could play the game of nigger at auditions with grace, facility, and style when it suited our purposes, to get the job, to soothe white fears, or to cajole another ounce of charity from white sympathy. But when the game was over and the purpose served, we'd put the pretense aside.

On the other hand, there were those actors who had played the game so long and so successfully that it had become second nature, had taken them over completely. Buffoons and clowns, we thought—we "enlightened ones" who looked upon theater as a tool for black liberation—we laughed behind their backs and called them "ooftah": theatrical house niggers, beyond all hope of redemption, with whom the white theatergoers flocked to Broadway to commune. White folks and black performers, in desperate symbiosis—how they needed each other! *Green Pastures,* I thought, was heaven for these two.

Green Pastures offered whites the kind of nonthreatening Negro religiosity they loved to see. Black folks were portrayed as children, kind, charming, warm, and winning, but also dependent, shiftless, and totally unable to fend for themselves. That's not who was in my church on Sunday morning.

Religion, to us—I speak from my own experience—was always a spectacle and a contest where the struggle between God and the Devil, between good and evil, had been going on forever. But to us, the struggle was personal; good and evil was synonymous with black and white. We were a people in bondage crying aloud for succor to the God who had safely brought his people out of Egypt and through the Red Sea into freedom. Our religion was there to tell us that the same thing would happen to us one day. Our oppression was a yoke we wouldn't bear forever; one day that was sure to come, the shoe would be placed on the other foot. We brooded about good versus evil all week long; then Sunday morning, right there in the pulpit, the preacher, the voice and servant of God, would bring it all to a head.

When the preacher got to the part of his sermon that showed most vividly the titanic battle between good and evil, we could hardly wait. First, he would compare us, and our suffering, with Jesus; we, too, were being crucified. We would groan and weep and shout with pity. Then the sermon would segue, and so would we, from gentle Jesus, meek and mild, who never said a mumblin' word, to God, the great avenger.

And God was something else! From "Father, forgive them, they know not what they do" to "Justice is mine, saith the Lord." "Ye shall reap what you sow." "The wages of sin is death." Verse by thunderous verse, in God's high and holy iambic pentameter, King James Version, the preacher would build his case against Satan, the sinner—none other than the cruel white man, who finally, with one mighty blow, was hurled down to a hell and brimstone!

The whole church would rise to its feet triumphant, that God, our sure defense, had, through the powerful words and images of the preacher, delivered us from the white man one more time, just like he delivered Daniel. We saw the white man, plain as day, right there before our eyes, groveling on his knees, begging us for mercy. Payback time and punishment for slavery and for everything that had been perpetrated against us. Oh, man! A good sermon could change us from victim into victor in the twinkling of an eye. Doing for the faithful what Joe Louis's fists had done that second time to Max Schmeling.

Seeing the white oppressor hurled from his throne down into the darkest pits of hell Sunday after Sunday was of the essence of our religion.

And that's exactly what was missing for me in *Green Pastures*. In my critique, I tried to explain, to cram it all in. I am not sure how much I succeeded. My instructor was impressed, and so was the rest of the class when I read it. Impressed, if not convinced.

CHAPTER 19

Hookin' Up

OSSIE: One day I received a wire from a producer named Garson Kanin, asking me to come to his office and audition for a part in a show called *The Leading Lady*. The cast had been chosen, and rehearsals set to begin, but Oscar Polk—the actor who had played Gabriel in the film version of *Green Pastures,* and who had been cast as the butler in this play—had stepped off the curb in Times Square, been hit by a taxi, and killed. They needed a replacement fast. I read for the part and was given the job immediately.

Garson Kanin and his wife, Ruth Gordon, the producers, were different in style and temperament from Shumlin, Merrick, and Wildeberg. They were not moved by the liberal impulse to improve society, as were Shumlin and Merrick, nor had they the desire to make money, which so obviously motivated Wildeberg. No, this pair was as dedicated to an intense professionalism in the theater as they were to each other, determined to work together at their craft when they wished. They worked together like a machine, not only on Broadway, but also in Hollywood where they were equally famous. I liked them right away.

One added pleasure was the presence in the cast of two authentic Shakespearean actors, John Carradine and Ian Keith. It was obvious from their conversation and from their demeanor, on stage and off, that these men belonged to a very special fraternity. They were forever quoting from the master or describing their adventures in various past productions. And they, of course, were personal friends of John Barrymore.

Poetry and its delivery had changed their lives, had carried them off to the top of a magic mountain, a plateau of transcendence from which they refused ever to come down. Listening to them confirmed for me the power and the purpose of language as a basic element in the exercise of power. It was a lesson I never forgot.

To men like Carradine and Keith, Shakespeare is too precious a secret to keep to themselves. They were always searching for listeners, somebody before whom they could present all those wonderful characters and recite all those wonderful lines—still urgent, still pulsing, still insistent, crowding a player's memory. These men could not converse without performing. In me, they found what they needed. They took me deep into their confidence. They told me everything they thought I needed to know about the good old days, about the craft, the technique—gestures, intonations, and all—and about those bibulous times when they drank Barrymore under the table. It didn't matter at all that they coached me for a performance that was never to happen.

The Leading Lady performed the usual previews, opening in New Haven, moving on to Boston, then down to Philadelphia. But the show needed additional work, so they sent us out to Chicago for another week.

There's something about being in a show that snatches you from hurry, giving a chance for peace, a place to rest, and think about things. Even time to think about maybe being married to Ruby. I sent her a wire and told her what I had been thinking. . . . It was from Chicago I sent Ruby a telegram proposing marriage.

RUBY: Something about his proposal struck me as an offer to save me from myself. I called him and said, "Well, okay, but don't do me no favors!" It wasn't what you might call a romantic moment.

OSSIE: *The Leading Lady* closed as soon as it opened and immediately after, we went into rehearsals with *The Smile of the World.* They not only hired me, but they also hired Ruby. I was the manservant and she was the maid.

RUBY: They asked you who you'd want to play the part.

OSSIE: And I said, "Ruby."

RUBY: I didn't even have to audition!

OSSIE: So, we were rehearsing *The Smile of the World,* and one Thursday, we had the day off. On that day, we went to New Jersey to be married. In Jersey, you could get married in one day. In New York, there was a three-day waiting period. My brother Willie stood up for me, Ruby's sister LaVerne stood up for her. LaVerne was as beautiful as Ruby was, very lovely, and a lady.

So we took a bus over to Jersey City, found a Baptist preacher, and went into his study in the church for the ceremony. As he was reading us the rites, he came to the question, "Do you, Ossie Davis, take this woman to be your lawful wedded wife?" Well, the reverend had big eyes, one of which wandered. One eye was looking at Ruby, and the other one was looking at Ruby's sister. I said, "I do." That was December 9, 1948. I thought it was a pretty good use of a Thursday.

RUBY: Neither of us recalls clearly the specifics of one of the most important days of our lives. As in a line from the play Ossie would soon write, everything was "haze and vaguey."

Our marriage was an insert into an already very busy schedule. We never sat down to talk seriously about what we expected from the marriage or from each other. It was an extension of a relationship that had commenced easily and inauspiciously, almost subconsciously, soon after we met. We had road-tested it with *Anna*. There was no big ceremony, no wedding gown, no church service, no pictures. There had not even been a discussion of where we would live. It felt almost like an appointment we finally got around to keeping.

After the "I promises," the "I do's," and the tears, the four of us got on a bus bound from Jersey City back to New York City. Willie and LaVerne sat on the bench seat in the back of the bus, and Ossie and I were on the long side bench. I wore a brown suit. Ossie wore a hat and carried his overcoat. There weren't many passengers.

For the whole trip, Ossie's body was twisted from the waist as he gazed out of the window. I looked out the window, too, and then I looked at him, out the window and at his pork-pie hat—back and forth like that. Neither of us spoke. He didn't look back at me.

A kind of low-grade panic came over me. So this is it. We are married. Related now. Connected. Forever and ever, maybe. I felt a silence all through me. The bus was moving, but there was no sound. "As long as you both shall live—" Maybe this is what forever feels like. Maybe I was just hungry. All of us should be hungry. It had been a long day even though it was just after noon.

We ate at a restaurant near my sister's apartment. After the meal, Willie offered to see LaVerne home. As we said our good-byes, LaVerne asked, "Where will you guys be living?" I didn't recall having discussed it, but he answered without hesitation, "At my place in the Bronx."

"Oh, yes," she said, "I've got that number." And we hugged, and kissed, and went our separate ways.

There had been confusion in my mind. I had wanted him to come live with me at my mother's apartment because his room in the Bronx seemed always in total disarray. When I first saw it, I thought of the Collier brothers who lived and were found dead in the middle of unspeakable clutter.

When I visited Ossie, he would have to clear spaces for me to sit and put my things on. Newspapers, books, magazines, toilet articles, clothes, orange peelings were everywhere. The space was not dusty or dirty, as I recall, only extremely cluttered. He was able to put his hands so precisely on anything he wanted to show or to read to me, however, that it occurred to me that the disorder I beheld was planned deliberately.

We went by taxi to Mother's place, where I packed a few things. He understood that there just simply hadn't been time to properly move, with rehearsals every day, and so much going on in both our lives. We had talked about getting an apartment, but we'd soon be traveling with *The Smile of the World* and that could last a long time.

I said to myself, "How could you think, Ruby, that he's even thought about moving in with you and your mother? What a thick-headed contemplation."

As we walked up the one flight to our love nest, I felt ashamed of my reluctance.

"We jumped the broom," he said. "May as well carry you over the threshold." And he did—into one of the cleanest, neatest spaces I could hope for. Not only that, but Pat, his landlady, had turned another room into a lounge area for us where she had prepared and left food and drinks.

"Well, you know I couldn't bring my bride into the place like it was before, now could I?"

I hugged him then, and started to cry. He pushed me an arm's length away, and looked at me a long time; and when our eyes met, we laughed, and laughed, and laughed.

We spent the evening calling folks and talking. Pat made us another fine meal, and we laughed and joked some more with Pat and her friend Roger. When we left them, we got ready for bed and went to sleep—Ossie on one side of the bed, and me on the other. After all, we had to get up early and go to work. That's what I think happened. Neither of us really remembers.

We don't recall telling anyone in *The Smile of the World* company that we were getting married. All day long, no one gave us a clue that they were aware that we were wearing that person-to-person glue. At the end of the day, champagne and a big cake were brought in. Ruth and Garson, along with the whole company, toasted us.

CHAPTER 20

Movies and Complications

RUBY: We blinked, and it was 1949. Twenty-six years old and no babies! After all, we'd been married several months, and I wasn't even pregnant. I had to know why. Schlepp, schlepp with the little vials of sperms, smears, and tests. Oh! He's okay. It's me! I've got a cervical ulcer. High-intensity person, what do you expect, Ruby? What do I do? Calm down. Okay. I'm calm. No. You have to get the thing burnt off. Oh, my God! I'm not going to make mommyhood. He'll need another wife. No. No, I'll get a co-wife for him—like in Africa. Are you crazy? Like in Africa?! Over my dead body.

Mother reminds me that I'd had some trouble in the womb department years ago. Yes, yes. I remember. I'd get knots in my stomach with pain and secretions, before and during exams, or in any time of stress. The condition had been developing all this time. Oh, my God!

Just what a bride needs to tell her gorgeous husband—"Look, baby, I'm all tensed out. No babies, ever." I mean really, God, get with it. Remove this cup. Oh, forgive me, I pray, as the gynecologist begins the first of a cauterizing series to un-ulcer me.

"You're so lucky," she said. "When this is over, I see no reason why you won't conceive."

"In other words," I stammered, "I couldn't, I mean, it was impossible before this?"

"Yes," she said, "there was like a barrier to the—"

"—to the little fishes," I exclaimed. Then it hit me. God is good. I mean, truly good. Who knows? Had it not been for my beautiful ulcer, I might have already babied up and made this marriage very difficult, if not impossible. Thank you, Lord.

After three months, we found ourselves, indeed, with child. It was a glorious accomplishment. With great joy, we tended our "bun in the oven." Ossie was working in *Stevedore* at the Equity Library Theater. I was getting unemployment insurance and going to the clinic at Columbia Presbyterian Hospital for checkups.

One day we got a call from an agent in Hollywood who had seen us in something, and was now offering to represent us in an upcoming film called *No Way Out,* starring Richard Widmark and Sidney Poitier. We were excited. We said we'd call her back because Dick Campbell had been our agent for *Jeb* and *Anna,* and we'd like him to speak for us. Dick said he had no authority in film and suggested we accept the offer. The weekly salary was $750 each. I was cast in the role of Sidney's wife; Ossie was cast as his brother-in-law, and the filming would begin in about three weeks. We didn't think to mention the fact that I was pregnant because I was scarcely a month into it and the filming would be over before I'd even begun to "show."

Four months passed, however, before the filming was set to begin. When the agent called to make final arrangements, we had to tell her about my condition. We all laughed a little, saying maybe the story could accommodate my reality, or perhaps the pregnancy could be a plot enhancement. I was barely showing, but it might be worth a mention.

Two days later, she called to say that, indeed, my pregnancy was a major consideration and, sorry, but the offer to play the part was withdrawn.

After all these years, finally, a first offer from Hollywood, and I had to be pregnant. Well rehearsed in angst, I cried and anguished, screamed and beat up on God. "Why? Why? Why?" became the refrain of more loud and prolonged boohoos.

That night something slight and pink slithered out of me. I decided to calm down, accept my fate, and go to bed. I had read that sometimes there is a staining with the first pregnancy. The next morning found Ossie and me hurriedly dressing to get me to the clinic. No staining, I was bleeding. Ossie had to leave after I was admitted to the hospital and assigned a bed.

About an hour later, after the bleeding had subsided, I was wheeled into an examination room. There I was prepped and propped in the stirrups, legs wide apart, and draped with a sheet. It seemed I had been staring at the ceiling—the lights, the clocks, and the hanging paraphernalia—for a very long time when the doctor came in. He was a startling, handsome blond, followed by a lovely brunette nurse. A smallness came over me. I wanted to be gone from this place, to close my legs, and to reclaim myself.

He glanced at my face, pleasantly enough, and pushed ever so gently on my belly. The nurse helped him with the gloves. The image of my mother cleaning the inside of a chicken before stuffing it came to mind. The nurse stood to one side for a few minutes, then went to another part of the room. Silence. The doctor's fingers were probing around inside me. He began to whistle. "Please," I yelled without making a sound, "don't whistle! Hurry up and be finished with me!" I glanced at him, but he was looking off somewhere. I bent my head back and I could see the nurse smiling. Settling my head, I caught his return smile and wink. Whistle. Whistle. They were flirting with each other! Probe. Probe. Finger, finger. "Stop it," my mind shouted, "That's too rough. Enough! Enough!" I felt like a helpless, ugly little colored girl at the mercy of unconcerned white folks. At that moment, one hot tear scooted into my ear.

Back in the ward now, I was sure that everything would be all right. No bleeding, thank you, Jesus. Forgive me, Lord.

I awoke a few minutes before 3:00 A.M. with cramps. I could see the clock in the nurses station. A blond nurse was seated, leaning back against a cabinet or a wall reading a magazine, *True Confessions,* as I recall. I pushed the buzzer. No response. I pushed again. She slapped the literature aside and came to me.

"I can't sleep," I said, "and I'm having cramps."

"I'll get you something to help you sleep," she said. She did. Still I didn't. The cramps were similar to menstrual cramps, only worse. Four more times, I pressed the buzzer; four more times she came, increasingly annoyed after each interruption. Finally, the cramps mercifully subsided and I fell asleep.

When I awoke, the ward was in full motion. A new nurse was on duty. I was not allowed to go to the bathroom, I must use the bedpan. As I began to use it, I felt something like a tiny elbow protruding from me. When the nurse answered the call button and looked at my situation, she ran back to the station and got on the phone. Split seconds later, a doctor, looking disheveled, as if he'd just awakened, dashed into the ward, pulling on his white coat. He gave a little squeeze to my abdomen, I felt the baby slip out of me and into the bedpan, which the nurse quickly covered with a white towel.

Another nurse was tending me as I sat up and asked, "Please, please, please let me see my baby." She tossed her dainty head as if to say, "Don't be ridiculous." My mind leaped to the floor, snatched the bedpan, and knocked her down, but my body let itself be wheeled somewhere to be squeezed again, cleaned, and wheeled back to the ward, where I stayed for two days.

When Ossie came to take me home, we were asked to visit the office of the head of the hospital. He expressed regret about the miscarriage. It was a boy, he said, and the hospital would like to keep the six-and-a-half-month-old fetus.

"In a jar, you mean?"

"Yes," he answered me. "But first I will need you both to sign this release." Burial didn't occur to us. We saw no reason not to, so we signed.

There were no rainbows. Despair. Flat out. I'd heard it overtakes women whose motherhood is too suddenly snatched. It clasped me like a huge reptile and almost squeezed my breath away. Signals got scrambled as my mind and body banged into my soul. I watched my belly disintegrate, bosom swell, burst and shrivel, arms grow weak, dangling useless from having nothing to hold. Comfort found no place to land on me and all silence was a wail. I ached beyond recognition of myself for that almost baby boy that my sight couldn't claim, even for a moment, to store with memory.

Ossie tried to make it better. He called friends to visit when he couldn't be there to cheer me up. It didn't help. I just wanted folks to go home. Cheer up, Ruby. If it's any comfort, it happens all the time. There'll be others. I found no solace in the fact that many thousands of women lose their babies. How can such horror be passed off as routine?

On the second day, I began to call my family and friends. I needed to come home to myself. I also called the agent and told her what happened. "Stay by the phone, Ruby. Give me your number. Can you stay by the phone?" After about twenty minutes, the phone rang; her voice crashed through my emotional barricades as she explained, "Ruby, Sidney's wife is cast, but I can get you his sister, and you'll be married to Ossie. Now how does that sound?"

OSSIE: Pick a day—any day—or any night for that matter; take it cold turkey, or filtered in, item by item, red hot off the radio; good news and bad following you around, waiting. Or pick up the pieces yourself, from *The New York Times, Daily News,* or *Daily Worker;* life coming on in pulses and heartbeats, even before daybreak; in *Life* magazine, in *Look* magazine and don't forget the newsreels. If it's black life, you want to try the *Amsterdam News* as you shuttle along on the subway, coming and going at sixty miles an hour, trying to hold it together.

Going where? Why, to the audition, of course; to the rehearsal, to the performance, yours or somebody else's. After the show comes the party for the good cause of the day, at midnight, at the home of somebody rich and conscientious, or at least prestigious. Robeson might be there, along with Orson Welles, and maybe Marlon Brando; raising hell, raising funds, eating grapes, cheese and biscuits, drinking wine and making speeches to save the life, protest the lynching, commute the sentence, stay the execution, or set the prisoner free. Josh

White may be sitting in the living room corner, picking the blues on his guitar and smiling with a burning cigarette behind his ear like a pencil.

The year 1949 was fraught with one urgency right after another: China falls to the Communists; Russia explodes the atom bomb; McCarthy goes to Wheeling, West Virginia, and announces he has in his hands a list of Communists working in the State Department; Ruby and Ossie are married as much as they can be living in somebody else's apartment on Forest Avenue in the Bronx.

We had lost our baby. My own disappointment was tempered by my concern for Ruby. She was inconsolable. As life and luck would have it, the agent called and we were off to Hollywood. The film was to be called *No Way Out*—a race drama starring Richard Widmark and Sidney Poitier. The word got out, in the newspapers: Fred O'Neal, Mildred Joanne Smith, Ossie, and Ruby were going to do a picture in Hollywood. Monty Hawley had once referred to us as "basement boobs," and maybe he was right; but look at us now, taking the train, not to California, not to L.A., but to *Hollywood*. Clickety clack. Maybe never coming back—oh, fabulous day!

We got on board at Grand Central, rode overnight to Chicago, and there had a ten-hour layover to wander the downtown streets, catch our breath, and do nothing in particular, except to keep our fingers good and crossed.

The day was hot and I was dry. There was a street vendor near Union Station selling Cohasset punch, a sweet, cooling, soothing beverage concocted with half a peach resting on a bed of cracked ice, awash in copious amounts of peach juice and some other liquid that I couldn't identify. It hit the spot, made the gullet smile, and cooled the body down. My last memory is of bottoms up, over the rim of the glass, watching the tallest buildings in downtown Chicago wobble and weave, then slowly fade from sight. Somebody, mercifully, got me back on the train.

Ruby and I had both been on Pullman cars before, the last time in *Anna Lucasta,* but this time was different. This trip felt like a wedding journey, our first joining to a job in Hollywood. It was Sidney's first film, too.

RUBY: Our agent had found us a lovely two-room spread in some-body's house—on Western Avenue, I think. We never saw the owner. The caretaker greeted us, showed us up a flight of stairs, and handed us some keys. We dropped our stuff; then she ushered us downstairs, talking steadily. "You and your husband will be quite alone. Please make yourselves at home," she said, making us feel again like newly-weds. "There is no basement, but this is the laundry room, and here in this closet is where we keep the ironing board, the dustpan, and the mop. When you come in at night, feel free to use the living room, and the patio is also at your disposal; and if you need anything, I live in the little house over there, and here is how you can reach me. The phone is right there past the stairs, and another one outside your bedroom. And this, of course, is the kitchen."

Kitchen it was indeed—spacious, sparkling, inviting, with an oven and a counter in the center, and large Spanish tiles on the floor. The chairs and the table were also Spanish, made of carved dark wood. She told us how to get to the grocery store, which turned out to be bright and airy, filled with all kinds of breads, meats, cheeses, and wines. The fruits and vegetables seemed bigger, more healthful, and more inviting than any we'd seen before.

I asked, "Who are the people in the pictures on the walls?" She named them all. They were mostly musicians who had stayed in the house over the years; some of them were women. The only ones I could identify were of Fats Waller, Duke Ellington, and Cab Calloway.

The caretaker said good night and left. And then it was just Ossie and me in this big house, our first time absolutely alone since we mar-ried. We turned on the radio, listened awhile to Jack Webb and his new show, *Dragnet,* fixed ourselves a snack, sat down at the table, had ourselves a glass of wine, lit our cigarettes, and looked at each other. This part of our assignment truly felt like another installment on a honeymoon much too long deferred.

The sound stage where we were filming *No Way Out* was cavern-ous. Here technology had reached the pinnacle of perfection, making the studio both soundproof and acoustically favorable. There were spinning red lights standing guard just outside the heavy doors—all this to make absolutely sure that no sound, or any other sign of life from the outside world, would ever get through to disturb what was happening in front of the camera.

The first day on the lot at 20th Century-Fox, I ran into Sidney, talking with Richard Widmark. When Sidney introduced me, the words that came into my head and flapped out of my mouth before my brains got in gear were, "Oh my, but you are so little." I, who had once been married to a midget, had the nerve to call him small. He was about five feet tall—at least a foot taller than Frankie. It didn't occur to me at the time but Richard Widmark was one of several short leading men in Hollywood—Jimmy Cagney, Spencer Tracy, and Alan Ladd, to name a few; but the way the cameramen framed their shots, you'd never know it from watching them on screen. You could swear that a five-foot-tall man was six-foot-two.

Since that time, whenever a stupid, thoughtless remark gushes forth from the mouth of a total stranger, I welcome it as penance for what I said that day. Richard was gracious, however, and didn't give me any knuckles to eat. Rather, he laughed. I've since come to see him as an actor of tremendous stature with power that has little to do with inches and feet.

Early mornings, riding through the city to the studio was a breathtaking experience. We'd make our way to Pico Boulevard, which was in walking distance, and take one of those beautiful red streetcars that were, at that time, the pride and joy of the city. All this was before the freeways had been built, before the auto companies had persuaded the city fathers to rip up the tracks, and get rid of the nonpolluting streetcars. We passed block after block of beautiful homes and estates as we headed westward on Pico toward 20th Century-Fox. The grass was very green, and the trees looked as if their leaves had been waxed— I'd never seen anything like it.

The studio was only a few miles from the Pacific Ocean and every morning there might be a little chill in the air, but every day was filled with sunshine, and toward noon, the weather was unbelievable. I could see why the place was named after the angels. Los Angeles, though, seemed to be wrapped in a sort of impersonal perfection; it seemed to be tied up in its own beauty and self-sufficiency. I was impressed, but

I was also uncomfortable. I didn't belong. I was a black girl from the bowels of Harlem, and something was missing for me.

When we had played in *Anna* downtown at the theater in 1947, we had lived in another kind of neighborhood, close to Central Avenue, where the people of color had a different lifestyle altogether. That was not this Los Angeles. This was the film city, the big time, the studio version of life outside Los Angeles. It was the Hollywood we had missed before.

At the studio, we were immediately struck by the fact that we didn't see any black people working anywhere. No technicians, no grips, no electricians, no props people. We didn't see any dark skins in the makeup and wardrobe departments or as hairdressers. From the minute we entered the gate in the morning till the time we left, we were in an all-white world, and that reality was hard for us to ignore. Almost automatically, we were concerned.

Shouldn't we take some kind of action, we thought—but what? Had the NAACP or the Urban League proposed it, we would have been the first to participate. We discovered, however, that Ossie and Ruby were not initiators, primarily; our role was followship and support, not leadership, in the Struggle against discrimination.

Besides, *No Way Out* was a daring, innovative, and worthwhile project, capable of stirring up controversy and raising awareness. Sidney's role in the film was part of the Struggle, too, but in another form. Playing a doctor, he was going to put his black hands on a white man, and when challenged, stand up for his rights, both as a doctor and as a man. If this film succeeded, it would open the door for others.

There is a time, a season for everything under the sun, I reasoned. The very fact that this film was being made at all was proof that someone at the top here in Hollywood was very conscientious, wanted to deal with prejudice and injustice, and was trying to make a difference. Joe Mankiewicz, the director, a sensitive and very aware person, was putting his career on the line. The cast was great. Everyone was absolutely friendly, pleasant, and eager to please. Don't make waves, I cautioned myself.

Remember, I told myself, this is not a one-room, no-script operation, like the ones you did back in Harlem for Toddy Productions. This was not Oscar Micheaux, or even Bill Alexander, who for all his professional life never had enough money, space, or connections to realize his cinematic dreams. Look what had happened to *The Fight Never Ends:* good film, good as anything Hollywood had to offer, but it never had a chance. All that work for nothing. And where did Bill Alexander wind up? Location unknown. Avoiding his creditors. Be cool, Ruby, keep your eyes open and your mouth shut, and see what happens.

OSSIE: I saw what Ruby saw, and felt what she felt; but I attacked the problem differently. Whenever I am confronted by the strange and the unknown—the potentially frightening—I always laugh. Loudly and frequently, whether I'm tickled or not, I roar with laughter. Not only does it relieve me of tension, but it also sometimes throws those who might not wish me well completely off guard.

On our very first day before the camera, I set out to make everybody on that set like me right away. The first scene was of a breakfast involving all the black actors from New York, and that gave me exactly the background I was looking for. The prop man served my plate, with a huge egg on toast, sunny side up. It wasn't a real egg, of course, rather a peach, cut in half to look like an egg, and covered with thick, gooey juice. The bacon was real enough, as were the french fries, with ketchup to match. I was playing Ruby's husband, a hungry truck driver with a hearty appetite who really enjoys eating breakfast. That was what the director told me, and that was all I needed to know.

First was the master shot. We played the scene from beginning to end, with me laughing, joking, wolfing it down, cleaning my plate, and asking for more. I stole the scene—everybody was watching. I was absolutely hilarious. I almost felt like rising and taking a bow. But that was only the beginning.

They shot the scene again, and then again. And each time, I tried to outdo myself. I was a hit. The prop man had found himself a buddy, and the crew was eating it up, having themselves a ball, laughing at what I was doing with my face, my hands, my fingers. The other actors not only asked for smaller portions, but also they spit what they hadn't swallowed into a bucket. But not me. I had an audience—good, friendly-faced white folks, laughing at everything I did—and I wasn't about to let them down. After three takes, though, I was beginning not to feel so hot.

The director, however, was very pleased. "Splendid everybody, just splendid. Now we'll move in for coverage."

RUBY: I could see Ossie slowly beginning to turn green. The director had not taken into account that we were primarily from the stage, and that we'd had very little opportunity to work before the camera. We were excited, nervous, and just plain inexperienced. Acting for film requires a different technique that is not learned by osmosis. It takes study, observation, and practice. I felt Ossie was ill at ease because he was going through a routine I'd seen before, when he wanted to please a lady, mostly. I'd noticed it, first, when he took me to his home in Georgia to meet his mother and his aunts. To show their love for him, they would prepare increasingly sumptuous meals, day after day in their various homes. Ossie would supply the jokes, the stories, the merriment, and an amazingly hearty appetite to express his gratitude. To fulfill his part of the homecoming ritual, he would always oblige.

His performance that first day on the set was more than an ingratiating display for the benefit of the whites present; it was his way of trying to put everybody at ease.

OSSIE: Whatever Ruby thought, she didn't seem very amused, or certain enough of herself to be of much help.

"Coverage?" I asked, not knowing what the director meant.

"Yes. The same scene, but now we move in close."

"You mean, we gotta do all that eating again?"

"Oh, yes," he said, explaining to me about two-shots and three-shots and, most important of all, close-ups.

"Close-ups?" My stomach was already churning.

"Yes, and I think I'll start with you. Remember, the camera is right down your throat, so give me the same gusto, the same hearty, hungry truck driver, dying to get at those eggs. Props, fix Mr. Davis another plateful, will you?"

Ruby was just coming into her own as a cook, and I loved coming downstairs to her bacon and eggs and coffee. But for the next week or so, I begged for grits and kippered herring. And she obliged.

RUBY: The day before the beginning of principal photography, some test footage had been shot for the purpose of examining our faces. The makeup people were not quite satisfied with me. They spoke aloud to each other while viewing the results.

"I really don't think she needs any makeup at all. Some powder? But these brows. Yes, let's take the brows down." I felt like a thing, not a person—a heathen from Harlem. Everybody out here is so beautiful. So trim, slim, and perfect looking. How can they bear to touch us black Neanderthals from New York?

Nevertheless, the makeup they put on my face each morning did please me; but hair was a different matter. On the trial day, I could sense that the hairdresser assigned to me was not well practiced in handling hair like mine. Despite efforts to relax, I grew increasingly tense. I found myself inquiring about a colored hairdresser. Was there one on staff? Finally, I suggested that perhaps it would be appropriate to bring in somebody who would be more familiar with my kind of hair. "Of course," they said, with a smile that seemed to spring from relief—"It could be arranged."

Elizabeth Searcy, a colored hairdresser, came that afternoon, which certainly made me relax, but not completely. I was still uncomfortable because I felt those in wardrobe straining to be normal, working with people that, were it not for their jobs, they would not touch. The incident with the shoes was proof.

In those days, an actor could be required to wear personal clothing if it did not have to be special—period, for example. I had brought some shoes and some dresses that I felt would serve. When reviewing a pair of the shoes, one of the wardrobe attendants, I noticed, had picked up my sling pumps and was dangling them from two fingers, trying to get the attention of another attendant. When she did, she raised her eyes heavenward as if to say, "Will you look at this?" After she caught my eye, she said, "Yes, these will do, I think."

"Well, what was the matter? Are they too old-fashioned? Too scruffy? Do they smell?" I wanted to ask, but I didn't. I felt the blood rise to my face and I had to remember my temper. That encounter, however, helped lead to a concern about clothes and appearance that remains with me. The only freedom from such worry came much later, when Celia Bryant, now deceased, began to supervise all work-related wardrobe and costume fittings. She was a designer who had worked with me and Ossie in almost all our productions, and personally, too, for many years.

Every day at work on *No Way Out,* I was conscious of the film's political and social themes. I was also vividly aware of the discrepancy between the fictional world of the film and the reality of racist discrimination on the lot, and in the film industry. The people responsible for getting us before the camera became more gracious and efficient, but remained unaware that they helped form the scaffolding of racism on which bigotry and exclusivity grows and climbs.

When listening to their self-congratulatory remarks about how marvelous a team they were, and sensing the enormous self-confidence that comes from steady work in a well-paying job, I wanted frequently to interject, "Yes, but black people are deliberately barred from participation in this image-making business. Do you realize that?"

I once asked a makeup technician why he didn't inquire about the absence of blacks in the unions? He said—and I believed him—that he hadn't given it much thought. But maybe he should, I suggested. Maybe more people could be "very nice people" in this world, just like him, if their good fortune, their opportunities for advancement in life, were not cut off because of their race.

That conversation took place nearly fifty years ago. Since then, some progress has been made in the film industry, but it has been slow and strained. Some bright promise is rimming the horizon, but I always want it to come up faster, and to benefit many more people than the select few.

Films like *No Way Out* have widened the crack in the door through which other cultures have entered the previously lily-white film industry, and I was pleased to have had even a small part in this one. It was the best I could do, I'd say, for a colored girl at the time.

OSSIE: As isolated as they try to make life seem in Hollywood, there are times when matters of great importance are somehow smuggled in. Suddenly you find yourself rudely confronted by the life you thought you'd left outside.

The scene about to be shot was a big one—a night shot where the bad white guys from Beaver Canal were supposed to raid the black community in answer to Sidney's insolence. I approached a group of actors already in costume and makeup, waiting around, talking. I ambled up, found a place at the edge of the crowd, and stopped to listen: "Paul Robeson laid it on the line." This comment came from a white actor whom I had not met but who looked important. I knew what he was talking about—the recent "speech" Paul made in Paris before the World Peace Conference.

There was much I might have added to the conversation, but though they seemed as partisan and as passionate in their commitment to Paul as I was, they were white. My worship of Paul Robeson came from another place, a blacker place, to which they did not belong. And I wasn't ready to share.

In New York, it might have been different, but this was Hollywood. Who, among all these strangers, did I know I could trust? Robeson was America's question mark. It was the time of the witch-hunt, of naming names, and pointing fingers. He couldn't come into the conversation without bringing the Struggle with him. And I didn't want the glorious Hollywood dream to end—I wanted to be loved, not controversial. I said hello to the guys and kept on walking.

Hollywood did accomplish one lasting thing for me, however. One morning I woke up with my mouth tasting like—I'd rather not say. I took what was left of a pack of cigarettes and flushed it down the toilet. I never smoked again. Hooray for Hollywood.

Our agent wanted Ruby and me back in a hurry. We didn't take the train; that would have meant five days of travel, so we took a plane instead. The total flying time from L.A. to New York was nine hours, with a refueling stop somewhere in the Midwest. There were two flight attendants—we called them stewardesses then—who gave us box lunches on both legs of the journey. The planes were not yet jets; they had propellers. On takeoff, you could see fire spitting from the engines;

they rattled and bounced us around a bit, and they made a hell of a racket. Nothing to do but fasten our seat belts and try to sleep.

Ruby and I were gypsies. No sooner had we set our suitcases down after returning home from one adventure than we were off on another—sometimes together, sometimes alone.

During this year of our first Hollywood film, I also worked in the Equity Library Theater production of *Stevedore,* with Jack Klugman and Rod Steiger, both of whom became stars on Broadway and in Hollywood; and with Lloyd Richards and George Roy Hill, who became well-known directors. Ruby drove all the way down to Florida A and M College with Powell Lindsay, who had directed her in another film for Bill Alexander, to work in an original play by Randolph Edmonds, a professor there.

We both did *Anna* again; this time it was a bus and truck tour, with a stop at a Baltimore theater, which had Jim Crow seating when we got there, but open admission when we left. In Montreal, the producer's girlfriend absconded with the payroll, leaving the company stranded—except for Monty Hawley, who could always pass for white; he found himself a French Canadian girlfriend who paid his hotel bill and set him free. We even played *Anna,* a drama, at the Apollo Theatre, Harlem's music mecca, three times a day, where the show ran fifteen minutes overtime, because folks laugh harder uptown.

CHAPTER 21

Giant Steps

RUBY: The decade of the 1950s was a time of giving birth and of getting born into a wider concept of ourselves as actors, and into a heightened sense of art and the Struggle as inseparable bedmates. It was a time of learning to work together, mapping strategy for riding five horses between us. Death came galloping hard into the family. Friends turned on friends, and people lost jobs, lost respect, lost everything they owned. Values got confused; Satan rode high in the saddle, and people who sat high were brought low. It was a decade of fear, a time for laughter behind closed doors. It was a time of insisting on the right thing: *Brown* v. *Board of Education* in 1954. Hypocrites and tyrants, Hoover and McCarthy, held people hostage. Resources were leached by the cold war, and people suffered. It was a decade of deeper involvement with labor unions, a decade of getting ready for the heroes, the confrontations, and the murders of the sixties. It was the decade when the public issues became personal ones for us, too.

In 1950, I was pregnant again, in spite of the doctor's advice to wait a year. This time, I was on my way to play Rachel Robinson in *The Jackie Robinson Story*. Needed: an actress who understands that the aim of this assignment is to make the ballplayer look good. As it turned out, Jackie Robinson didn't need my help. He didn't need me to simp my way through the picture as so many female actors of the day, who played the "good girl," seemed required to do. Recently, Ossie and I watched the picture again on television. I was struck by the innocuous nature of my performance. The Rachel Robinson I met at the time of the shoot was feisty, joyous, earthy, and tremendously supportive of me. Neither the dialogue nor my interpretation of the character fully reflected the woman I met, who was to become my friend.

One day Rachel gave me Sharon, their baby, to hold. Although it didn't show, I was three months pregnant at the time. That moment, which somebody luckily photographed, felt like a rehearsal for my own impending motherhood. But I kept my secret.

Working with Jackie was no problem at all. He put me completely at ease. As an actor he was earnest, honest, and pleasant, but there was a certain edginess to him. In one scene, for example, I had to massage his shoulders, which I didn't want to do because I've always been sensitive about my rough hands, which were then also cold. When I put my mitts on that man's shoulders, he jumped, turned abruptly, and glared at me. Silence. At that moment, the director didn't seem to know what to do, nor did anyone else. The thought flashed through my mind to excuse myself so that I could find some lotion, soften my hands, and warm them. It was a low-budget picture, however, so I didn't want to use up costly minutes and people's patience fooling with my fingers in the ladies' room. I laughed a little laugh, but nobody laughed with me. I rubbed my hands together furiously to generate some warmth. Well, the sound of that action was like two pieces of coarse sandpaper in heat. I blew into my hands, rubbed them together again, and put them back on his shoulders. This time he relaxed, and we went on with the scene. That was the only rough moment I had with Jackie in the picture.

Through the years, the Robinsons and the Davises became friends.

We seldom saw each other socially, but we did meet in many places, on many platforms, in support of some aspect of the Struggle in which we both believed.

OSSIE: We knew about the Hollywood Ten, about hundreds of people in the industry being hauled before the House Un-American Activities Committee and forced to name names or lose their jobs. We knew about the Rosenbergs, and about the loyalty oath you had to sign to work in television. But we tended to look upon it as just another example of those national excursions into insanity so sadly characteristic of our country from time to time. (Of all countries, I guess.) But then, they reached out for Paul, and that was different.

J. Edgar Hoover called him the most dangerous black man alive, a threat to the American way of life, who had to be stopped, one way or another. Many Americans, who had been so proud of Paul's status as a spokesman up till now—white folks who used him as the prime example of what America had accomplished in the way of race relations, and black folk who used him as the prime example of what we could do given half a chance—found themselves embarrassed, if not frightened. His oft-expressed sympathy for the Soviet Union and for socialism, at a time when the Cold War was getting hotter than ever, struck them as treasonous, and made him more of a liability than an asset in their eyes. They decided it was safer, and more convenient, to sail with the ill winds blowing against him.

To much of traditional black leadership, Paul represented a danger to black interests, which depended heavily on white friends in high places, like Eleanor Roosevelt, who, after Paris, had bowed to pressure herself, and spoken out against him. Walter White, Jackie Robinson, Adam Clayton Powell, Mary McLeod Bethune, A. Philip Randolph all joined the chorus. Charge and countercharge, magnified by a press that was already hostile and prejudiced, inflamed the atmosphere. The situation grew from bad to worse, becoming so tense and explosive that, in Peekskill, New York, where Paul had gone to give a concert—as he had done many times before—a riot occurred, which put his life in danger. Many of his friends feared for his safety, and suggested he lower his voice, concentrate on his singing and performing for a while, and leave the speaking alone.

But in 1950, the Korean War began. And though Truman had desegregated the U.S. Army, which made him very popular with a lot of black folks, it didn't impress Paul Robeson at all. He loudly and openly criticized President Truman, and attacked American foreign policy. It wasn't long before the State Department relieved him of his passport.

Taking his passport was an effort to silence Paul, to take away his power to move the masses who loved him around the world. And to silence Paul was to silence the legions of us who thought and felt as he did. A furious campaign was launched to win him back his passport. And the way to win was to rally the masses he loved to his defense.

New York, not Hollywood, was still headquarters and nerve center of the entertainment world, and that was where we chose to take our stand. This was, from the outset, more than a fight for a passport; there was a strong sense, rather, that history's ancient promise of freedom and justice for all was hanging in the balance—even the basic meaning of American democracy. So a state of war existed between us and the status quo—those men of means and power who correctly felt that Paul was a danger to them, and to their postwar effort to reconstruct the world.

We didn't have the vast media resources they had at their fingertips, but we had Paul. He was our instrument as well as our cause. The harder they fought to keep Paul quiet, the harder we fought to magnify his voice. The mass rally, the picket line, the demonstration became the basis of our strategy and the first line of our defense. We had to keep the masses, not only the workers here in America, but around the world, on our side.

So always there were meetings, public and private, caucuses, and sessions behind closed doors where plans were debated and strategy worked out. Ruby and I were caught up, as were the rest of our peers and fellow artists, right in the eye of the hurricane.

Some were there whose every waking moment belonged to the Struggle, whose whole life was defined and consumed by the Struggle;

they were ready to drop everything when the call went out. Ossie and Ruby also, but only up to a point. Oh, we accepted responsibility, we came to the meetings faithfully, we took part in the discussions, which were sometimes heated, and we accepted our assignment. We were good MCs, working well together. But then we went home, leaving the Struggle behind us. Burning the midnight oil—that was for the leaders, not for us.

But if a quick articulation of the gathering's objective, a succinct statement—off the cuff, on the spur of the moment, though occasionally prepared—was needed, I was your man. Or if you wanted somebody who could stand on the flatbed of a truck in Harlem at midday and recite Margaret Walker's "For My People" so that the passersby who heard her stopped to cry, Ruby was your woman. So it went in the battle to get Paul's passport.

RUBY: When I returned from Hollywood, I was faced with another momentous development. Not only would the baby be coming in about six months, but also the whole section in the Bronx where we roomed with Pat and Roger was condemned, and was going to be torn down to make way for a housing project. We had to move.

Back in the Bronx now, my routine changed drastically. It was time to look for a place to live and to get ready for the baby. My life took on a different rhythm. Instead of feeling like an actor, I felt like a typical, picture-book housewife, barefoot and pregnant, waiting for my husband to come home from work. I cooked and helped Pat sometimes with the housework; I knitted baby booties, sewed and embroidered receiving blankets, baby pillows, coverlets, and so on. I went regularly to the prenatal clinic, and I got a chance to see more of Mother and my sister, LaVerne.

Ossie, however, wasn't a typical husband. He didn't work in a factory from nine to five; he was working on Broadway in *Wisteria Trees* with Helen Hayes, Vinie Burroughs, Maurice Ellis, and all the other beautiful people.

After a while when he came home, I began to feel that he less than adored me. "Was it because I was getting misshapen-looking, greasy, fat, and frumpy?" I wondered. Or—oh, horrors!—"He doesn't love me anymore!" He was surrounded by beautiful, interesting women at work, six days a week, and I was losing him to the charms of hussies hell-bent on snatching him from me. I was convinced of it when one day he came home and, out of the clear blue sky, suggested that I put on some lipstick. I went into the bathroom we shared with Pat and Roger and had a boohoo heyday. During the course of this self-pity party, I happened to glance at this broad in the mirror—hair, face, nails, clothes—I was a mess! Ruby, I told myself, this will never do.

A man is an elementary creature. Beauty is only skin deep? Don't you believe it. Beauty is in the eye of the beholder? Well, that depends upon the quality of vision in the eye that is doing the beholding. Beauty radiates from the soul? Well, I'll buy that, but until the rays hit him, I better do something with my hair, hands, feet, clothes, shoes, etc. Besides, if he's looking at another woman—even thinking about it—I will have to kill the perpetrator of my misery and/or the father of my child. And another "besides": Ruby, you will feel better.

So I stopped knitting, sewing, and working on my layette, waddled on out to the makeover place, and got myself together. One day I stayed so long at the beauty parlor, getting my hair styled, along with a manicure and a pedicure, that he had to leave for work before I got back. That night when he came home, he said he had been worried because he didn't know where I was. I hadn't fixed his supper, and I'd left no message. I told him what I had been doing. I told him why. He said I didn't need to do that. He said, "I love you, baby; don't care how bad you look." He told me I was crazy to think that he would two-time me. I cried and told him how ashamed I was to even think that he even thought about such a thing. Then we forgave, and hugged and kissed each other, and went on to sleep.

In the middle of the night, though, I happened to wake up. I turned to look at my sleeping lover, and I said to myself, "No, Mother, I just don't happen to believe that all men are dogs, though in some cases, dog might be an improvement. But, God Almighty, they are some elementary creatures."

I didn't want to waste money buying cute maternity clothes because we had to save to buy a house. I sewed up a few things to tide me over, and bought one fairly decent dress. Ossie even gave up the fifth of Seagram's he used to buy every week for our gin and tonics. At the suggestion of Maurice Ellis, known as Stretch, who was working with Ossie in *Wisteria Trees,* we decided not to get an apartment, but rather to buy a house, maybe out on Long Island.

"You don't want to move out on Long Island," Stretch said. "Everybody's moving out there. Besides, I hear that whenever there's a storm, all the basements leak. Why not up in Westchester? I know this real estate broker up in Mount Vernon. I'll introduce you to her."

OSSIE: The broker showed us several places before the one she and Ruby finally settled on. I wasn't any help at all; gladly, I left all aspects of the choosing up to Ruby.

Actors' work is unpredictable, so we decided to purchase rental property. A two-family house with a tenant to pay rent would guarantee that we could at least pay the mortgage on the steep cost of this $13,000 house. Getting hold of that kind of money was a problem. We borrowed from Ruby's parents, but that wasn't enough. We needed a mortgage, and thereby hangs a tale.

I had gone to Josh Logan and Leland Heywood, producers of *Wisteria Trees,* but they couldn't help. Then we tried a big bank downtown, but their policy was never to lend to actors, black or white—or so they told us. Once again, Stretch Ellis came to the rescue. He told us about Carver Federal Savings and Loan, a new bank up in Harlem, owned and operated by black people. We went to Carver and got a loan of $6,500, a second mortgage was arranged with the sellers, a German couple, and the deal was done.

RUBY: Ossie took me in a taxi to Columbia Presbyterian Hospital about nine o'clock in the morning, August 16, because the contractions matched the rhythms that they said would indicate it was time to come in. There wasn't much need for a husband at this point, but I didn't expect Ossie to disappear so quickly or so completely.

They prepped me and put me in a gown. After examining me, they told me I had to walk because the baby wasn't quite ready to come. Out in the corridor, hour after hour, I was part of the heavy-bellied traffic walking to encourage our babies to come out and get going with this life. One by one, a doctor would examine us to see if we were sufficiently dilated—two fingers, two and a half fingers, three fingers—whatever that meant. The baby still was not ready to come; back to the corridor. What is the child waiting for? One by one, my walking associates disappear. They don't come back. They've gone to the birthing room.

Finally, it is late at night, and I am by myself, walking that corridor. Then, a real bad cramp. I tell the nurse. Examined. Okay, it's time. Get her to the birthing room. Get her on the bed. I lay there. I hear women moaning, crying, screaming, and some are cussing. "Oh, come on, ladies," I say to myself, "face it. It's hurting time. You got to grit your teeth, and if you can't grin, bear it. Stop the hollerin'! For crying out loud, quit the hollerin'!" Suddenly a pain comes to me that makes me feel as if I am on a rack being pulled apart at the pelvis. "Whoa, whoa," I try to whisper, but something comes out of my mouth like a roar and a shout. "WHOA . . . WHOA . . . WHOA!" By the time I am wheeled to the delivery room, I can only hear myself bombarding the three o'clock morning air with screams that must be coming from somebody else. What could Eve ever have done to cause such indescribable pain to be visited on her and all her sisters and daughters forever! I am given some medication. The incredible pain begins to subside.

I wasn't a private patient. I came through the clinic. As such, I discover, I'm also the center of a lesson on how to inject the anesthetic into the spine to eliminate the pain of childbirth. A doctor indicates the exact location in my spine to insert a needle. There is some discussion. The needle goes in; its contents are emptied. More discussion. I lie down. Nothing hurts anymore. I push when I'm told. Soon, a tiny brown baby comes out of me. She is so small. My heart reaches out to her. The umbilical cord is cut. She is cleaned, wrapped, and given to me to hold. My arms seem so skinny. Will milk really flow from these meager breasts? It just better. No bottle for this baby. This child is mine forever!

OSSIE: Having an actual baby was, for a man like me, like any other function—so normal and so natural that it almost seemed to happen by itself, very much like our marriage ceremony, a routine that required no second thinking. You had sex, and pretty soon, willy-nilly, there was the baby and that was that. I had no inkling that that simple act and its consequences had changed our lives and our relation to each other—that I had entered a domain for which I was little prepared. Yes, there were certain basic skills that I'd acquired as the eldest child helping Mama with the other siblings. I knew how to wash diapers and change a baby, but didn't everybody? This baby was a cute little extension of my own ego.

It never occurred to me that some day, and soon, she would cease being a baby, an adorable object to hug and kiss and coo over, and become, instead, a child, independent in the sight of God and man, with sniffles and dolls and colic, and a burgeoning need to be somebody, separate and distinct, whom the world was going to call Nora. It never occurred to me that I would become, not her owner, but her parent, her father, which is a different thing entirely.

RUBY: During the growing-up years that sped by so very fast, Mother would keep people's children from time to time. It was one of the ways she increased the family income. We would treat the older children as if they were part of the family. I remember the lovely Mitchell girls, Rosemary and her two sisters. Most of all, I remember George and Arthur Stewart.

Their mother, Bertha, was the kind of woman who comes to mind when someone says, "Now that woman is a character." She was a skinny brown woman with missing front teeth, who covered her mouth when she laughed, who walked fast and had a devilish, quick wit. Her lover, or common-law husband, was a Scotch-Irishman who adored her and the two sons she bore him. I thought she treated him shamefully. We all felt sorry for Mr. Stewart, who asked Mother to keep first one, then the other of his sons soon after they were born. Bertha refused to marry Mr. Stewart and nobody seemed to know why. We children liked both of them. She came to see the babies almost every day, sometimes with Mr. Stewart. Our mother was really their mother for a long time, however.

I should have learned something from watching Mother work with those baby boys, but I didn't. I loved dolls as a youngster, but I don't remember feeling any attachment to real babies. When my sister, Angelina, married Carl Roach, and their first child, Michelle, was born, I only saw the new baby a few times.

How unfortunate to be in school so many years and not be required to take even one course devoted to parenting, motherhood, management of the home, and above all else, to some basic relationship training. What is a husband? What is a wife? What about sex? What is the importance of family? Work? Community involvement? The information that is handed down by word of mouth, learned in books only, or heard on the street is insufficient.

My first deliberate instructions relating to taking care of a tiny baby were given during the last month's checkups at the clinic before Nora was born. They continued while I was in the hospital, at which time the new mothers were also advised to nurse their babies for at least three months.

I hadn't counted on nipples that could become sore, that would crack and bleed. The nurses were especially gentle, showed me ways to heal, and reassured me the baby would not starve in the process. When the row of babies was wheeled into the ward, my eyes went straight to mine because she was the tiniest; so fragile, I thought, as she was handed to me. The nursing was painful, and I wasn't sure she was getting enough.

In the middle of the second night, I wanted to hold her to reassure myself. I started for the nursery, but I was stopped at the door.

"I just want to see if my baby's still alive," I said. "She is so small."

The nurse said, "Oh, she'll live. Little ones like that do very well. Don't worry now. Go back to bed." I did, but, unable to sleep, I got up again, intending to make my way back to the nursery. Hopefully, no one would be there. There were two nurses there now. One was changing a diaper. The other was headed straight toward me. I ducked into a lavatory. I'll wait here a moment, then go on back to bed, I thought. My heart was racing and I wasn't sure why. I wasn't doing anything illegal. I just wanted to locate and look at my baby even through the glass partition.

Glancing out of the lavatory window as I turned to leave, however, my heart almost stopped. Across the vast courtyard, a brightly lit window arrested my attention. There were two men in white coats and—was that a corpse on the table? I quickly tiptoed back to the ward to retrieve my eyeglasses from the bedside table. Between racing and stopping, it's a wonder my heart kept on pumping.

Back in the lavatory, I again turned my attention to the window that seemed like a monster eye in a dark, dark night. I saw a head being sawed open, hands pulling the skull back and reaching inside, brains put on a scale, then dumped in something. I watched in fascination as first one organ, then another was weighed and disposed of in the same manner: heart, liver, lungs. The men seemed to be enjoying a lively conversation, interspersed with laughter. It seems to me that they were also smoking cigarettes.

When I finally crept back to bed, filled with the horror, the sadness, the pity, and the wonder of that incredible and fascinating procedure, I realized that I had been witnessing an autopsy—a routine procedure, I cautioned myself. No need to do trauma here. The physical body—after years of being hidden in darkness and mystery, of being subject to careful study, to indifferent or responsible feeding and tending—this holy vessel, this temple of awesome life force is now so much guts turned inside out, exposed to fluorescent lights, and relegated to garbage. It happens to everybody, and eventually we all must bow down to the winners, the worms.

Such extraordinary occurrences—death and birth! How can such exalted events be so taken for granted? It is as if the Creator played Her best hand all the time. It's like using the really good glasses, the sterling, and the Wedgwood china in the backyard or every day.

I quit my vigil at the window and went back to bed, as the night cracked and the lighted window went black. I was awakened the next morning by the nurse who said she could let me sleep, but she knew I would want to wash and have breakfast because the babies would be coming in soon.

When Ossie came to take us home, I wasn't ready—I really didn't want to leave the security of the hospital. There was talk about my staying another day, or going home without our baby, Nora. "We like our babies to be at least five pounds," we were told. Nora was four pounds, fifteen ounces. "Naturally they lose a few ounces after birth, but she's gained back all but two ounces." We were given cards, menus, flyers, start-up maternity kits, medications, and formula directions in case I decided not to nurse.

I was not what you might call a relaxed mother. I prayed. I had almost every page of my Dr. Spock book dog-eared. I wanted to do it right. *Relax,* everybody said, including Dr. Spock. Enjoy! Okay. Where do I go for relaxing, enjoying, laughing lessons? Bathe the baby. Oil. Fold diapers. Nurse. Burp. Clean the poop. She's still so little. To my friend, Yvonne Machen, I said, "Don't smoke, Mache. That is why she's so little. I smoke!" On a bad day, it could be as much as half a pack.

Ossie was a gem. So calm. He seemed to know about babies. He carried Nora in one hand a lot. That made me nervous. What about supporting her head? I didn't count on his long finger serving as a splint behind her neck. With one hand, he'd put her on his shoulder.

Daddy brought Mother to the Bronx to see us and the new baby. Mother helped me get the laundry together and gave me much reassuring advice. When we told them the baby's name, a shadow seemed to flit over Mother's face. At that moment, I gave myself a mental uppercut. Why hadn't I named her "Emma"? It would have pleased Daddy, too.

OSSIE: On September 1, less than two weeks after Nora was born, we moved from the Bronx to our two-family house in Mount Vernon. Mrs. Bachmann, the former owner, and her husband had left the house immaculate in every detail, thankfully, because we didn't have any money to put into painting and decorating.

The move itself was simple in execution, but most profound in implication. We moved from being merely actors and activists toward being parents, neighbors, homeowners, members of a community. Most of all, we were a family, which was what God, society, Daddy, Mama, Reverend Whitaker, and the Black Experience had expected and trusted us to become. I took on my role as husband/father, for which I had been rehearsing all my life, passed down to me by my father, which I in turn would pass down to my son. None of this was on our minds as we entered our new home and our new life.

We started out as something of a curiosity, having moved into this mostly white, working-class neighborhood. We didn't even own a car, or any of the other trappings associated with people in the theater and in movies. When we explained to Mom Boucher, our closest neighbor, in response to her inquiry about what we did for a living, she said, "Oh, things will work out and you'll get a regular job soon. Meanwhile, every little bit helps." We were welcomed and our neighbors soon became our friends.

Five Cooley Place is situated on the side of a steep hill, but the area at the back of our house was flat enough for a garden, and there were three peach trees, which still bore beautiful peaches. The neighbors to the left were Irish, gregarious, and friendly. Lou Thomas, Mom Boucher's son-in-law, was in love with all things growing. He had long admired our garden space, and since he only had a small plot, we invited him to make use of ours. Immediately he took charge and grew food for both our houses, teaching us a great deal in the process. To the right were the incomparable Oakleys from Jamaica—Fred, Ida, and their daughter, Dorothy. There were the Brubachers, the LaSoursas, the Hunts, the Hamlins, the Wagners, the Woods, the Baptistas, the Ramseys, the Newmans, the Jacksons, the Nardozis, the Annunziatas, the Saunderses—and so many more. A multicultural assortment of good neighbors and friends.

We didn't own a refrigerator at first. The ice box took a twenty-five-pound block of ice, and that did the job. We washed diapers by hand, rinsed them, boiled them, and hung them outside to dry on a clothesline, which ran from the back window out to a tree.

The furnace burned coal, which was delivered into the basement . by way of a chute, where I shoveled it into buckets, took them down another flight of stairs to the subbasement where the furnace was, and dumped them into the bin. I quickly learned to set the thermostat, to bank the fires at night, and to drain the radiators. I had never been responsible for anything like this in my life before, but I wasn't daunted.

The house was old. Some rooms had only one electrical outlet in the baseboard. Obviously we needed more, but local electricians were charging seven dollars to install an outlet. Ruby's brother came to the rescue. Edward taught me to do simple wiring and troubleshooting—to hang doors, to repair a broken sash cord, to unclog a drain, to unstop a toilet, and to do other simple plumbing repairs. I learned fast, and further, I could always count on luck and a continuing sense that I was one of God's favorite people, and that everything was going to work out just fine. It usually did.

Three blocks away was the A & P, where we did all our shopping. Between us and the store, however, was an overgrown plot where people used to dump things. I often took the shortcut, and on my way home, would retrieve various items I could use in the rudimentary workshop I'd started just beyond the furnace room. I had found boxes, blinds, old frames, and pieces of furniture among other things. A stage-hand from *Green Pastures* brought me a good saw and some other tools. I used to take some of the junk I'd found (a large ice box on one occasion), bring it home, dismantle it with my pliers, my hammer, and my screwdriver, saw the wood up, and refashion it into something else we could use. We still have three items—a clothes hamper, a chest of drawers, and a cabinet—that I built from wood and metal scraps.

My experience as the firstborn, and therefore Mama's helper, was put to good use in attending to Nora. I not only took the two o'clock feeding, but also I was a very light sleeper, and at the first whimper, I was out of my bed and into Nora's room in a flash. I learned to decode the noises she could be expected to make in the course of a night, and to sense immediately which ones demanded personal attention. There were times when it wasn't the sound from her room that woke me up; it was the silence. I would wake in the middle of the night and rush to see if our firstborn was still breathing.

Ruby, meanwhile, seemed to take to the mechanics of motherhood, wifehood, and housekeeping like a duck to water. Underneath the smooth facade of domesticity, however, a rebellion was brewing.

RUBY: I've read about retreats, spas, places where people can go regularly to treat their bodies and their minds by the still waters, with soft music, soft voices, gentle hands that relieve tensions and calm the spirit. Praise God, I've known some people whose life's work consists of such ministrations.

I've imagined another kind of retreat, however, especially built for black people from all levels of the economic and social ladder. It would consist of a compound of houses with three soundproof rooms. The first would be the largest because it would be heavily padded. It would be the shouting, screaming, tear-out-the-hair room. In it, you could howl, cry, curse, demand answers from the ancestors, and question the Divine. Concerns could go from ancient to current. One could pound on, fling oneself against, or climb the walls until completely exhausted. Satisfied.

In a connecting cubicle, one could shower, dress in a long white robe, and then move to the middle smaller room in which would be a chair and a padded mat on which to sit, or kneel, and talk aloud to Jesus, or to the divinity of choice. Silent meditation might be preferable at this point. The third room might be only large enough to shed the robe, don street attire, and grab the briefcase, pocketbook, shopping cart, or whatever belongings were set aside when one first arrived.

I needed to visit such a compound about six weeks after moving with our new baby to Mount Vernon. It was early afternoon and Ossie had gone to the theater.

Nora cried and cried, and nothing I did made her stop. I nursed and changed her, held and sang to her, sat and rocked her—to no avail. What should I do? Call Mother? Call the hospital? Call the new pediatrician? What will I say—"My baby is crying"? That's what babies do sometimes—they cry. But not this one, not this long. The pins are all in good order. I'll call our new neighbor, Mrs. Saunders, who lives one block over; that's what I'll do.

As I leave the room to go to the phone, a feeling of panic comes over me, and I begin to cry and pound my fists against the wall. Nora suddenly stops crying. I rush back into the room, pick her up and see that she wants to nurse again. She is hungry! My sweet little baby is hungry! I get the paraphernalia I'd brought from the hospital—instructions, bottles, and cans of milk—and make my first batch of formula as fast as I can. I calm myself and give Nora her first bottle, which I continue once a day until she's about three months old.

Most women can have a baby. Becoming a mother is something else. Most women can have a wedding, but not every woman can be a wife.

I knew I was in trouble as a "loving wife" while washing up our dinner dishes one day as Ossie sprawled in the living room with his newspaper. There seemed to be no end to the work—cooking, washing, ironing, nursing, shopping. It seemed to last all day until late into the night. I was feeling stressed and resentful—"OSSIE!" The call was like a high note struck on an oil drum with a hammer, and he came, pronto, thinking something was wrong. Well, it was but I didn't know where to begin.

This incident occurred in the days long before the women's lib movement, when women began to question their role in marriage, in family, in the workplace, and in the community. Although they hadn't yet articulated it, women were also beginning to search for themselves as distinct human beings, with aspirations, ideas, goals, and talents as worthy as those of any man.

An argument can be fun, can be stimulating, and can lead to greater conflict or to greater understanding. Arguing is an art. Between husband and wife, it is a vital form of communication. Things get said and done in an argument that no other level of exchange could accomplish. When the inside gauge says *stop,* however, it's best to cool it; zip your lip and wait for another day.

I kicked off the dialogue, "You know, I've had some kind of job as far back as I can remember, but this housewife business is the hardest job ever. It is eternal, with no vacations, no social security, no pay, no nothing. Everybody takes you for granted. When you met me, I was an actor. I'm not giving it up. I'm not going to spend my life doing dishes. I think you should know that!" I ventured loudly but without much conviction.

"Why are you jumping up and down like that?" he replied. "Who asked you to?"

"I want to take a workshop in acting with Paul Mann, and you're just going to have to help me do it."

"Help you? Don't I take out the garbage? Don't I boil the diapers—hang 'em out on the clothesline?"

"I'm talking about *me,* now, because it seems to take my life and your life to make your life!" I had just thought up that brilliant summation for the frustration I was feeling, and it sounded pretty good. "I never get a chance to lounge around after dinner with a big, fat cigar or—"

"What are you talking about? I'm sitting on an orange crate. I haven't smoked a cigar since God knows when—"

"Except for going to the store, I don't leave this house. You never take me anywhere. I haven't even—"

"What do you mean, 'take you'? You can take yourself. . . . What am I doing, standing here, arguing with you? You sound as if you're about to have your period. It makes you mean."

"There you go. Whenever I come up with a legitimate complaint, you blame it on my—"

"Do you want a divorce?"

This was another brilliant non sequitur. "Who said anything about a divorce?"

"You know what? Maybe you should have married Stanley."

"Stick to the point. You're not being logical, and you know it."

"Since when did you know anything at all about being logical?"

"Look, I took a course in logic at Hunter College, and one way an adversary tries to win an argument is by not following through with the main point of discussion. What made you bring up Stanley? I never loved Stanley, and you know it. What's Stanley got to do with you and me?"

"Too bad they didn't teach you at Hunter how to get to the point of why you had to call me in the first place."

"I'll tell you why I called you: I think that after I do all this work around here, and fix dinner, that you could at least help me with the dishes!"

"Dishes? For God's sake, Ruby, is that what this is all about—dishes?"

Ossie comes from a background where women generally were not treated as equals. They were expected, rather, to be the workhorses and do all the donkeywork. No matter the economics involved, the man was king. I come from a background where women, at least, tried to assert themselves, even if, in the end, the realities of the workload mitigated against the likelihood of success. I had never witnessed the kind of equality that I envisioned.

Pressing on to make my point, I said, "I never get a chance to read the papers anymore. I'd like to get up from dinner, read, take a nap, do what I feel like doing. Sometimes you act as if I am running a hotel and you are a guest—the king, or something. And as I've heard it said, 'A king is a son of a bitch—even if he's your own husband.' "

Marriage is rampant with galloping contradictions. We, as women, sometimes tell ourselves that we will demand respect, stand up for our beliefs, be true to our deeper instincts for self-preservation—ready to do battle in defense of our hard-earned rights.

Then, a smile, a dozen roses, a wink, and a pat on the butt, and we just giggle like foolish schoolgirls, blush, and abandon ship. At a critical moment, we will stumble into a blatant contradiction that defeats good judgment, sanctions an unfair tradition, or sinks us deeper in some spiritual and mental rut. Then it's all the way back to square one.

In an earlier argument, I had found myself protesting that religion, intellectual curiosity, and information are not the sole provinces of men. Yes, the Bible conceivably was written by men, and that possibility alone may explain some of the lopsided concepts about women, for which everyone is paying a deep spiritual and psychological price. Certainly it is time for women to take a crack at the "eternal verities."

I reminded Ossie of the time, shortly after we met, when he introduced me to his learned friend, Medas. In a conversation, I had dared to interject my philosophical observation on some opinions of the sages from long ago, and both of them became suddenly silent, looked at each other, then at me—Medas in amazement and Ossie in embarrassment. I was being put on trial and the verdict was in. I was being put in my place. What arrogance! I had thought, but I said nothing.

Another confrontation ensued when I simply said to Ossie, "I saw you with Jane—how dare you! Flirting—with my best friend!"

"Ruby, sweetheart—"

"Don't deny it. I saw you . . . saw you with my own eyes."

"Well, let me know when you see something with somebody else's eyes. We could get you into the *Guinness Book of Records,* at least," he said.

"Funny, funny. You are so funny when you don't want to deal with the facts. That's right. Change the subject. Ha, ha."

"Let me tell you something, Ruby. I don't say you'll never have cause to be jealous, but it won't be because of some woman."

"Don't tell me it'll be because of some man."

"No. See that thing over there?" He pointed to his portable typewriter. "That's the only thing you'll ever have to be jealous of. Don't ever try to pull me away from that. I'm a writer. That—is all I care about."

"You mean, first the typewriter—then me?"

He didn't answer. Slowly he turned, with an almost holy demeanor, and retreated from my presence.

That was our first full-fledged quarrel—toe-to-toe—since we were married. God knows, I gave it everything I had.

Finally, he came back into the kitchen, looked at me, and laughed. Yes, he would help with the dishes, keep the baby while I took classes in acting, and I must share with him whatever I learned. He went back to the living room and to his papers, looking quite superior, as if the contest had ended in a draw. But I knew surrender when I saw it. In my unbiased opinion, I had won.

But that was in the past; those early battles were just warm-ups, preliminary workouts, rehearsals for how to be married. In arguments to come, we would frequently yammer, expostulate, and test each other's mettle. Most often, we would reconcile before we fell asleep. The next day, we might have a good laugh before he would present a proposal for improvement of whatever it was that prompted the fight.

In our relationship as warriors and gladiators, most of the time problems would get solved and meaningful changes would be made. He was and is a sensitive, intelligent, and mostly logical person who realizes that being a really good male, in today's context, takes practice, much effort, and great flexibility. He acknowledges, too, that generally, the faults of women pale in comparison with the faults of men. We both agree that, whatever the situation, if marriage is to survive, it's going to take men helping women and women helping men to see the truth, which alone will eventually set us both free. All of us, of course, are in transition, and are in need of some honest reckoning with personal contradictions that can plague our relationship.

OSSIE: Ruby wasted no time in getting back to her first love, acting. She registered for classes with Paul Mann. I stayed home with the baby until she returned, then we had dinner, and I caught the train for work. *Wisteria Trees* was playing at the Martin Beck, the same theater where we had opened in *Jeb*.

CHAPTER 22

Tall Targets

RUBY: I had promised myself to stick to the nursing routine for at least six months, but I got a job in a film about Abraham Lincoln, *The Tall Target,* starring Dick Powell, and I decided to abandon my noble determination. Had I continued thinking that my less than gushing supply of milk, plus the one bottle of formula the pediatrician suggested, would be sufficient, my baby might have suffered severe psychological problems arising from frustration and hunger, and slowly starved to death.

I shall be ever grateful to whoever was responsible for casting me in *The Tall Target* because that assignment was one of the two in my baby's first year that helped save her life. A few weeks later, I packed myself and my little baby, and once again headed west to Hollywood.

"You better stay home and take care of that baby." I was shocked to hear Mother utter those words. She, who had talked all through my life about getting an education, having a career, making money, being independent. She had spoken about her regrets, her choices, and her sacrifices. It would take a few more years for me to fully understand what I felt was her denial of everything she had told me about having a career, and being a wife and a mother.

No husband, no children at home now, Mother still lived in the large apartment on St. Nicholas Avenue. Except for her living space and the largest bedroom, she rented the rest. She played the horses enthusiastically, as well as the numbers, and kept a few children that she couldn't turn away. To travel with me, and take care of Nora? No, she couldn't do that right now. I thought, why did I even suggest it? The minute the inquiry left my throat, I wanted to recall it. I needed to do something for *her* now. It didn't occur to me that she might want to resume her own career as an actor, and that I might help her do it. I wish it had.

I had met Lil Hill in Los Angeles during the filming of *The Jackie Robinson Story*. She was a fast talker, a fast walker, and a fast driver. I genuinely liked her energy and her enthusiasm about life. I had phoned before leaving New York to tell her I'd be coming to Los Angeles soon, bringing my baby. Did she know a good place to stay where a baby would not be a problem? And did she know of someone who could take care of her on the days I worked? She knew people, yes, but she'd like to help me personally. She had a big house; her children were all grown and gone. Both of us were welcome to live with her, and she would care for the baby while I was at the studio.

The room she rented me and Nora was spacious and beautifully decorated. I didn't have to report to work for several days, which was lucky for me because it gave me more time to check out Lil and her qualifications as a baby-sitter.

In *The Tall Target,* as the slave companion and traveling mate to the character played by Paula Raymond, I was very well dressed. One of the costumes I wore had been made for June Allyson for another picture. Her name was sewn in the neck of the garment. For the sake of conversation, I guess, I remarked to Dick Powell, who was June Allyson's husband, how thrilled I was to be wearing his wife's dress. He said, in effect, "Oh, come on now, Ruby." It was my first feeling of somebody saying to me, "Please, cut the bullshit." I'll never do that again.

Another close call in Nora's first year occurred during the filming of *The Tall Target*. My call to be on set was at 5:30 A.M., but it was decided around noon that I wouldn't be needed for at least another three hours. I could wait, take lunch, or leave. A car could take me home and stay with me until notified to bring me back. I was overjoyed at the prospect of seeing Nora and relieving Lil for a little while. I changed back into my street clothes and headed home. When I opened the door, I expected to see or hear Lil. There was no sound in the house. I rushed upstairs to my quarters. The baby wasn't in the crib sleeping. I called out. No answer.

I came back downstairs to the kitchen, made myself a snack, read the paper, secure in my mind that Lil had gone out and taken Nora with her. "Did she take her in the car?" I wondered. "Or go walking with the carriage Lil had lent us?" I went out the back door to the garage. The car was not there, and I didn't see it on the street. As I headed back into the house, I saw the carriage, but I didn't think the baby was in it. I was about to close the door, but— Wait. Did I see the carriage move? Yes. It was shaking.

I leaped down the steps, across the yard, looked in the carriage, and there was my baby! She had evidently turned herself over from her back, gotten wedged between the side of the carriage and the mattress, and was struggling to get her head free. I could tell she had been crying for quite a while. She was wet, cold, trembling, and taking small, jerky gasps of air. My baby! Thank you, Lord, for bringing me home. After I changed her, fed her, and just held her for a while, the call came for me to return to the studio. Since Lil had not yet come back, I packed some necessities, left her a note, and took Nora with me to finish the day. Elizabeth Searcy, the hairdresser, found a woman to come to the set and watch Nora.

Lil apologized profusely. I was so upset, I can't even recall her excuse to this day. I took Nora with me to work every day until I finished the picture.

OSSIE: In 1951, while Ruby was off in Hollywood doing *The Tall Target*, I was on Broadway in a revival of *Green Pastures*, the very play that I had so vehemently criticized in my drama class at Columbia as being "ooftah." William Marshall played De Lawd and I was Gabriel, his right-hand man in heaven. Bill's opinion of *Green Pastures* was even more withering than mine, but it was a job, and we were not about to turn it down. No way we could change the dialogue, which we found offensively sentimental and condescending, in the same class as any blackface minstrel show. Nonetheless, Bill and I came up with a way we thought would infuse the stilted, childlike language with revolutionary fire and brimstone.

There is one big, angry scene in the play where De Lawd has to castigate the world for its sins, which gave Bill a chance to use that magnificent voice of his—which could melt the fire curtain if he wanted to—to full advantage. But he needed to be inspired to do his best. So, every performance, just before the big explosive moment, I would choose the latest atrocity imposed somewhere in the world on black people and whisper it into Bill's ear, to give him a revolutionary motivation. I would keep talking while Bill pumped up his anger. Then Bill would rise to such ear-shattering heights that nobody sitting in the audience—which was usually white—could help but feel the lash of his vocal venom.

Night after night, performance after performance: the Scottsboro Boys, the Rosenbergs, the apartheid state in South Africa, J. Edgar Hoover, and the name of anybody who had dared attack Paul Robeson—I would feed him his dose of verbal arsenic, and that mighty voice of his would shake the rafters. Bill finally got so hoarse, we had to stop.

And there were other duties. I had been elected Equity deputy— every Broadway company has one, whose job it is to see that the rules of our union, Actors Equity Association, were strictly being observed by management—an assignment that I, as an amateur Marxist practitioner, took quite seriously. My talent for being a bit pompous and self-righteous shows up, first on my face; I exude an aura of high moral purpose, which Bill Marshall and William Van Prince, another actor friend, recognized at once. They would find some minor infraction of Equity rules—or create one—then send for the Equity deputy. Also, there were five beautiful young dancers, vying to be treated like stars in an already overcrowded dressing room, who kept me hopping. I must have made a major ass of myself, scurrying about representing the Negro working class in a major Broadway production.

Actors Equity Association was the heart and soul of Broadway—and its conscience. It was a sort of command center in the sometimes vicious and bloody fight against McCarthyism. Whereas in Hollywood actors, stars, and celebrities seemed to be stumbling over each other, rushing to clear their own names by pointing the accusing finger at their friends and associates, on Broadway, it was different. Though we, too, were a community besieged, we held ourselves above such perfidious behavior. We knew how to defend ourselves and how to fight back.

No. Broadway was not Hollywood. We had organization, we had a philosophy based on what we considered to be our First Amendment rights, we had a galaxy of heroes, including Paul, and we had an objective, which was to fight the witch-hunt and get rid of McCarthyite witch-hunters. We knew how to compose a leaflet, call a rally, stage a demonstration, and make a rousing speech at the quarterly meetings of the union, or downtown on Centre Street, on the steps of the United States Court House. We even knew how to raise money.

John Randolph, who was always a walking storehouse of information, up to the minute on any cause he thought worthy of our attention, was also a floating bill collector and treasurer for those causes. It was always a pleasure to run into John somewhere along Broadway as you were sure to do, even though you never left him without making a contribution to something or other. He had the biggest and friendliest smile you were ever likely to bump into, and he could explain the most complex issue, why it needed our support—including our money—without breaking stride as we walked.

And if, heaven forfend, John Randolph should happen to miss you, there was always Bill Ross, better organized, but less talkative than John. Bill also was the shepherd of many causes. So he would have one pocket reserved for the Society of Soviet American Friendship; one for Rosa Lee Ingraham, black mother in jail in Florida for killing a white man who attacked her; one for the Rosenbergs; and one for miscellaneous causes. Bill was good at asking people for money, but when it was appropriate, he also gave. One day, when a close vote was expected on the floor of the Equity meeting, Bill Ross slipped me nine dollars without my even asking so I could pay my dues right then and vote. Bill is long since dead and gone, but I still owe him much more than money.

Equity was our little corner of the public forum, an arena of debate and agitation around some of the most momentous issues of the day. We actors looked upon ourselves as crusaders as much as artists, with a mission to take the lead, helping to shape the future of the postwar world. Many a battle over racism, segregated theaters, McCarthyism, the cold war, and nuclear hysteria was fought out on the floor of our union meetings. As deputy, I felt it was my duty to attend. And it was there that I first became a dues-paying union man, and met actors and stage managers who remained my friends for the rest of my life.

One of the features of the quarterly Equity meeting was John Effrat's reading of the names of those who had died since the last meeting. A funereal hush would fall over the meeting, no matter how loud, angry, and passionate the debate had gone but a moment before. There was something almost religious in the sonorous but honored pronunciation he gave to every name. I never failed to sit there and wonder how my name was going to sound on that day when John Effrat would say, "Ossie Davis," for the very last time, and my long membership in the union would come to an end.

In the midst of it all, I was possessed of a new idea for a play. Early mornings would find me up and at the keyboard of my portable, hunting and pecking. But that was just for starters. Much of what I wrote was written backstage; on train rides into town; waiting to make a speech; on the backs of menus, letters, envelopes, and phone bills—or someone else's manuscript.

The theme of the play was loyalty, and it was based on an incident that took place in Brownsville, Texas, where, in 1906, some black soldiers of the 25th Infantry Regiment, stationed at nearby Fort Brown, had been mistreated.

A few of the soldiers, fed up with the constant harassment they continually suffered at the hands of the townspeople, decided to take matters into their own hands, and retaliate. Disobeying military orders, they rode into Brownsville and shot up the town, killing one white man and destroying some valuable property. When the company officer, who was white, began to question the men, trying to determine what had happened, and who had done it, he ran into a stone wall. The entire regiment chose to face disciplinary action rather than tell. Even when President Theodore Roosevelt threatened that every man of Companies B, C, and D would be discharged without honor unless they talked, the men held fast. They'd rather accept military dishonor than betray their comrades.

Such a depiction of black men, sticking together, sacrificing their careers to support each other—black men who are so often accused of disloyalty to one another—would be salutary and most inspirational for black people. Also, this was the time of the witch-hunt. People who had bonded together in the past were now spilling their guts, accusing one another before the various committees. Now was the time to show the world what true loyalty meant! That was my mission, my self-imposed assignment. I ran to the 42nd Street library, dug up everything I could find on the case, including big, thick transcripts of the original Army hearings, and buried myself in research.

All during *Green Pastures,* I spent what little time I could spare working on *Clay's Rebellion,* the title of my new play. After *Pastures* closed, I got a part as a walk-on in a play called *Remains to Be Seen,* and that was perfect. I had one entrance, and only one line: "You got my fingerprints!" to a detective in passing. I was on and off in less than five minutes. The rest of the time I had to myself, writing, reading, rewriting, in my dressing room backstage.

It occurred to me that if I went to the library on matinee days to do my research immediately after I came off stage, instead of hanging around for curtain call, I could spend more time with the books. I tried it once or twice, missing the curtain call entirely. Nobody said anything, or seemed to be paying any attention, so I decided to press my luck and proceeded to miss them all. It worked for a while, until I was sent for—and questioned—by Howard Lindsay, author of the play and also the star.

I eagerly explained that I was a playwright, just as he was, and that, in my opinion, curtain calls were not all that important anyhow. He agreed. He knew what it meant for a playwright to be completely absorbed in his work, and wondered why I bothered to show up at all. Why not just forget *Remains to Be Seen* altogether? That way, I could spend twenty-four hours a day at the library, if I wanted to. He said he would be happy to arrange for me to leave the show. I told him that from that moment forward, I would be glad to show up for curtain call.

I recently found that manuscript, reams of withered paper in a ragged manila folder, covered with my handwriting, though some of it had been typed. The subject still intrigues me. Someday soon, I hope to read again what I wrote so long ago. Maybe now, I'll know how to make it work.

RUBY: I swear, toddlers know when they are looking good. Nora made my sewing machine needles sing, making clothes for her. She seemed to enjoy the fittings and the modeling for me.

One day, soon after she learned the magic of her feet, we went walking. She was in a dancy-prancy mood, outfitted in a dress I'd made with a bonnet to match. I took the stroller because I was going to the store, and keeping up with her would be easier during the shopping, or in case she got tired walking.

She looked at herself in the mirror before we left, clapped her little hands, and hugged me around the knees. I put her in the stroller at first, but she soon let me know she wanted to walk, which she did surprisingly well, I thought. She seemed so happy with herself.

At one point, we began to play an "I'm-gonna catch-you" game. She'd run away, turn, and let me catch her, or when I would stoop down and open my arms, she'd squeal with delight, and run in for a hug.

As we neared the railroad station, I decided to put her in the stroller. It was getting late and I wanted to get to the store and back home. I said, "Come on now, baby, let's ride for a while." As I looked up, I saw her running away from me as fast as she could. She turned into the area leading to the train station. I called her, stooped down, held out my arms, expecting her to turn, see me, and run in for a hug.

(229)

She turned, all right, but instead of running toward me, she started backing away, laughing and jumping backward. Directly behind her was a steep flight of concrete steps leading down to the platform where the trains pulled in.

Each time I reached for her, she squealed with laughter and backed away. She was now almost at the edge of the top step. One more move backward, and she would tumble down all those stairs. A voice sounded in my brain, "Leave her! Leave her! Walk away and leave her!"

I ran back to the sidewalk. A man was passing. I said, "Please, mister, talk to me." I babbled something about my baby. He looked at me in surprise, uncertain, unnerved perhaps, by this crazy woman seizing his arm.

He removed my hand, and with a quizzical look, slowly walked away from me. By then, the ruse had worked. Nora was running after me as fast as she could. She fell and cried out, "Mommie." With every ounce of my strength, I ran back and scooped her up. I screamed and sobbed with relief, squeezed and touched her, kissed her, and thanked God over and over for directing me in that critical moment when there was no one around to catch her, or to break her fall, should she have tumbled down those steep, concrete steps. What terrible injury she would have sustained!

To this day, the thought of what might have happened still haunts me. I came to the realization that nothing in my life could replace my children. My family makes all that I could become or accomplish worthwhile.

CHAPTER 23

Connections to the Left

RUBY: Commies here, Commies there, Commies under the bed and in your hair. Commies crawling through the government, rampant in the arts, plagues of Commies everywhere.

At first, Ossie and I didn't believe in the seriousness of the madness. After all, six million Jews had so recently been killed. The pall of that horror still hovered over the world's consciousness. It was too soon for another wave of persecutions, especially one fomented in the United States where only eight short years earlier, our country had been a crucial factor in defeating the Germans, liberating Europe, and in opening and emptying the death camps.

The Soviet Union had contributed so very much to the triumph over racism and Hitlerism, but now in the blink of an eye, the Soviets went from being regarded as our brave allies to agents of the "evil empire" that must be obliterated. Our nation became obsessed with the idea of tearing down the political system spawned by the people with whom we had recently spilled so much blood. Anyone who was even marginally inclined to support communism had to be destroyed as well.

Everybody knew about Ethel and Julius Rosenberg, who were accused of being spies who had given the secret of the atom bomb to the Soviet Union. When the case first appeared in the news in 1950, I felt no special interest, accustomed as I was to stories of witch-hunts, blacklisting, persecution, and discrimination. To those people newly exposed to the victimization system, I thought, "Welcome to the club. This is what blacks have suffered, and continue to suffer, in varying degrees, all the time."

Some of the details of the case, however, began to stir my conscience. A mother and father were about to be killed. Spies are executed in time of war. We were not at war. I was baffled. What was going on behind the headlines here?

I had been warned that speaking out could cost me jobs and adversely affect my career. Ugly things were beginning to happen to free-thinking people in the business, especially in Hollywood; well-known writers and actors were refused work, and lost access to a livelihood.

Ossie and I were disturbed and saddened by what was happening to the country. At best, we felt we were barely on the periphery of the Hollywood/Broadway acting scene. Why should we be nervous about our association with people accused of being Communist?

I don't remember how I happened to be asked to speak at a rally to secure clemency for the Rosenbergs on March 29, 1953, at Carnegie Hall. I'd been attending workshops conducted by Sidney Lumet, the director, where I met Lee Grant and other progressive-minded actors. Perhaps one of them had suggested me. I do know that I was tremendously moved by the fact that two small children might be left without their parents. I was aware of so many instances when Jews had joined in our Struggle for justice, protesting the persecution and the murder of blacks. My deeper self felt an obligation here.

Ignoring my reticence to make political pronouncements, I agreed to speak. I profoundly believed that, no matter what, the Rosenbergs would not be killed.

That night after the Carnegie Hall affair was over, I came upon Howard Da Silva in the hall outside, arguing heatedly with a newspaperman, who implied that I must have been coerced into making the speech. Da Silva, whom I had not yet met, called me over and I set the record straight. "The decision to speak was mine," I said, and hurried off. The next day my name appeared in Ed Sullivan's newspaper column as a "fellow traveler." I was now a "pinko," a Communist sympathizer.

OSSIE: I remember that slightly differently. Two things. First, you and I hadn't had a job in a while. They were having a rally and asked us to come. We talked about it and said, we're not Communists, we don't know Ethel and Julius Rosenberg, and besides, all that "red" stuff—we might lose our jobs.

Ruby said, "Hmmm. What jobs?" So Ruby went to the rally. The anti-Communists were in total control of AFTRA, the radio and television union, which meant that anybody who had the slightest smell of being a radical was left out of everything. So a group of people in the union decided to get together and challenge the slate of officers. Lee Grant was one of the challengers along with John Henry Faulk, Charles Collingswood and his wife, and Ruby Dee.

The names were listed in "Red Channels," a newspaper column, and heads began to roll. John Henry Faulk was snatched off CBS. Others lost their jobs, and the newspapers took it up. Ruby was one of the people whose name Ed Sullivan used. When your name appeared in "Red Channels," you were fair game. So Ruby was the most notorious left-winger in our family because Ed Sullivan and others made her so. That's how she became involved.

Years later, when I found out the Rockefeller administration in Albany had a dossier on me—I didn't even know the state kept dossiers—I got a copy of it. One of my crimes, for which I was called a "fellow traveler," was that I was known to associate with Ruby Dee!

RUBY: Sometimes at night, when we were alone, we'd talk about the new plague in the nation being treated as if it had been sent by God. Some people fought back, of course, but it was difficult not to join the intimidated and the awestruck. We'd talk also about the ridiculous nature of what was happening, and despite it all, there were times when we would sneak a hollow howl. "How can you be red when you're so black?" Were it not for the real sadness and horror, it appeared absurd.

OSSIE: When Jackie Robinson had gone down to Washington to testify against Paul Robeson, it hurt us deeply. We understood that he did what he thought he had to do. How could he turn against Paul, who had been so instrumental in getting Jackie admitted into the game?

And Jackie wasn't the only one. There was Langston Hughes, who had to publicly eat his previous words to square himself with the House Committee; there was Josh White; and there was Canada Lee, who couldn't find a job anywhere and died of a broken heart. Some of these black heroes had to publicly attack Paul Robeson, or at least swear that Paul had duped them. We thought about it, the agony and the shame of it all; we talked about it, and some of us wrote about it.

My thoughts were expressed in a one-act play called *Alice in Wonder,* about a popular black entertainer, Jay Weatherscott, being groomed as the first Negro performer chosen by the networks to star in a weekly radio broadcast. He is asked by the networks to go to Washington, and to testify against a black vocal artist and political leader of great renown who had been accused, as Paul had been, of inciting treason and sedition.

This time I had much better luck with the dialogue. I showed it to Ruby. She liked it and agreed to play the part of Alice, Jay's wife, who walks out on him because of his actions. The script was rough and needed work, but I had just taken another job in summer stock. Ruby and Julian Mayfield, an ardent leader in our little group of black performers drawn up in a circle of defense around Paul, agreed to work on the play while I was out on the road.

RUBY: Take me out. Take me out. Take me out. Inside my head, the command flashed, printed in bold white capital letters on a black background. As I returned to consciousness, I became aware that I was in the hospital, my body naked from the waist down, moving in rhythm to the words. People were talking excitedly. That is all I remember of the moment—the birth of my second child. However, I do remember the circumstances leading up to the moment.

I was about a week into my last month of pregnancy—May 1952. I had been painting the dining room, and was almost finished when, luckily, Lance Taylor, one of the actors from *Anna Lucasta* and our good friend, stopped by to bring us a piece of art he had fashioned from a sheet of copper. Ossie was away on tour.

After letting Lance in, I resumed the work. He said, "You're making me nervous on the ladder. Don't you want me to finish the job?" I laughed and told him to relax, because this baby wouldn't be coming for another three weeks. Suddenly my water broke. I was amazed and embarrassed. I grabbed my prepacked bag and Lance drove me to the hospital.

I was once again a clinic patient and the subject of study for some interns whom an attending physician was instructing. I was soon ready to deliver, and the anesthetic was administered, not to the spine, but this time, through a mask on my face—it was gas.

I had discussed childbirth without anesthesia, but the baby was several weeks early, and Ossie was out of town. He was disappointed to have missed taking part in the birth of his son.

At first the baby looked like my brother Edward; then, as he got older, I could see he had his daddy's mouth, eyes, and sunny spirit. I named him Guy in the hospital because I had always liked that name, and Ossie didn't want a "junior." I called him Victor, too, to soften the macho-ness of Guy. I had thought of my father's name, Marshall, but I'd dismissed it because it sounded military. This time I sensed my father's disappointment. Guy and his grandfather turned out to be very close. In fact, Guy often referred to himself as Guy Marshall Davis. I know Daddy was somewhere smiling when many years later, Guy and his wife, Dorothy, named their son Martial.

Guy was a happy baby who rarely cried. He seemed delighted just to have been born. He was only a few months old when I began work on a play Ossie had written.

I am a natural collaborator. There is no great virtue in that fact; it just comes with the territory of me. Ossie, on the other hand, is much more possessive of his developing ideas, much more secretive and protective of his inner processes than I am.

(235)

It is not difficult to imagine, therefore, that our working together would be challenging. I thought of him as being too tight; he considered me too loose, because I never come to any firm conclusion that I would not readily abandon, faced with a better conclusion. I have little loyalty to the detailing of an idea, only to the idea itself perhaps. When he would become defensive after some remark, question, or point of disagreement I might put forth, I would feel duty-bound to explain why I thought as I did.

In our early efforts to work together, sometimes an issue would degenerate into an argument about his defensiveness and my uninformed criticism. The moments would not be happy. The next day, more than likely, I would retreat from some judgmental posture I had taken, and apologize—for not commenting first on the positive aspects of whatever was being discussed. He, in turn, might point out the virtue in some suggestion I had made, and elaborate on it. In that way, we worked things out—and still do—usually at breakfast when much of our daily communication takes place. Occasionally, I have been so impressed by something he has said that I've regretted not having recorded him. I do believe he possesses a brilliant mind, a great sense of humor, and a profound grasp of history.

I was pleased and surprised when Ossie suggested that I work with our friend, Julian Mayfield, to shape his play *Alice in Wonder,* which Mayfield and Maxwell Glanville were producing. Ossie was on the road in *Jezebel's Husband.*

Julian, who was also a playwright, and I had an easy time of it because Ossie had written so much that our job consisted primarily of cutting and rearranging the material. Julian was also a collaborator by nature, so he was a joy. Then, too, we weren't discussing anything we had written. This was Ossie's play, and he wasn't around to question our choices or to disagree. We felt free to do the best we could with what we had. Ossie later said it wasn't too bad.

OSSIE: I had been cast as house servant and tourist guide to an Old Testament prophet, played by Claude Raines, also featuring young Ben Gazarra, in *Jezebel's Husband.* Raines, who possessed one of the most magnificent voices for an actor I had ever heard, was one of the kindest and shiest men I have ever met. There was about him, and his work, an air of melancholy loneliness, a quality that distinguished him on the stage, playing an ineffectual prophet dominated by his greedy and ambitious wife, Jezebel. It was easy to see that the sad and flowing music of his speech was not an affectation, and that he was indeed a lonely, private man.

One day, in New Haven, Connecticut, where the theater was located, in one of those huge, glass high-rise buildings, home of a major insurance company, he had stayed in after the matinee, sending out for a sandwich, as was his wont, and so had I. We were quite alone, and after a bite or two, which he didn't seem to enjoy, he started to talk.

His daughter had come to visit from Hollywood, and was now out with his wife, who was not her mother, shopping. He humorously complained that the two of them had much more interest in each other, more like teenage sisters than stepmother and daughter, than they had in him. They seemed, according to him, to bring out depths of extravagance in one another, and all they wanted of him was to pay the bills. He laughed, taking no care to hide the pain of this double rejection, and I laughed, too.

He seemed compelled to talk, and so I listened as he spoke of his childhood in England, his schooling over there, how he had come into the theater, and had finally come to America. I got no hint in any of this that he had ever been loved, even by his parents, or ever had a friend.

He talked to me of Shaw and Shakespeare, and of the difference between their respective plays about Cleopatra. He spoke of other plays he loved and told me why. Richard II, the butterfly king, seemed one of his favorites. And then, almost imperceptibly, he started to recite:

> *"Now mark me how I will undo myself:*
> *I give this heavy weight from off my head,*
> *And this unwieldy scepter from my hand,*
> *The pride of kingly sway from out my heart;*
> *With mine own tears I wash away my balm,*
> *With mine own hands I give away my crown,*
> *With mine own tongue deny my sacred state—"*

I see him now as he stood then, against a loaded bookstack, which served as a divider in our impromptu dressing room, still in his prophet's simple, rough, dusty, bone-colored robe that came down to the sandals on his feet, looking off—far off—into the encircling gloom. His eyes were bright, a smile of irony was seated on his face, as his low musical voice swept Shakespeare's words and images before him. Sadness was there, but no tears were in those eyes—no tears at all. But as I listened, there were tears in mine.

The witch-hunt reached its climax with the Rosenberg case. The trial, though sensational in its own right, had to compete at a time when the Hollywood Ten and the Smith Act had already claimed our attention. It was only in 1953, when the courts decided the Rosenbergs must die, that the enormity of what was happening became apparent, and panic set in.

A campaign to secure clemency was launched immediately after the verdict. It seemed ridiculous that two people like the Rosenbergs could know enough about making a bomb to steal the secret and give it to the Russians. And even if they had, we didn't want them to die. We identified with the Rosenbergs because they were of the Left, they were obvious targets for the FBI, and they were Jews. Even so, their case was only one of the many in our orbit—until that rally at Carnegie Hall.

I wasn't at the rally. Either I was working or I was baby-sitting the children. It so happens that in the audience were Howard Da Silva and Morris Carnovsky, who were in the process of casting for a play, *The World of Sholom Aleichem*. What they saw and heard on stage from Ruby Dee that night changed our lives forever.

CHAPTER 24

The World of Sholom Aleichem
and Beyond

OSSIE: Ruby and I have been regarded as successful actors working continually in the entertainment industry for over fifty years, and many assumptions about us—some quite incorrect—are based on that longevity. We have survived, of course, and that has counted for much of the attention; but we are not "stars," nor are we "celebrities" in the common, tabloid sense of the word. Neither of us has appeared in a "breakthrough" role, or series of roles that finally elevated us to the ultimate heights of stardom.

Ruby, who has been at it longer than I, has achieved higher status than I as an actor. Both of us are in the Broadway Hall of Fame and in the NAACP Image Award Hall of Fame; we are recipients of the President's National Arts Award. The closest we came to "stardom" was in 1960 when we both were on Broadway in *A Raisin in the Sun,* and even there, I followed in Sidney Poitier's footsteps. We showed up there again for nine months in my own *Purlie Victorious,* but that was more of a curiosity than a hit—it never really "took off." We simply called ourselves laborers in the field of the arts.

Ruby took on the roles of Lena in Athol Fugard's *Boesman and Lena* and Julia in Alice Childress's *Wedding Band.* Though neither play made it to Broadway or Hollywood, critics and other givers of awards recognized both plays as major contributions to the theater.

Some other roles of major consequence were, first, as Mary Tyrone in a 1982 television production of Eugene O'Neill's *Long Day's Journey into Night,* and then as Amanda Wingfield in Tennessee Williams's *The Glass Menagerie* at the Arena Stage in Washington, D.C. Both roles had been created by other actors, at other times, in other places.

My last histrionic fling was as Midge in Herb Gardner's *I'm Not Rappaport,* a role created by Cleavon Little, which I later reprised in the film with Walter Matthau. So how to explain our somewhat inflated status in the public mind?

If Ruby and I are half of what people think we are, it is not because of what Hollywood or Broadway had to offer. The opportunities that have knocked on our two doors, though theatric in nature, came mainly from somewhere else.

We survived—no, more than survived—we triumphed, thanks to a strategy that assured us the victory: Simply, we learned how to belong to the people for whom we worked—mostly black people. They were, and still are, the audience that never made us rich, but never let us down.

It all began with *The World of Sholom Aleichem,* in May and then again in September of 1953 at the Barbizon-Plaza Hotel.

This production was one of Broadway's answers to the Hollywood blacklist. Two of the guiding spirits were Howard Da Silva and Morris Carnovsky. Both had made reputations for themselves in the Group Theatre in New York and had worked on Broadway before they had gone on to Hollywood, where they joined a host of other busy character actors.

But along came the witch-hunt, and when they, at the top of their careers, were summoned before inquisitional committees, they had refused—without any subterfuge or evasion—to cooperate in any fashion, thus in essence destroying their careers. They returned to New

Kince Charles Davis, Ossie's father (*standing center*), with friends. (Dee and Davis Archive)

Laura Cooper Davis, Ossie's mother, in Mount Vernon, at the family's first house, 1952. (Dee and Davis Archive)

Gladys Hightower, Ruby's birth mother. (Dee and Davis Archive)

Edward Nathaniel Wallace, Ruby's father. (Dee and Davis Archive)

Emma Amelia Benson, Ruby's mother. (Dee and Davis Archive)

Ossie, age twelve.
(Dee and Davis Archive)

Ruby, age thirteen, at summer
camp in upstate New York.
(Dee and Davis Archive)

Ruby and her family: (*first row, from left*) Ruby, LaVerne,
Edward; (*second row*) Toni (Edward's wife),
Daddy, Angelina. (Dee and Davis Archive)

Ruby as Cobina (*with bouquet*) in her first play, *On Strivers Row,* American Negro Theatre, 1940. (Morgan and Marvin Smith)

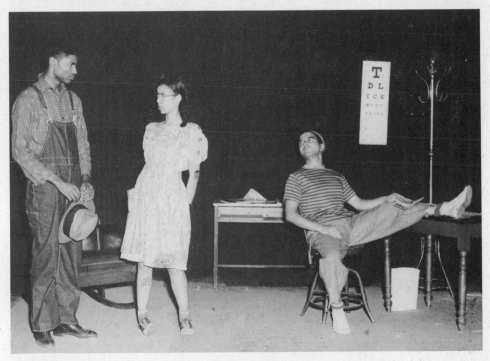

Ossie in *Black Woman in White,* Rose McClendon Players, 1941. (Dee and Davis Archive)

Ruby, the proud graduate of
Hunter College, 1944.
(Dee and Davis Archive)

Ruby working as a wirewoman during WWII at Western Electric Kearny
Works in New Jersey; used as 1996 advertisement for AT&T.
(AT&T Archives)

Ruby at Local 1199 event with Eleanor Roosevelt; Leon J. Davis, president of Local 1199, at the podium; and other union officials. (Dee and Davis Archive)

Ruby and Ossie in *Anna Lucasta* press photo, 1946. (Dee and Davis Archive)

Ruby Dee, publicity headshot, autographed to Ossie. (Lucas & Monroe)

Ossie, publicity headshot, autographed to himself, 1946. (Morgan and Marvin Smith)

The Three Annas: (*from left*) Isabelle Cooley, Yvonne Machen, and Ruby; as an anniversary stunt for *Anna Lucasta,* each actor performed in one act, 1946. (The House of Patria)

Backstage with Howard Da Silva at the Barbizon-Plaza Theatre in *The World of Sholom Aleichem,* 1953. (Myron Ehrenberg, Scope Assoc.)

With Jackie Robinson in *The Jackie Robinson Story,* 1950. (Eagle Lion Films)

Ossie with Lena Horne (*right*) and Josephine Premice in the Broadway musical *Jamaica,* 1957. (Friedman-Abeles; Billy Rose Theatre Collection; The New York Public Library for the Performing Arts; Astor, Lenox and Tilden Foundations)

With Nat King Cole in *St. Louis Blues,* 1958. (Courtesy of Paramount Pictures)

The family on a break during the filming of *A Raisin in the Sun:* (*from left*) Nora, Ruby, LaVerne, Ossie, and Guy, 1960. (Courtesy of Columbia Pictures)

With Sidney Poitier in the 1961 film *A Raisin in the Sun*.
(Courtesy of Columbia Pictures)

With the cast of *Purlie Victorious*, Cort Theatre, 1961. (*From left*) Beah
Richards, Helen Martin, Godfrey Cambridge, Ruby Dee, Ossie Davis, Cy
Herzog, Roger C. Carmel, Sorrel Brooke, and Alan Alda. (Adger Cowans)

Dr. Martin Luther King, Jr., on the hundredth performance of *Purlie Victorious*, came backstage for the celebration, 1961. (Dee and Davis Archive)

Strollin' on Broadway, 1961. (*Ebony* magazine)

Ossie on the picket line, protesting the lack of Negro actors in Broadway casts, April 1962. (*Amsterdam News*)

(*From left*) A. Philip Randolph, Martin Luther King, Jr., Ruby, and Ossie. (Russ Carter)

With Duke Ellington, backstage at Lincoln Center.
(Ann Meuer)

Ruby in
The Balcony, 1963.
(Continental Pictures)

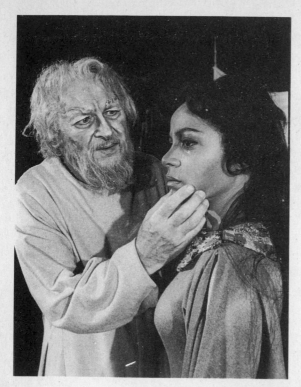

Ruby as Cordelia with Morris Carnovsky in *King Lear*, American Shakespeare Festival, Stratford, Conn., 1965. (Friedman-Abeles; Billy Rose Theatre Collection; The New York Public Library for the Performing Arts; Astor, Lenox and Tilden Foundations)

Ruby as Kate and John Cunningham in *The Taming of the Shrew,* the American Shakespeare Festival. (*Jet* magazine, July 22, 1965)

Ossie and Sammy Davis Jr. in *A Man Called Adam,* 1966.
(Embassy Pictures)

Ruby with Jules Dassin in
Uptight, 1968. (Courtesy
of Paramount Pictures)

Ossie and Samuel Goldwyn, Jr. (*right*), on location in Harlem, as Ossie directs *Cotton Comes to Harlem,* 1970. (MGM Clip+Still)

Ossie in the television series *Bonanza,* 1969. (Gary Null; courtesy of Bonanza Ventures, Inc.)

Ossie signs autograph as daughter LaVerne looks on, 1960s. (Dee and Davis Archive)

Ruby with Zakes Mokae and James Earl Jones in *Boesman and Lena,* Circle-in-the-Square, 1970. (Friedman-Abeles; Billy Rose Theatre Collection; The New York Public Library for the Performing Arts; Astor, Lenox and Tilden Foundations)

With Harry Belafonte and Sidney Poitier in *Buck and the Preacher,* 1971.
(Courtesy of Columbia Pictures)

With James Broderick in
Wedding Band at Joseph
Papp's Public Theater, 1972.
(Friedman-Abeles; Billy
Rose Theatre Collection;
The New York Public
Library for the Performing
Arts; Astor, Lenox and
Tilden Foundations)

Freedomways magazine benefit, 1972. (*From left*) Esther Jackson, Diahann Carroll, Norma Rodgers, Ruby, Ossie, and Julie Belafonte. (Dee and Davis Archive)

In Nigeria, with cast of *Countdown at Kusini,* 1976. (Courtesy of Columbia Pictures)

Esther Rolle as guest on *The Ossie Davis and Ruby Dee Story Hour,* a radio show syndicated on sixty-five stations nationwide, 1977. (Dee and Davis Archive)

With David Wolper, producer of *Roots* and *Roots II,* in California, 1978. (Dee and Davis Archive)

With Sterling Brown at Howard University for the television show, *With Ossie and Ruby,* KERA-TV, 1980s. (Moorland-Spingarn Research Center, Howard University)

Back in the stacks at the Schomburg Center for Research with James Baldwin (*center*) and some Schomburg officials, after an interview for *With Ossie and Ruby.* (Dee and Davis Archive)

Ruby celebrates her birthday with the Broadway cast of *Checkmates* and the mayor of New York. (*From left*) Marsha Jackson-Randolph, Paul Winfield, Ruby, Mayor David Dinkins, and Denzel Washington, 1988. (*The Black American*/Saigda)

Ossie and Guy, as featured in the book of photographs *Fathers and Sons,* 1985. (Steven Begleiter)

"An Evening with Ossie and Ruby," Wichita State University, 1985. (Dee and Davis Archive)

Ossie and his sister Essie.
(Dee and Davis Archive)

In New Rochelle aboard *The Ossie Davis* with grandchildren and Ossie's
mom. (*From left*) Jihaad, Muta' Ali, Ossie, Ruby, Ihsaana, and Laura Davis.
(Gannett Suburban Newspapers/Wendy Vissar)

With James Garner in Hallmark's *Decoration Day,* 1990. (Hallmark Hall of Fame Productions)

As "Mother Sister" and "Da Mayor" in *Do the Right Thing,* 1989. (40 Acres and a Mule Filmworks)

At the Cannes Film Festival, 1989. (*From left*) Ossie, Joie Lee, Richard Edson, Spike Lee, and Ruby. (40 Acres and a Mule Filmworks)

With Samuel L. Jackson in *Jungle Fever,* 1991. (40 Acres and a Mule Filmworks)

With Nelson Mandela at the premiere of *BOPHA!*, at Planet Hollywood, New York, 1993. (Jonathan Snow)

Ossie with President Bill Clinton at the White House for a Celebration of Baseball, 1994. (White House Archives)

Ruby and Ossie as the 106-year-old Mother Abagail and Judge Parker, in Stephen King's ABC miniseries *The Stand,* 1994. (ABC/Mark Seliger)

Guy, Ruby, and Ossie in *Two Hah Hahs and a Homeboy,* Crossroads Theatre, 1995. (Larry Brown)

Performing her one-woman show, *My One Good Nerve,* at A.C.T. in Seattle, 1996. (Chris Bennion)

The children and grandchildren in New Rochelle, 1993. (*First row*) Jammal, Jihaad, Brian; (*second row*) Guy, Martial, Dorothy, Ihsaana, Hasna, Wali; (*third row*) Muta' Ali, Nora, Bill, Imani. (Dee and Davis Archive)

Ossie and his brothers, William (*left*) and Kenneth, with their mother, Laura Davis, on her ninety-fifth birthday, July 9, 1993. (Adger Cowans)

The whole clan together for Laura Davis's ninety-fifth birthday, July 9, 1993. (Adger Cowans)

After receiving the President's National Medal of the Arts Award, 1995. (*From left*) Guy, Ossie, Ruby, Nora, and Hasna. (MH Photography)

Ossie and Ruby in the television special *Of Courtship and Marriage,* reciting poems by African-American authors, 1964. (CBS)

York where the climate for work was still open in theater, if not in radio and television.

They were casting a play, *The World of Sholom Aleichem,* which was based on two short stories and several folktales translated from the original Yiddish and dramatized by Arnold Perl. One story, "Bontche Schweig" by Itzaak Peretz, was about a poor Jew who has died of starvation and inattention, and has gone to heaven where, before an overworked Jehovah, he is eloquently represented by a defending angel. Howard and Morris had heard Ruby speak against the death penalty for the Rosenbergs at Carnegie Hall, and offered her the role of the Defending Angel.

The pay was minimal, hardly enough for one actor to subsist on. So wherever possible, hiring was done in pairs—Howard and his wife, Marge Nelson; Morris and his wife, Phoebe Brand; since there wasn't a part for me on stage, they made me the stage manager. Sarah Cunningham, Will Lee, Gilbert Greene, Vincent Beck, Herschel Bernardi, and Jack Gilford made up the rest of the company.

Each day of rehearsal brought Ruby and me closer to another definition of what theater could be. As Howard Da Silva put the cast through its paces, it was also an intensive exploration of "the method," an acting technique with which we were generally familiar, as it was greatly respected by those from the Group Theatre.

My job, in part, was to watch the performance, giving the cues for changes in the lights and sound. This production did not rely on sets or upon scenery, but rather on lighting and on music. The magic of the show depended much on a very delicate touch, on timing, and on tempo from the stagehands, as if they, too, were musicians, and I, their watchful conductor. The music was lilting, modest, brave—and Yiddish, suggesting with a certain degree of sadness that an entire world, a culture, a treasured way of life was disappearing, even as we watched, never to return.

The theater was in the basement of the Barbizon-Plaza Hotel. The stage was small; there was never enough space backstage, or enough dressing rooms for the actors. Nevertheless, we opened to good notices, and business was brisk at the box office. Once more, Broadway, or more precisely, off-Broadway, had thumbed its nose at the blacklist.

We all had jobs. And there were other ways by which we could supplement our modest incomes.

Professor Fred Ewen, who had been kicked out of Brooklyn College during the witch-hunt, had a brilliant idea: to present actors reading from the works of the great playwrights, novelists, and poets at the teachers union. To carry great literature directly to the workers, according to Fred Ewen, was a serious artistic responsibility binding us as actors to the working class, and therefore to the Socialist revolution, which, though starting in Russia, was bound to change the world. Fred chose the material and Howard directed it. This time, I was included, not as a stage manager, but as an actor in the small band of troubadours that included Howard, Morris, Phoebe, Margie, and Ruby.

In addition, Howard and Morris accepted other paying engagements at synagogues and community centers. Once or twice when they were unexpectedly called back to Hollywood to do bit parts for some courageous independent producer, they sent us in to do the gig instead. Now it was one thing to work in a synagogue alongside Howard and Morris, but doing it without them was something else again. Howard was very reassuring. "You don't have to read from Jewish material. Do things from your own culture—something you love."

We couldn't have been more warmly received. We felt that we were among people who understood and appreciated what we had to share. Since then, we have had many occasions to appear on our own at Jewish centers and synagogues, adding to our basic repertoire works we found that were specifically Jewish. One was of Binem Heller's "Pesach Has Come to the Ghetto Again," a poem about the Warsaw Ghetto in 1941, where the outnumbered Jews fought the Nazi army to a standstill. Later we included works from other cultures as well.

So, the work that sustained us in the industry did not always come from the industry itself. These appearances taught us how to convert any space into a theater and thus to make our own job opportunities. Two notebooks, two music stands or podiums, and our passion for great literature are all that was required to create a kind of people's theater.

I had known about Jews all my life, having first encountered them in the Bible as they swept across the pages of the Old Testament. I got a bit closer when I worked with them in the garment district. But it was only as I looked out on stage from my stage manager's chair, night after night, and watched the play about the people from the Polish city of Chelm—the city of fools—that the wall between us came tumbling down. During the run of *Sholom Aleichem,* the extraordinary power of theater to educate as well as to entertain was brought home to me.

I knew that Chelm was home, and all the fools who lived there were my relatives—their folly and their peculiar wisdom opened the doors of kinship. I never grew tired of their antics, seeing in the maddening illogicality of their culture, the wonderful down-home madness of my own. I laughed the laugh of recognition, and ultimately responded, eight years later, with *Purlie Victorious.*

Some other benefits, however, came to us much sooner.

Local 1199, Retail Drug Workers Union, represented mostly Jewish, Hispanic, and Negro people who worked in drugstores and pharmacies. Moe Foner, executive secretary of the union, was himself a victim of McCarthyism, having been dismissed from his post as a teacher at City College before going to work for 1199. He was looking for a way to bring culture to the workers, and wanted a program for Negro History Week. Madeline Gilford, a performer and the wife of Jack Gilford, one of the actors in *Sholom Aleichem,* told him about us.

We went to see Moe at union headquarters, and had a brief conversation. We liked his questions, he liked our answers, we all shook hands, and the job was ours. Moe left the program entirely up to us. Our experience with Fred, Howard, and Morris encouraged us to base our offering in current events, directly related to the issues from which the new Negro history was being made.

On May 17, 1954, the Supreme Court handed down one of it most momentous decisions ever, *Brown* v. *Board of Education,* which outlawed segregation in the public schools.

America, stunned, as after a hurricane, gathered to assess the impact—writing, talking, debating—trying to decide what was to be next. I hungrily read it all, hoping to find a centerpiece for our program. I found what I wanted in the people of Clarendon County, South Carolina, and in Reverend Joseph DeLaine, a respected leader in the black community.

Nobody was out to make history, certainly not to change the ways of segregation; but the white parents there had thirty buses to carry their kids to and from school, while the black parents had none. DeLaine, a teacher and a preacher, tried to get them one and wound up losing his job and his credit, having his church burned down, and having to escape for his life, at eighty miles an hour. Several black parents, represented by Thurgood Marshall and the NAACP Legal Defense Fund, sued on the basis that their rights to equal treatment under the Fourteenth Amendment were being denied. The case, known as *Brown* v. *Board of Education,* was one of five winding up before the Supreme Court, which had just ruled unanimously in favor of the black parents. The dramatic sketch that followed almost wrote itself.

Not only was I the writer, I also directed; we asked Bill Marshall to play DeLaine, while Ruby and I did all the other characters. We called it *The People of Clarendon County.* The audience in the crowded 1199 union hall was deeply moved by our presentation. Moe was so pleased, he not only gave us the fifty dollars apiece he had promised, but also asked us to do the same kind of show for the union's next Negro History Week program.

So began one of the most fruitful and rewarding associations of our lives. Moe proved to be a friend, and his commitment to bringing music, dance, and theater into the lives of workers was right up our alley. Soon we were being called on for other cultural functions at the union. In the process, we got to know not only Moe, his wife Ann, and his illustrious brothers, Phil and Henry, but also Leon J. Davis, president of the local, and his wife, Julia. Its progressive policies on race and gender equality made it a pioneer in struggles yet to come. So, when Martin Luther King, Jr., called 1199 his favorite union, we knew exactly why. In more ways than one, Ruby and I, except for paying dues, considered ourselves members of 1199.

The production team of *Sholom Aleichem,* which included the writer Arnold Perl and the producer Bernard Gersten, had a rather large ambition. They were looking for works from other cultures—Irish-, Italian-, and African-American. Their object was to present a more inclusive America, different from the image one would generally get from Broadway. I started in immediately to write a play to submit to them for next season.

It was to be a very angry play, harking back to the time I had been picked up on my way home from school by the police in Waycross, and taken into the station house where they had laughingly poured syrup on my head, while I was laughing, too. After all these years, the incident still rankled. I wanted to express my suppressed rage and indignation.

Every morning I would be up and writing feverishly. I began to notice that all the black characters in my play—especially Little Willie, my hero—tended to be noble, holy, and wonderful; but all the whites were mean and evil, and hatefully racist. But that didn't bother me. Writing page after page of venom, rage, and hate—from black and white—was therapeutic and deeply satisfying. But when I read it back in the cold light of day, it wasn't satisfying at all.

The meaner I made the white folks, the more they became, not humans, but caricatures. And even worse, my Negro characters, too, lost their humanity. The more I vented my righteous indignation and raw anger, the more outrageous and ridiculous they became.

Here indeed was a paradox. These people were my natural enemies; they could and often did kill one of us without a moment's thought, with no regret. I should have been able to hate them as I felt they hated me. Yet I couldn't. Was that what it meant to be a nigger—a person who when confronted with his enemy's throat, instead of baring his blade, could only laugh? Or was I within glimpse of some profound truth about the mystery of oppression and its effects on human behavior?

I wanted in my play to bring the South to judgment, to weigh its racist arrogance in the balance, find it guilty as charged of every crime committed against me and my people, then punish it. But no matter how angry it made me, I couldn't read what they were doing to the superinnocent little black boy without laughing out loud! What was my sense of humor trying to tell me?

Meanwhile, every night on stage, a solution was trying to reach me. As I visited again with the delicious fools of Chelm, I found that same ineffable contradiction: that we were both—I and my fellow fools, in a way that was as Jewish as it was black—laughing to keep from crying. My play began to change. My characters from Waycross were beginning to sound like the people of Chelm; and then they became, in the end, something else entirely. That something else would finally be called *Purlie Victorious*.

In 1955, Howard and Morris put together a summer stock repertory company that was to appear at Crystal Lake Lodge up in the Catskills. Ruby and I, along with Ruby's mother, Emma, Nora, now five years old, and Guy, age three, went upstate to Crystal Lake to work with the company.

Among the plays on the menu, there was *The World of Sholom Aleichem,* Chekhov's *The Cherry Orchard,* and *The Prodigious Snob,* adapted from Molière by Miles Malleson. This time I was an actor, playing the part of Semyonov Pistchik, a peasant friend of Madam Ranyevsky in *The Cherry Orchard.* I was awful. Howard Da Silva, not the most patient of men, lost his temper several times. Not only was I patient, but I also smiled a lot. It didn't help. In fact, it made things worse.

Acting, for me, was pure imitation. I did on stage what I was told to do—no more, no less—and that drove Da Silva crazy. It wasn't so bad when I was playing characters that closely resembled the man I really was, like Rudolph in *Anna Lucasta,* or Gabriel in *Green Pastures,* but Semyonov Pistchik was a Russian peasant. I hadn't the slightest idea what that meant. My true interest has always been writing, not acting, and I had no desire to make myself an actor. The simple idea of listening to what is being said to you on stage, pondering the information, then speaking in return, was totally foreign to me.

Howard tried to bully it out of me, once pushing me against a wall and threatening to knock me on my no-good, shiftless ass! I couldn't help myself, I had to laugh. I almost fell on the floor. Howard sensed that I had talent, that I was sensitive, that something in me was native to the stage. He tried as many ways as he knew to shake it out of me. I tried as hard as I could to be responsive. But being responsive to me meant being, not creative, but obedient, like a trained parrot. Howard finally gave up altogether. As for me, I remembered the instructions and kept trying, every chance I got, to execute them.

During that summer, two process servers showed up at Crystal Lake and proceeded to hand out subpoenas for a hearing before the Rapp Coudert Committee, which was investigating Communist infiltration into New York's summer camps. It didn't take them long to locate Howard, Morris, Phoebe, and some others who accepted their subpoenas and went on about their business; but it wasn't so easy to locate Ossie Davis and Ruby Dee. We were there, right in their faces all the time, but they couldn't see us. We were colored and they were expecting white, and nobody at the camp would tell them any better. They even asked us if we'd seen Davis and Dee, and we said no.

The play that night was *The Cherry Orchard,* and Ruby and I were listed in the cast. They saw our names; they knew we would have to appear—they'd catch us then.

They sat down front, and when the curtain went up, they saw where they had gone wrong—that actors could be colored as well as white. They'd wait till after the curtain, and then they'd grab us. And that's where they made their second mistake. The cast and crew— Connie Bromberg, the stage manager, in particular—aware of what was happening, decided, with our permission, that we, too, could play the game of cat and mouse.

When the play was over and we had taken our bows, the two process servers came backstage looking for Ossie Davis and Ruby Dee. Connie told them that we had already dressed and left, but the two guys weren't buying. They had been watching the exits; they knew for certain that we were still somewhere on the premises, and so they stumbled and mumbled around, searching, but everywhere they looked, they came up empty. It was after midnight when they finally left.

Connie turned out the lights, then knocked on the top of the large wicker laundry basket—which the two angry men had passed a hundred times—and let us out of our hiding place. The coast was clear, and we were free to go.

A car, with the motor running, was waiting in the parking lot, with the actors crowding around, laughing, joking, crying, and waving good-bye—to see us off, back to Mount Vernon.

It was easy to imagine, as we looked back and saw the lights of Crystal Lake fading into the distance, that we could hear the music—that happy-sad, ironic Yiddish music—also fading away. A long good-bye to Chelm and all its people—a long good-bye to *The World of Sholom Aleichem.*

RUBY: Ossie, I don't remember being in the laundry basket. We talked about hiding there, but we both couldn't fit in it. Perhaps you got in the basket while I was someplace else waiting; then they had another idea.

I remember Connie took us down a road to a barn, where we hid in the loft. I'm sure of this because I had to go to the bathroom and there was no facility. Also, I remember thinking that Connie was being dramatic. He seemed like a character in a story of the Underground Railroad and I thought about his father's adventures as a leftist. We were not so much afraid as not wanting to spoil his rescue mission.

When we left the barn, it was near dawn, and everyone was gone. Perhaps you saw the actors gathered in the parking lot at an earlier point, but I recall that Connie had to find transportation for us. It had been a complicated, yet very amusing night.

OSSIE: Just goes to show, indeed, it takes the two of us to get this story told.

In 1954, *Brown* v. *Board of Education* put the spotlight on the South, black and white, and the whole world waited with baited breath to see what the reaction would be. A list of Southern legislators tried to render the decision null and void. They signed a statement that was summarized by the title of a book, *The Deep South Says Never.*

In the summer of 1955 in Money, Mississippi, Emmett Till, a fifteen-year-old black boy, was killed and his body thrown into the Tallahatchie River. The murder brought matters to a head. It was to the Left what the firing on Fort Sumter had been in 1861—a declaration of war.

The Till story was a natural fit for Ruby and me in our work with Local 1199. Once again, I read the newspapers and the magazines, wrote our second script, and staged it for the union's 1956 Negro History Week celebration as *What Can You Say to Mississippi?* We asked Sidney Poitier to do the reading with us. It was very effective. We were pleased, but also dissatisfied. What good would a fifteen-minute dramatic sketch do for Emmett Till, his mother, his family in Chicago, or the people on the spot in Money, Mississippi? It seemed so puny. White Mississippi had spoken both for itself and for the rest of the white South. What we didn't know was that the black community down South had already begun its response.

Four months after Emmett Till was murdered, Rosa Parks made a response not only for herself but for the entire black community. On December 5, she was abused and arrested for refusing to give up her seat on a bus to a white man. A boycott, calling for all Negroes to stay off the city buses in Montgomery, Alabama, was organized to protest Rosa's treatment—a boycott led by a young Baptist preacher named King. The black South had finally responded to the challenge. Thousands of black people answered Martin's call, refusing to ride the segregated buses, choosing to walk, if they had to. The battle was on.

We in the North immediately saw the situation and grabbed the opportunity. Something big was happening in Montgomery, something new and daring, affecting us all. Funds must be raised, lawyers hired, briefs filed, transportation provided. Rallies must be held, pamphlets prepared, calling for public support. Dr. King and Reverend Ralph Abernathy became the new potential heroes of a brand-new people's movement. But who were they?

The picture of Rosa Parks being fingerprinted was simple, powerful, speaking for itself, summing up the Negro experience in America. In our considered opinion, expressed around the dinner table at 5 Cooley Place, the call for Negroes in Montgomery not to ride the buses made all kinds of sense. It made us glad. It made us proud. It was about time, we said, talking back to the television set. We blacks had taken about as much as we could take.

Martin Luther King was something else again. He was composed, patient, and reasonable, with a manner that was respectful and polite.

Here was something more than Reverend "Pork Chops"—more than hellfire and brimstone. Here was a man with a considerable command of the English language, who knew how to capture the national attention.

He and the TV cameras seemed made for each other. But his philosophy of nonviolence seemed dangerous nonsense to many of us in the North, where the money was, and where the political and social support could and should be mustered. We needed desperately to talk to this young man.

Local 1199 was the first union to issue an invitation to Martin Luther King, Jr., and Ralph Abernathy to come North. Abernathy came; Martin couldn't make it. We in the North, including Ossie and Ruby, could only wait our turn.

A few months later, there was a "hurry up" call from Reverend Doles, the pastor of Grace Baptist Church in Mount Vernon. Martin Luther King was in town and was meeting with some ministers at Abyssinia Baptist, Adam Clayton Powell's church in Harlem. Would we like to drive over with him and check the new man out? We jumped at the chance. On the way, Reverend Doles reiterated his concerns about King; he had as much trouble swallowing the doctrine of nonviolence as we did.

The meeting was not in the sanctuary, but rather in a smaller room upstairs. The three of us found places in the back against the wall where we could sit in judgment.

Somebody introduced Martin, there was a thin, polite smattering of applause, and he began to speak, starting off slowly, knowing that he was on trial before a cold and skeptical bunch of preachers, each one seeing himself as a better man than Martin.

Martin modestly and politely thanked the few ministers who had come to bid him welcome, almost apologizing for taking up their time. He explained the boycott and the small part he and Ralph Abernathy had been called on to play in getting it started. He laid out, in that mellifluous, rolling baritone of his, the long litany of indignities that black folks had suffered in Montgomery, and talked about unearned suffering being redemptive, about nonviolence being a way to pressure the Christian white man. He mentioned Thoreau, spoke of what happened in India, thanks to Mahatma Gandhi, and wound up quoting Jesus Christ himself.

You sensed at once the man was a master of black sermonizing, knowing just what to say and how to say it. Doles, who was normally restless and fidgety, started out sitting between Ruby and me, listening in silence, like the rest of us—and watching like a hawk.

As Martin picked up speed, erecting one tower of rhetoric after another, signs of grudging approval, almost involuntary at first, began to echo from one side of the hall to another. Reverend Doles got so excited, he forgot himself and leapt to his feet, as did most of the ministers, shouting back at Martin. Suddenly he was running down the aisle, winding up in the pulpit standing next to Martin, urging him on! Other ministers followed, swarming up into the pulpit, grabbing Martin, shaking his hands, and trying to hold him close.

It was perfectly clear—nonviolence notwithstanding—that we in the black church, and in the black community, had found ourselves a new leader!

CHAPTER 25

The Plot Thickens

OSSIE: Work and activism were not our only concerns, nor even always our major concerns. In the most natural, easygoing way, we were becoming a family. The children saw to that.

Ruby and I, moving from a common culture as well as from instinct, accepted them as the center of the spinning whirlwind that was our lives. We enjoyed their presence among us, and they returned the favor. We had no trouble fitting them into our schedule, and they always seemed to have plenty of room for us in theirs. To come home was always a joy, for they would be waiting and ready to pounce. My hat was barely off before the horseplay would commence, which inevitably wound up with me being wrestled to the living room floor, with Nora and Guy swarming all over me.

Or, we would play a strenuous round of "bookity, bookity," with Guy sitting on one knee and Nora on the other, bobbing up and down as fast as my pounding feet and ankles could manage to gallop. Or sometimes around the piano, I'd play my heavy-handed chords in

E-flat major (the only key I know), composing melodies, with gibberish lyrics to match. We'd play games, telling tales and doing dances that have been in the family forever.

And on and on and on—till Ruby would call us in to dinner.

We never allowed the children to think we had a life of which they were not the center. Wherever we went, if it was possible, we took them with us: rehearsals, performances, rallies, demonstrations, picket lines. When it was necessary to leave them with Evelyn or Mrs. Adkins, the wonderful ladies hired to help us with them, we made sure they understood where we were going and why, and what we proposed to do once we got there. The children were growing, and we were growing, too. Soon it would be time for Nora to go to school.

But before school, there was something equally important for the children and that was church. Neither of us was overly religious and we were not churchgoing people at all. Religion was something we never even discussed. But the time had come to fix the children in their identity, to stabilize their concept of themselves, to tell them, and show them who they were—to make them Negro.

I hadn't thought about religion, the church, or God as a serious object of contemplation for a long time. I hadn't missed the connection, but that was personal. The family needed a church—a black church— because it was the church, through the years, that had held black people together, and therefore held our history and our collective consciousness as a people. The church was a repository of all we thought precious and worthy to be passed on to our children. Religion—the black church—was something we owed our children as much as we owed them food, clothing, shelter, love, an education, and shots against measles and smallpox.

Ruby, of course, sensed it first, that trying to teach them at home was not enough. The children needed a church where they would be able to see black people in positions of power and authority. I had no objections, so Ruby found a church, Grace Baptist of Mount Vernon, and took Nora and Guy off to Sunday School every Sunday—but only for a while. She said that with all her other wifely chores, I should at least give her a hand in that, and I agreed.

So every Sunday morning, I would take the children—but only as

far as the door, where I turned them over to a Mrs. Welles, the super-
intendent. I told her I preferred to wait outside until the service was
over, and then I'd pick them up. Mrs. Welles was a most generous
woman, patient and understanding, but this she didn't quite understand.

"Come on in, Brother Davis," she said, "you don't have to stay
outside. You can sit in the back of the sanctuary. God ain't gonna bite
you."

I liked Mrs. Welles right off, but not enough to explain my situation to her, that I was still having some trouble with my own religious
convictions. When I walked away from the church, I had no intention
of ever coming back. But that was a matter between divine providence
and myself. My children had nothing to do with it. I certainly didn't
want to deny them the rich, emotional nourishment I had found in the
church when I was a child, just because I had had a difference of
opinion with the divine. So, in spite of Mrs. Welles's hospitality, I chose
to wait outside.

Outside was all right in the summer and the early fall, but when
winter came, I found myself much more amenable to her invitation. I
came inside and sat in the back, but that was awkward—me alone,
sitting on the back row where everybody could see me. There was an
adult class held in the sanctuary, so I decided to sit in with them. It
was impossible to sit with ten or twelve other grown-ups and stare
straight ahead like a dummy, not saying a word, especially since I had
once been a Sunday School teacher myself. Soon, in spite of myself, I
was a regular in the class, asking and answering questions, and offering
comments. Before long, whenever the teacher was absent, I would be
invited to take over.

Mrs. Welles, who could play me like a fiddle, soon offered me the
hook: "Wouldn't it be nice if, in addition to the one male teacher who
taught the grown-ups, they had another male teacher, especially for
that unruly boys' class in the basement? Boys like that should have a
man to teach them instead of all these women, don't you think?" I told
her that I would gladly teach the boys if, first, she would tell Reverend
Doles, the pastor, that I had no intention of joining the church.

I had no idea how much I had missed it. How good it was to be a part of the fellowship again, especially with Guy and Nora there, to mix again with the congregation, to hear good singing and good preaching, to meet Reverend Doles, and to get to know him better. A young man, he impressed me very much. To sit again at the feet of Moses and David and Jesus, and most of all to hear the old King James iambic pentameter, rolling from the pulpit straight at me.

RUBY: Ossie has never been infected with the disease of ownership, as far as I can surmise. That applies to clothing, to housing, and to money, more or less. I admire and envy that quality in him because the habit of getting and holding on to things is mad-making. We live in a very "thingy" world, however, and I've not found a way around the accumulation of many "things." As Ossie has quoted through the years, "Whatever you own owns you."

After we managed to get our first mortgage, a sense of pride in ownership began to overtake me. Our house and the land around it were on a hill, and our property extended from Cooley Place in the front to Lyons Place in the back—a complete block. My status as landowner made me blossom inside as I planted grass and flowers in one part of the front yard in which stood a majestic oak tree. On the other side of the walkway, just below the porch, lilac bushes grew. Such a sweet smell in the springtime! Beyond the house was a vegetable garden to the right, and peach trees and blackberry bushes to the left. Near the side of the house, steps led down to Lyons Place.

Across the street from our house, there was a four-story apartment building. It seemed to be the practice when we first moved in that all kinds of people—children and adults—would take a shortcut through our yard rather than walk around the block to get to the factories, to the streets, and to the commercial areas beyond Lyons.

Unacquainted at first with the demands and prerogatives of ownership, I would chat sometimes with the passers-through. Then it occurred to me that we were landlords, with tenants and obligations to maintain the physical condition of the property. I stopped the chatting and the smiling, and had signs made: NO TRESPASSING. KEEP OFF THE GRASS. PRIVATE PROPERTY. NOT A THROUGH STREET. These signs were placed in front and in back of the property, and initially, they were respected, but before long, I began to see more trespassers, some of whom I didn't recognize.

I decided to enclose our property. Through the Yellow Pages, I located and hired a company that installed chain-link fences to seal off our property at the front and at the back. They suggested that we purchase the fencing with sharp wire edges to ensure that no one would try to climb over it. Gates with strong locks secured the entrances. The trespassing ceased.

Several years later, one warm spring day I was working in the kitchen when I heard Guy, then about seven years old, call to me. He sounded like he was in trouble and he was. Blood was spurting from his inner right arm near the elbow. I applied a tourniquet to the upper arm and rushed with him by taxi to the Mount Vernon Hospital, where he received many stitches. It was a large, ugly wound—the result of his trying to climb over the barbed-wire fence.

I thought that maybe he had been defying logic or gravity—as boys sometimes do. I recalled an earlier incident when he had injured himself and his sister playing with rocks as if he expected them to bounce. Fortunately, those incidents weren't serious. This one was. My goodness, I thought, must boys always be boys?

"But, sweetheart," I said, "why didn't you use the gate? That's what the gate is for, baby. You open it and you walk through."

"Mommie," he said, "the ball went inside the yard, and I couldn't find the key." I usually kept the padlock open and the key in the mailbox on the porch, but it wasn't there. I didn't know where it was, or why the gate happened to be locked. I only knew I had put up a fence to protect our property from trespassers—and who got caught on it? My own son.

OSSIE: In theater and film, employment is a sometime thing, no matter what your color. Ruby and I had the advantage, being two; when one of us wasn't working, the other one usually was, but there were times when both of us were jobless, and this year, Christmas of 1955 was coming much faster than was income. Lou, our next door neighbor, knew I needed a job, so he suggested that I try the post office, where I was to ask for Mr. Brown, the man in charge of hiring temporary workers. Mr. Brown took me on.

I was given a bag loaded with mail, and a man drove me across the tracks to the white side of Mount Vernon. He showed me where I was to get my second load, and my third, when I had delivered the previous ones. I liked Mr. Brown, who was black like me, and I wanted to show him I could cut the mustard. I pitched in, did my job, and did it thoroughly—too thoroughly, in fact. Finding and filling mailboxes, ringing doorbells, knocking on doors, asking questions, trying to locate the person whose name was on the letter—you might have thought I was a police detective. I forgot all about the time, and ended up way behind schedule. I would have been fired after the first day, had not Mr. Brown been a kind, patient, and understanding man. He told me not to waste time trying to locate every single person.

"It's Christmas, Davis. Find a place on the premises, leave it, and move on," he said. I wouldn't be surprised if some of those people never got their mail. I only know I left it in the vicinity.

We paid the mortgage and some other bills, with enough left over to subsidize Ol' Santa by becoming big spenders at the Salvation Army store. We enjoyed giving a second life to salvageable toy trucks, carriages, wagons, cars, trains, and tricycles. We'd hide them in the basement, and when I had the time, I would do my magic. Mostly a little paint was all that was required. For structural alterations, out would come my tools. Other toys were all my own creations: a rocking chair, a crib for Nora's doll, a carved boat with a propeller driven by a wound-up rubber band for Guy.

We'd wait till the last minute, when prices were drastically cut, to buy the tree, for maybe no more than fifty cents. Then, staying up all night, and with the help of lights and all kinds of decorations, we'd work to transform it into something magical to behold.

Once the tree was up, we would wrap and spread the toys and gifts around it. Next morning, after breakfast, the children would come to the tree. We knew from the looks on their faces, the squeals and shouts, the wiggles, the dances of pure delight, and the hugs, that Santa's visit had been a big success.

In 1956, I was back at work on Broadway as an assistant stage manager with a walk-on as a black lieutenant in the Army in *No Time for Sergeants.* My very light duties during the show left me plenty of time to write. And Ruby was pregnant again.

RUBY: A few years ago, I was asked to contribute an article to a book of collected accounts on the subject of abortion. I wrote the article, then phoned the editor with apologies because I had changed my mind and decided that I didn't want to be included in such an anthology.

Since my own experience in 1954, about two years after our son was born, I've been reluctant to write or to talk about abortion. To tell the truth, I am ambivalent and peculiarly uncomfortable with the subject. In the late 1980s, I was asked to speak at a prochoice rally. I accepted, I suspect, because I was still trying to sort things out.

There was something about the tone of the gathering that bothered me. Number one, I didn't think there was anything about abortion that one could praise or celebrate. The flat-out rah-rah atmosphere disquieted me. Even with some legislative victory, I still wanted everyone to feel somewhat uncomfortable.

I do understand the necessity of abortion in instances of rape, incest, incurable diseases of the fetus in the womb, or if the mother's life is in danger. Even for reasons with which I might disagree, however, or might not understand, I am adamant in the belief that every woman should have the right to a legal, safe abortion, should she so decide, which is why I agreed to speak at that rally. A woman's decision to terminate a pregnancy in the early weeks is a deeply personal choice. I've wrestled all my life with the pronouncements of absolutes. Despite the trauma to all concerned, to mandate a woman's choice is a form of slavery.

"Ruby, I thought you were concerned about overpopulation. You said you and Ossie only want two children. It's not fair to babies to drop them and leave them to the care of strangers because you want to work. . . . Going from howling, 'I'm barren, I'm barren,' to baby-making machine. With all the modern techniques to avoid getting pregnant, here you come again, getting ready to join the big-belly brigade.

Look, hussy, if you spent more time with those books you've got stacked up everywhere, and less on your back, you wouldn't be in this situation. You'd better speak to that man also. Having babies is a very serious, two-butt proposition. It has very little to do with being good parents. Any female can have a baby, but it takes more than just being able to spread your legs to become a mother." I said all this to myself before anybody else even thought about saying it to me.

I knew many women who had had abortions. They were illegal, but they were common. And many women died. My sister had one. She and her devoted friend had known each other a long time, and he wanted to marry her, but she didn't love him. She never got the choice again. Abortion? She knew someone. She would go with me.

The fact that I am a survivor of an abortion attempt didn't call out to me through the years to affect my consciousness in that moment when I found myself on a bed in a dark room of a tenement. I had tried drugstore remedies, herbs, poultices; had flung myself wildly, dashing upstairs, bouncing on my behind downstairs, and had swallowed all kinds of concoctions I'd read about based on old wives' tales and witches' brew. I had made up my mind to do it and had shut off all debate.

Pay the woman. Catheter inserted. Go home. I am given instructions and pills. She said, "In three days, you won't be pregnant anymore."

I don't know when my father first told me that he and Gladys had tried not to have me, but it fed my abhorrence of the act. You just can't know whom you're eliminating. It is deeply disturbing in that effect because, of course, I can't imagine not having been born. I've known several women who tried to abort, but were unsuccessful. They had some of the most beautiful babies one can imagine, grown now into intelligent, loving children.

I didn't want to be a housewife, cooking all day long, washing, ironing, shopping in secondhand stores, patching, sewing, and living life scraping the bottom of barrels. I had known such families, and being with some of them would make me so sad. My Aunt Josie had a joyous family of thirteen children. The older ones seemed always to be working along with their mother and cooking food in large pots. We always had a good time when we visited them. I loved her but I didn't want to be like her.

Since I was a girl, the idea of people having babies just because they could seemed unwise. The world is too small, I thought. For some people, having lots of children is their only insurance. Maybe one of them will become rich and give their parents a good old age.

When we become a more life-affirming society, when war, poverty, economic uncertainties, and greed no longer threaten the stability of the family, perhaps then we can tackle—with love, faith, and common sense—the finiteness of the earth and its resources in relation to all creatures.

The day after the catheter, I proceeded with my normal household routines. The third day, I began to bleed. I felt awful, and went to bed. I had told Mother and Daddy what I had done after the first day. Without comment, they came, packed the children, and took them to Mother's. They wanted me to go to the hospital. I refused. I begged them to leave me alone. I would be fine, I protested. They left.

The next morning, the passage of massive blood clots left me feeling faint, in pain; the thought that I could die came to me. I banged on the floor and on the radiator, hoping to attract the downstairs tenant. There was no answer. I called Mrs. Saunders, our friend on Fulton Street, and told her I was in trouble. She promised to get a doctor right away. I hung up. As I tried to get back in bed, I remembered the front door was locked. How would the doctor get in? I crawled on my knees to the front door, finally reached the knob, unlocked the door, and crawled back to bed.

Soon the doctor and Mrs. Saunders arrived. After a few questions, the doctor gave me an injection. Mrs. Saunders cleaned me up and changed the linen. The doctor examined me thoroughly, silently; then he talked to Mrs. Saunders and gave her a prescription. She fixed me something to eat, then went to get the prescription filled. By and by, I felt as if I was floating on a cloud. The pain went away. I felt tired and so lucky to be alive.

Ossie came back from the Catskills where he had been on location shooting a film, *The Joe Louis Story*. The next day, my body expelled the flesh, completing the process. Ossie and I were silent together for a long time that day. We prayed and asked God to forgive us.

For many years after, I included in reading concerts around the country, on campuses and in theaters, a poem by Gwendolyn Brooks titled "The Mother," which begins:

> *Abortion will not let you forget.*
> *You remember the children you got*
> *That you did not get.*
> *The damp, small pulps with little or no*
> > *hair,*
> *The singers and workers who never*
> > *handled the air.*

A couple of years later, we decided we should have another baby. Three children. As actors, life is so uncertain. Life is uncertain even if you are not an actor. We've managed well so far. With trust in God, move forward in faith, we tell each other.

Juanita Poitier, my dear friend and Sidney's first wife, exuded a kind of self-confidence and regality that I admired. It was she who told me, "Ruby, oh, for heaven's sake! You don't need to go to the clinic to have that baby. Look, go to my doctor."

So, during my third pregnancy, I was the private patient of a doctor whose offices were on Park Avenue, and who catered mostly to white patients. Also, this doctor scheduled his deliveries. Babies didn't come at odd hours—just whenever they felt like it. Near the ascertained time, the doctor would call, perhaps once a day, with specific questions.

Finally, one day after our talk, he scheduled my delivery for nine o'clock the next morning. I was beginning to experience some mild labor pains. The morning came, and Ossie and I went downtown on the subway. We had spent the night in the city at Rosemary Mitchell's house. She was one of the children Mother had kept long ago and we had become friends.

From the subway we took a taxi, but we arrived at Beth Israel

Hospital fifteen minutes late. The doctor glanced at us without a greeting as he hurried about his business. We were reminded that he had other appointments. I could see that he was annoyed. The contractions were becoming more severe, but I was not in major agony. He gave me an injection; I was prepped and taken to the delivery room.

This delivery was the first time I was aware of all that was going on. The anesthetic was given only periodically in small doses through a mask on my face, and I remained conscious.

Later, when the doctor, dressed to travel, came to my private room, the first words out of my mouth were "I hope I didn't make you late." Then I carried on about the traffic that had delayed us after we got the taxi. He didn't seem to know what I was talking about. He kissed my cheek, and told me about my beautiful, healthy baby girl. I was relieved when he left because I knew he had an appointment.

I didn't say anything about my new baby, or about how happy I was that my husband had waited and seen her already; this was the earliest he had ever been present when I was giving birth. Instead I repeated, "I'm so sorry I was—I hope I didn't make you late." What a lie! What a liar you are, Ruby. To hell with his appointment.

I didn't like the idea of making my baby come tick-tock, by the clock. I wanted to feel that it was time—because nature said so—not because he had to squeeze me into an important, busy schedule. Needle. Spread. Drop. Tick-tock. And besides, she wasn't really ready to be born.

We named her LaVerne, after my sister. I was overjoyed to have her. To finally square my account with God. Even in the womb, this baby asserted herself. Once, I felt her raise her head up as if she were looking around and then just plop it back down. Her kicks were as strong and determined as she is to this day. She was the biggest of the three.

I hadn't expected to be so delighted that this last child of ours was a girl. When I brought her home, Guy and Nora were so excited. Nora wanted to hold her right away, and when I told her that she couldn't hold the baby right that minute, she began to cry. As I took LaVerne into the room to get settled, Guy said, "Don't cry, Nora. You've still got your Betsy-Wetsy doll."

LaVerne had her father's mouth, but there was something about her that looked like Gladys and the Hightowers.

Soon after LaVerne came, a job that I couldn't ignore presented itself. There was no more leeway to hesitate and equivocate. Nursing this baby became an option we couldn't afford.

The same thing had happened when Guy was born. I was looking forward to a few months to just be a mom, when Hollywood intervened. With him, it was *Take a Giant Step,* by Louis Peterson, a black author whose play was made into a film by the newly formed company, Hecht, Hill, and Lancaster, which took pride in producing stories with themes generally ignored by the Hollywood establishment. With LaVerne, the job was in the film *Edge of the City,* with Sidney, John Cassavetes, and Jack Warden. I once again wrestled with the conflicts of being a working mother.

I had been lucky that my parents, especially Mother, helped out when she could, and that Mrs. Saunders sent eighteen-year-old Evelyn Thompson to help with baby-sitting chores. We needed someone every day and sometimes around the clock.

Growing up in Harlem, I remember seeing black women standing on corners, watching cars whizzing by. One of the cars slows down. One of those women approaches the car and some words are spoken. It is explained to me that the lady just got a job. She was going to somebody's house to do day work—to clean, wash, iron, maybe cook for somebody. Somebody white.

My mother rented rooms to a lot of ladies who worked sleep-in. They didn't have to stand on corners for day work. They lived where they worked, and came home to my mother's house on their days off— Thursdays and every other Sunday.

There was one lady who didn't sleep in; she worked for different people every day. One day she got sick and asked Mother if I could go in on a Monday in her place. Mother and I said yes, so she called her employer and set it up. She got paid by the hour, so I worked as slowly as I could. I wanted to make all the money I could for the sick woman before next Monday. That same day, the employer called to tell the lady not to send me back ever again. If she had to be sick, just don't come anymore, the woman said. She would get somebody else.

All around me was talk—sometimes with humor, sometimes with anger—about "that woman I work for," "that family," and "my people." Sometimes somebody quit, walked out for any number of reasons, including "that woman tried to cheat me out my money," or "I work so hard, but I don't get enough to pay my bills!" Sleep-in seemed to be the best way. Maybe you could put away a little something, having no rent to pay.

Before I could imagine, it became my lot to need someone to help me with the basic drudgeries of life, to need a day worker, a maid. I became an employer.

I had not read books on the subject of female descendants of slaves who needed maids. (There ought to be one.) As a person of pigment, it became a sweat-popping challenge to figure out how to make mental adjustments to the fact that I needed a stranger to help me live my life in the U.S. of A.

My first "girl" was an out-of-work actor I knew named Jackie André, who volunteered to help when I was with Frankie Dee. "You're going to need somebody to help you keep that big house he bought you," she said. She could work two days per week for an hourly wage. It would have cost more, but she knew that, like her, I didn't have a job and was going to school. I didn't realize I needed help until she mentioned it. Having a—I mean, having someone to help me hadn't occurred to me yet. Having a . . . a . . . a maid? Well, Jacqueline was not a maid; she was a friend, giving me a hand.

When she first started coming, I was ill at ease, and at the same time, glad to see her. She knew many of the aspiring performers better than I did. She knew a lot about the theater, too, so we spent several hours just sitting and talking. When she'd start to do a chore, I'd interfere to denigrate the necessity of getting to work. "Let's have some cocoa," I'd say; then I'd make and serve it, and we'd continue to talk.

After a while, she'd get up, put our cups in the sink, and say, "Well, I'd better get to work now. Something special you want me to do?"

"No, no. Whatever you do will make everything better than it was." After several cocoa times when life stories, actor intrigues, and being-colored clinchers had us both exhausted, she said, with a bit of annoyance, "Ruby, you're not paying me to sit and talk. Relax. When I don't have a job in a play, I do housework. I'm my own boss, and I know how to do it. Take it easy. No sense in both of us pulling this slave." She laughed as she took some shoes and some rubber gloves from a little satchel.

"If you want to go shopping or go see a movie, that's okay," she added. I started to protest and she put up her hand. "And I'm honest, too," she said. "Believe me, I understand."

It took many years for me to become comfortable hiring people to work for Ossie and me. I had to get over the embarrassment caused by even needing somebody. Many women had careers, raised their children, and cherished their husbands at the same time. So what is so different about you? I asked myself.

I often got knots in my stomach while the assistance I needed was being delivered. I would be relieved only at the end of a work period when payment was made and the door was closed on the matter. How dare I own more than I can take care of myself? How dare I need someone to wash my dirty clothes, and change my babies' diapers, and cook, or help me cook my meals?

The whole saga of slavery, the denial of opportunity and even of one's own self-worth, hounded the hell out of me. Jumbled and twisted in my mind was the abominable horror—from the beginning of re-corded time—of people snatching people of a different race, tribe, sex, location, or language, and assigning to them some label of inferiority, which justified the use of their persons, their gifts, their labor to satisfy greed, lust, and laziness. Now here I come, descended from slaves myself, a new-day version of a slave master. True, I paid the going wages, but was it enough?

My sensitivity to the injustices and hardships endured by black women through the years forced me to look deeply into the business of "hiring help." Black women at the bottom of the wage barrel per-form some of the essential work that frees others of us from the drudg-ery and the details of staying alive. The contemplation had no bottom. If there are those who depend on us for a living, we in turn must depend also on them. The President of the United States needs somebody to free him to be President, the clerk with a family needs somebody to help her be a clerk, and the maid often needs somebody to free her to be a maid.

The contradictions and unreadiness to turn parts of my life over to strangers eased as I remembered Mother telling us that when she was a girl, many young women earned their way through school by doing housework.

"That's it!" I thought. What bothered me was the idea that drudgery had no outlet; that nobody cared whether a bottom line worker advanced in life or not; that there had to be some active effort to hold servants in place, especially if you're just a woman, and a black one at that. But if I say I need your help, and I'd also like to know what your vision of yourself is in the future, then part of the payment for your helping me live my life is that maybe I can help you enrich yours.

"Do you want to go back to school? We can make some arrangements, perhaps, for you to go to night school or summer school to earn a few credits toward some degree. How about learning a trade or a skill?" With the initial offer of employment, I asked these questions to let the prospective employee know of my desire to buy their time and their services, not for salary and benefits alone, but in addition, for some modest interest in them as a human being with goals.

Two young women we employed have gone to summer school, working toward a bachelor of arts degree. Another has taken a business course. Most people who have helped us stay with us a number of years. We become partners in our need for help from each other.

In the process of building a foundation for our family, we became landowners and employers, and we also established friendships that, as it turned out, would last a lifetime. Sidney and Juanita Poitier were two such friends, who became part of our extended family.

I first caught sight of Sidney Poitier with peripheral vision, out of the corner of my eye—a tall, dark, neat young man in a short, navy blue coat and black pants. He was sitting alone on our tour bus, hands in his pockets, staring out the window. I hadn't known him at the American Negro Theatre. Perhaps he came along when I was off somewhere. Somehow he was traveling with us on the bus and truck tour of *Anna Lucasta.* We seldom spoke to each other. He seemed shy, withdrawn, and preoccupied. Sensing my attention, he turned, looked at me pleasantly enough, but he didn't smile. He simply turned back to his view out the window.

Over the years, I would play his wife or his girlfriend five times in film and once on stage; we would become neighbors; our families would become friends; some of his children would call Ossie "Uncle Ossie" and me "Aunt Ruby," and our children would address Sidney and Juanita likewise. I treasure the times when he would come barefoot to our house and the three of us might wind up in the kitchen, joking, laughing, and discussing some issue of the day.

He had married gorgeous Juanita Hardy two years after Ossie and I married. They were in Los Angeles with Beverly, their first daughter, when he called, asking us to please find a place for them, maybe a house, because they'd be coming east. We found a place not far from us.

After Pamela, Sherry, and Gina were born, Juanita, who worked in real estate, among other interests, decided to move to a larger house almost two hours away in Pleasantville. She had become my best friend, and although I joined in her enthusiasm for the move, I didn't want them to leave Mount Vernon. Since Carlotta and college, I had not felt as close to anyone as to Juanita. I missed shopping under the bridge, all the baby talk, and the woman talk, discussing aspirations, making plans, hobnobbing with all the girls—Tina Sattin and Delores Harvey among them—and especially Jean Walker, who worked for the Poitiers.

Jean had lived with Sidney and Juanita since their first baby was born, and had remained with Juanita even after their divorce, helping to raise the children, cook, and keep house, attending to the family in so many ways. Our family, too, loved Jean—a giving, caring, constantly involved and reliable member of their household—who sometimes looked out for our brood if we found ourselves in a pinch.

After the move, we still managed to get together, only not as often. Our families visited several times a year and most every Thanksgiving. Sidney was becoming very busy with his career, which kept him away from home quite a bit of the time. He began drifting away from Juanita. The two of them felt like family, and I didn't want them to split up, but I didn't know what to do. I constantly conjured up scenarios in my head that I thought might keep them together. Ossie reminded me from time to time that although they were younger than we were, they were grown, and to butt my mind out of their business.

We loved them both, but I especially had to cut the strings on my unexpected concern. Sidney and Harry Belafonte had become like younger brothers to me, but the time had come to let Sidney go. Juanita was hurt, of course, but among the things I learned from her in handling my own affairs was how to recover and carry on.

I could go deep into depression whenever an actor I knew gave up on New York and moved to L.A. for good. How could any sane person leave the hot-cold, riotous-quiet, dangerous-safe, dirty-clean New York for picture-book-perfect L.A.—where the houses don't even have basements?

The dissolution of the Poitiers' marriage disturbed me deeply. It added to the feeling of desperation and helplessness that settled over me as I saw love turn sour among close friends. Why did Juanita have to move so far out of New York? Why had the beautiful model allowed herself to gain so much weight? Could it be true? Yes, judge the book by its cover. Who cares if beauty is only skin deep? That may be deep enough for a man, especially a young one. In retrospect, my mind and heart turned constantly in varying degrees to breakup after breakup within a few years between people who felt like family.

I remember one night at the Palm Café on 125th Street in Harlem when Lonnie Sattin described in tender detail his passion for his wife. Ossie was deeply impressed. "Just watch," I whispered to Ossie. "Methinks the brother doth protest too much. One of the surest signs of nonlove is this too great public acclamation." (Ruby, take note!)

Then through Sidney, I first learned that Harry was leaving Marguerite, whom I had known many years. She had lived next door to my Aunt Cassie in Washington, D.C. Sidney had already left Juanita. Another performer friend of ours, with a magnificent tenor voice, also left his wife. These were close friends who had not only left their wives and children, but had married white women. It was happening all over. Walter White, national executive director of the NAACP, quit his wife, remarried white, and was forced to resign. As all of these men left their black wives and immediately or eventually married white women, I wondered, could I be next? (Oh, woe!)

Private, dark, resentful thoughts scurried around in my mind despite all attempts to travel the path of calm logic and understanding. They were thoughts never to be expressed aloud or betrayed by attitude or gesture when meeting the new mates of black friends who were still very dear to us.

I can understand how some black men and white women, too, in the U.S. of A., suddenly faced with freedom of choice and newly won rights, will choose to look for each other all over the place. In a sense, that is what integration truly means. The laws against people loving and associating as they choose are barbarous, ludicrous, stupid, titillating, and spring from minds that are monumentally immature.

Earlier contemplations, however, came with fangs. How dare you white women raid the black woman's nest, flaunt your perfumed, ivory skin, fling your flaxen and raven hair in the eyes and noses and mouths of our beautiful ebony men, assaulting all their senses? You have left us in mourning with our husbands still alive.

As for you black men now lost to us, however, you have emblazoned in the minds of your daughters the bitter thought that true beauty does not shine in earth-colored women with wooly hair. You have forced a defiant strut to the stride in order to help ward off demons that would sag our shoulders, slump our spirits, and make us believe that you don't love us anymore.

Such were my thoughts for the longest time. Time, however, brought me to another level with respect to interracial liaisons. It brought me to a genuine appreciation of Sidney's new wife, Joanna, and of Harry's Julie. They are concerned and beautiful women whom I am proud to know. Their new families seem whole and loving, following in the tradition of men and women who mate and marry as their hearts and minds lead them.

I realized that throughout our history, some white women and men have joined the ranks of people from all races who have sacrificed resources, reputation, and—more often than is acknowledged—their lives in service to their very best instincts in securing justice for others. Through my years, I've come to know several white women who have met and eventually married black men, whom they literally and figuratively rescued from the gutter, men rejected everywhere. They nursed them back to health and to belief in themselves, and guided them, in many cases, into fulfilling careers.

Racial separation is deliberate, and taught for nefarious reasons. Racial harmony is possible and mandatory if our species is to vanquish its common enemies and survive.

CHAPTER 26

New Work,
New Territory

OSSIE: I had never been in a musical before *Jamaica* in 1957, and I
had much to learn. It seemed that the dancers only came to life when
they took center stage, the spotlights hit, and the band played. There,
solo and ensemble, they exemplified grace, and thrust, and a brilliant
liquidity of motion. Some nights, they brought the audience to its feet!
But when the number was over, the curtain fell, they suddenly became
as empty vessels. Whatever lightning flashed but a moment before was
left behind.

Singers, too, and members of the chorus, on stage seemed to be
different people—parts of a mighty voice that shook the rafters, who
often, after the song was over and mouths barely shut, disappeared
before your eyes. This also applies to some actors I know, who seem
to come alive only through the role they happen to be playing. That is
not the way it was with Lena Horne.

Lena was more than a talent; she was an institution, as famous for
her advocacy, her membership in the Struggle, as for her singing. A

woman first, but that was just for starters; she knew how to protect herself in the clinches as if she were her own daughter. There are those who, having been stung by Lena's verbal punches, swear the woman is made of iron. Well, that may be so, but such female iron is elegant, and calls for lovers. Approach the lady with flattery or with flowers, tell her she's beautiful, and how much you admire her, but unless you speak from a basis of true respect, you'd better duck.

It was impossible to be in *Jamaica* without having some of Lena's sexy magic rub off on you. It certainly did on me.

Ricardo Montalban was a gentleman, *un caballero mas grande,* from ancient Mexico, adding an Old World charm to a New World hustle and bustle.

Joe Adams was strictly black L.A. He had been a disc jockey, then was featured as Husky Miller in Otto Preminger's *Carmen Jones,* and this was his big debut on Broadway. Joe wasn't quite satisfied with his acting, and he turned to me for help. In exchange, he offered to update my masculine image, instructing me in the intricacies of shoes and shirts and ties and slacks and blazers.

He thought it was time for men to wear cologne, and following his advice, I went to the drugstore to buy some. When I put it on, I smelled like a lady. "That's not cologne, that's perfume—they'll call you a sissy." He suggested I empty it down the drain, but I poured out only half, then refilled the other half with Listerine. First, I gargled, then put some under my armpits. It was the best I ever smelt in all my life.

Josephine Premice was *Jamaica*'s "Woman Exotique." She knew everybody in the business, and knowing her, I got to know them, too. She and her husband, Tim Fales, were most gracious hosts when we visited them while in Rome a few years later.

Also, there was Yip Harburg, and the pleasure of his company and his voice. Yip, who wrote the song "Brother, Can You Spare a Dime?" was, in my opinion, more than America's greatest lyricist; he was a poet—and a bit of a preacher. He wrote the book, with Fred Saidy, for *Jamaica,* as well as the lyrics. To hear him stand by the piano serving up his own words was a surprise and a revelation. Nobody—

not even Judy Garland—could sing "Somewhere Over the Rainbow"
like Yip Harburg. He almost made you cry.

It was late in 1957 when I got the message from Mama that Daddy
had taken to his bed. He was a diabetic, and the doctor had long
warned him that the insulin he had to inject every day, which was
from pigs, would eventually destroy his kidneys, and that's what
gradually happened. I knew from the tone of her letter that I'd better take a day or two off from *Jamaica,* and go home for a visit
while there was still time. Ruby was working in a film, so I traveled
south alone.

Mama and I met at the door, and she hugged me. She was already
beyond crying public tears, and she was glad to see me. My two brothers and my sister lived not too far away. I was the last of the children
to come home. A natural quiet attends a place where a man is sick unto
death; and more than that, a sort of peace had settled over the house,
as if time had stretched out a covering wing as we prepared for a
timeless ritual.

I put away my things, and then she took me to the room where
he was lying with his eyes closed, but not asleep.

"Kince," she said, "here's Brother," then turned and left.

His strength was gone but something strange and sweet had come
to take its place. He opened his eyes enough to acknowledge me, smile
a little smile, then closed his eyes again. I sat beside his bed for the
longest time, holding his hand, father-to-son communion, listening to
him breathe.

Sometime later, when twilight came, Mama came back to the door.
"Come on, Brother, it's time for you to eat." She fed me well. Cooking
had given her something useful to do. We sat and we talked, until talk
became superfluous. We never once mentioned Death, but Death was
on our minds.

Neighbors and friends came by, and Mama made them welcome,
presiding over their comfort. Once again, it gave her something to do.
There was no sadness in the house, only a deep, hospitable respect for
the inevitable event.

The little black train is coming
Get all of your business right
You better set your house in order
'Cause the train may be here tonight.

As Mama used to sing the old folk song.

And so we chatted about Daddy, his life, the funny, wild, im-probable deeds that he had done, and those widely inconsequential things that culture and custom provide us Southerners for just such times as these.

I stayed the night, but had to leave the next day. Late the following morning, I went into his room to say good-bye. He stirred when I came in; I took his hand, sat down, and he talked a little. His voice was thinner than I'd ever heard, but his face seemed satisfied, and I felt the peace and the love that flowed between us.

He asked about the children, and about Ruby, and said how glad he was that I could come. He went on for another moment or two, and then his voice halted, and there was silence. When he resumed, the focus had shifted. I remembered those many walks we took together when I was a boy, and we were in the thicket, hunting roots. I recognized that he was no longer talking to me, but speaking to God, as one might do in private, reminding Him that he, Kince Davis, was still His obedient son, deserving of His mercy. Some further words were uttered, beseeching his Friend's forgiveness, then a praying phrase I used to hear him say: ". . . thy will, Oh, Lord, not mine . . ." Daddy's eyes were shut now, to me and to the world—the words were meant for his Maker and his God.

And I, as I had done so many times before when the two of them got private, finally withdrew, tiptoeing quietly to the door, from which I turned, took one last look, and said, almost beneath my breath, "Good-bye, Daddy." In January 1958, he died, and I went south again.

～　　～　　～

RUBY: In 1959, I was playing Sidney's wife in *Our Virgin Island,* a British film shot in St. Thomas and St. Croix. Sidney and John Cassavetes were the leads, with Virginia Maskell, "Bare Breasts" from England, as the love interest.

I called her "Bare Breasts" because on warm mornings when we went by boat to the little island where a good deal of the shooting took place, she removed her top and let the sun and the breezes play in her hair and caress her bosom. There was no self-consciousness in it. She just did it. I tried to be cool, as if this is just what any young English girl in this position would do. After all, her country had colonized all those parts of Africa, which in all its most voluptuous innocence, must have been an inspiration. At any rate, the whole event had a sensuous quality about it, a great generosity of spirit.

It was the second time I had worked with Cassavetes. He was an actor's actor, a dedicated professional, full of honest surprises. Later he would be recognized as a gifted director who created a distinctive cinematic style from an ad-lib, ad-hoc approach to filmmaking. He was a seat-of-the-pants producer, with a gift for mining improvisations. Locations could be almost anywhere, including his garage. *Shadows, Husbands,* and *Faces* are three of his works that critics came to treat with respect.

During the filming of *Our Virgin Island,* I frequently got a chance to listen to him share his thoughts. He had an intense sense of humor. Occasionally we talked, and I expressed my still gestating urge to make film adaptations of books by authors I admired. How do you go about that, huh? How? I asked him.

"Just do it," he once said.

Before the shoot was over, he came to my quarters one day and gave me a 16-millimeter Bolex camera. He had just bought a new, more advanced one, he said, naming the model and the accessories. Though I was utterly surprised, I protested that he ought to let me buy it.

"Nah, nah," he said, "I don't need it anymore. See? It's a great little camera—just the thing you might need to try out some of your ideas."

He gave me the instrument with two additional lenses, a viewfinder, and a light meter, all enclosed in a marvelous leather case. I began to carry it everywhere because, in a way, it began to lead me. I became keenly aware of places and ideas for stories and movies—originals and adaptations. At first, I just had fun with it. I filmed the clouds from airplanes, the children and their friends playing in snow-drifts, workmen building a wall in our yard to keep the dirt from sliding down. Years later, I shot more footage on vacation in Mexico; in Italy where Ossie was filming *The Cardinal*; I filmed Mother and Daddy as they visited Angelina and Carl in Burlington, Vermont. (They kept moving north, from the Bronx, to Pelham, to Kingston, to Vermont, and finally to Canada.) I planned to do something original with this footage. Measuring light, distance, angles, and practicing shots preoccupied me now.

Cassavetes showed me a few things, and I was anxious to get it all down pat. I also learned a lot from reading the literature that came with the camera as well as material from camera stores and the local library. The Bolex was a wind-up job, like a clock. This camera opened me up to myself in many ways, and to new worlds of literature as I tried to find the books that I would turn into plays and films. I went crazy with the discovery of authors I'd never heard about in school.

The Bolex, however, was only a camera. It couldn't record sound, as video cameras do today. I felt I needed something to round out the pictures I planned to be shooting. I needed sound. First thing I knew, I went into a store and bought an Ampex sound system, a tape recorder, an amplifier with speakers, a long cable, a microphone, a stand to hold it, a tripod for the camera, and a bank of floodlights. We completed the process by buying a Bell and Howell 16-millimeter film projector, and we were on the way to our very first production.

OSSIE: Paul Robeson was still headmaster of our little circle, and the fight to get his passport, still very much on the agenda—a matter that split good people, even his friends. Local 1199 was in the very thick of the struggle, but Actors Equity, our union, was a better place to fight.

During the late fifties, near the end of a hot and heavy regular meeting, I arose under the call for new business and made a motion that Actors Equity support Paul Robeson in his fight to regain his passport. The effect was electric. The motion was quickly seconded, and the floor thrown open to debate. My motion caught everybody by surprise, including me. The vote was a landslide: seven to one in favor of the motion, which was also surprising.

Most of the members knew Paul, certainly by reputation, and most objected to the way he was being treated. But the witch-hunt was still in progress, and raising your hand in an open show of support for Paul Robeson could cost you your job.

Of course, votes from membership were not binding on the council, and as we expected, the council hastily nullified the vote, declining to move in the matter of Robeson's passport. But the damage had been done.

A public hearing was held in the federal court at Foley Square to investigate the dangers of Communist subversion. Subpoenas were issued, and this time, the process servers didn't miss. Ruby and Ossie were among the first witnesses called.

Members of our group immediately went into a defensive posture. Meetings were called to discuss and debate how best to defend ourselves. Ruby stayed home with the children, but I went. Ruby was appalled that we had to waste our time—and money—running around like chickens with our heads cut off. Still, she knew how serious this could be, and that, foolish or not, if we didn't show up, they could put us in jail for contempt.

Lawyers were summoned to help us plan our response to the question, which had become the litmus test of our times: Are you now, or have you ever been, a member of the Communist party? Some were advised to plead the Fifth Amendment on the grounds of possible self-incrimination, while others, like Ruby and me, could answer as we chose.

Came the day of the hearing, there was a crisis at 5 Cooley Place. Evelyn Thompson, our baby-sitter, couldn't come, so Ruby suggested I go on ahead, and tell the Committee what the problem was, and that she'd be there as soon as she could manage. I didn't like the arrangement. I told her maybe we should take the baby with us, but Ruby wouldn't budge. I reminded her of what might happen if she didn't show; then I went alone down to the federal courthouse on Foley Square.

The place was crowded; people were coming and going in and out of the hallways; photographers snapping pictures, reporters asking questions, people speaking into microphones. Everybody but me, it seemed. I was ignored completely. I looked around for whoever was in charge—someone to whom I could explain Ruby's absence—but everyone was much too busy to listen.

Most of the people called were small fish, not a real headliner among us. The really big catches, the stars and the celebrities, had already been called, or cleared, or denied their jobs. It turned out to be a quick foray into Broadway, meant to intimidate the theater, whip us back in line, like Hollywood.

I kept an anxious and expectant eye out for Ruby, hoping she would show before her name was called, and it was discovered that she was absent. The inquisitional process was completely devoid of excitement or suspense. The pickings were slim, and the Committee was in a hurry. Paul Mann, Ruby's acting teacher, was called early in the proceedings:

"Are you now, or have you ever been, a member of the Communist party?"

"Mr. Chairman," Paul rejoined, "this Committee has no right to question my beliefs or my affiliations—"

"The witness will answer the question: Are you now—"

Paul cut him off, "Mr. Chairman, I have a statement—"

"Never mind your statement. Either answer the question or step down. Bailiff!"

"I have a statement, Mr. Chairman," Paul persisted, holding up some papers and waving them around.

"One more word, and I'll hold you in contempt. Bailiff, get this man out of here. We ain't got all day!" Paul was pulled from the witness chair and quickly hustled away.

I wasn't as ambitious or as defiant as Paul, but I, too, had a few observations I wanted to share with the committee.

"Get him the hell outta here, Bailiff!" I was ejected, too.

A short while later, I looked up and saw Ruby at the foot of the long flight of steps leading up to the courthouse. I ran to meet her, took her by the arm, and brought her to a Mrs. Scotti, who turned out to be the coordinator. I told her that my wife had finally showed up, and that her lateness was not an act of defiance or show of disrespect to this committee. I tried further to explain about the baby-sitter, but Mrs. Scotti cut me off.

"Forget it," she said. "The hearing is over now. Maybe some other time."

She left us standing on the courthouse steps, looking a little foolish. Our grand defiance never had a chance.

CHAPTER 27

Big Breakthroughs

What happens to a dream deferred?
Does it dry up
Like a raisin in the sun?
Or fester like a sore—
And then run?
Does it stink like rotten meat?
Or crust and sugar over—
Like a syrupy sweet?

Maybe it just sags
Like a heavy load—

Or does it explode?
—LANGSTON HUGHES

RUBY: I should have already read the play that had been sent to me a few days earlier, so before getting out of bed, before the demands of the day gobbled up my time and attention, I did. I had to give an answer about whether or not I wanted to be a part of this project sometime before noon. It was not an easy play to read. It had emotional depth, rich dialogue, and a great sense of truth. Here were engaging characters with dimension and distinct personalities. I couldn't remember reading any play like it. I was moved and excited, filled with questions and some reservation as I got up, contemplating the title, *A Raisin in the Sun,* taken from the Langston Hughes poem "Dream Deferred."

Lloyd Richards, whom I had known as a teacher at Paul Mann's studio and as an actor, was to be the director of this new play by a young author, Lorraine Hansberry. Although he didn't specify which part he had in mind for me, I knew it was Beneatha, the restless, ambitious younger sister of Walter Lee. Lloyd called about noon for my reaction to the play. Would I be interested? Oh, yes. I was delighted, ecstatic. When was it to go into rehearsal? . . . And I loved the part of Beneatha—so fresh, challenging, and different from anything I'd done before.

"No, no, Ruby," Lloyd began, "forgive me for not making it clear. I want you to look at Ruth, the wife. You'll be Sidney's wife. He's agreed to do Walter Lee."

My heart flopped over and sank. Ruth? It seemed I'd been playing that same character, more or less, in almost everything I'd done since *Anna:* as Ossie's wife in *No Way Out;* as Jackie's wife in *The Jackie Robinson Story;* twice as Sidney's wife in *Go, Man, Go* and in *Edge of the City;* and as Nat Cole's betrothed in *The St. Louis Blues.*

I tried to persuade Lloyd to see that I could do Beneatha, but he insisted that he needed a special kind of actor who linked all the characters, who was an engaging person on her own, and who, in a sense, was the tapestry against which all the other characters came to life. It was a flattering appraisal of what I had to offer. Although sorely disappointed, I agreed to play Ruth. No matter what, I very much wanted to be a part of *A Raisin in the Sun.*

Phil Rose was the producer, and the first reading of the play was held at his house. The cast included Sidney Poitier, Claudia McNeil, Diana Sands, Lou Gossett, John Fiedler, Ivan Dixon, Lonne Elder, Glynn Turman, and me. Bob Nemiroff, Lorraine's husband, was also among those present that first day.

Lorraine was so young, I thought. She looked like a teenager, but there was a definite air of maturity about her. Hearing her speak, I quickly forgot about her youth. She spoke with an authority, tinged with wit. I felt I was in the presence of a superior intellect. Clearly, she had written herself in the character of Beneatha—iconoclastic, impatient, and brilliant. I realized, as I listened to Diana Sands read the part, that Lloyd was right. Although I believed I could play the extraordinary Beneatha, I was relieved that the challenge would not be mine. I also realized that I was most comfortable listening to Lorraine as she discussed or argued some point with people I judged to be her intellectual equal.

I shall always remember our meeting after the first preview in New Haven. Lloyd had been rehearsing the play as a straightforward drama. We explored the truths of the characters, and the realities of the circumstances. We actors respected Lloyd's patience, and his persistence both in pursuing Lorraine's vision and in incorporating the distinct talents of the cast. And he was in the process of making history as the first black director of a drama on Broadway.

That first audience, however, let us know that *A Raisin in the Sun* was more than a drama; it was a comedy-drama. Sidney and I opened the play. We had scarcely begun the opening scene when the laughter began—a reaction for which we were not prepared, as I recall.

At the next rehearsal, Lloyd injected a new rationale into the action. I felt flustered. Had I been doing something wrong? What he was saying to me now seemed partly a contradiction of some elements on which we had previously agreed. As I tried to accommodate the new instructions, I began to cry. I recovered quickly, and the unusual rehearsal continued.

When it was over, Lorraine met me on stage, and asked if she could do anything, or explain anything, to make it easier to accept Lloyd's new, altered directions. At that moment, I felt uncomfortable, patronized, and incapable of expressing my dilemma. I soon realized that Lloyd was simply trying to get us to embrace an added facet of Lorraine—her sense of humor.

To accommodate the change, there only needed to be an adjustment in attitude. I think Lloyd could have skipped all the explanation and justification, though, and simply said, "People want to laugh at this particular dramatic reality. Lighten up, Ruby. Let them."

On the other hand, I should have remembered that part of the creative process is arriving at solid conclusions that sometimes must be changed or abandoned in an instant.

That reminds me of the time when we often did staged readings. One night we were reading a piece about a black youth involved in integrating a lunch counter in the South. Ossie had written the piece for District 65, the Retail Workers Union, for Negro History Week.

Frequently in such performances, a few actors played many parts. At one point, early in the drama, Will Geer took the role of a black grandmother, and the audience howled. Now Will Geer, a white actor and a friend, was a folksy, gregarious person with a sense of humor and a distinct cracker drawl. I remember the shock of hearing people, not titter, but guffaw during our serious presentation.

The four of us looked at each other, read the looks, and immediately turned our serious drama into a satire. The reading was an enormous success.

OSSIE: *A Raisin in the Sun* was a hit. Broadway ate it up. I liked it, too, but Ruby and I had a basic bone to pick.

In our opinion, this play was meant to be a warning, as Langston's poem suggested. Walter Lee Younger was a frustrated young black man whose dreams of better things for his family had been too long deferred, and he was on the verge of exploding, either into crime or into revolution. Lorraine didn't say which, but she did imply that if America wanted racial peace, something drastic had to be done about the hundreds of thousands of Walter Lees all over this country. That sentiment, in our opinion, expressed the author's clear intent. But somehow, in the production, that clear intent became subverted.

Sure, Walter, goaded by dreams of what he could not have in America because of racism, was about to explode; but not to worry. Lena, his mother, the strong and domineering head of the household, was totally in charge. America could depend on her to keep Walter under control, no matter what. The people who filled the theater night after night had nothing to worry about.

The play that had started out as a fire alarm ringing in the night, a wake-up call that America desperately needed, had somehow been transmuted into a domestic comedy-drama about a family's urgent need for decent housing. Their solution to the race problem was simply to exercise their right to buy a house in a white neighborhood.

All this being said, *A Raisin in the Sun* was still a most important work, a vital part of the message America needed to hear, and a part of the Struggle. It was a dramatic breakthrough, no matter how you looked at it. We finally accepted it as that.

In August 1959, Sidney left the show and I took over the role.

I owe Lloyd Richards big for a simple piece of instruction. Just as I was about to go on stage one day, he asked me to do something— something I couldn't handle at the time, but it turned out to be the key that finally unlocked the cell, and set me free to become an actor.

"Ossie," he said, "do me a favor. I want you to go out there on that stage; I want you to confront Claudia McNeil. Forget the lines, forget the character, forget how Lorraine has written the scene, forget the rest of the play. Just make her give you the money, you hear me? Don't leave that stage until she gives you that check for ten thousand dollars!"

The money Lloyd was talking about was the proceeds from a life insurance payment, which Walter Lee needed to invest in a liquor store. In the scene, as written, Mama turns him down.

If only I could have done it. If only I could have become enraged—really fought with Claudia—it would have made the scene between us, not only real, but electric. It would have scared the hell out of the audience, and nailed them to their seats. Unfortunately, for me, I had never been enraged in all my life! I could only fake it, imitating Lloyd and Sidney. And the audience can always spot a fake.

Now, of course, forty years later, I can do it. Now I know exactly how to do it. Rage? I've finally got the hang of it now. And if ever I get another chance to play Walter Lee Younger, I'm going out there and *make* Claudia McNeil give me that damn check for $10,000. That's what acting is all about!

Though rage was not available to me at that time—I could not fly off the handle, like most people—anger, I had, but not enough for an actor. I don't remember ever losing my temper, nor has ambition, jealousy, or revenge pushed me into action. Inaction is the way I prefer to meet a crisis. I am emotionally slow, to the point of being dense. Staid, almost to the point of being stolid. When the role I am playing calls for aggression, I have to squeeze my innards mighty hard, like a rooster trying to lay an egg.

Ruby, on the other hand, is a natural and intuitive defender of the innocent and of the helpless. Ruby, spontaneous, gloriously impulsive; She of the instant reflex—as Claudia McNeil found out one matinee day.

It was vacation time, and Diana Sands had been replaced in the role of Beneatha by Billie Allen, her understudy, for two weeks. There is a scene near the end of the first act that calls for Lena, the mother, played brilliantly by Claudia McNeil, to lash out in anger and slap Beneatha hard across the face. Now, most actors know how to pull a punch and fake a blow, but Claudia—powerful and heavyset—had never bothered to learn.

So every performance, she would haul off and slap with all her might. Diana knew how to duck and roll with the slap, but Billie didn't. We tried to teach Billie Diana's technique, but she never got the hang of it. That matinee, Claudia, as usual, had almost knocked Billie to her knees when Ruby stepped into Claudia's face, and growled under her breath—right there on stage—"You hit that girl one more time like that and I'll knock you flat on your ass!"

Claudia, almost shocked out of her senses, nearly forgot her lines, but being the trooper that she was, she bravely carried on. Then, when the curtain came down, she crumpled like an accordion and fell to the floor in a faint. And there she lay until the stage manager finally found some smelling salts and revived her just in time for the second act.

Claudia was a heavyweight, flat of foot and solid. Ruby was a bantamweight, at best, but in a fistfight, I'd back Ruby Dee every time. Luckily, it never came to that. Claudia hauled Ruby before Actors Equity, complaining about her "most unprofessional behavior," and at the union's insistence, Ruby apologized; but Billie never had to stumble again.

~ ~ ~

In 1960, while Ruby and I were in *Raisin,* a strike on Broadway brought all the curtains down for a week or so. Ruby and I, being ardent unionists, were in the thick of the action, but we were glad when the strike was settled and we got back to work. A few days after the play resumed, I got a letter from a teacher at a public school on West 48th Street. She had been planning to bring her entire class to see the play, but the strike had intervened, closing the theater on the very day that they were set to come. She wondered if I would be so kind as to at least come by the school and say hello to her class. I said yes.

The school decided to take full advantage of an actor's appearance, so instead of a visit with just one class, they arranged an assembly with rows and rows of students gathered in the auditorium. It should have been a snap. By now, Ruby and I had appeared at many schools in Mount Vernon and New Rochelle, where we recited poetry, told stories, and swapped jokes with the students. Our purpose was to give our own children and other children of color something seldom found in the regular lesson plan—something black.

The routine was familiar. I took my place on the platform, and while the principal introduced me, I checked out the students, sizing them up, figuring out which selections from my repertoire I would offer them this morning. However, as I spied them out, I became aware that something was different. There was none of the buzz and wriggle that usually sweeps across a vibrant student body when visitors come. They sat there rather stiff, dutiful, silent, and respectful, like little inmates in a prison under orders to be quiet and not move an inch.

The applause was not spontaneous, sounding rather as if it had been rehearsed. Their faces told me nothing. I was not used to such eerie stillness; but I'd worked with kids before, and I thought I knew exactly what to do.

The trick, of course, is to wean them from their teachers, to free them from the bonds of politeness and good manners, and to get them to laugh on their own. I cleared my throat and let go:

> *My ol' mule got a grin on his face*
> *Been a mule so long*
> *He forgot about his race.*

Big Breakthroughs

I'm like that ol' mule
Black, don't give a damn—
You got to take me
Like I am!

Usually, kids are not expecting grown-ups, especially dignitaries, to say words like "damn." It shocks them. They look quickly at their teachers, then at each other, and then they laugh a little nervous titter that soon becomes a roar. That's when you know you've got them. But this was different, a little like performing for the dead. The students, watching their teachers for guidance, politely applauded, then resumed their iron-faced look of false politeness. My pride was sorely hurt, my ego undone. I decided to bring heavier weaponry to bear.

It was all a matter of surreptitious bonding, of showing the children that I was a child like they were, and that I was on their side in the battle between students and teachers. I and that roomful of children, rebels all, in glorious conspiracy against all the grown-ups in the world. And "Casey at the Bat" was just the thing to do it.

"Casey," one of the greatest performance pieces I know, is about the overconfident baseball home-run hitter who struck out in the clutch. It's a simple piece that gives the actor a chance to use his voice and his body movements. If "Casey" couldn't do it, no one could!

I never worked harder in my life. I crossed my eyes, I mugged, I stuck out my tongue; I shouted, I whispered, I groaned; I made animal noises that sounded almost like farts, I worked them, I wooed them—I almost herniated myself as I tried to bowl them over. Little by little, they started to laugh as children ought to laugh, just a little at first, but by and by they forgot their teachers altogether and joined me in the great melodramatic conspiracy to be joyously, deliriously, and childishly happy.

Then, of course, having led them to the brink of rebellion and insubordination, I had to bring them back, sober them up, and return them to the authority and to the control of their teachers. I told them about my teachers—about Wilhelmina Gaines, who taught me to love the English language; about Lucius Jackson, who introduced me to "Casey at the Bat"; about Mary Lee Hall, who taught me the joy of reading and telling stories. I told them that the teachers were their friends, always ready to help them, no matter what. I could see the teachers breathing a sigh of relief and gratitude.

After the children had returned to classes, the principal apologized. Most of the students had immigrant parents, had come to school with latchkeys on a string around their necks, and because they were hungry, they were more interested in lunch than in learning. They had never seen a live actor before; hence they didn't know how to behave, so they just sat there, doing as they were told.

I understood, but I did not like at all that first joyless look on their faces, and I was determined to do something that would open them up to the joys of reading and writing, and to the joys I knew at school when I was a child. And if they could not afford to go to the theater, I was determined to carry the theater to them. I asked the principal if I could come back and bring Ruby with me. He said yes.

I took the trouble to reassure the teachers once again, reminding them that I was on their side. Although I could reach those kids in ways that teachers couldn't, my job was not to usurp their authority, but to reinforce it.

Within the spectrum of teaching styles, Ruby and I still consider ourselves positioned somewhere between bootleg educators and adjunct professors. Our primary function remains—to help the teachers teach.

RUBY: We'd heard about this project Max Roach, the master drummer, was working on with Abbey Lincoln, a compelling blues and jazz singer. Max and Oscar Brown, Jr., had written a piece called "Freedom Now Suite," which I first heard when I attended a benefit concert one Sunday afternoon. "Freedom Now Suite" was unique, fresh, and timely. It fit right in with what was happening in the civil rights movement. It had history, passion, a cry for Freedom Now for African Americans, and also a salute to African tribes, languages, and countries, some of which had recently been liberated from British and French colonialism.

It worked well as a concert, but I had a much grander vision in mind. I saw it as a film that would fuse music, dance, and text to create a new cinematic experience. Short, pungent, but eloquent and as hard-hitting as anything Malcolm and Martin were saying. I approached Max, told him what I had in mind, and he bought the whole idea. Ossie agreed to write some additional material to tie the whole thing together, and Sidney agreed to direct it. We called the project *Uhuru!,* which, in Swahili, means "freedom."

Max brought in Coleman Hawkins, a master saxophonist, and Michael Olatunji, a Nigerian percussionist. Abbey, of course, was vocalist, along with Oscar Brown in his own inimitable style.

We rented a studio and came out with a stunning twenty-five-minute soundtrack. Unfortunately, the production of the music alone exhausted completely our meager supply of capital. We tried to interest other investors, but we forgot one thing: We were not producers. Another thing we forgot: We were not financially intelligent. Our finances disappeared like snow on a summer's hot rock. There was no time now to go to school and learn to be filmmakers and producers.

We never finished the film, but Max has staged "Freedom Now Suite" several times with Ossie as narrator. Changes have been made to fit new times and circumstances, but as Max presents it, making majestic statements on the drums, it is still a powerful piece of music. My dream of being a filmmaker would be deferred, it seemed, but my inner and outer vision had been irrevocably changed.

A Raisin in the Sun closed in June 1960, and Columbia Pictures immediately adapted it for film. After the success of the play, Ossie and I began to get more work in television. PBS, then known as TV-13, had a series called *Play of the Week.* In one episode, "Black Monday," a story about black students integrating a white school, we noticed a young white actor in his first TV role. He was a "gorgeous blond," and a really good actor, I thought. His name was Robert Redford. As I watched him play a racist rabble-rouser, it hit me like a revelation: "This actor is going to be *big!*" No matter, I thought, so am I.

Myron McCormick, who was also featured in "Black Monday," had come over to me during a break and said, "Ruby, you are a genius, you know, a great actress." I really hadn't assessed myself at that point, but I goosepimpled. I think he's right. Oh, God! Two geniuses in one family. Can the world stand it? One of us will just have to commit "genius-cide."

The possibility of being one genius short, however, arose when my husband of twelve years, for whom I had borne three children, sat on his lips when the suggestion was made that I be allowed to audition for the part of Lutiebelle Gussie Mae Jenkins in his soon-to-be produced farce, *Purlie Victorious.* Everybody always looked upon me as a serious dramatic actress. No one, including Ossie, had ever seen me do a comedic role. This oversight alone was a resounding refutation of my greatness and evidence that his guardian angels were doing double duty at the time because he still lives. I hesitate to contemplate the status of our marriage today if I'd had to beat down competition for that part. *Purlie Victorious* brought us to a new level in our artistic life together.

OSSIE: Though I write a great deal in the morning, and in between scenes backstage when I'm working, most of my creative labors are carried out in the back of my moving mind. I know from experience how to hang on to a scene I am working on in the midst of all kinds of distractions, or how to put it aside for a moment, a week, or a month, then pick it up exactly where I left off. It was certainly that way for the five long years it took me to write *Purlie Victorious.*

My most intractable problem was with my little hero. What should I have him do? What should I have him say? What kind of punishment was horrible enough to avenge the syrup poured on his head in a Waycross police station? The more I let him have his way in my imagination, the more he rebelled. Finally, I was forced to let him do it his way, following along as he changed his name, and his object, moving away from anger and revenge, and off toward laughter.

I might have been still wrestling with the problem had not Lorraine Hansberry and *A Raisin in the Sun* come along. The overwhelming success of that play suddenly made everything possible. I felt a sudden, powerful surge of encouragement, as every other black writer in the country must have felt. If Lorraine could do it, why couldn't I?

Her achievement gave me—and the play I was writing—a purpose. I forged ahead and soon the work was done. That elation that comes from having finished something you think is big and good and important was finally mine. There it was, *Purlie Victorious,* a full-length play, able to stand at last on its own two feet. I had gone out in search of a hero and had finally come back with a fool. But what a fool! Laughter was the straw that broke the camel's back.

I never show my work until I'm finished. Ruby had no way of knowing my play had changed. She still expected the noble little mistreated colored boy from Waycross.

Satire is not for the cynic. Only the lover should be allowed to laugh at the ways of his people. I thought I had pulled it off, but the unexpected laughter threw Ruby completely. She was appalled. The characters were offensive, the language demeaning.

"Ossie, these aren't people; these are stereotypes, a minstrel show that white folks love to laugh at." I could see in her eyes how much it hurt her to have to tell me this, but we've always tried not to lie to each other, no matter what. She had read it, more or less, as a straight drama.

I tried at first to explain what it was I was trying to do with the stereotypes. I was trying to turn them inside out and upside down, embrace them as if they were indeed true-to-life. I made no headway at all, and I began to feel uneasy. Laughter, for all its curative powers, can also be destructive. It was only when I took the pages and read them to her myself that the change came. In a flash, she was howling with laughter. Good, clean, healthy black folks' laughter—laughter *with,* not *at* black folks. I was deeply gratified by her response.

Still, Ruby had a point. The 1960s were a time of revolution. Black folk were determined to change the image by which we were perceived, to put folk humor aside and put on war paint, so that white folks should be under no illusion that we were joking. We had to present them with our sternest face. And that's the kind of play I had tried so long to write; but I had ended up with laughter instead of revenge. Was *Purlie Victorious,* with all its laughter, its gags, its schtick and one-liners, an act of betrayal?

Nothing black in a racist world takes place in a vacuum. A play cannot be just a play, left by itself to succeed or fail; its very presence must reflect the current state of black affairs. By 1961, civil rights had forced its way to the top of the national agenda. We blacks had a sense that we and our agony and our fate were being taken seriously in a way that had never happened before. Surely, now was the time to be serious, demanding, and a little bit dangerous. This was surely not a time to laugh. Or was it? How could we convince white folks that this time we meant business, this time was no joke, if they saw us laughing? Should we present a more angry, revolutionary face to the world, rather than one of continuous merriment and tomfoolery, as Purlie would seem to suggest? What place has laughter in a revolution?

To further test the waters, one Sunday afternoon we invited some of our fellow black warriors over. Present were John O. Killens, Loften Mitchell, William Patterson, our Communist guru, and his wife Louise, and Jim and Esther Jackson from *Freedomways* magazine. Once again, I read the play myself. The laughter bordered on hysteria. We began to suspect we had a hit.

I had twenty-five copies of the play made and carried them around to my friends on Broadway. Howard Da Silva read it and fell in love. I think Josh Logan, whom I remembered and admired from *Wisteria Trees,* was a sentimentalist as far as the South was concerned. My guess is that my *Purlie,* with its savage humor, put him off entirely; I'm not sure he understood the nature of the humor. But Phil Rose, who had produced *A Raisin in the Sun*, did. He offered to produce the play on Broadway.

What more could a playwright want? I insisted on Howard Da Silva as a director and got him.

If Howard had come to me and said, "Ossie, I want someone else to play the lead in *Purlie Victorious* because you can't, because you're the worst actor I have ever met," I think I would have said, "Okay, Howard, if that's the way you feel." But Howard, no matter how I must have disappointed him, never gave up on me. That might have surprised many people who knew us both.

Howard, as a director, was not kind, or sentimental, or forgiving. He was dictatorial and opinionated. There are actors, some of them damned good, who went to their graves hating his guts. He could be crude, rude, sarcastic, and insulting, yet he was, in my opinion, one of the greats. For every actor who couldn't abide him, there was another who would have died for a chance to work with him. One of my few regrets is that he did not live to see me arrive as an actor.

One day in the middle of rehearsal, Howard was working with Ruby and me on stage while he sat way in the back of the house, watching and listening. It was a simple scene, which, since I had written it, should have presented no problem, but nothing I did was pleasing to Howard. He had us repeat the scene over and over, trying to get what he wanted, to no avail.

Finally, he shouted, "Stop, stop, stop!" He ran down the aisle, up onto the stage, and confronted me. "Ossie," he shouted, "that is not the author's intent!"

"Well, what the hell is?" I replied. Then he patiently told me the meaning of what I had written, but didn't know how to handle as an actor. I tried it again, applying his instructions. This time it worked. Even so, I never did a performance that really satisfied Howard. However, the critics, in general, were pleased. Still, their pleasure did not resolve the question: Is laughter proper in a revolution?

We never had the benefit of out-of-town tryouts, but we did have previews, which gave us a chance to test the show before a live audience prior to the official opening. Our first live performance was before the Congress of Racial Equality, which had bought the house for a benefit. These were our friends, our comrades in the Struggle; they wanted to laugh—that energy we could feel—but they didn't know whether it would be proper. We were more than a little disappointed at their tepid, nonparticipatory response.

On the other hand, Roy Wilkins, executive secretary of the NAACP, was so impressed he sent a letter to the heads of all the branches, urging them to see the show.

On opening night, we felt we had a winner. Afterward, Dr. W.E.B. Du Bois, who was ninety-three years old, climbed the stairs to our dressing room to tell us so. And later in the run, we got the same supportive response from Martin Luther King when he came to see us on the occasion of our one-hundredth performance.

The most convincing show of support came from the most unlikely of sources: Malcolm X, Black Muslim leader and spokesman for Elijah Muhammad. It was most unusual for him to come to a performance because Elijah Muhammad forbid the Muslims to attend theater. Malcolm came backstage, and talked to Ruby and me. He said he liked the show because he felt that black folks laughing at white folks was revolutionary—the highest kind of Struggle he could imagine. Malcolm's opinion was welcome, but not completely surprising. Not to us. We'd already met Malcolm at least three times before this occasion.

CHAPTER 28

Struggle, Realities, and Art

OSSIE: In 1959, a documentary called *The Hate That Hate Produced* appeared on CBS television. It was about a new phenomenon on the black horizon: the Black Muslims. Here in the middle of the swelling tide toward integration was a burgeoning, blistering island of black nationalist dissent. They were separatists, and they called for five states in the South to be turned over to the black man immediately and without condition as reparations for slave labor. As for nonviolence, the Black Muslims considered it ridiculous, advocating an eye for an eye and a tooth for a tooth.

These ideas, shocking as they were, were nothing compared with the man who gave them utterance: Malcolm X. He was a man lean as a rain-beaten bone, and mean-seeming as a rattlesnake—even his horn-rimmed glasses were meant to upset the black middle class—with a shock of reddish-blond Negro hair cut just a size too short.

Ruby's and my first response to Malcolm was not to pay too much attention. He was black, but he wasn't Baptist, Methodist, Pentecostal,

Presbyterian, or even Episcopalian. He was a Black Muslim, something we had never heard of before. We fully expected that he, like so many others before him, would prove a nine-day wonder, flaring up for a brief moment in the national attention, then disappearing just as fast as he had come.

But Malcolm didn't disappear. He hung on, kept getting louder and more insistent. The man turned out to be not shallow or foolish, but knowledgeable. His voice was strident, but serious, his manner, finger pointing and accusatory. Not only did he stick it to the white man, calling him a blue-eyed devil; he was equally sharp with black folks, accusing us of loving the white man more than we loved ourselves. He seemed to think Martin Luther King, Jr.'s philosophy of nonviolence was exactly what was wrong with "the so-called Negro leader."

Our growing curiosity was further stimulated by the fact that Ruby's brother, Edward, had become a Muslim. It was easy to see the positive effect Malcolm was having on him. He told us of some of the inner workings of the organization, about the effect Malcolm was having on Harlem's street people, on drug addicts and criminals and hustlers who normally preyed on the community. People from the gutter, under Malcolm's prodding, had turned their lives around. This was the part that interested us the most. Not since Father Divine in the 1930s and '40s had anyone had such a redeeming effect on the disaffected masses. This was more than even Martin was doing.

Malcolm was an expert on the damage that slavery and racism had done to the black man's image of himself. He was equally expert in what had to be done to remedy that egregious lack of self-esteem. He knew it would take more than civil rights legislation, jobs, and education to really save the black man. And he knew that none of the traditional organizations that serviced the Negro people—black churches, colleges, sororities and fraternities, the NAACP, the Urban League— was capable of doing what needed to be done. He felt, as did some of us, that to ask a man who had already been beaten up and beaten down to be nonviolent was only to change black pathology into another religion.

Malcolm, for all his fiery rhetoric and his exotic Muslim philosophy, was addressing burning issues that neither Martin Luther King nor the Communists were addressing. Was he a clown? Was he a demagogue? Was he a hustler? Or was he on to something very, very important? Whatever he was, it soon became clear that here was someone who seriously had to be dealt with. Ruby and I decided, as had always been our policy with other black leaders, to check him out.

Edward had for some time been urging Ruby and me to come to Mosque No. 7 over in Harlem and listen to Malcolm. We finally agreed.

It was a Sunday night service and Ruby's father had decided to come along. They patted us down at the entrance along with everybody else, and we went in and found seats in the crowded auditorium. Malcolm arose to speak. Like Martin, he was a master of oral communications. He knew the music of black speech and how to play an audience like an instrument. His sentences were clear, pithy, and to the point, with images fresh from the streets of Harlem. The room was full of believers but this was more than preaching to the choir. He knew how to command attention, to make us listen. He combined profound scholarship and understanding of national and international issues with a refreshing wit.

Several things were immediately obvious about the bright, irritating young man to whom we were listening. First was his extraordinary intelligence and learning—the man surely read everything; second was his absolute devotion to "the Honorable Elijah Muhammad," whom he equated with God. He tended to repeat his major points because, as he told Ruby afterward, he wanted to make sure nobody missed them. It was absolutely impossible not to like Malcolm X.

The revolutionary laughter he so admired in *Purlie Victorious* seemed to puzzle others. The question the play asked, according to one critic, represented its final test: Could black folks and white folks sit side by side in the same theater, and laugh at a play that poked fun at both sides of American racism? We believed that it could and should be done, but white Broadway thought otherwise. We thought that the audience that had had such a long and passionate love affair with *A Raisin in the Sun* would surely take to us, but it was not so. The regular Broadway audience—the mostly white carriage trade—was not comfortable in the presence of such raucous laughter.

At the suggestion of Sylvester Leaks and John Henrik Clarke, we turned specifically to our own people, the Negro audience, and they responded. Their trade alone kept us afloat for several months, where otherwise we would have been forced to close. For a while, there were rumors that the play might win a Pulitzer Prize, but that was not to be. So, after eight months, sometimes running at a loss, we were forced to close. But in short order, the entire production was on its way to Chicago.

Although *Purlie Victorious* hadn't made a dime on Broadway, what happened in Chicago caused investors to take a second look.

The original booking was for two weeks at the Edgewater Beach Hotel, but business was so good, they moved us to the Civic Theatre, where we stayed for two months. The question arose: Why not send Ruby and Ossie on a national tour?

Ossie and Ruby were more than willing, and the money was already in place. Raymond League, a young man we had met in Chicago, gave up his public relations job and moved to New York to set the wheels in motion. Things went swimmingly until we had to face one question: What to do with the children? Nora was eleven years old; Guy was nine; and LaVerne, the baby, at age five, was ready to register and enter kindergarten at Graham, the grade school in Mount Vernon. What to do with the children?

There were options, of course. We were not the only people in show business faced with this challenge. First, we could hire a tutor and take them on the road with us. Can you imagine anything more awkward? Or, we could have hired somebody to stay home with them and act as surrogate parents until the tour was over, a year or two down the road. Or—and this was the one we chose—we could forget about the tour and all the money and the honors it would bring, and take care of our own children as parents are supposed to do. That was that. We walked away from our great opportunity, *Purlie Victorious,* and never looked back. But there was Otto Preminger waiting to come to our rescue.

I first met Otto Preminger on Irv Kupcinet's TV talk show out in Chicago while we were doing *Purlie Victorious.* The topic of the show was Malcolm X, and I was surprised at Preminger's open and perceptive attitude. He seemed to have given the subject considerable thought. In his opinion, Malcolm was not a terrorist or a hate-monger, merely out to upset the white community. Rather, he saw him as a revolutionary who happened to be black, and Preminger seemed not only to respect Malcolm, but also to admire him.

When asked his response to Malcolm's description of the white, blue-eyed devil, Preminger brushed it off as pure sophomoric nonsense. It didn't scare him at all. When my turn came, I talked about our show, *Purlie Victorious,* in which Kupcinet was a heavy investor, and I hardly mentioned Malcolm. But I didn't forget Otto Preminger, and it seems he didn't forget me. Later, back in New York, I got a call from Columbia Pictures asking me to come downtown and audition for a film, *The Cardinal.* The producer and director turned out to be Otto Preminger. He offered me the part of the Negro Catholic priest, with a parish in Louisiana, who was having trouble with the Klan. The film was to be shot in Rome around Easter time and that turned out to be good news for the Davis family.

My first day before the camera was in an interior scene where Father Fermoyle is to introduce me to the papal secretary. Fermoyle was being played by Tom Tryon, whom I had only met that very day. We were seated, Tom and I, in front of the secretary's desk, both of us dressed in priestly vestments. I noticed as we were waiting for the camera to roll that under his robe, Tom was trembling violently. I thought he was ill, got to my feet, and asked if I should call the director.

He snatched me back down into the chair and whispered as a man will do when he's deathly afraid, "Please, please, please. I don't want Mr. Preminger to know. I'll be all right!" He pulled his legs tightly together until his knees stopped trembling. When the scene was over, he apologized and confessed that being near Otto always affected him that way.

I had heard stories about other actors who felt the same way— scared to death of Otto Preminger. Yes, Otto could be awful. I saw him lose his temper one night at a church full of Italian extras who had had a little too much wine for dinner, and giggled during that hallowed moment when Father Fermoyle was being elevated to cardinal. Otto cursed them for their boisterous, disrespectful behavior in English with a heavy German accent that was then translated into Italian by the local assistant director, where something was evidently lost. The harder Otto cursed—and he cursed until he gagged and had to sit down—the louder the extras laughed.

Otto never treated me that way, however. Rather, for some reason, he went out of his way to be truly gracious to me and to my family. We remained friends until he died.

Much of the film actor's job is waiting to be called. Rome was no different. Ruby and I and the family stayed at the Hotel Albergo. The hotel was small, but neat, clean, comfortable, and the meals were good. Nobody else from the company was there, but that didn't matter. Otto Preminger himself had called and spoken to the manager; they treated us like people of great importance.

Usually, a car would pick me up early in the morning and speed me to the set, and Ruby, Nora, Guy, and LaVerne would have Rome all to themselves. But sometimes the car would be delayed till late in the morning. Everybody at the hotel thought I was really a priest.

One day while I was waiting, already dressed in my priestly garb, Ruby and I decided to bring the family downstairs and have our breakfast. The sight of a Catholic priest openly parading a wife and children was too much. Everything came to a stop as the other patrons stopped and stared. At first, I hadn't the slightest idea what the furor was all about until the hotel manager explained, both to me and for the benefit of the other residents, that I wasn't a real priest; I was only an actor.

On another occasion when I had to wait, Ruby and I were in the lobby with the children. By now, everybody was in on the joke and they used to tease us. I was sitting in the lobby when suddenly I heard a voice, a voice from out of the past, and to this very day, I can't explain why—I started to tremble.

The voice was Southern, white, angry, superior, female, condescending, and full of complaint. I never turned to see who was speaking; somehow I didn't dare. Suddenly I was sitting there short of breath and sweating. Ruby, alarmed, asked me what was the matter. I couldn't tell her. I didn't know myself. After a while, the encounter at the reception desk was over. The voice had disappeared and I was myself again. But Ruby kept pressuring me, wanting to know what was wrong. My car arrived and I was glad that I had to go to work. It gave me an entire day to try to figure out what had happened to me.

Sure, I know the game of nigger and how to play it. Many a time from infancy, I suppose, I have played it in self-defense. It is a game in which, to make the white folks happy, you deploy yourself as something less than a man; rather, you play the fool, or a bumbling clown, an incompetent, quite incapable of taking care of yourself. It's a game that denies us power, then uses our powerlessness as proof that we are inferior and in no way to be considered a threat. It is a role such as any competent actor might play while the curtain is up and the necessity to survive is the issue at hand; but when the play is over and the curtain goes down, he puts the role aside, drops the accent, abandons the limp, removes the makeup, takes off the costume, and again becomes the man he always was.

The art of pretending to really be a nigger is much like that game. In the presence of the supremacist, you do what you have to do in order to survive: You grin, you shuffle, you lie. Most of all, you pretend in important ways to be helpless, absolutely incapable of standing on your own feet and making your own decisions, deferring always to the judgments of the supremacist, agreeing to let him—out of the kindness of his heart—do your thinking, and seeming to welcome his unsolicited supervision. This behavior confirms his need to believe that Negroes haven't got sense enough to survive on their own without him. But then, when the white man is gone, the way is clear, and the danger is passed, you're supposed to drop your obsequious behavior, take charge of your own affairs, and resume your role as a man in your own community. Or so I thought.

But suppose when the danger is over and the time comes to take the nigger off your face—like an actor removes his makeup—the face you then reveal is still a nigger? Suppose, like an onion, the more nigger you peel away, the more you find hiding underneath, layer after layer after layer, until finally suspicion becomes certainty: If ever you were a man, you're not one now, nor will you ever be again. Manhood was something you bartered away for peanut brittle, and some friendly pats

(301)

on the head at the jailhouse in Waycross, Georgia. . . . Maybe it was impossible to play at being a nigger without in the end becoming the nigger you played.

I mean, here I was, safe and sound in the bosom of my family, thousands of miles away from segregation and lynching and the Ku Klux Klan, yet the sound of a woman's accent—a woman who didn't even know I was there in the lobby—was enough to make me panic.

Paul Laurence Dunbar was right when he wrote: "We Wear the Mask." What he didn't say was that, in turn, The Mask Wears Us!

RUBY: The house in Mount Vernon had seemed spacious compared with our rooms in the Bronx. We needed the space because Ossie's mother was coming to live with us and Guy had to have his own room now. Even so, we clearly needed more space for separate rooms for the children, for Mama, for an office for Ossie, some private space for me, and space for all the books we had already begun to accumulate.

My friend Juanita came regularly to help me find another house. She was key in helping me to decide on an old house almost as big as hers, and situated on one and two-thirds acres in New Rochelle. It had been unoccupied for more than a year and was in need of much remodeling. We became excited by the possibilities. Juanita wouldn't hear of such talk about not being able to afford the upkeep.

"Oh, Ruby. You're going to need this house." She helped me gain the confidence to tell Ossie this was the house I wanted. Ossie offered no objections and expressed no concerns. He approved the choice. He knew I loved fireplaces, which we certainly did not have in Mount Vernon. This place had four. We needed them, too, because it turned out to be a big, drafty house, on one of the coldest hills in New Rochelle. The original papers for the house had been lost in a fire at city hall, but we learned that the house was about seventy years old.

An acquaintance who had heard about our impending move called to warn us against it. "Why?" I asked.

"We'd like to see you move into the Wykagyl area, where there aren't any black families," she replied. "The area you've chosen is great, but it's already well integrated."

"I want my children to feel safe. I want to feel safe. I'm away so much, I want to be friends with my neighbors. I don't want to be tolerated, on my best behavior, always seeking my neighbor's approval. I want to be able to knock on a door, assured that my neighbor would more likely welcome any one of the family. Or if I should need help . . ." On and on I babbled. "I admire the pioneers who risk so much in the process of integration, but I cannot break that ice. I realize the sacrifice in services and facilities, the discrepancy in tax dollars spent, but we'll just have to struggle harder where we are. Thanks, but no thanks. We just don't choose to struggle on this front."

We kept the house in Mount Vernon, and rented the three apartments. At Nora's suggestion, we chose a holiday, February 22, 1963, to move to our new old house. Mama, Ossie's mother, cooked our first meal in the fireplace because the kitchen was being remodeled.

CHAPTER 29

Marches, Movements, and Martyrs

OSSIE: The March on Washington in 1963 was very clear about its two objectives: jobs and freedom. The two belonged to one another. It is, of course, much nobler, more romantic, and more glamorous to suffer, bleed, and die for freedom than it is for a job, but jobs can feed a family, and freedom to starve was not what we had in mind. The right to be free was established in the Thirteenth, Fourteenth, and Fifteenth Amendments to the Constitution. And even though the right to a job was not protected by the Constitution, we felt it should be. Hence the final title for the grand convocation at the Lincoln Memorial: The March on Washington for Jobs and Freedom.

On the day of the march, August, 28, 1963, the people began to assemble with the dawn at the foot of the Washington Monument. Our assignment, handed to us the night before by Bayard Rustin, the man who put the march together, was to emcee the entertainment—Pete Seeger; Peter, Paul, and Mary; and Odetta—until it was time to march to the Lincoln Memorial, where the program was to be held.

It was easy to know by the way the crowds of people seemed to materialize out of nowhere that the march would be tremendous. A sense of We, the People was rapidly gathering steam right there before us. You could see it in the thousands of upturned faces; you could feel it in your pulse and in the rising waves of excitement and applause from the multiplying crowds. Somebody passed me a note and asked me to announce: Dr. W.E.B. Du Bois, the undisputed father of the Struggle that brought us here, had died the previous night in Ghana, West Africa. I don't know whether I called for a moment of silence, or whether such a call was necessary, as we stood for a moment in all our thousands with bowed and thankful heads.

The plan had been that We, the People would gather at the foot of the Washington Monument and then, at the signal, march in our clustered glory along the mall to the Lincoln Memorial where the program proper was to be held. But the signal never came. All of a sudden, Ruby and I saw that the people were beginning to leave—the March on Washington for Jobs and Freedom, all by itself, was already under way. We abandoned the platform and fell in line. What happened then is history that every schoolchild knows.

What is not common knowledge is that Malcolm X was also there, pacing back and forth behind the scenes. It is easy to think of Malcolm and Martin as polar opposites, and in many ways, they were. But they understood each other's role in the Struggle and, I think, had a healthy, if distant respect for each other.

The euphoria that followed the great success of the March on Washington was well deserved. Two hundred fifty thousand people moved into and out of Washington, D.C., in perfect peace and harmony. The doomsayers' dire pronouncements that chaos, disorder, and even bloodshed would occur had not prevailed. The unfinished civil rights revolution had become the number one item on the national agenda and our efforts had put it there. After the march, the leaders of the movement were invited to the White House to meet with President Kennedy.

Martin's "I Have a Dream" speech was still ringing victoriously in all our ears. We all had a dream! But the dream was not to last. Nineteen days later, on a Sunday morning in Birmingham, Alabama, the South struck back: Four little girls were killed by a bomb placed in a church. And as if that wasn't tragedy enough, on November 22, 1963, President John F. Kennedy was killed in Dallas, Texas.

Then it was Lyndon Johnson's turn and we were a bit surprised. Johnson seized on the grief of a shocked, frightened, and guilty country and used it to political advantage. In 1964, the Civil Rights Act passed, and in 1965, the Voting Rights Act was passed. Then Johnson issued an executive order calling for for affirmative action to encourage and promote Negro business, and he declared a War on Poverty, instituting programs, reminiscent of FDR's New Deal, for rebuilding our cities, guaranteeing jobs—the kinds of jobs we desperately needed—for everybody for years to come. The call for jobs and freedom that had brought us to Washington in 1963 had finally been answered. Or so it seemed for one brief, shining moment. Johnson had seized the initiative and was ahead of the pack running the ball down the field.

But then came Vietnam, and little by little, the dream turned into a nightmare.

RUBY: August 28, 1963, was one of America's great days—everything seemed possible. Artists were there in force. Harry Belafonte, Lena Horne, Sidney Poitier, John O. Killens, Mahalia Jackson, Marlon Brando, Burt Lancaster—just to name a few. Martin Luther King had gone out of his way to make us welcome.

This time was different from the first time I had "marched on Washington." In 1957, on the third anniversary of the *Brown* decision, I had joined a prayer pilgrimage of about twenty-seven thousand people. It wasn't large, but it gave momentum to the voting rights initiative, and people came from all over the country. Ossie was working and had to miss it, so I went by myself.

A group of us artists, actors, and singers took the train from Penn Station and traveled down together. As I recall, this was the first time that Sammy Davis Jr. was among us. He was asleep for most of the trip down, but before we reached D.C., we got a chance to talk, mostly about why it was so important for people like us in show business to take part in demonstrations and so forth. He was well informed and genuinely concerned.

The labor leader A. Philip Randolph and Roy Wilkins of the NAACP had organized the program, and had invited Dr. King to speak. I thought he looked so young, but he was impressive as he led the battle cry, "Give Us the Ballot!"

We entertainers weren't among the leaders. We stood with the rest of the crowd—people from black schools and churches, labor unions, sororities and fraternities—determined to gain our civil rights. We wanted to join hands with others. Unity and strength mattered a great deal.

Six years later, with ten times as many people present, Martin and the planners of the March in '63 proved that the artists indeed had a special place in the Struggle. We were out front, a part of the program.

To recall is sometimes painful, but it had to be the fall of 1964, a few months after Malcolm returned from Mecca, that M. S. Handler of *The New York Times* hosted a gathering of a few friends for him, and we went. He'd changed, yes. He'd met many Muslims who were white, and he'd let go of his idea that all whites were "blue-eyed devils." He made it clear, though, that his focus on justice for black people had not changed. He would review his alliances, formulate a program, and continue in the Struggle.

It had to be the fall because Lorraine was still with us. She hadn't gone to the hospital that final time until late 1964.

In a recent conversation I had with Juanita, she remembered that it was in August, late summer, 1964. During those radical and revolutionary times, Juanita and I often talked about what we as a group needed to do. She was also an activist and often gave fund-raisers at her home in Pleasantville. We liked her place because it was big, but not easily accessible to the uninvited.

The two of us talked about organizing a summit where all the prominent black leaders in the Struggle could meet in an informal atmosphere, talk, map strategy without press participation, without cameras—let down our hair. We made the arrangements and carefully invited the possible participants. There was Dorothy Height, Whitney Young, Malcolm, King, Lorraine Hansberry, Roy Wilkins, A. Philip Randolph, Ossie, and me. Sidney came later. Jean and Gladys, a friend who helped Juanita on special occasions, prepared the food and the refreshments.

Malcolm was the first to arrive. He was smiling as he unfolded his long, lean body from the car. A shotgun stretched casually under the rear window in plain sight. Martin couldn't come. He was in jail. He sent someone.

There was an uneasy feeling as we gathered. No agenda had been set. Juanita and I had worked up a few introductory remarks. They weren't necessary. The discussion took off easily and enthusiastically, as if each person present had been planning such an occasion. It was decided that it was necessary to formulate a Declaration of Human Rights for Black Americans. It was suggested that Malcolm go to certain African heads of state to make certain that we could count on their support, if such a document were formulated. Could the gathering here become the nucleus of a small organization, working behind the scenes without publicity and fanfare, that would develop a strategy for accomplishing and securing civil rights for blacks and for all Americans? We began making preparations.

I remember our last visit with Malcolm. He didn't come in the front door; he came in the side entrance near the kitchen. He spent the time in the dining room, sitting in a chair that he placed against a wall that faced a door on one side and a window on an adjacent wall. We had eagerly anticipated the visit. I'd been thinking much about recent events following President Kennedy's assassination, Malcolm's remarks about the death, and threats against Malcolm's life. Elijah Muhammad had silenced him for speaking to the press against his orders. I felt the very real danger surrounding him. During the visit, I suggested places where he could go into hiding. My secret wall loomed in my mind as a very real possibility.

We talked for about an hour; then I asked Ossie to excuse himself for a minute. We went upstairs to our bedroom where I asked Ossie about the wisdom of suggesting my hiding place, should it become necessary.

"No, no, no," Ossie replied adamantly. "Malcolm could never hide behind a wall. Please, don't mention such a thing." I then told him about the $5,000 I had squirreled away. Surprised, but pleased at the prospect, he said, "Yes. Offer it."

I went to get the cash. It wasn't there. It had been several years since I had hidden the money. Oh, yes. I remembered I'd moved it. That place had not seemed secure anymore. I pulled the new spot apart. It wasn't there, either. "Please, Ossie, stay down with Malcolm. I'm sure I'll find it, I'm sure." Scurry, scurry, scramble, scramble, scramble—like a pack rat—the sound of my own activity driving me to distraction. I can't find the escape funds.

What the hell—where the hell did I put them? I rush back downstairs, thinking I'll have to send a package. I'll ask Malcolm where to send it, how to send it. No. A check won't do. I don't believe there's $5,000 in the account.

I get downstairs, Malcolm is at the side door, about to leave. He and Ossie embrace. He pecks my cheek. He's saying good-bye. I know. I'll get it to my brother, who lives near Malcolm. They're friends. Take care, Malcolm. Be careful, my brother. He's across the yard and gone. I love you, my brother. All the years of planning, just for such times as this, and I can't find the funds. He's gone. Out into the danger. Into the enemy camp without the funds.

Two days later, it came clearly to my mind, the marvelously logical location of the emergency money. My father had given me his mother's last pair of boots, and I had hidden the $5,000 in one of them. "Running money," I had called it.

That experience reinforced in my consciousness the futility of worrying in advance. The bombs don't drop on people who own bomb shelters, and if they do, they are dining in a restaurant that gets hit. Be sure to carry matches, and you'll find yourself drowned. Your bottles with the good water that you set aside for the time when the reservoir gets polluted, or when you find yourself parched in a desert, are available only in the mind's eye. I've thrown out the grain because the bugs got to it, the honey got hard, the canned goods swelled up, and the batteries corroded in their battery packs. Even little crawlies got into the dried fruit and vegetable capsules. Bugs, of course, if necessary, could be consumed for protein. I gave away my Chinese kerosene stove for cooking. If it's "the fire next time," maybe a little spark will land so you can get the grits cooked. If I'm lucky, the world won't come to an end without my being able to locate the pocketbook with the credit cards and driver's license for identification. If it's some tribe of white folks, or any other kind of mad folks coming at you—not much action here, but you could try to get your rocks, or your rifles, pitch or shoot and run like hell.

Seriously, I've learned this about preparation for disaster, that except for a tested working relationship with Divine Spirit, there is very little else. We've got to remember and hold on to the thought. "Vengeance is mine," saith the Lord. I find that comforting, given today's crop of enemies. More and more they are not readily identifiable. They don't always wear uniforms and they could be anybody. I'm willing to be patient and wait on the Lord, but I sure hope I can witness the punishments and retribution—even if only through a keyhole.

In January and February of 1965, only months after our summit, death strutted through our ranks, and plucked first Lorraine, who died of cancer; and then Malcolm was shot. It was October of that same year that Gladys, my birth mother, died.

OSSIE: The last time we saw Malcolm, he came to our house in New Rochelle, and he came alone. He sat across from Ruby and me in the dining room with his back to the wall, and he talked. He didn't come for advice, he didn't come for sympathy or consolation, he didn't come to listen, he came to talk. Quietly, reflectively, in his heart's own way, this talk bonded him to us forever. Very simple, very clear—a man who at last could put himself and his time into perspective. He spoke of Elijah Muhammad but without rancor.

Malcolm at the end was a hunted and a haunted man, running, running, running for his life; his home firebombed, his wife and his children stranded in Queens at Edward's house. Still, he was not deterred from his main objective: to bridge the gap between him and the rest of the civil rights movement with an organization that would give him a broader base from which to operate, the details of which he planned to unveil that Sunday afternoon at the Audubon Ballroom, where he was assassinated.

Malcolm had invited us to the Audubon that day, but we had a previous commitment downtown and had left the children in Harlem with Mother. When we returned to pick them up, the kids told us that something had happened to Malcolm. We turned on the television as a bulletin interrupted the ballet. Malcolm X was dead—shot down in front of Betty and the children. We were stunned and deeply, deeply saddened. That night, we drove back into Harlem and walked the streets, mingling, talking with the crowds about Malcolm's death and what it meant to black people.

The situation was hostile and explosive. To make matters worse, on Tuesday, the mosque on 116th Street was firebombed, after which a contingent of white, helmeted police in riot gear was bussed into Harlem every morning to patrol the streets. Fear and sorrow were mixed with a desire to give Malcolm a decent funeral, if we could.

Percy Sutton, Malcolm's friend and lawyer, went from church to church trying to secure a place for Malcolm's funeral, but most of them said no—it was too dangerous. Finally, Bishop Childs offered his small church on Amsterdam Avenue.

Sylvester Leaks, speaking for Percy Sutton and Malcolm's family, asked me to give the eulogy, and I asked him why . . . "Why me?" The answer was that Ruby and I were widely known to have been among Malcolm's earliest friends and supporters. Also, I was a man with whom nobody in this shooting argument could quarrel. Ruby and I were honored to accept.

Tension continued to build in Harlem, and on Friday night before the funeral, we received a call from Edward suggesting that maybe we had better stay away from the funeral. Ruby and I stayed up late talking things over—not about whether or not we would go—only about what to do with the children.

Saturday wasn't much of a day, as I remember, no sunshine at all. The funeral was at ten o'clock. We drove in early, parked on a side street, and went inside the Faith Memorial Chapel. Ruby and I sat in the pulpit. Our job was to read the messages that were pouring in.

At the proper time, I arose to give the eulogy, trying to be simple, plain, honest, and sincere, saying by way of farewell what, in my heart, I believed Harlem wanted me to say. Afterward we followed him to the cemetery where the professional gravediggers were waiting. We said no, and took their shovels from them. Malcolm was ours, and if he had to be buried, we would do it.

RUBY: The sixties was a time when death put on red and blood flowed all over our consciousness, haunted our dreams, threatened our sanity, smeared the great documents. We looked over at Asia, saw the war coming, and looked away. It could only confuse the issues, bankrupt the resolve of the would-be righteous. We marched on Washington for jobs and freedom. But where were the jobs to come from? Nobody suggested the specifics. Lyndon Johnson said he would take care of all the specifics, and we believed him.

He stood at the rostrum at Howard University, looked straight into the camera, and said, "We shall overcome," which were the words of our theme song, and we believed him. He went to the University of Michigan and called for a War on Poverty; but then he found another war in Vietnam, and Lyndon loved that war more than he loved colored people. And we still believed him.

We got the freedom side of it, the Civil Rights Act of 1964, the Voting Rights Act of 1965, his call for affirmative action—but where were the jobs to back the whole thing up? By the time we peeped his hole card, and Martin called his bluff, it was too late. A new day was born but it couldn't be aborted, and the demons were smarter. They took the lid off the pot, looked at the stew that history had been making, and said no, no, no. Not freedom. Not now. And the peashooters started popping and lopping off heads. And the greedy took the new technologies, locked arms, threw goopher dust up the nostrils of the ba-a-d young people to cool down the clamor, neutralize the discontent, fry the spirit of the reformers, and tighten the grip on the globe to prepare it for the new march—this time, to the order of the global market billionaires. And you knew, by the way we looked at each other, that black folks had lost again.

As actors, you *gotta* perform in a Freedom Riders benefit concert at Scarsdale High School, even if the American Legion won't let them use the facilities to benefit communism. With the Negro American Labor

Council, CORE, and the Committee for the Employment of Negro Performers in 1963, you *had to* picket the hit shows on Broadway—*How to Succeed in Business Without Really Trying* and *Subways Are for Sleeping*. In television, it was shameful that at that time there were virtually no blacks on the soap operas, despite the fact that they were heavily viewed by blacks. With that same committee, at the Judson Memorial Church, Ossie *had* to call upon black Americans to fight discrimination in the industry with boycotts.

Four little girls were killed in Birmingham, Alabama, and the Association for Artists for Freedom was formed. James Baldwin, John O. Killens, Clarence Jones, Ossie, me, and others joined hands and hearts to propose a Christmas boycott to protest the Birmingham church bombing, and to make "our Christmas gifts contribution to civil rights organizations, and other institutions working to build and strengthen the moral and religious fiber of our nation." We *had to*.

When Malcolm was killed, Juanita Poitier, Betty Lomax, Tina Sattin, Sylvia Woods (of the famous Harlem restaurant Sylvia's), Delores Harvey, and I had to form the Concerned Mothers to raise funds for a house for Betty Shabazz and the children. Dr. Billy Taylor, Nina Simone, Michael Olatunji, and others had to participate in fund-raising concerts. There was no question of alternatives.

The four-century war against discrimination feels eternal. Is there a time in life when it will be won? I believe so. This costly, dangerous tool of separation hurts everybody. It's like a poisonous snake wrapping around us body and soul, and only the Struggle keeps it from tightening its coils in a death squeeze.

The 1960s were a busy time, and besides the recognizable employment, we were dashing around the country on the "Odd Job Circuit" with our notebooks, meeting all kinds of people, and sharing, collecting, and reading new and old literature; and when we couldn't find exactly what we wanted, we wrote original material.

I made many guest appearances on various television series and in 1965 landed two roles played in repertory at the American Shakespeare Festival in Stratford, Connecticut: Cordelia with Morris Carnovsky in *King Lear* and Kate in *The Taming of the Shrew*, which made the cover of *Jet* magazine because it was the first time a black actress appeared in a major role there. In the summer of 1966, at the Ypsilanti Greek Theater Festival in Michigan, I appeared in Euripides' *The Oresteia* with Dame Judith Anderson, as well as with Bert Lahr in *The Birds* by Sophocles. Back home that same year, I did *The Incident,* a film with Brock Peters, Martin Sheen (his first, I think), Tony Musante, Beau Bridges, and Ed McMahon. Despite the hectic pace, certainly not the rule, going from job to job, the Struggle continued, and we continued to play our parts within it.

CHAPTER 30

Sex Comes out of the Closet

OSSIE: As the civil rights movement was creating revolution in the political and social spheres, another revolution was taking place, creating a very wide change of values; it was called the sexual revolution. Ruby and I are certainly not experts on human sexual behavior. We are normal man and wife, I suppose, which means we married for sex as much as for love. Ruby—my beloved, my betrothed, and finally my wife—was, and still is, my sex object—just like yawning nature intended—of whom I thought I would never get my fill! So it is with all people, more or less, who are in love. But as everyone knows, sex, even at full blast, is not enough to sustain two blazing, blinding appetites, no matter how marvelous and ethereal it appears at the very beginning. It is no substitute for food and rent and work and a weekly paycheck, which define the world in which two lovers must live.

No. Man does not live by bread, or love—and certainly not sex—alone. All honeymoons must finally be abandoned, as other things come knocking at the bedroom door.

Ruby and Ossie are as average as bread and water, not pioneers, or brave explorers of new connubial territory, or defiant rebels who have found something together that makes the two of us special. Our limits were the limits of tradition: one man, one woman, one marriage, forever and ever. That we should now be saluted for spending fifty years together is a sign of how the times—not we—have really changed.

That we arrived at fifty years together is due as much to luck as to love, and a talent for knowing, when we stumble, where to fall, and how to get up again. We two scavenged among the changes thrown up by the sexual revolution that swept across the country, to find what suited us, and what could be left alone.

On this we can all agree: Marriage is an institution in serious need of repair, but we can't fix it by fiat or decree. Change, to be healthy, must be preceded by a time of tasting and testing—of trying things on for size. We, and some of our peers, saw that a fundamental part of the revolution in which the world was engaged also brought with it a new dispensation between man and woman, rushing into being right in front of our eyes, changing the world forever in its wake. There came the pill and other forms of contraception; altered attitudes toward the sex act itself espoused from the point of view of the scientist as against the moralist; and the changing status of women, who, under the First Amendment and the cult of the individual, began to fight for an orgasm equal to that of the male. All this, plus the newly legal availability of hard-core porn, not only on the newsstands and the top shelves of the local library, but also right up there on the screen larger than life, forcing everybody—lovers, husbands and wives and parents, the police, the church, and the state—up against the same concupiscent wall.

Good conversation is often a testing ground for new ideas—ideas that are carried straight from the breakfast table into direct action. That's how it was with us.

Love, sex, marriage, children, and home had finally produced a family—a family that was stable and secure. And that was as good a place as any to stand and fight. Thou shalt not abandon the family, nor the family abandon thee! Once Ruby and I understood and accepted this as the new criterion, the rest was easy.

But not as easy—not really—as it sounds. It was a proposition not without risks, and certainly not without precedent. We had to work the whole thing out between the two of us. That took both time and patience.

Our work often took us away from each other, and put us in intimate contact with very attractive people for long periods. I had been "attracted" several times over the years, but not involved, and I felt sure that Ruby, working with some very handsome men, must have had the same kind of feelings. Both of us seemed to know how to deal with temptation. We had been married about fifteen years and had every intention of staying that way. Like many other people, I'm sure, we discussed the nature of marriage from time to time, what it was and what it wasn't—especially in the light of the current revolution—and what constituted proper behavior for a husband and a wife.

It occurred to us, from observation and from reasoning, that extramarital sex was not what really destroyed marriages, but rather the lies and deception that invariably accompanied it—that was the culprit. So we decided to give ourselves permission to sleep with other partners if we wished—as long as what we did was honest as well as private, and that neither of us exposed the family to scandal or disease. We had to be discreet and, if the word can be apt, honorable in our behavior, both to ourselves, to whomever else might be involved, and most of all, to the family. And for the most part, we were.

RUBY: Remember, Ossie, you once said to me, "The only way to truly own something is first to let it go?" I don't remember which philosopher you were quoting, but it sounded deep.

OSSIE: It was deep, and I was quoting myself. But how does this apply to sex and marriage?

RUBY: Well, I had been accusing you quite a while of paying too much attention to this girl—this grieving widow—and it took a long time for the anger—jealousy, I suppose—to claim my tongue, but when it did, it was mean—I mean *mean*. After the tirade, I was ashamed and wished I could have stuffed all that venom back where it came from, or better yet, have destroyed it.

OSSIE: She was a friend, and she was in trouble. I stumbled into the problem, and, frankly, didn't know how to back out.

RUBY: You could have introduced me to the heifer—

OSSIE: Heifer? Ruby, how can you call her a heifer, she was a friend.

RUBY: A friend sometimes turns into a heifer—and I could have straightened her out, because sometimes that "damsel in distress" program can lead to complications that a mere man cannot even remotely handle.

OSSIE: How about that night you danced with my old Army buddy—laughing and pouring champagne in his glass as if only the two of you were on the premises?

RUBY: You didn't want to dance and I did, and he was so—look, you're changing the subject, just like you always do.

OSSIE: Changing the subject? He was about as subtle as a truck. Kept his big eyes glued on you. Lucky for the two of you that I'm not a jealous man.

~   ~   ~

RUBY: It's true. Deep down, I don't believe Ossie is jealous. But I am. The world is full of beautiful people, and it is delusional to think you're the only person in the world to find your mate attractive. Ossie is outgoing, gregarious, with a good sense of humor, and a vibrant respect and appreciation for women. It was easy to imagine that—as enthusiastic as he always was—he might be going overboard with one of the ladies, a possibility I had taught myself to live with. But his husbandship was solid and responsible, and he never gave me serious cause to regret or to complain.

On top of that, ideas about sex, marriage, and family—as we were constantly discussing at the breakfast table—were changing rapidly. Extramarital sex was almost becoming the norm. The notions of couples just living together, having babies out of wedlock, deliberately choosing to be single parents, were no longer shocking to me. We found ourselves tolerating behavior from our children that wouldn't have been so easily tolerated when we got married.

Ossie has a sure sense of himself. Feelings of insecurity as a woman would attack me from time to time, however, and jealous suspicions would spoil my peace of mind and rob me of my sleep. He says it was my idea that we should free each other from the vows of "keep you only unto him/her as long as you both shall live," allowing ourselves to have other partners if we so desired. Maybe it was. I only remember being determined not to be the fence blocking his view of the greener-looking grass on the other side. We talked about people we knew who had broken up, and we talked about not wanting to lie and cheat and tear up our heads longing for closer but forbidden contact with other people.

At first I told myself that this extramarital "arrangement" would, at least, lessen the temptation to be suspicious and jealous. And when I asked Ossie, "What happens if you really fall in love with this other somebody you're messing around with?" He answered with a question, "If that should happen to you and you ran off with another man, I wouldn't care, as long as you let me come with you. Would you do that for me?"

He was half laughing when he said it, and maybe he was bragging in his arrogance, but I believed him. It was his way of stating—bottom line—that our marriage was secure—that neither of us would be willing to let go of the other, no matter what. Yes, I finally agreed—the only way to really hold on to something is first to let it go.

Soon after our arrangement, Ossie got a job in *The Hill,* a Sidney Lumet film, starring Sean Connery, being shot in England and in Spain, and was away for two months. He wrote often, upbeat, inspiring, naughty letters full of news designed to keep me laughing—but stimulating, too. I kept busy, and tried to keep my mind off the possibilities suggested by marital freedom with a husband so far away for so long. I didn't try hard enough, however.

I never got the feeling that I was having an affair. It seemed more like a role in a play I could be rehearsing—the "other woman," heifer, hussy, adventurer—so much more exciting than the wide-eyed, nice little wifey at home type (closer to what I really was) or the drudge behind the ironing board of life praying for her man to do right (something like Ruth in *Raisin*). Here I was busting out like those "whores" Mother used to accuse Daddy of. It really didn't seem like me at all, not at first. Somebody else was walking around in my skin.

He was a classical musician, living with his wife and two children in the Bronx. He made most of his living playing weekend gigs and recording sessions with small jazz groups and studio bands. Ossie had known him in the Army, and introduced us one night when he came backstage after catching us in *Purlie Victorious*. He was among those friends who used to visit us when we first moved to New Rochelle, where he had relatives.

He wasn't exactly shy, but he didn't talk much. Always helpful, always polite. He had good taste in art and seemed honestly impressed when I showed him some sketches I had done. About as tall as Ossie, he had graying hair and warm friendly eyes. I liked him very much, and I knew soon after we met that he liked me. Ossie noticed it, too, and the three of us became friends. He was an honest and open person we could depend on, especially when Ossie was away.

One day I found myself reading part of a letter Ossie had written me from Spain, in which he touched on the possibilities for him of our "arrangement," and thanked me for agreeing to it. When I began babbling an explanation of the "arrangement" to this man, it occurred to me that I was issuing an invitation. He interrupted me to say how envious he was of the way things were between Ossie and me, and how he wished—Without completing the thought, he stuttered an apology, confessing how long he had loved and wanted me.

In my immediate need to let go of the demons of fear, insecurity, and doubt about the "arrangement" with Ossie, I found it easy to push aside common sense.

I am not a musician, but I love music. I used to read it fairly well and would spend hours at the piano trying to master compositions that I'd studied as a child. I used to practice when the children were in bed, and when no one was around to hear the mistakes and endless repetitions. After he discovered my hidden hobby, he began to work with me occasionally. I appreciated his patience and encouragement. Music, however, wasn't the only thing we began to share.

There was a certain feeling of guilt and shame that followed the times we were together. I found I had to lie anyway, not to Ossie, but to him. I couldn't for the life of me say what I was feeling in the aftermath. "Oh, please, I like you, yes. We've had a good time, but for God's sake, man, go away now and leave me alone."

I missed the spirit, the intelligence, the knowledge, the conversation, and most of all, I couldn't laugh with him. I couldn't admit that I was using him for personal gratification and—as I later realized—for revenge against Ossie for saying yes to the "arrangement." I couldn't say, "Please don't love me! You can't leave your wife and children. Don't you even think it."

The rendezvous was over. I knew that whatever adultery was, it wasn't freedom. His marriage had been troubled for many years. He wanted comfort, advice, someone to talk to. But where there are great needs, rejection—however packaged—can be devastating. I, too, have needs. I need somebody to laugh with, to share values and life commitments, and to grow old together with. I need Ossie, for God's sake.

OSSIE: She was a professional nurse who went with the cast and crew to Almeria, Spain, where we were filming *The Hill,* and I had learned to like her very much. She was English, as was everybody else on the shoot except Sidney Lumet, the director, and me. She was not much taller than Ruby, a brunette, well read, with a marvelous sense of humor. She liked me, too. She was single and free and there was nothing to stop us from being intimate but the fact that we were the kind of people we were. Five weeks we were in Almeria, growing closer together, and by the time we got back to England to work in the studios there, we knew that our mutual attraction was more than casual.

She came to dinner with me in my hotel in London and afterward we went up to my room to discuss our options. Not wanting her to think for a moment that I was just another philandering husband, I felt impelled to tell her about the openness and freedom in our marriage; that though Ruby and I had agreed that we were free to sleep in other beds, we felt duty-bound to be considerate of other people's feelings. Nervous people talk too much, and so with us. We filled the night with civilized conversation. She deeply admired my candor, and said more times than once that Ruby must be an extraordinary woman.

On we went, talking, talking, talking—meanwhile, our passion slowly leaked away. Neither of us knew exactly how to crank it up again, get to the point, and take advantage of this freedom I thought I had. Ultimately nothing was left between us but awkwardness—and a clumsy silence that finally tied our tongues. We managed, not the kiss of fire that I had been expecting, but a small show business peck upon the cheek. She smiled, I kissed her hand, and then she left.

A short while later, Ruby joined me in London, and we moved from my hotel into an apartment lent to the two of us by Eslanda, Paul Robeson's wife. Spacious, magnificent, with many a work of precious African art and sculpture. In the living room was a huge chair, carved splendidly from some exotic African wood. Every time I saw that chair, I was tempted to sit in it. But I knew I was not Paul Robeson, that my behind was not big enough or important enough—certainly not royal enough—to sit on the throne of the mighty. So I always managed to sit down somewhere else.

But I still felt attracted to this other woman. So I talked it over with Ruby and asked her to intercede on my behalf. Ruby did. She explained that whatever might happen would be all right. But this time, the lady said no. So, she had her feelings and I had mine, but never the twain did meet.

I never regretted that both of us said no. To the end, I remained appreciative of her friendship. Before we left, I wrote her a nice long letter. Though I was very fond of her, I never wrote her a sonnet.

RUBY: Sex can sometimes seem the most important thing in the world, especially when you're young.

OSSIE: I agree.

RUBY: Slip a notch or two in time, you'll be old, and it's still important. But answer the question: Was it worth it, or wasn't it?

OSSIE: Extramarital sex? It has its points, but not as a permanent arrangement—ultimately it's too dangerous. People can get hurt. Families destroyed, children ruined forever.

RUBY: Whatever you may have gained for the moment, there's a whole lot more that you can lose forever.

OSSIE: Lose? Like what? I don't think I lost—

RUBY: I did. I let parts of myself out that I can never call back in again. Good name, self-esteem, reputation. Somebody, not deeply connected in any other way, now knows too much of where I live—all the places, all the ways. You know what I mean?

OSSIE: Yeah, I think I do. But looking back, I'd say no matter what did or did not happen, we freed each other. And in doing that, we also freed ourselves. We turned each other loose and set great wheels in motion once again. I found myself having to compete with other men for my own wife's affection. It was a humbling, but also a stimulating experience. I'm glad we did it, but I am equally glad it's over. And what of it all is left? Memories, experience, and some minor pieces of erotica—sonnets, free verse, letters—exchanged between us, which I fear, being a prude and a puritan at heart, we'll really have to burn. And deservedly so. The important thing is that we paid our tribute to sex without having to lie to each other. And as for our children, and our grandchildren, and all our friends and peers who may think we betrayed them—we make no apology, and we don't have to lie to them, either. Sex is fine, but love is better. That's the most important part of being free.

In light of what we learned, is extramarital sex something we could recommend as a regular part of marriage? Not now . . . not anymore. Not since AIDS has entered the equation, and genital herpes, syphilis, and other venereal diseases, which, according to the latest reports, are on the verge of becoming epidemic, especially among the young. A new puritanism—even sexual abstinence except for married folks—may be indicated. The freedom to mingle and mate is now proscribed, not so much by the priest as by the surgeon general. Everything else sexually is now on hold.

~ ~ ~

Though I wisely managed to avoid adultery, my trip to England and to Spain was not without sin. During the five weeks we spent in Almeria, shooting exteriors, the little Spanish I knew made me a people's hero. The English are generous with their language, but they seldom bother to speak anybody else's. So most of the translating between the actors and the locals who worked on the set was left to me. If there was a problem, the people on the set would come to me and I was often able to straighten things out. The fact that I was the only black man on the film added to my celebrity. Word about my color and my facility with the language got out and about around the town.

A film always attracts curiosity seekers, so every day some of the locals would gather to watch us work. One day, I was told that the mayor of Almeria was visiting the set with his family, and had asked specifically to see me. He wanted to shake my hand. This posed me a quick dilemma. The year was 1964, Francisco Franco was still in power, and the mayor was an open and avowed fascist. I, Ossie Davis, with my knowledge of history, my hatred of dictatorship, my memories of the Loyalists, and of the Abraham Lincoln Brigade, shake hands with a fascist?

I felt like making a speech denouncing the mayor and all those like him for what they had done to freedom and democracy in their country. I didn't. I was brought into his presence. He said a few smiling words, welcoming me to the city. I didn't say a word, but I smiled right back. The same little grin perhaps that a little black boy had given his police patrons back in Waycross. I shook hands with the rest of the mayor's family and got rapidly back to the set, vowing that I would never tell anybody what a bloody, cowardly traitor I had been. I never told that story, and said to myself, I never shall. What would my grand-children think?

CHAPTER 31

In Control, but Still in Crisis

RUBY: I don't mind being second choice. The ability to find other choices, to create options, is a vital prerequisite for a good collaborator. I have the capacity to see more than one side of a subject, to weigh matters and make choices based on their value in relation to what's at stake.

Jules Dassin had come back from Paris to do a remake of the 1920s film *The Informer,* which had starred Victor McLaglen. With Paramount Pictures as the producers, he planned to adapt the original script for an all-black cast.

Ossie had agreed to meet with Jules to discuss the adaptation. Jules knew Ossie couldn't do it because he was about to do *The Scalphunters* in Mexico with Burt Lancaster, Shelley Winters, and Telly Savalas, but he wanted Ossie's input and opinion. Ossie suggested we both go to the meeting at Jules's quarters on Fifth Avenue in New York because we had already talked about the possibility that I might be helpful in coming up with concepts for the rewrites. I had wanted to try my hand at writing a screen adaptation for a long time. And I was pleased that Ossie had this kind of confidence in me.

At the meeting, we discussed the script's treatment of the Irish rebellion against the English and the ways it mirrored the black-versus-white struggle in the U.S.A. In black communities all over America, there were riots and social upheaval in response to the Vietnam War. We all sensed my enthusiasm for the subject and its particular relation to the black Struggle. We also were excited by Jules's awareness of the parallels, and the fact that he, as a white producer, wanted blacks to write the film. It was agreed that he would work with me in bringing an authentic sound to the language and to the feel of the events.

Five days a week, I went to the apartment where Jules lived with his wife, Melina Mercouri. After consultation with Jules, I was sequestered in a room and I began to write *Up Tight!*, the title we chose. He would describe the scene that had to be written, and after a time, depending on the complexity of the scene, I would deliver it to him, and begin work on another scene as he read and critiqued the previous one.

It was satisfying and surprising work. I learned something about myself. As a writer, I could deliver to order. It seemed easy. I could imagine scenarios quickly and in detail. My own involvement as a black woman, and as a human being in the Struggle, afforded me a wealth of people and experiences to draw on. If some detail needed to be altered, dropped, or substituted, I usually had several other options to suggest. I think Jules was pleased.

As the time to begin filming approached, he included me in the casting process. He talked about giving me a writing credit. I don't recall the details of our contractual arrangements. At any rate, Julian Mayfield, with whom I had collaborated in a rewrite of Ossie's play *Alice in Wonder,* was chosen to play the lead, Tank. It was also agreed that he would work with me on the script, as Jules was busy with other aspects of the shoot. Once again, our collaboration was a highly productive one. He said he had not known what a good writer I was. That pleased me enormously.

Jules cast me as Tank's girlfriend, Laurie. We began shooting in Cleveland, the city where I was born. It was an exciting company. The location was stunning in its reality. There was an enthusiasm in the community and the work was exceptional. Jules was a sensitive, active, committed, involved, dynamic director.

During the filming, Martin Luther King, Jr., was assassinated. Principal photography was almost complete. Immediately, Jules picked up the company and went to Memphis, Baltimore, and Atlanta to capture footage on the aftermath of the tragedy. He would work it into the film. Given the story's focus on revolution, Paramount wanted to pull the film so they could cut out any inciting, inflammatory images. Jules, however, quickly took the film to Paris to complete it, then brought it back when it was ready to be distributed.

It was by no means a slick evocation of revolution. I was most proud of having been a major part of the screenwriting effort, and deeply grateful to Jules for the opportunity to strengthen my faith in my unproven gifts as a writer.

∾ ∾ ∾

One of the reasons I will always cherish the city of Chicago is that there I met Dr. Alvenia Fulton, a naturopath and holistic practitioner. We were performing *Purlie Victorious* at the Edgewater Beach Hotel back in 1962 when the entire cast was invited to visit her store and have dinner in her home. She prepared an unusual, most tasteful meal. It wasn't until it was over that we realized that no meat had been served. The meat substitutes were delicious, fulfilling, and only a small part of the vegetable feast, topped off with a marvelous dessert and a truly believable coffee substitute.

That dinner was the beginning of a long relationship in which she changed my way of thinking about food. She not only showed me better ways to prepare and enjoy it, but also introduced me to the concept of food as medicine. She gave me a new respect for the miracle that is the human body and how better to care for it. She also taught and wrote about the miracle of fasting and cleansing. During the run of the play, she took several of us through a short fasting and cleansing program for the first time. At the end of it, I truly felt mentally sharper and more physically alive than I'd ever known I could feel.

Through the years, we remained in touch and she ministered to my needs as best she could long-distance. I improved the way I fed and cared for my family, and introduced her to as many people as I could.

Prominent among her friends and associates was Dick Gregory. Together, I believe, they worked on several projects, and she became one of the inspirations for his highly successful Bahamian Diet program.

Despite all that I respected about her work, I didn't live in Chicago, and I continued to see the kinds of doctors I'd known all my life. When I'd receive an analysis, I'd discuss it with Dr. Fulton, she'd make a recommendation based on diet, and suggest that I try it before embarking on the drug-based program. I was falling between two stools. There was Dr. Fulton, Alvenia, my friend, who was black, ancient, endowed with the wisdom of God and man—a commonsense healer whose successes as a holistic practitioner were greatly respected; and there were the doctors I'd known, mostly male, mostly white, whose main medical principle was "cut it out" or "drug it out."

When the obstetrician whom I had been seeing since the birth of my last baby suggested that I see a prominent surgeon and a friend of his, I was taken aback at first. He wanted the surgeon to examine a very small lump in my left breast. Then I remembered that my doctor had discussed uterine fibroid tumors long ago, and in turn, I had discussed them with Alvenia. He had said not to worry about them, but Alvenia suggested a program that would shrink or eliminate them. I followed her advice. Several years later, he told me that the fibroids were almost gone. During this time I'd also read of her success eliminating lumps from women's breasts without surgery. I thought I'd see the surgeon, then call Alvenia.

Mother had always said, "See a surgeon long enough and he will find something to cut." Never cut me, I thought, as he made his examination, and as I was being X-rayed.

The next day, he called to ask how soon I could come into the hospital. He wanted to get a look at that lump.

"It won't be possible for about two weeks," I said. In my mind, I was traveling to see Alvenia that next day.

"Two weeks is too long," he said. "I need to look at it much sooner than that. How about tomorrow?"

"Tomorrow?" My heart almost stopped.

"Is your husband home?"

"No, no," I lied. "He's not at home. When he returns, I'll have him call." After hanging up, my mouth turned dry with fear. I blurted out to Ossie what the doctor had said, and told him I needed to see Alvenia.

Some of the color drained from Ossie's lips as he said, "No, Ruby, I think you need to see the surgeon."

Muriel Rahn, Dick Campbell's wife, both of them long and dear friends, had only recently died from breast cancer. We both stood silent, remembering how close the diagnosis had been to her death. Alvenia's remedies took time. Could I risk it? Did I have time enough for even a second opinion?

Ossie called the doctor. I didn't go for the biopsy that day, but I went the day after. Ossie was to stand by in case the lump was malignant and the breast had to be removed. He would have to give permission.

Pills. Needles, people talking, asking questions. Count backward? I know that routine. I will not go under, get knocked out, surrender to oblivion. Why don't I get off this table, grab my clothes, and hightail it to Chicago? Stop asking silly questions, making idle talk. Go to a surgeon often enough and cutting will be done.

I woke up with my left side securely bandaged and a thin tube guiding pink fluids draining from me into a plastic bag. It was a realization that stunned and saddened me beyond description. My left breast was gone.

I imagined it slopped into a huge sack of defective body parts to be used in a landfill or dumped into the ocean. Wouldn't the fish turn up their noses at a dish of rejected, infected, defective body parts? I tried to make myself laugh, "Well, it's gone now. Tit 'twas now t'ain't." It didn't work. As I put my hand on the place where a breast had been, I exploded into desperate and prolonged grief.

A numbness had overtaken me by the time the doctor came to the room to check me out. I couldn't speak or look at him. He told me how lucky I was that, between him and the obstetrician, that cancer had been discovered while it was still the size of a pinhead. I tried not to break out into a fresh boohoo, but I did.

"What's the matter?" he asked. "Afraid men won't look at you anymore? If I had my way—I've seen so much—I'd have them removed from babies."

Later, in his office, I had come prepared to take care of my account. The woman who handled the bills said, "Doctor has closed your account. There will be no charges." Immediately, I returned to his office, and as calmly as I could, thanked him and explained to him that I was not in need of charity, that I always paid my bills. "That's all right," he said. "We don't require payment sometimes. Consider it a gift."

All that happened in 1967. Thank God, there has not been a recurrence.

Since that time, stories of women healed of breast problems using Dr. Fulton's system based primarily on supervised cleansing and eating regimens have come to me from a number of sources. The lumpectomy procedure that has become a standard option today was only on the verge of being introduced then.

Too many times over the years, I've regretted not having first consulted Dr. Alvenia Fulton, a black woman who carried with her age-old alternative solutions to modern problems. I'm still wobbling on the fence, reluctant to jump down on one side or the other, waiting to commit to a medical system that embraces the best of all known disciplines. About a year later, I saw Alvenia in Chicago and told her what had happened. She looked at me with understanding, but I felt the disappointment, too, as she said, "Well, that's behind us. Let's see if we can't keep that from happening again."

OSSIE: Nearly four years had passed since the March on Washington. Black leadership had been patient, but they couldn't wait for Lyndon Johnson to come back from Vietnam. Just as they had feared, they saw the inner cities—first in Watts and New York, then in Cleveland, Detroit, and Newark—begin to explode. A. Philip Randolph drew up a Freedom Budget. It called for government to make a modest investment: $10 billion a year over a period of ten years for a jobs program— all in the spirit of the President's War on Poverty. Randolph showed him how to have his war against the Vietcong in Asia and the one against poverty here at home. But Lyndon never responded to the proposal.

The black leaders felt that Lyndon, though a man with good intentions, had become hooked on the war in Vietnam, and that the victory he so eagerly sought was getting further away every day. Still, they had no jobs to carry back to their burning cities, so all they could do was wait.

Martin waited, too, as long as he could, but he couldn't wait forever. Finally in 1967, he attacked the President's war policy. When Martin declared his own war against Johnson's war in Vietnam in a speech at Riverside Church in New York, the time of his own death was exactly one year away. The place would be Memphis.

Ruby and I had answered the call from Harry Belafonte, who had arranged for Nelson Rockefeller to provide a plane for a whole contingent from Broadway to travel to Memphis and join Martin in a massive march in support of garbage workers who were striking for better pay and working conditions. The march had been set for Monday, April 7. We made the march, but Martin wasn't there. They had shot him down on Friday, April 4.

We went to Atlanta to attend the funeral, and then we came back home. Tension was high, feelings were strong, explosions rocked the cities. I made two placatory speeches, one at the New Rochelle High School, and the other at a Central Park rally that threatened to get out of hand. Two months later, on June 5, Robert Kennedy was shot down in a hotel in Los Angeles. Nobody asked me to rally or to speak, and I was glad. There was nothing more to say.

There are those who say the Southern way of life is based on grits, and the glory of grits lies in the heat. A cook could lose his job—or a portion of his behind—for ignoring this.

The year was 1968, the time was June, the month Bobby Kennedy was killed, so soon after Martin Luther King. The nation was dazed, the South sullen and defensive, and in Shreveport, Louisiana, where the film *Slaves* was being shot, the tension between the whites and blacks was hot and rising. The stores downtown were being picketed by a Committee of Youths, under the aegis of the NAACP. Everybody was looking for something dire to happen. It was rumored that Shreveport was a bastion of the Ku Klux Klan, which was already pissed off. The film we were making was based on *Uncle Tom's Cabin*.

Ruby and I had split the family in two; she taking LaVerne to live with her in Los Angeles where she was a regular on the series *Peyton Place,* and I taking Guy with me to Louisiana. We left Nora back in New Rochelle with Mama.

The cast and crew were living at the Ramada Inn, and early every morning before the drivers came to ferry us to the set, we would eat breakfast in the dining room. Breakfast was mainly whatever else you chose, served up with grits. The waitresses were teenagers with accents you couldn't cut with a butcher knife.

One day I got down to breakfast before Guy and was working on my grits and sausage and eggs when he sat down beside me and ordered the same. The place was full. A lot of truck drivers on the interstate stopped in for breakfast, too. Guy and I were the only black folks in the place. All those Southern white accents talking about King and Kennedy—and sometimes looking straight at me, I thought—put me on the defensive. But I had been among hostile whites many times before, and as a Southern black, I knew the drill.

We had been four or five weeks into production and nothing untoward had happened yet. So far, so good.

The waitresses were ripening adolescents, giggling and flirtatious as they hustled from table to table with their bouncing boobs and their loaded trays. After all, they were serving actors, and who knows, they might even be picked for work as extras themselves.

Guy's breakfast came, but his grits were lumpy and cold. He put the plate down rather noisily, I thought, and called the waitress back. She asked, from across the room, what the matter was. He replied, from across the room, that the grits were cold. She returned to our table, talking all the while in that Southern twang about how busy everything was—that twang that had almost destroyed me that day in Rome. She ascertained that the grits indeed were cold and asked what Guy wanted her to do about it.

"Take 'em back and heat 'em up again." Guy's voice was simple, clear, direct, and full of masculine self-assertion. I looked around to see if any of those truck drivers were listening. I had never in all my life spoken to a white woman with masculine self-assertion. Back home in Waycross where I grew up, that could have got me killed. It just wasn't done that way, and I began to sweat.

I started, almost instinctively, to intercede, to take the conversation away from my son, and say those words the way that I'd been taught: politely, if not obsequiously, verbal hat-in-hand, with laughter that was quick to apologize. But, choking on my own grits, I looked at Guy, and found I couldn't do that. I couldn't infect my son with the disease I knew was in me. I couldn't pour the sacramental syrup on his head. I swallowed hard, stared at the food on my plate, and kept on eating, although by now, my own grits were cold and lifeless.

Soon the girl returned with a plate full of steaming hot grits, talking loudly as she sat them down on the table. She apologized and said she did not blame him. Nothing in this world was as awful as a plate of cold grits early in the morning. And what her Papa would have done if that had happened to *him*!

She alerted all the other girls in the dining room, and made it her special business to see to it from then on that Guy's plate of grits was always as hot as could be.

A few days later, I had to fly back to New York on business, and I wanted very much to take Guy with me. Though it was June, and Shreveport was the South, we were shooting a night sequence, and it could get cold at night. There were many young people who were on the crew, some of whom had come from as far north as Canada. And to avoid the cold, these young people, boys and girls, Guy among them, would crawl into an old automobile between setups, pull a blanket over them to keep warm, and sometimes even fall asleep. Word was out that this fraternization under the blanket was rubbing the Ku Klux Klan—some of whose members were working on the production—the wrong way. They were planning to do something drastic about it.

I didn't forbid Guy to crawl into the car with the other kids, although I wanted to. I felt as long as I was there to keep a watch, he might be safe. If not, at least I would be there in his defense.

I was tempted to order Guy to go along with me back to New York for that one day, but after wrestling with myself, I decided at least to let him make his own decision. I told him about the Klan and the rumors I had heard. He told me that he, too, had heard them, that he would think it over and let me know.

The next day, when I arose early to pack for the plane, he told me he would stay and take his chances with the Klan, then went off to get his early morning grits. I went to New York. It was not an easy trip. I didn't sleep at all, and I returned as fast as I could the very next day. Nothing had happened.

I was proud of my son, proud that in spite of what he had heard, he stood his ground, and in doing so, he reminded me of my daddy. I was equally proud of myself, that whatever the Old South had done to me, it wasn't contagious—it hadn't rubbed off on my son.

There should be enough kick in an ice-cold martini in a short, thick glass offered to you by Sam Goldwyn, Jr., to make you a man of decision on the spot, but I said no, I wanted to check it out with Ruby first. Sam was producing a film to be based on a popular novel about two detectives, written by Chester Himes, called *Cotton Comes to Harlem,* and he had originally offered me and Godfrey Cambridge the roles as the two detectives, Coffin Ed Johnson and Grave Digger Jones.

The movie adaptation had been written by Arnold Perl, an old friend of ours from the days of *Sholom Aleichem,* but Sam wasn't satisfied; the script wasn't black enough. He phoned me from Hollywood to ask my opinion. I made a few suggestions, and I told him not to worry: Godfrey and I would take care of the blackness when we got before the cameras.

Sam asked if I would put my suggestions in writing, which I did, and sent them off to him. He was so pleased with the changes I proposed that he wanted more. But there is a limit, soon reached, to the number of changes a movie script can take before it begins to lose its original flavor. I warned Sam that that was happening, but he didn't care. He wanted the script to be authentic in its representation of black life, and asked me to continue what had now become a major rewrite. I asked him why wasn't he dealing with Arnold Perl, the original screenwriter. He told me Arnold was hot to do a film about Malcolm X, and had no more time for or interest in *Cotton.*

I took a room in a Hollywood hotel and set about seriously revising the entire script. I had an office right across from his at the old Goldwyn Studios on Santa Monica Boulevard, where I would work on my revisions, then take them across the hall for his review. During all this time, Sam continually nudged me about who might be a good director. I paid him little attention—that was up to him as far as I was concerned.

Finally, my work on the rewrite was done, and Sam still had no director. I didn't have time to worry about that, being busy as I was working in television. We kept in touch by phone, however. It was while I was working on *Night Gallery,* a new television series (hosted and written by Rod Serling, the writer of *Twilight Zone*), that Sam invited me to his house, fed me martinis, and then made the announcement.

"Ossie, I've found the director. I ran him by United Artists—they're financing *Cotton*—and they've agreed."

"So who is this director?" I asked, taking another slurp.

"You are. Here. Let me freshen your glass for you."

I called Ruby. She read the script. It didn't knock her over, but why not?

I gave Sam my answer, and we immediately agreed on Raymond St. Jacques to take my place as Coffin Ed.

The best thing I've ever done as a director was *Cotton Comes to Harlem.* The film has been credited with being the first commercial Hollywood film to prove that there was a considerable market for black films, even if white folks decided to stay away. It was also credited with helping United Artists and Hollywood pull themselves out of a financial hole.

One of the deciding factors for me was that the entire film was to be shot in Harlem. I was comfortable in Harlem; people knew me there as one of the homeboys. I wasn't white. I wasn't an outsider. People would be glad to see me working there because I was Ossie Davis, the man who had eulogized Malcolm X. The community would treat me as one of its own. I could depend on their welcome to smooth the way, and make things easier for the shoot. But the second day out, that theory was sorely tested.

The shoot was to be a collision between a speeding police car driven by Godfrey Cambridge and a wagonload of watermelons; it was to take place at the intersection where 153rd Street comes to a stop at Eighth Avenue. Most of the morning was spent making things ready, and by ten o'clock, we were almost ready to shoot. The script supervisor, Judy Tucker, who was white, was sitting near the camera while I was lining up the shot when somebody threw a whiskey bottle half-filled with water and hit her in the head, knocking her out cold.

Pandemonium. Fear. Panic. The policemen assigned to protect us ran up to the roof looking for the perpetrator, who was nowhere to be found. Sam, who was on location with us, started to call off the shoot. In spite of Ossie, Harlem was too dangerous. By this time, Judy had fully recovered. She refused to let us take her to the hospital, and insisted the shooting go on. We finished lining things up and got the first shot in before lunch.

A few weeks later, a group of young men marched onto the set and sat down in front of the camera. They identified themselves as young black filmmakers and proceeded to state their grievances. Sure, they acknowledged, there was a black director, and a lot of black actors were working, but what about the crew—the gaffers, the carpenters, the prop men, the scenic designers, the set dressers, and the drivers? They demanded answers, or else there'd be no more shooting. Not in Harlem.

Neither Sam nor I was completely surprised. We'd heard that something of the sort was in the wind. Unions in the film industry were, and some still are, notoriously racist. They have New York production over a barrel. Sam had tried to put some black crewmen on the picture, but the unions wouldn't hear of it. Maybe this work stoppage would make them more amenable.

No union jobs were available, but at least we were able to get some jobs for black apprentices. This was my first meeting with Cliff Frazier, who was a sort of consultant and spokesperson for the young intruders. I joined Cliff in the formation of Third World Cinema, meant to provide training and qualify young people for jobs in these various specialties.

The fight to get black jobs in white Hollywood is a never-ending battle played out in many ways, some quite subtle. There is from time to time a big brouhaha—sometimes it gets quite excitable—over whether or not a *white* director can really ever make a film truly representative of *black* lifestyle and *black* culture. This question, in my opinion, is more about jobs—and ultimately about power—than it is about race.

I like very much the way Sam Goldwyn dealt with the question. Though Chester Himes, the original author, is black, the screenplay for *Cotton Comes to Harlem* was written by Arnold Perl, who was white. This fact didn't bother me, and I know of no one else, black or white, who was bothered by it. I was ready to work in the film without a qualm. But Sam, for reasons I have never questioned, insisted on incorporating a black man's opinion into the script. Then he insisted that I, a black man, direct it. A white director could well have directed *Cotton,* perhaps even better then I, but Sam wanted something else— something else he thought that I could give. I'm very glad he did.

RUBY: Although Ossie and I had both been invited in 1969 to attend the Sixth International Film Festival in Moscow, such a trip seemed impossible. I was working for a radio station in Boston, WGBH, and Ossie was busy directing the film *Cotton Comes to Harlem,* but James and Esther Jackson, founders of *Freedomways* magazine (which was closely associated with Dr. W.E.B. Du Bois), had been instrumental in securing the invitation, and they were insistent: This opportunity was too important for us to miss and they suggested that I go to the festival alone. I asked Ossie how he felt about it, and he agreed.

From the moment I gave my consent, confusion reigned. I was to leave the Sunday of the July Fourth weekend. I needed to renew my passport, obtain a Russian visa, and book my passage by plane. The Jacksons lost no time in making arrangements. Jim went to Washington himself to get my Russian visa, returned with it on Sunday morning, and the plane left with me aboard on Sunday afternoon, via Air Canada to Montreal, London, and finally to Moscow.

On the plane I assiduously studied my Berlitz book, *Getting Along in Russian,* and regretted deeply that I had not learned the Russian alphabet, so different from ours. There was a very nice businessman on the plane who gave me his card and reassured me that, were I in trouble, he could help me. On Monday, at 4:00 P.M., Moscow time, I arrived at the Moscow airport.

Moscow. The prospect excited me. It had been the home of Alexander Pushkin, a black Russian. Pushkin, a poet, had been deemed by some scholars to be one of the glories of the Russian language. And here was I in Pushkin's old hometown.

There were about forty-five people from the United States in the delegation to the film festival, including the three official delegates and seven special advisers. The rest of us were just members. I remember seeing Jack Valenti, the president of the Motion Picture Association of America, and various other important people in film, but I found myself most of the time in the company of Lucy Kroll, John Phillip Law, Albert Johnson, Gail and Sidney Lumet, Lillian Gish, and David Wolper. I knew Lucy Kroll better than the others primarily because Jules Dassin had wanted James Earl Jones to play Tank in *Up Tight!* and Lucy Kroll was his agent.

I had not known David Wolper previously, but we were thrown together at various functions, so we soon got to know each other, and frequently we had dinner at the same table, where one evening I inquired about his connection to film. He very graciously explained that he was a filmmaker, particularly of documentaries, and he gave me his card.

I was embarrassed when the next morning a large envelope was delivered to my quarters in the hotel containing extensive materials relating to David Wolper, his company, and his widely acclaimed films—many of which I had seen, such as *The Making of the President, Four Days in November* (about the JFK assassination), *The Race for Space, Hollywood: The Golden Years,* and *The Underwater Sea World of Jacques Cousteau.* He had come to Moscow as a member of the U.S. delegation to sell and buy films.

Then my mind lit up like Rockefeller Center on Christmas Eve. David was just the man I had been looking for ever since I discovered the world of black writers and their works, which offered the possibility for the kinds of roles that inspired me to be an actor in the first place. Luckily for me, he hadn't resented my talking about books, films, ideas, and the frustration of being a black female actor. Rather, he seemed interested in what I had to say and talked meaningfully about issues of race and the challenges inherent in making the kinds of films I envisioned.

Among the books we discussed, books that I thought would make great films, were Zora Neale Hurston's *Their Eyes Were Watching God* and Margaret Walker's *Jubilee.* I also spoke of a book that hadn't been written yet, and of the man whom I had seen mesmerize listeners in two living rooms, one belonging to Lucy Kroll. The master raconteur was Alex Haley. Before the festival ended and we headed back to the States, I made sure that David Wolper would have a lot to think about as he left Moscow.

In August, the following month, Ossie and I and the children were guests of Calpenny Films, Ltd., headquartered in Lagos, Nigeria. Francis Oladele, head of Calpenny, wanted Ossie to direct a film there and suggested that he come for a weeklong visit. Ossie asked if he could bring the family along, and Francis was more than happy to oblige.

Moscow and Lagos were both providers of awesome experiences for me. I was fascinated by the contrasts in people, terrain, rhythms, sizes, colors, architecture, businesses, smells, sounds, languages, and, above all, expectations. I realized almost immediately in both cities that I'd been romanticizing race, political systems, and people. No matter what I felt, no matter how eager I was to understand and identify, I remained a foreigner in Russia as well as in Nigeria. Political systems cannot be reduced to generalized notions of some sort of utopia or hell. Human affairs are far too complex for that.

The ordinary Soviet people that I met sensed that I came from somewhere else. So did the people in Lagos. Strangers stopped me in Moscow to congratulate me on my country's landing on the moon. What in the world did *I* have to do with white folks landing on the moon? The Nigerians referred to their countrymen from other tribes as strangers; so how in God's name would they refer to me? I was told that they referred to African Americans using a phrase that sounded like *ayen bo doo doo,* which, in translation, meant "black white people."

It was altogether an astonishing learning time as I, a black American woman born in Cleveland, tried to touch hands and minds through a language that I couldn't learn fast enough in Moscow and through a culture cut too deep to heal in just a week in Lagos. Face it, Ruby. Put your history back on and be yourself—from Africa long ago.

OSSIE: In August of 1969, when the family hopped a plane for Nigeria, West Africa, it would be twenty-five years before we took a major trip together again, and it would be our last trip overseas together. The occasion was to prepare for my second directorial assignment, a film to be shot in Nigeria based on *Kongi's Harvest,* a play by the internationally known playwright, Wole Soyinka, who happened to be in jail at the time. A civil war was raging, Wole had said aloud that he thought the whole thing foolish, and the military government had locked him up.

Yes, I had enjoyed my stint as a director of *Cotton Comes to Harlem*. The exercise of power and authority was intoxicating, but I wasn't drunk. Directing calls for a vision and an itch, a dedicated focus, energy, the ability to be mean and stubborn if you have to, and at times, a little devious. Qualities I thoroughly understand, but do not have. What I do have is the ability to be too easily persuaded. I find it hard to say no to someone else's expectations.

That someone was Francis Oladele, a Nigerian film producer, married to Jeanne Jackson, the sister of Maynard Jackson, then mayor of Atlanta. Francis and Jeanne lived with their family in Surulere, a suburb of Lagos, Nigeria's capital.

Francis was determined to make the film of *Kongi's Harvest*. He already had a Swedish film crew under contract, but he wanted a black director, which meant his choices were limited. There was Gordon Parks, who had directed *The Learning Tree*, based on his own book; Melvin Van Peebles, who had just come home from France where he had made *One Potato, Two Potato;* and I.

Oladele not only knew the facts and figures of American film production and distribution, but he also knew his own market—how many film houses there were in Nigeria, how many seats they contained, and what percentage of those seats he had to fill to make a profit. The Lebanese controlled most of those film houses and most of the films came from India. He proposed to change all that.

He pointed out that Nigeria offered the kind of varied locations that places like Yugoslavia did, which American and European producers could use: urban, seashore, desert, jungle, rolling hills, and plains. I was impressed. The thought of Africans and African Americans joining hands across the ocean intrigued and then seduced me. I felt that whatever future Africa might have in world affairs would happen first and foremost in Nigeria. Why not begin with film?

Nigeria had gained its independence from Britain in 1960, and had seemed to be the one country on the continent that was poised to become a big power. It had the resources, the people, and the potential wealth for becoming an influential modern state that would serve as a shining example to the rest of Africa, and to black people all over the world. But the civilian government had been overthrown in 1966 by the military, and now the country was engaged in a war. That explained the potholes and traffic jams.

Nigeria had been put together by the British in the 1860s to supply the cotton mills of Manchester, which had been cut off from their supply by the American Civil War. The population was composed of Yoruba, Ibo, Hausa, Fulani, and other tribal groupings easily played off, one against the other. Now the Ibo in the east were in a war to separate themselves into an independent state. But the military government had launched a campaign to preserve the integrity of the country. "To make Nigeria one is a task that must be done" was the national slogan. The fighting was essentially over, and Nigeria had emerged intact.

Making a film there seemed more than a job; it was an act of super patriotism and race loyalty.

We arrived over Lagos at night. The blackout was on; still there was a strange pattern of ground lights as we flew in low over the city. On the long drive in, we passed hundreds of tables set up on the sidewalk, with flickering candles barely enough to light the bananas, kola nuts, and other small items for sale.

We checked in at the Ikoyi Hotel, which was not very different from the best hotels anywhere. I had of course been in Africa before, but to Ruby and the children, it was a first, a chance to see an entire country owned and run by black people.

It seemed as if Nigerian drivers had to negotiate through traffic jams, from one pothole to the next, by verbal intimidation. Francis Oladele was slightly demonic in his driving as well as his conversation, and was master of both. From Ibadan, home of the University of Ibadan, we went on to Ife where we met the *Oni,* a traditional tribal ruler whose word was law among the Yoruba. Then we traveled to Abeokuta, where we saw the Olumo Rock, a site sacred to the Yoruba. It is said that it was here that the Africans made their most ferocious stand against the invading English in the eighteenth century.

Initially, Ruby and I were slightly sentimental about Nigeria. We particularly wanted the children to see it as we saw it: Africa, the motherland, which we expected would welcome her long lost children with open arms, ending forever the historical trauma of slavery. Home again, like the Prodigal Son, we fully expected that old umbilical cords would be reunited, and we would be greeted with the fatted calf.

The Africans we met had no such special sense of kinship. To them we were friends, yes, relatives, yes, but mostly we were Americans who happened to be black—rich customers to be haggled with and catered to, like everybody else. Still, for the Davises, history was being remade. There was a pride in being in a place where black people were running things, even if their methods differed from ours. We came. We saw. We returned to America just a little sadder, but wiser. The full recovery from slavery, racism, and colonialism would take much longer than we thought. But on the whole we liked what we had seen— and we could wait.

January 1970. The war was over, Nigeria was once again at peace, Wole Soyinka had been released from prison, and we were ready to go into production of *Kongi's Harvest,* which was about an African dictator and the struggle to depose him. Wole was to play Kongi.

Soyinka—who subsequently won a Nobel Prize for Literature— is one of the best writers in the English language, and not at all sentimental about Africa, as some of us Americans were. To us, all the ills Africa suffered came directly from slavery and colonial dominance by the European powers, and we felt that once the bonds of colonialism were broken, Africa would quickly take her place among the nations on an equal footing, morally, spiritually, economically, and otherwise. Wole seemed to see it differently. His works imply that Africa is not Europe, rather that Africa has to find a way into the twentieth century that is strictly her own; and that she has a very long way to go in order to finally arrive at who she is. And history seems to have borne him out.

Kongi's Harvest was written in English and it should have been easy enough to take my cast and my crew from one scenic location to the next and come up with a dramatic, colorful film. But it was not. First, the crew was Swedish and all my directions had to be translated. Then, quite a few of my actors were not comfortable in English, which to some was a second language, not their native tongue. And though they were fluid and plastic in their normal speech and movement, absolutely delightful to talk to and to interact with, the moment the camera rolled, they lost their naturalness and fluidity, and became like puppets with a British attitude and accent. Try as I might, I was seldom able to get their naturalness and spontaneity. I got what they had picked up watching English films.

When principal photography was finished, I flew to Stockholm to edit it. Then it was exhibited in New York and in a few other cities, where it did not do well at all at the box office.

But the most unkind cut of all was what happened in Nigeria. Most of the Lebanese distributors and film house owners there had no interest in encouraging indigenous filmmaking. Francis had to fight like hell to have his film shown in his own country. Even there it failed.

When Phil Rose, who produced *Purlie Victorious,* approached me about making the play into a musical, I didn't want to hear it. I don't particularly like musicals, never did, never will. I was quite pleased with *Purlie Victorious* just as it was. But Phil is, first off, one of the nicest human beings you'll ever meet and I owed him plenty: Without him, *Purlie Victorious* might never have come to life at all, certainly not on Broadway. Also, I was convinced that he'd never raise the money to mount the production. So I told Phil to go right ahead, hoping he would fail, and went on about my business, which at the time was directing *Cotton Comes to Harlem.*

Phil is a stubborn and a determined man, not to be underestimated. He pulled together a new creative team: Peter Udell, a lyricist, and Gary Geld, a composer, and together they shaped *Purlie Victorious* into a musical and called it *Purlie.* My only contribution to the production was to supply Phil with the names and telephone numbers of two actors working with me in *Cotton*—Melba Moore and Cleavon Little.

Purlie opened in March of 1970 while I was away in Nigeria with *Kongi's Harvest,* and it was a smash hit. Broadway seemed to love it. Ruby sent me the notices, and included in her letters her own positive appraisal. I didn't get to see it until sometime in May, and what I saw I didn't like at all. Even to this day, my opinions haven't really changed. I love the people in it. I respect them for their effort and their devotion. I loved even more the royalties coming in every week. All that was wonderful and much appreciated. But my own true heart will always belong to the original play. What had been in the original script a subtle satire, based on the folklaughter of the real inhabitants of a culture, was now a blatant cartoon, played for laughs, that had little to do with the real lifestyle of the people being portrayed.

The black response to segregation in the South was embodied in a culture of subtle hints, and sly innuendoes, not flat-footed, heavy-handed slapstick such as the musical offered. There is, for instance, a song in which Ol' Cap'n is invited to "come kiss our black behinds," which even now causes me to shudder, so contrary is it to the surgically delicate humor of the moment's original intent. It is an insult, not a spoof. I sat there, when first I heard it, wanting very much to stop my ears and hide my face. It is one of the most egregious pieces of bad taste I have ever witnessed in the theater. Artistic overkill, smacking of rank amateurism. I was horrified!

Had I been there, as I should have been when the work was being put together, I would have insisted those lyrics be withdrawn. Nevertheless, *Purlie* was a huge success. It made Phil back his money and paid me handsomely as well. Even now a royalty check comes in from time to time. But my fundamental loyalty is still to *Purlie Victorious,* which I truly believe—I say this without false modesty—will one day be recognized as a minor classic in the genre.

CHAPTER 32

The Family Comes
of Age

OSSIE: In 1970, the war in Vietnam came to our house in New Rochelle on the very day Ruby and I were to receive the Frederick Douglass Award for "distinguished leadership toward equal opportunity"
from the New York Urban League.

Guy, who was eighteen at the time and eligible for the draft, went
with a schoolmate to sit in at the draft board, which was situated in a
tall building across from the post office. Guy has always been his own
Lone Ranger, keeping his own counsel; none of the family was privy
to his intentions. A neighbor brought us word, and I hurried downtown
to see what was going on.

Shortly after I got there, the police came and arrested not only
Guy and his friend, but also his friend's father. I wanted the world to
know that Guy had a father as well, so I stepped up and got myself
arrested, too. We were taken before a sympathetic judge who released
us on our own recognizance; then we were freed to rush downtown to

join Ruby and the girls at the Urban League awards dinner. We arrived just in time.

Though we always tried to show up as a family, the children made sure that they were not swallowed up by the public gush that often surrounded their parents, finding a way to maintain their own sense of themselves as individuals. For instance, Guy would seldom sit at the same table with the rest of us, preferring to wander off and establish himself at some other location. LaVerne would always insist, "Daddy, mention my name, but don't tell them it's me." Nora seemed to have caught on to how the game of celebrity parents was played and soon became the one who took charge of operations. It didn't matter as long as we were together.

It was a brand-new world, changing every day, and Ruby and I, as parents, like the rest of grown-up America, had to try to show our children how to live in it. That took a lot of guessing, improvising, and trying various lifestyles on for size. We took a lot of chances, but we never bluffed, or postured, or pulled rank unless we had to. Together we met the cataclysmic changes rushing at us from all sides—efforts to unionize the hospitals; the antiwar demonstrations; the dogs and fire hoses in Birmingham; the funerals and the turmoil when Kennedy, Malcolm, and later, King, were assassinated. The children were always eager and full of questions. We had no ready answers, but we tried.

Once when I was co-chairman with Dick Gregory of the Committee to Defend the Panthers, somebody sent me a threat through the mail promising that on a certain day Dick and I would be killed. We turned the letter over to the police; they came and spent the appointed day at our house with the family and me.

On another occasion, when I was chairman of the Committee to Defend Angela Davis, and Angela was acquitted, there was a big rally in honor of the occasion at Madison Square Garden. I made my speech standing in a bulletproof glass booth, and the family was right there to see me do it.

We saw it all, we faced it all, we came through it all together.

Sometimes it wasn't easy. Like the time we found marijuana in somebody's pocket. Ruby and I had to do something, but we didn't know exactly what that something was. We met with the children in the basement and laid our cards on the table, describing to them in language they could understand what the situation was. We were not accusatory, or judgmental, and we didn't claim moral authority backed up by the law and God Almighty. Everybody had a chance to speak, to ask questions, to state his or her own position on the question of drugs and of sex.

Then we shared with them our conclusion: If they wanted to smoke pot, they could do it here at home. If they had to have sex, have it here at home. There was to be nothing they could find in the world outside the door that they couldn't find at home, nothing they could do out there that they couldn't do under our roof—with this one proviso: No matter what, we would always hang on to each other; we would always be a family. It well may be that in dealing thus with our children, we broke Mosaic law and the moral code. If that's the case, we did it in defense of the family.

In 1971, Shirley Chisholm of the Congressional Black Caucus called on me to help her solve a problem. The caucus, which consisted of the thirteen newly elected black members of Congress, had just been formed, and their first annual dinner was to be held on June 18. Naturally, no one congressman could be called upon to give the keynote speech without insulting all the rest. They needed somebody from the outside, somebody who was not a congressman, not even an elected official. I accepted the invitation.

I am more at ease speaking extemporaneously because then nothing comes between me and the audience, not even my speech. I do it all from memory, fired up by a sort of verbal spontaneous combustion that rises up and sweeps my thought along on a torrent of words. That does not mean that I forgo preparation. There's usually reading to be done, unless I am very familiar with the subject, and sometimes I even make notes; then I memorize them. A rehearsal of sorts is provided by the give-and-take with Ruby and the children at the dinner table. And often, some of what I say has come directly from them.

Whenever I make a speech, I always try to come up with a different angle from the usual fare, to find a phrase that will express succinctly the basic thought that I am trying to impart. The speech to the Congressional Black Caucus was second only to the eulogy for Malcolm X as the most important speech I ever made. This excerpted transcript contains my call to black leadership at that time:

It's not the man, it's the plan. And for those of us . . . still caught up in the dreams that rhetoric will solve our problems, let me state it another way. It's not the rap, it's the map. . . . At the time when Dr. King died in 1968, he was in the process of organizing his forces and calling upon his people to come one more time to Washington, D.C. And I have a feeling that had he come that time, he would not have said, "I have a dream," he would have said, "I have a plan. . . ." That plan that he had might have made the difference. . . . It is a great misfortune that we never had a chance to get from [our previous leaders] just what the plan was that they had in mind.

And that's why tonight, the burden of my appeal to you . . . is to give to us a "Ten Black Commandments"—simple, strong—that we carry in our hearts and in our memories no matter where we are, [we can] reach out and touch and feel the reassurance that there is behind everything we do a simple, moral, intelligent plan that must be fulfilled in the course of time. Even if all our leaders, one by one, fall in the battle, somebody will rise and say, "Our leader died while we were on page three of a plan, now that the funeral is over, let us proceed to page four."

. . . From our noble thirteen, we need that they think the problems out, that they investigate the possible solutions, that they codify their results and then present their programs to us, the people, so that we may ratify what they have thought and organized and left to us as a program of action . . . If a storm of oppression should wipe us out, all out but one family, and that family was crouching somewhere in the dark, one brother would reach out to another and say, "Hey, hey man, what's the plan?"

RUBY: That glorious trip to the Moscow film festival in 1969 yielded another blessing: I got to know Lucy Kroll. About a year later, she called to say that James Earl Jones would be playing Boesman in *Boesman and Lena,* a work by the acclaimed South African playwright Athol Fugard. She asked if I would like to read the script and consider the role of Lena. I confess I didn't understand the part at first. Ossie read it, and talked about its very real social, political, and gender significance. He helped open my eyes to the beauty of the text and to the genius of the author.

The work in *Boesman and Lena* became one of the most satisfying investigations of a character I'd ever done, thanks in part to John Berry, the director, and to Ossie. The word "investigation" may be only halfway accurate. The acting process is more reciprocal, I think. You dig as far as you can into the character, while at the same time, the character digs as far as it can into you. The rehearsals and the discussions about apartheid, coupled with my own familiarity with the frustrations of racism, the brutality of sexism, and the desperate need for comfort and joy that we all share—all this began to wear away and to crush out my reserve, anxiety, and uncertainty until, finally, I relaxed in gradual surrender.

The door to myself flew open one day, and Lena walked in and climbed all over and through me, holding me fast from the beginning to the end of the performance. After the final curtain, she would let go, and I would feel happy and relieved. Lena was an extraordinary, multidimensional person, carrying me into places in myself where I had never been, stretching me enormously as an actor.

OSSIE: There are certain times when the actor is said to be "flying." A feeling of awe possesses the observers, who hold their collective breath, as at a baseball game when a pitcher is on the verge of a no-hitter. None of the other players says a word, not daring to break the magic spell at work. That's what I felt the night before the opening of *Boesman and Lena.* Ruby wasn't Ruby anymore! Bare-footed, bare-legged, standing arms akimbo, talking, laughing, crying, barking, as I had never seen her before, she was Ruby, of course, but it was more than Ruby. She was totally incandescent, as if a fire was blazing in her belly, spilling out from her eyes. I was stunned and so was the audience. There was no way any of us could explain what was happening on that stage.

I returned the following night, which was the opening, June 22, 1970. Ruby was wonderful, the critics raved, she was nominated for an Obie, and she ultimately won the Drama Desk Award for her splendid work that night. Excellent though it was, it was not like the performance I had seen the night before. That had been like voodoo, when the mystical god comes and rides the bucking believer, like a monkey riding a goat.

RUBY: On the morning of July 14, I'd arranged to meet an acting coach recommended by, I believe, the stage manager for *Boesman and Lena*. I awoke feeling anxious about my mother, who had called out to me on the previous night as I was getting into the shower. I called to Nora, "Go see what Gramma wants." She did, and returned to me, saying, "She said she's all right now—never mind." I hurried through the shower and quickly went into her room. I stood there, watching her sleep for a few minutes, regretting that I had not come when she first called. She seemed peaceful, so I turned out the light and left.

The next morning when I came downstairs, she was dressed and sitting by the large window in the kitchen looking out. Her face was somewhat drawn and wistful, I thought, as we greeted each other; then she continued looking out the window as I prepared a pot of cereal. When I brought her a bowl, she refused it, which unexpectedly infuriated me.

"Mother, Nora said you didn't eat your dinner last night. How do you expect to feel good, to live, without eating? You won't see a doctor; you won't eat. What is it, Mother, are you trying to die? Well, I won't let you. Kitty [who was one of the roomers still living in Mother's large apartment] says maybe you should give up the apartment. I haven't time to talk to you now, all right? I've got to go downtown, but I'll call you before I go to the theater. Maybe we can talk about it then." On and on I went; she scarcely said anything, glancing at me occasionally, as if something of far greater importance than apartments was on her mind, then turning away again to look out the window.

It was a strange day. All I remember about the appointment with the coach is that he had me walk around and around the room calling my own name. It was an unsettling sensation—me calling out at the top of my voice, "Ruby, Ruby, Ruby, Ruby!" I felt stupid and somewhat apprehensive. I wished I hadn't made the appointment, and before it was over, I left.

I also had an appointment at the Algonquin restaurant to lunch with Raymond League, who, along with Jean Murray, the first black woman on CBS late evening news, had founded the first integrated advertising agency, Zebra, some time ago. He wanted to discuss an idea for a new ad campaign and thought I might assist him. He and his former wife, the actor Janet League, had been instrumental in promoting *Purlie Victorious* at the Edgewater Beach Hotel in Chicago, helping to stretch the run from two weeks to two months, and had come to New York to help us plan the road tour. When Ossie and I decided not to tour after all, they had stayed on.

That meeting was also depressing as it turned into a surprising account of the intrigue, duplicity, and deadly threats surrounding the dissolution of his company, Zebra. I lost track of the time.

Suddenly I remembered I'd promised to call Mother and excused myself. Ellen Brickers, who managed the office, answered the phone. "Please put my mother on," I said. I waited. Yes, Mother was moving so much slower these days, I reminded myself. A few days earlier she had slapped at me, and had missed—much as she had done when I was a child, but without missing. Something was wrong. Maybe some of the blood vessels in her brain were giving way. I thought she may be drinking a little too much.

Ellen came back to the phone. "She's sleeping in front of the TV. Your father is talking with your husband. Shall I wake her?" she asked.

"Yes, yes," I said. "Wake her because I promised we'd talk today." Silence on Ellen's part. "Never mind." I said. "Let her sleep. I'll see her in the morning. Or maybe I'll call her later, when I get to the theater. Yes, maybe I'll call later." I never did.

OSSIE: That morning, I drove to a clinic in the Bronx at Montefiore Hospital for a routine X-ray and lab test that would only take a few minutes, and at Mother's request, I took her with me. I could tell from her little grunts and from the awkward way she walked that she wasn't feeling well, but I agreed that perhaps the ride, getting her out of the house for a breath of fresh air, might do her good, as she suggested.

When I got to the hospital and parked, she asked me to recline the seat so she could lie back as she waited for me to return. I asked if she'd like to come in and talk to my doctor at the clinic, but Emma didn't believe very much in doctors. No, she didn't feel like moving, rather she'd just lie back and listen to the radio in the car while she waited.

I was soon done and drove home, slowly this time because I could see she was not comfortable. I helped her back inside the house and guided her to her favorite seat in the dining room. She groaned in pain; then she sat. The chair was a recliner, so I helped her to get comfortable and went on about my business. I was beginning to worry a little, wondering, as Ruby and I had done several times before, how to get her to accept a visit from a doctor.

I was busy with God knows what when Nora came to me in a hurry. "Daddy, Grandma's lying on the floor in the bathroom!" It was the small bathroom in the vestibule. I rushed in and found her curled up like a baby lying on the cold tile floor where she had fallen. I took her into my arms, remarking in my mind at the strange look in her eyes, her pupils open and dilated and empty—empty in a way I'd never seen before.

I carried her to the long couch in the living room, while Nora ran across the street to a neighbor, Sylvia Gennis, a doctor, who came running. She hopped onto the couch, straddling Mother, pounding away at her chest for five minutes or so. It was no use, of course. Emma was dead.

I went to the theater that night and watched Ruby do Lena again. Two friends of ours came back to her dressing room. We dropped them off in Harlem; then, on the way home, I broke the news to Ruby.

RUBY: That night I was surprised to see Ossie at the theater. When he told me Mother had died, then I knew why the day seemed so off center. I felt my heart trying to leave my chest.

OSSIE: Ruby didn't respond, almost as if she hadn't heard what I was saying, just sat there as I drove, looking straight ahead, but saying nothing.

~ ~ ~

RUBY: I have this deep thing about horses, but I didn't know it until I had to learn to ride one. The occasion was preparation for a role in the film *Buck and the Preacher*. Again my name was Ruth, and again, I was Sidney's girl. I started with riding lessons at a stable in New Rochelle, and was surprised at how easy and natural it all seemed.

When we got to Durango, Mexico, where the film was to be shot, Sidney, Harry, and I rode every day, just for the fun of it. It was an exhilarating sensation after my butt toughened up, and I could ride flat out with the guys and not get left behind. I took to it as if I had done it before, the horse wranglers told me, as if I'd been a horsewoman in some other life. I loved the horse I was assigned to ride and she seemed very much to like me.

One day I was riding alone at a fairly good clip when the horse, all on her own, came to a sudden stop. No one was in sight for as far as I could see. What could be the matter? I slapped her neck with the reins, kicked her in the sides with my heels, and tried to make her go, but she wouldn't. She stood stock-still. I stroked her, and talked to her, and looked around to see what might have spooked her—a snake, perhaps. No. I got down, looked around again, and there on the ground, just a few feet behind us, were my eyeglasses. I had not missed them, nor heard them fall from my pack into the soft desert sand below, but she did. I thanked her, gave her a great big hug, remounted, and we were soon on our way again, galloping past the low-growing cactus as fast as we could go.

On the days Harry, Sidney, and I rode together, I felt as if we were people from another time, characters out of a fairy tale—like the Three Musketeers or something.

Before the beginning of principal photography, Sidney took over the directing from Joe Sargent. I'm not sure of the reason. I was surprised, having no idea of Sidney as a director, but I thought he was most impressive. He seemed well prepared every day, and gave all his actors a great sense of confidence in his vision and in his direction. It was immediately obvious that he knew what he was doing. Frequently he and Harry would confer. They seemed to work so very well together. Their friendship was beautiful, in front of the camera as well as behind it.

Julie Belafonte, Harry's wife, played an important role as a Native American, and I was so pleased that we could hang out together—and shop, enjoy the desert, the people, the sights and sounds of old Durango. Ossie visited me for about a week and it felt a little like old times when we all hooked up with Sidney, who seemed relaxed, even though he had his hands full. I had lots of time so I took painting lessons.

On another horse-riding adventure, I came upon this place where there were children with no clothes, some scantily clad, with runny noses, and a mother looking bewildered because I had presented myself as she was cooking something over what looked like a hole in the floor. It was as if they were living on a plantation or like animals in a cave. The man who owned the land was incensed that I was talking to them. I found myself explaining that I was lost. I noticed that the landowner had a modern kitchen, but the peasants were nearly destitute. I later thought of that saying, "*Pobre México*, so close to the U.S., so far from God."

I wonder whatever became of that horse. I think about those days sometimes, about the rich Mexican landscape, and about the poverty I stumbled on from atop my horse as I rode into an incredible sunset.

～　　～　　～

OSSIE: Picket lines, congressional hearings, and letter-writing campaigns threatening to boycott Hollywood could only get us so far in our search for jobs on both sides of the camera. The answer was always "Of course, we'd like to hire you black folks, but the unions won't let us. And even if they did, where would we find black technicians, prop men, costumers, and makeup artists? Where?" The situation was a catch-22, as always, but this time we had a plan.

First, we would train black technicians on our own, then pressure the unions to let them in. Meanwhile, knowing that this process took time, we decided to produce black films on our own. The key to all of this was Cliff Frazier. He rounded up a group of people, white and black, who were willing and qualified, and started Third World Cinema in February 1971.

Students were selected, first come, first served, on the basis of written applications followed by interviews, and once admitted, were rigorously trained in every aspect of filmmaking, except acting. There were courses in writing, directing, sound recording, lighting, and operating the camera. Cliff was always job oriented, and after a few years, it became apparent that television, not moviemaking, was where the jobs were, so we decided to put the emphasis there. There are many professionals holding down important jobs in television today who got their starts with INCA, the Institute for New Cinema Artists, the training arm for Third World Cinema.

In addition, Third World Cinema co-produced a major motion picture, *Claudine,* with Diana Sands signed to play the title role, co-starring James Earl Jones. Diana became ill as soon as the shooting started. Diahann Carroll, however, replaced her.

RUBY: There are some spirits that stride boldly over the horizon and claim life with gusto. Diana Sands was one of these people. She came sure and laughing, taking hold of what she came for with both hands. She played Beneatha in *A Raisin in the Sun,* giving us the essence of Lorraine Hansberry, the author, in her portrayal. She was like my baby sister—a tomboy and a lady practical joker. I saw behind those eyes, however, that she was scared, and heard behind the hearty, full-mouthed laugh that she desperately wanted somebody to love her; and if it didn't happen soon, she was going to beat up pillows and moan and cry in the night.

Near the end, when the mark of death at the hands of cancer had put her in Sloan-Kettering, I saw her, even as she lay on her dying bed, running backward with that same energy and dispatch that marked everything she did—going the other way, becoming child, waxen baby, disappearing over the same horizon, becoming spirit again—letting go, one by one, all the hands that tried to hold her. She was a glorious actor, full of the joy of life, as well as much of its sorrow.

OSSIE: After Daddy died, Mama had bought a house in Tuskegee, Alabama, to be near Essie, my sister, who worked for the Veterans Administration Hospital at the university. And there she stayed for five or six years until she began to have trouble with her gums. Local treatment proved fruitless, so she came to visit with us and to consult with specialists in the New York area. The condition proved to be chronic, and finally we persuaded her to stay with us so she could be near treatment. It turned out that a good grandmother—somebody to help look after Nora, Guy, and LaVerne while Ruby and I were working—was just what the family needed. So Mama moved in and became a functioning part of the family.

Back in 1963, when we moved to New Rochelle and decided to hang on to the house we owned in Mount Vernon, we became absentee landlords, and that gave us a problem. For years we went from one set of unsatisfactory tenants to another, until finally the house in Mount Vernon stood empty. We persuaded Nora to move in and house-sit for a while, but after she left, we were faced with the same old problem of finding a tenant who could be counted on to keep the place in good order. We wondered if we could ask Mama to move in and keep an eye on things until we could either rent it well or sell it. That option immediately raised another problem

Mama was in her late seventies. How would she know that she wasn't being rejected? That we weren't tired of her, and secretly trying to get her out of the house and out of our lives forever? We spoke first to her dentist, then to her gum specialists, and to another doctor treating her for her heart. None of them was sanguine. Some were dead set against it. Finally, we explained our predicament to Mama herself, reassuring her that we still loved her, that all we wanted was a small favor, and that as soon as we could settle the matter, her place with us would be waiting, guaranteed for the rest of her life. Please, Mama. Please?

Mama agreed to try it. She moved into the house in Mount Vernon, took it over completely, and has been there, queen regnant, ever since. We think she loves the place.

RUBY: John Henrik Clarke was the editor of *Freedomways* magazine, and he recommended me for an assignment as a book editor. It was an offer I couldn't refuse. Joseph Okpaku of the Third Press first came up with the idea of a book of poetry for children, ages eleven to seventeen—the "between cycle" people.

As our children were growing up, we often made appearances in elementary, junior high, and high schools. It always seemed easier to find material that would appeal to the very young in elementary school, and to young adults, than to the group of which Clark spoke.

Mercifully, it occurred to me to collect material from the targeted age group itself. I approached Ann Williams, a guidance counselor at Albert Leonard Junior High School in New Rochelle, whom we had grown to know when our children were students there. She put us in touch with teachers who encouraged students to submit poetry. I was moved, amused, and greatly impressed by the candor, the humor, the simplicity, and the profundity of the work we received. These blossoming writers were questioning the nature of existence, searching for personal definition, or cynically dismissing some traditional values. There were also poems describing poverty and discrimination, as well as self-critical and judgmental expressions, abstractions, some nonsense, some humor, and a riddle or two.

Nora, Guy, LaVerne, a few of their friends, and several adults, including me, are featured in the masterpiece I called *Glowchild and Other Poems*. Some of those young poets are now published, like Gordon Nelson, Calvin Anderson, and our daughter, LaVerne, whose name is now Hasna Muhammad.

Nora taught me how painful it can be to be young, and the time in life finally comes for freeing your hair from braids, for high heels, pretty dresses, parties, and boyfriends. I was excited, too, even with budding hormones beginning to dictate new attitudes and behavior that I had to get used to. Nowhere in school do you learn how to deal with your child becoming her own boss and acting as if she knows as much as most adults—maybe even more—especially more than her mom.

Over the years, I remember delivering this admonition to the three of our children: "Okay. So maybe this is your first time on this earth.

I don't know. But this trip, I am the mother. This family arrangement is not a democracy. It's mostly a dictatorship. I've never been a mother before, either. But since I was here first, and I run the joint, I will listen to your side of any issue and consider what I think makes sense. The final decision, however, is mine and I expect to be obeyed. That is the basic meaning of mother and child. I love you. I will listen to you. But I am the boss!" It worked for a while.

As I look back now, we weren't too bad as parents, but I feel that part of education should include an exploration of what it means to be a parent. Parenting is too important for complete on-the-job training.

Some things definitely found me unprepared. Once there was a dance at the high school for which we helped primp and prime Nora. When it was time for it to be over, I waited with excitement for her to come home. I was not prepared for the look of unhappiness as she came through the door and hugged me.

"Mommie. Nobody asked me to dance," she said. "Only the pretty girls, the ones with the light skin and long hair, were asked to dance."

I almost cried. My beautiful brown daughters would find out about color, and soon the ugly specter of racism would dig its claws into their minds and souls, and the struggle for their value as human beings and as black women would begin. A kind of fury overtook me.

"Before I see them question their beauty, their worth, their capacity to be loved, we'll send them abroad to school—to Germany, to Switzerland, to France," I said. I mentioned these countries first because I'd known a number of girls who went to such countries and married white men who adored them. They were black or brown, beautiful or plain, but they found love and fulfillment. "What is with this demon of color and hair?" I asked, as if I really didn't know the answer from the depth of my being.

It was difficult not to let our fears clutch us—especially when the children made decisions and choices with which we did not agree. It was all I could do not to bring out the passports again years later when Nora told us she was getting married. Her husband-to-be was a Nigerian living in America. He was intelligent, attentive, and a hard worker—with just the right skills to help us build the family production company we envisioned. Nora seemed to like him, but I had to work hard to dispel my initial reaction to him. After all, this was Nora's business, and that was all that mattered, I told myself.

The night before the wedding, I couldn't sleep. Instead, I laid my plans. Several days earlier, I'd secured several thousand dollars in cash—enough to buy clothes and pay for hotel space until we could plan the next move. The more I thought about this marriage, the more unacceptable I found it. Nora must not persist in this marriage. I won't let her. I found in Ossie no ally for my fears, "It's Nora's choice, Ruby. I beg you, don't interfere. We've prayed on it."

The next morning, just before she began to dress for the wedding, I spoke to her one last time as Miss Davis. She didn't seem shocked when I told her of my reservations about the marriage, that it didn't feel right, that if she said the word, the wedding need not happen. I shall never forget her patience and her love as she reassured me and brought me back from a sweaty hysteria on that sweltering September day.

Only now does it occur to me that the madness of that time was a reenactment of my own nightmare, my own desperate wish not to marry Frank Brown. There had been no one around to show me how to avoid it. It was like being buried alive and screaming for help with no one there to hear you. Nora's marriage lasted less than a year.

~ ~ ~

Alice Childress was one of the first members of the American Negro Theatre. She was the original Blanche in *Anna Lucasta,* and a good actor. It is as a playwright, however, and as an author of short monologues, that I remember her best. *Wedding Band* is her most produced play, and I was Julia Augustine in the first four presentations.

I always got the feeling that Alice really had another kind of actor in mind for Julia, and I understood that without it ever being said. I'm aware of another occasion where an actor was cast, but it wasn't working out. Because I'd done the role before and time was running short, it was decided to send for me. My heart went out to Alice. She truly wanted someone, say, like Alfre Woodard, who wasn't old enough then, to have been a choice. If I were casting Julia, Alfre would fit the bill—earth-brown, sensitive, with a solid blackness about her, and sweet, but capable of getting down and dirty, too.

Wedding Band was a challenging play. The story caused eight local TV stations, mostly in the Southwest, to ban the show for content. It was an interracial love story, tender, sad, and, also in that aspect, vicious. But the most profound lesson Julia taught me, as an actor, had nothing to do with race.

When it was being televised for ABC in 1974, I discovered for the first time that it is possible to work twenty-five hours straight without any sleep. Joseph Papp, founder of the New York Shakespeare Festival, directed the teleplay with Alice Childress, as they had also co-directed the stage version at the Public Theater, and he was way behind schedule. We had to finish by morning and that was that. We dared not sit or lie down or stop talking or stop moving around for too long; and we ate only enough to put something besides hot coffee in our stomachs. Tempers were tightrope taut, the work was intense, but we did it because we had to.

Looking back, I think the relentless nature of the work added an excitement to the finished product. I really didn't know I had it in me, or why all of us didn't drop dead. I count *Wedding Band* among some of my most rewarding work.

～　～　～

OSSIE: Aaron Beckwith, a producer at CBS television, read *Glowchild,* Ruby's book of poetry, and took it to CBS to see if they were interested in using it as a basis for one of their young folks' specials. CBS said yes. Guy wrote the music. Nora's husband was our producer. I supervised the writing of the script, and then directed it, retitled *Today Is Ours.* The entire family and many of their friends were used as actors.

We shot the interiors inside Grace Baptist Church, in the same hall where, some years before, Mrs. Welles had staged her famous Christmas pageant with live sheep, and a most recalcitrant donkey who seemed to understand only Italian cuss words. Our pastor and some of the congregation were also involved as actors. In the vacant lot, where we shot the exteriors, we had to move the snow.

Nora, who still has a beautiful voice, sang one of Guy's songs in the production, and LaVerne, now Hasna, recited one of her poems. Harry Belafonte was our guest star. CBS aired it February 23, 1974, as one of their specials for children, but grown-ups told us they liked it, too. The Davis family was very pleased. It was the last time we appeared together on camera in the same production.

RUBY: It was January, cold, with snow on the ground. We had four days to shoot children having fun in a playground that belonged to a "Scrooge spirited" landlord, played by Harry Belafonte. We had rehearsed the indoor scenes and recorded the music, some of it performed by our truly gifted son, Guy, for this, his first professional assignment.

We knew this part of the shoot would be a challenge, but it wasn't like we could change the location to a basement or something because our story was built around real territory—sky and other elements of the unmistakable outdoors. There were fourteen children that Ossie, who is not exactly an outdoorsy, sportsy, fun-and-gamesy-type guy, was trying to make look as if they weren't freezing. It was necessary, no doubt about it, to shoot, reshoot, and then reshoot them "chillun," so that maybe eventually they would look thawed out and like they were having fun.

My heart went out, however, to Ossie, the director, when he called for another retake, and one of our own babies yelled, "What, Daddy, again?" Something in the tone of LaVerne's question made us realize that at least one of our children would not follow in our footsteps as a thespian.

We were so glad that Harry had agreed to be part of our project. He was a great mean old landlord. By the story's end, the children charm him into letting them use his land for a playground. Eric Saunders, one of the young actors and a musician, became our other son-in-law a few years later. In addition, we arrived at a new appreciation of Nora as a singer and as an actor.

Although we hadn't planned it, the whole family was engaged in one project based on material written by their peers in a book their Mama had compiled that was turned into a television special their Daddy had directed.

CHAPTER 33

A Teaspoonful of Power

RUBY: My father, though easygoing, generous, and affectionate, was a mischievous man who walked like his feet hurt. One day, a few years after he retired from the railroad, I'd prepared breakfast and he came to the house. I was glad to see him looking better than I'd seen him looking lately. I prepared one of his favorite breakfasts—eggs, grits, and coffee. We got to talking about Mother, and laughing about her luck with the horses and numbers, and how she'd use her winnings to make the family more secure.

"Your mother, Emma, was something else," he said. He began to get emotional. I felt uncomfortable. Then out of the clear blue: "I'd have never run around on your mother, with all those women, and stuff, but, boy, when she was through in the bed, you know what I mean? That was it. No matter what was happening with me," he said, "Em would turn over, or even get up and leave. She just wasn't much into that sort of thing."

Well, it was out. He'd said it—what I felt he'd been trying to tell me many times before. I didn't know what to say, or how to say it to this womanizer, this baby maker, this dog—as Mother had called him. I wanted so much to hug him, and tell him it was all right, that I understood. I broke the silence that followed by asking Daddy if I could get him anything else to eat. He said no and pushed his plate away.

I thought of Mother, who had been dead four years. Mother, the stern disciplinarian who was perhaps insecure, with times as tough as they were. I could have blurted out something like that to give him the forgiveness he needed from me, but I didn't. I didn't hug him, or tell him how much I loved him, either. I didn't know that that was our last meal together.

A couple of weeks later, Daddy went to the hospital—something the matter with his heart. The doctors had him taking seven or eight different pills. I'd expressed my concern, but I wasn't in touch with any naturalists like Dr. Fulton in Chicago, except by phone and by mail. I should have flown to Chicago and talked to her directly, but I didn't. She sent me some remedies, and made other suggestions, but they seemed impractical. Besides, I didn't want Kate, Daddy's wife, to think I was butting in and trying to take over. In addition, Ossie was going to Hawaii for ten days to work in the television series *Hawaii Five-0,* and I was getting ready to go with him. Most of all, though I had seen a bed sore on Daddy's rump that bothered me and I had spoken about it to the nurse, it never occurred to me that Daddy was all that sick.

There was a young friend of ours, Diane Edwards, who worked as a private nurse. She volunteered to keep an eye on Daddy while we were away. That reassured us all.

During one of my visits to see him in the hospital, he talked again about women. Rather, about a woman—a married, respectable pillar of the church—who had seduced him as a boy. He was sorry he hadn't told his mother. Perhaps I should have pursued the subject, asked him all the questions he seemed to be inviting—something that would have left him with some kind of peace and absolution, but again, I couldn't find the language, couldn't bring myself to say anything.

Another time—the last, I think it was—he sat up from a reclining position, and said simply and quietly, "Look, there's Emma. There's your mother standing over there."

I looked and asked him, "Where, Daddy? What's she wearing?" He didn't answer but kept smiling into the corner where, I'm sure, Emma was smiling back. That should have alerted me, should have told me something was wrong with his thinking. Senility, perhaps. I'd be sure to tell LaVerne the next time I saw her. I hugged him, but I don't remember if I told him that Ossie and I were going to Hawaii. It didn't seem all that important.

We went to Hawaii, where much of what I did was to watch Ossie work. We made it to the beach a time or two, but nothing spectacular. Ossie's no mermaid when it comes to large bodies of water and neither am I. He didn't even bring a bathing suit. Sometimes the most delightful thing a woman can do when she gets away from home is just to rest, no matter where she is. And rest is what I did most of the time.

Diane Edwards met us at the airport when we returned to tell us that Marshall Edward Wallace, my father, had died. Kate, his wife, who was in the cancer ward at that very same hospital at the very same time he was, died about a month later.

I don't like it—this looking back—to discover how life sometimes can blind us, and how death sometimes can make us see.

∾   ∾   ∾

After Moscow, David Wolper kept in touch, and on at least two occasions, invited Ossie and me to his home in California. One morning he called us in New York to inquire about that story about the generations I'd described to him in Moscow. I was a little disappointed that he wasn't asking about Margaret Walker's *Jubilee* or Zora Neale Hurston's *Their Eyes Were Watching God*. I so much wanted to play Janie. I quickly banished the ache and explained that we hadn't heard from Alex Haley lately, and presumed he was somewhere putting it down on paper. "Here, let me give you his phone number," I said.

I've been enormously pleased to read and to hear Alex and David give me credit in print and on platform for being godmother of sorts to the *Roots* phenomenon on television. David suffered some anxiety as the project was being written. No one, not even he, I suspect, anticipated its enormous success. For many reasons, including a heavy schedule on the lecture circuit and other commitments, we could not be in the first part of *Roots,* which aired in 1976, although Alex had suggested I make a choice as to which of two roles I might like to play. I'm happy, though, that "my hand dere" in the 1979 sequel, *Roots II: The Next Generation,* as Queen Haley, Alex Haley's grandmother.

OSSIE: My first memory of Alex Haley was at a meeting of the Black Academy of Arts and Letters somewhere in New York City on a Sunday afternoon. Ruby and I wandered around, shaking hands, chatting aimlessly, laughing with our friends, sipping wine, and eating hors d'oeuvres. In one room, we came across a group of people standing around a short, brown man with glasses holding a glass of wine in one hand and talking. We drifted into the crowd of listeners and soon found ourselves enchanted.

The man—we didn't know him then as Alex Haley—was a writer telling of a project he was involved in that called for a tremendous amount of research. He was out to trace his family tree as far back as he could, and was sharing with all who would listen some of what he had found. This was the first time I had heard of Kunte Kinte. It certainly was not to be the last.

Roots was one of the most watched television series ever, and there are many theories as to why it was so popular. Mine has to do with how blacks are perceived in the general American culture. Ralph Ellison asserted in his book, *Invisible Man,* that in order to accommodate slavery in the midst of a free society, American culture had to cultivate a certain spiritual, moral, and even material blindness concerning Negroes. Certain stereotypes had to be created that enabled the mind to perceive a vicious contradiction, and yet come away from the deception feeling pure and innocent.

But all of this had changed with the coming of the civil rights revolution when black folks, by our own push and insistence, had burst free from the portable oblivion to which America had consigned and confined us, and were insisting on being redefined. If blacks were not the images that whites had held sacred all these years, then who the hell were they? History had asked that question before, but it had to be answered differently this time, and it had to be answered at once! Alex Haley happened to be a part of the answer.

∽ ∽ ∽

RUBY: I used to think of sorority girls, when I thought of them at all, as young, middle-class girls, generally bright, well turned out in flippy skirts and saddle shoes, more or less, looking like cheerleaders. At Hunter College, I didn't know girls who belonged to sororities. Living an all-gears-engaged lifestyle off campus left me no inclination or time to investigate the matter.

Although I'd never been a joiner, I liked the idea of women banding together in friendship around a specific interest, or for any other reason. Outside of Carlotta, Barbara Smith, and one or two other girls, I didn't have pals, girlfriends, hanging-out relationships.

In 1974, I received a letter from Dr. Jeanne Noble of the Delta Sigma Theta sorority, headquartered in Washington, D.C., inviting me to become an honorary member. The invitation became more appealing as I thought about the mountains of work by dynamic authors that I wanted the world to know, and the whole field of images about black people waiting to be rescued from neglect. I also considered my own desires to be connected as an actor, and as someone responsible for bringing such images to the table. Surely among the 85,000 members, there would be women with like ambitions.

The induction ceremony was an inspiring affair. I was now a member of the enormous body of black women united in a sisterhood. I felt that the possibilities for some of the most meaningful experiences in my life were before me—and they were.

Delta Sigma Theta had just formed a new Commission of Arts and Letters, consisting of journalists, craftspeople, visual artists, actors, musicians, and others with and without celebrity who could suggest a more vital role for the sorority to play in the arts. I was invited to join it and I did. Among its members were Paula Giddings, author of *When and Where I Enter,* actor/director Micki Grant, who was also the author/composer of *Don't Bother Me, I Can't Cope,* and Lena Horne. Soror Noble chaired the commission.

The president of the sorority was Lillian Benbow, a warm, down-to-earth, elegant, dynamic woman who had great visions for the Deltas. She believed African Americans should have greater control of the images by which our families, especially our children, are governed, and she believed that as a public service organization, the sorority could broaden and improve those images.

To that end, Sorors Benbow and Noble requested a meeting with Ossie and me to discuss the idea of the Deltas producing a film. It was a tremendous idea. How did they propose to accomplish this? What film did they have in mind? Where would the money come from? Who would produce it? Ossie reminded them that he was not a producer. However, if a production company were to be set up that included the sorority as co-producers, he would be amenable. The Deltas agreed. They wanted us to be involved. There were many meetings with advisers, attorneys, and unions. Before money could be allotted to begin the project, we had to form a company to which the sorority could relate. We named the family corporation Rolling Ventures: R for Ruby, O for Ossie, L for LaVerne, another L for our son-in-law, I for nothing, N for Nora, and G for Guy. I had thought up the clever anagram.

While Lillian and Jean prepared the national headquarters and the chapters for the new venture, and secured investments, Nora's husband had found a script by John Storm Powers, an adventure film with political intrigue and a location in Nigeria. He had connections in the fledgling film industry there. Costs would be very low compared with any location we could find in the U.S.A. We could headquarter in Lagos, at the modern, convenient Ikoyi Hotel.

The film was to be called *Countdown at Kusini,* written by Ossie Davis, based on the book by John Storm Powers, and produced by Rolling Ventures and Delta Sigma Theta sorority.

OSSIE: In many aspects of my life and my career, I didn't pick the job that I was chosen to do; the job, instead, picked me. That's certainly how it was with *Countdown at Kusini.* A director was needed, and ultimately a producer. If I didn't do it, who would?

Not only did my son-in-law, the company manager, promise us the benefit of his kinship and connections in Nigeria, but also I was chairman of the American Delegation to the Black and African Festival of Arts and Culture, known as FESTAC, soon to be held in Nigeria, which gave me access to power in high places. Surely things would go well. The hell they did!

The money the Deltas had raised to produce the film, though substantial, covered only a portion of what would be needed. But we thought that if everything happened according to plan, and everybody watched their p's and q's, we could pull it off. There was no margin for error and no room for maneuver—circumstances that flew directly in the face of accepted Broadway and Hollywood wisdom, which says that anything that can go wrong with production will go wrong, especially if it costs money and the budget is tight. Things started to go wrong the minute we got there.

When the crew arrived in Nigeria and saw the working conditions, they insisted on more pay. Another big jolt came in the way the whole operation was perceived by the Nigerians. We had been promised that most of our necessities would cost us very little, or would come to us free of charge, as people would be persuaded to donate their services. Dancers would dance, drummers would drum, singers would sing, and villagers would dress up in their finest costumes just for the honor and the pleasure of being in a picture, particularly one being made by Africans and African Americans.

Local customs and considerations didn't help much, though. On one occasion, I was sent for by an official of FESTAC in the middle of the shooting. I was put into a car and hurried to his office, where he introduced me to two young Nigerian ladies who wanted to be actresses in the film. I promised to see what I could do and hurried back to location.

On another occasion, we were to film a scene in a village some distance from Lagos. We set up for the shot; then we were told we had to wait for the arrival of the chief, which took half a day. When the chief came, he refused to give his permission until he had been paid.

We ran out of money early on and had to constantly call Lillian Benbow to send us more. We piled up hotel bills for the crew on our credit card. And most of all, we relied on our friend, Joseph Krusch, who had become our tax attorney in 1960. From his office in New York, Joe began to guide us the rest of the way.

Finally, principal photography was finished. Ruby and I took a plane out with a stopover in Conakrie, Senegal. While waiting for the next leg of our flight back to New York, we met Muhammad Ali, who just the previous night had defeated George Foreman in Zaire and regained his title as heavyweight champion of the world.

Back in New York, there was still work to be done, and money to be raised. Once again, Joe Krusch and Lillian Benbow came up with the money. Joe introduced me to Herbert Lennard, a Hungarian film distributor, who put in his time and money. Meanwhile, every week there was a payroll to meet. I borrowed money from a labor bank on Moe Foner's recommendation and some from Freedom National, a black bank in Harlem. The Deltas found Pedco, a funding mechanism of the Presbyterian Church, from which we borrowed upward of $25,000, which enabled us finally to finish the film.

We heaved a major sigh of relief, and at last we could relax, ease up, turn loose, take some time to catch our breath. No such luck. Producing a film is one thing; distributing it is another. Our most momentous struggle was just beginning.

With *Countdown at Kusini,* we wanted to make a good film that would be artistically satisfying and that would make money for the sorority, competing with the blaxploitation films that were making serious money for the studios. Delta Sigma Theta—not Hollywood, for once—would own and control what motion pictures were saying about black people and also make a profit. The revolutionary thing was not how the film was made, but how it was to be marketed. It should have worked; all we had to do was to budget the whole thing backward.

If each of the 85,000 Delta sorors paid admission of $7.00 at the box office to see their own film, the gross would be $480,000. If we could produce a film that only cost, say, $200,000, they could turn a profit of $280,000 from Deltas' patronage alone, with the rest of the gross being a box office bonanza. It was as simple as that, and just as impossible.

Though we made a film completely independent of Hollywood money or influence, we still had to use Hollywood's distribution system. And that, in the end, was what killed us. There are about eight major distributors, who, once they agree to distribute your film, must make deals with the exhibitors, the people who actually own the theaters where the film is to be shown. For the Deltas' marketing scheme to work, a major rearrangement in the traditional Hollywood distribution system would have been required, and many a better film than *Kusini* has been sunk without a trace in the tug-of-war that obtains between distributors and exhibitors. But how were we to know? In fact, we thought we were lucky.

David Begelman, who at that time was head of Columbia Pictures, had been a personal "friend" of ours since the days when he had been our agent at Creative Management Agency. We were happy when he flew to New York to meet with us. Lillian outlined her marketing plan: Opening night in every major market was to be hosted by the Deltas at a big gala. Such an event would guarantee maximum press coverage, most of it free. Then the Deltas would mobilize their membership, who would not only see the film, but also visit schools and churches to stir interest and spark attendance by the rest of the black community.

David seemed very excited by the whole idea and told us that Columbia would be glad to cooperate in such a venture. He allocated $350,000 for prints and advertising, and sent us a check for $75,000 as a down payment.

The Deltas were out in force at each opening, in Memphis, in Atlanta—all across the country—holding their gala openings one by one. That part worked to perfection; but, contrary to our expectations, the exhibitors seldom ran the picture more than a day or two, certainly not enough time for the Deltas to get their members and their friends to the box office. By the time they had rounded up their membership, the picture had opened and closed. The Deltas' marketing strategy never had a chance. The remaining $275,000 that we were expecting from David Begelman and Columbia Pictures never materialized.

To this day, I cannot explain why *Kusini* failed so swiftly and completely at the box office, but because it carried our names, and because its funding came out of the pockets of the thousands of black women who believed in us and in the project, I wish that I could.

RUBY: It has been almost twenty-five years since *Kusini* was originally released, and in my mind, I often rewrite the story surrounding the making of it.

As if in answer to my longing to produce and perform in films adapted from black literature, Lillian, Jean, and the Deltas dropped their proposition in my lap.

I try to forgive myself for not shouting, "Hold on! I can tell you what we need to do. We must find a much simpler story, one close to the sensibilities and concerns of black women. Let us commission one of the countless sisters who are writers to write an exciting adventure, love story, mystery, or a compelling combination of all three. Let us make a film from a real story—a great women's story. Yes! I will be in the film, but let me be part of the production team as well! In this brave first effort, let us locate in somebody's garage, basement, country home, or get permission from the city for a vacant corner lot—like a Cassavetes would do it, getting the unions to do waivers, and perhaps contribute. Furthermore, it can be accomplished with the original investment. We will stretch the dollars and make them cover."

I try to forgive myself for throwing up my hands and going all faint, whispering, "Oh, no, not me. I'm just an actor—I mean, actress. Let my husband, let my son-in-law, let the men do it," then scurrying back to my "female burrow," and waiting to be summoned and given orders.

Will there ever come such a time again in my life? I was so close to making my gender proud, and I muffed it. Racism and sexism erode self-trust, and no matter what we say, make us do less than we know, and betray who we are.

∾   ∾   ∾

OSSIE: In 1975, Ruby and I found ourselves with a weekly radio show, and it was certainly no small operation. The National Black Network had offices and studios in downtown New York, and its programming was carried by local stations all across the country. We even had a sponsor, Kraft Foods of Chicago. We called it *The Ossie Davis and Ruby Dee Story Hour,* and it attracted a large audience. We produced the show, basing our format loosely on the kind of shows we did on college and high school campuses.

First, there was a section for short stories, folktales, and poetry, from works by African, Caribbean, and African-American authors.

Then we interviewed celebrities such as Sidney, Don King, Patti LaBelle, and Maya Angelou. We also highlighted moments from black history and affairs, and read letters from our listeners. Most of the letters came from teachers, who used our show as topics in their classrooms; from students; and from Black Mom and Pop. Though we were aware of the hunger for material about the black experience, we were still surprised at the volume of mail we received.

RUBY: Vince Saunders and Sidney Small ran the station. Our contact at Kraft was most patient and encouraging as we worked out the kinks, week by week, with our neighbors and friends, Arden and Clem Cumberbatch. How fortunate we were in this collaboration because they knew the older as well as the modern authors, were articulate writers themselves, and understood what we wanted to do.

When we instituted a contest called "Write On," giving $500 cash prizes for the best poems and short stories, we were overwhelmed. NBN had to hire several extra hands to handle the mail. The winners were brought to the studio, where we read their work over the air and gave them their checks.

When I was a child, it was mandatory that I took piano lessons. I remember the remarkable patience of piano teachers and all the practicing it took. Even today I'm still trying to play the songs I practiced years ago. The only difference is that today practicing is like taking a small vacation. I can tune out all the other concerns when I try again to play "Rustles of Spring," "Für Elise," some Scott Joplin, or, if I really need a long trip, some Gershwin.

I am considered a dramatic actor, and over the years, I have collected a few other feathers in my motley cap: In 1978, James Hicks, one of the editors of the New York *Amsterdam News,* invited me to write a weekly column, which I called "Swingin' Gently." James and Esther Jackson again enabled me to serve as contributing editor for the new *Freedomways* magazine. Although I've been writing poetry since I was about eight years old, the point is that nothing in my background told me that I would be qualified to write a musical. I called it a poedansical—poetry and music—and titled it *Twin-Bit Gardens*. Joseph Papp gave me a workshop at the Public Theater in New York and I was on my way. But on my way to where?

OSSIE: Ruby has a very different way of perceiving things. Hence her way of conceiving things as a writer differs also. So when she showed me a piece she was working on called *Twin-Bit Gardens,* I saw right away that she was onto something.

Joe Papp's workshop encouraged Ruby to keep on working. Later, she asked Guy to write the music for the piece, which he did. She changed the title to *Take It from the Top!* and took it to Woodie King, who produced it in January 1979. It played according to Woodie's schedule, then word of mouth caught on, and by the the end of the run, people were being turned away from the box office. Ruby obviously had the makings of a hit, and Woodie asked us to extend the run, which, naturally, we wanted to do. However, we had a series of engagements from which we could not extract ourselves, so we had to close the show.

That summer, Woodie brought in Ashton Springer, another producer, and they suggested that we try the piece out in Philadelphia's Playhouse in the Park. We were there for two weeks.

Ruby' s latest and best version was never shown in the New York area. We had expected that the large black population, church people in particular, would be a natural market for a play about God and angels. We were wrong. The church audience was not used to seeing God portrayed as we portrayed Him.

Her musical romp about the end of the world, and other business, is based in biblical myth, but it takes place in the world of high technology, and spoofs pop culture to render a social critique and a spiritual optimism. The play opens with God having given up on the human race because of their seemingly mindless march to destroy the planet Earth and their refusal to heed His Word, so He schedules Armageddon. But there's one angel whose job it has been to save souls, who just can't give up on humanity. When she gets busted for trying to save souls on the sly, she makes a deal with God that saves the world from destruction. Echoing a phrase that is well known to all performers who strive in rehearsals to perfect the scene, the musical arrangement, or the dance step, God's final decree to the citizens of Earth is to check themselves, and then "Take it from the top!"

It is a magnificent piece that yet awaits another chance to be mounted.

CHAPTER 34

We, the Family, Become a Company

OSSIE: It happened indirectly, and it certainly wasn't intended, but the 1980s was the decade in which the Davises began to reassemble and redefine themselves—not only as a family, but also as the creative labor force behind Emmalyn II Productions Company, Inc. We chose that name in honor of Ruby's mother, Emma, and of our children; one letter is taken from each of their names; L from LaVerne; Y from Guy; and N from Nora. Originally Joe Krusch set it up for tax purposes, but it soon began to actually produce programming for television. The corporation was composed of Ruby and me as officers, employees, and stockholders, and the children who were appointed members of the board and part of the company.

RUBY: These members of the board weren't just our kids; they had all come from a few places and had been through things. When they were six, seven, eight years old, they had walked picket lines, and through their parents, they had hobnobbed with progressive people, black and white. They had witnessed, although they may have been too young to register it, Ossie's and my work with the kind of people, mostly Jews, who had fought for the eight-hour workday, the forty-hour week, for safe working conditions in factories, against the poll tax, for antilynching laws, and so forth. They had eaten late night dinners at many benefits for the NAACP, the Urban League, CORE, SNCC, SCLC, at special drives to raise money for somebody's bail, to pay attorney's fees, or at fund-raisers to help correct some injustice.

In those days, we worked a lot for no money—sometimes we'd get a twenty-five-dollar honorarium—and provided our own transportation. To get us all to whatever site, we went on the train or we borrowed Daddy's blue Oldsmobile, which he finally gave to us. Feeding our kids was often part of the deal, and if we hadn't gotten around to giving them dinner, they would tear up the hors d'oeuvres. As they grew older, we took them with us less. By the time they took their seats on the board of Emmalyn II Productions, they knew the importance of labor unions, churches, and good schools, and they knew the value of protest. Above all, they knew the double-sided nature of being an American and being black.

OSSIE: From lap babies to board members, the transition seemed swift. Nora was just a handful of baby, two weeks old, when she trekked with us from the Bronx to Mount Vernon. Quick to smile—and to learn—with little dimples and flashing teeth—gregarious she was, and outgoing, with an instinct to mother anything that moved. Good at collecting people and organizing group activities, she became the driving force behind the "theater" that she and the children set up for themselves and their friends in the basement. There was never any doubt that she would follow in her parents' footsteps and take to the stage.

She went from New Rochelle High to Vassar College in a time of turmoil and experimentation as academia tried to adjust to an alien presence on formerly all-white campuses. The black girls found themselves being treated by the white girls as all scholarship students, who were welcomed as a "learning experience." An overly earnest tolerance seemed to prevail and deeply clouded the morale of the black girls. What happened next resulted from a failure to communicate. Something had to give, and something did.

Early one morning, I got a call from Nora, announcing, "Daddy, we've just taken over the main building." I was not at all surprised. She asked me to notify the parents of some of the other girls who were sitting in with her, and promised to keep me informed. She later transferred to New York University School of the Arts Institute of Film and Television, from which she graduated.

She had held a number of jobs—at the Studio Museum in Harlem, with Carl Byoir Associates, an advertising agency, and in single copy sales at *Essence* magazine. During this time she decided she wanted to look at becoming a performer.

After discussing her options with us, she enrolled in an acting class. Since she had grown up around people in theater, we felt she was aware of the very competitive and hard realities of the business, and we said little to dissuade her. About three months later, however, she called for a meeting with us to announce that she had thought further about the matter of becoming an actor, and had changed her mind.

Bright, energetic, intensely committed, Nora is the thorough professional in whatever she undertakes. She became an associate producer for our company, handling contracts, catering, airline tickets, and hotel reservations. Her hand was in everything, from the conception and design of a project, writing the text for the viewers guide, to dealing with actors, writers, and musicians, as well as with the unions and whatever else the company might need to meet its goals. Her second husband, Bill Day, whom she married in 1981, also became a functioning member of the team. They have quite a brood, Brian, Jammal, Imani, and Bill's eldest, Allena, and her children.

Guy has always been a creative, independent, iconoclastic soul, completely involved in moving his own agenda, with a strong sense of timing and direction as it applies to the way he has chosen to live his life. He never seemed lonely as a child, or much in need of any attention from others. We always suspected that something good was going on inside his head behind his private wall that didn't need assistance, but he never said. Like Nora, he, too, could be affable, gregarious, and compatible, but also self-contained and self-directed.

He spent two years at Pace University, then switched to Hunter College, Ruby's alma mater, majoring in music. He refused to get the last seven credits needed to graduate, much to Ruby's chagrin.

Along the way to his true calling, Guy had worked in a glass factory and had been a cabdriver. Today he is an accomplished acoustic blues guitarist. I've seen him tame a large audience sitting outdoors on a hillside; I've also seen him work a room of two or three "after midnight" customers down in a Greenwich Village nightclub, with the same easygoing authority. In both cases, he gave his best. I like his low-key equanimity and his give-and-take camaraderie with audiences. He performs as if he is carrying around in his head and in his heart a strong sense of pickers from generations past who are still watching—still listening—Huddie Ledbetter, Blind Lemon Jefferson, Robert Johnson, and Pete Seeger from today as well. It's their approval that Guy seems to be seeking. His artistry, his faithfulness to the masters finally led him to Memphis and the W. C. Handy Blues Award.

When Ruby decided to turn her play into a musical, *Take It from the Top!* though Guy's forte is the blues, he turned out to be an extremely flexible and eclectic composer. He was featured in the film *Beat Street,* produced by Harry Belafonte, in the soap opera *One Life to Live* for ABC; and in 1990, he wrote and starred in his own drama, *The Trial.* When Emmalyn II began to produce for television, Guy, our composer-in-residence, wrote the theme for our first venture, *With Ossie and Ruby.*

RUBY: Guy has worked with us many times as a composer and as an actor. He wrote the music for all our shows, and often performed it. We were especially pleased with his work at Crossroads Theatre in the 1995 production of *Two Hah Hahs and a Homeboy,* an evening of storytelling, humor, and song that featured just the three of us. I've received numerous invitations to present that show, but Guy travels so frequently, performing quite often abroad, that I could never coordinate our schedules. He also stays busy recording original compositions and has several CDs that are selling quite well.

Incidentally, Nora and Guy both met their future spouses at the Studio Museum in Harlem. Guy met and married Dorothy Désir, a curator and adviser to artists, in 1989. They have our seventh grandchild, Martial.

OSSIE: LaVerne started out as our small, in-house enigma with wide eyes and an inquisitive demeanor, more subtle in character and complex in personality than the others, requiring something a little special in the way she was attended to. Even the signal kicks in utero were strong and therefore misleading—the doctor predicted she would be a boy. Seldom obvious or overt in her demands, she was always, nonetheless, insistent; it was up to us to decipher what she really wanted. Being the youngest, it was perhaps natural that she would be a rebel.

She was smart as a whip, but—like many children of her troubled generation—was fervently antiestablishment in her opinions, skeptical of white America, and hard to persuade that college was a necessity. She agreed to attend—but only as a favor to her mother. LaVerne had majored in film and television at SUNY-Purchase, then transferred to Sarah Lawrence. There she was fortunate enough to study literature with the famous authors Alice Walker and E. L. Doctorow.

The sixties and seventies had been for young black Americans a time of rebellion for some, of revolution for others, and of religion for all the rest. Our children had to sink or swim in the turbulent currents that swirled through those years. We had struggled to bring them up as Baptists in Grace Baptist Church in Mount Vernon, where I was one of their Sunday School teachers. But with Malcolm X and Martin Luther King, with Angela Davis and Stokely Carmichael, with the Black Panthers and the Black Muslims as their idols and their icons, their moral and spiritual world offered choices their parents had never known. Suffice it to say: Not one of them remains a Baptist today.

I questioned Nora, being considerably curious and concerned as to why she and Guy and LaVerne never went back, and she told me that the pastor's laying on of hands was not, in her words, what she believed "Jesus had in mind." I hastily dropped the subject. I couldn't defend the pulpit to my children any further. Morally and spiritually, they were on their own.

LaVerne's spiritual journey—and maybe her liberation—took her further away than the others. She changed her name and her lifestyle— her dress, her dietary habits—and converted to Islam. We had no problem still including her, but she had to make some tough decisions about how she and her family could relate to the rest of us. We were all in for some rocky and uncertain times.

After graduation, she became a teacher in a public school in Mount Vernon, with a special interest in what the black children were being taught. She wrote plays on African-American history for her classes and became a published poet; with a profound interest in multiculturalism, she adopted a new way of looking at race relations in America, and began work on her doctoral degree. Whenever Emmalyn II Productions had a project that required research, we turned to Hasna Muhammad, and she responded.

RUBY: LaVerne was the daughter who had informed me that college was "irrelevant."

I said, "I can't help being your mother, but if you expect us to be friends, you better get that degree."

The day she graduated, she handed me her diploma and said, "Here, Mom. I guess we can be friends now," and bounced off. So I took it and kept it. About a year later, she asked me for it because she wanted to get her master's degree. Today she is an assistant principal in Orange County, New York; she is Dr. Muhammad, having recently completed her Ed.D. at Teachers College, Columbia University.

That reminds me of a similar story about Guy. Who was it that I couldn't get to take piano lessons? His sisters took lessons and practiced without a fight, but Guy absolutely refused to study. When a kid refuses to do something, you may just as well hang it up. It was a defeat for me then, but who turned out to be the musician in the family? Guy.

LaVerne and her husband, Eric Saunders, became Muslims before they were married—became Hasna and Abdul Wali Muhammad. I don't recall that they renounced Christianity; but in addition to the Bible, they read the *Qur'an;* she wore the veil and the traditional clothing, and he wore the *tarbuush* and the traditional clothing. They were becoming different people.

They referred to folks like Ossie and me as disbelievers, or "kafirun," prayed five times a day on prayer rugs, ate no pork, used no utensils contaminated by pork, and one day, they informed us that they were giving up their apartment and moving to a Muslim community in Brooklyn. Ossie and I went slack-jawed for a while, but except for the derogatory nature of the word "kafirun," we were cool. We were glad they weren't into drugs, in jail, or caught up in some of the popular craziness into which some young people stumble while looking for right turns to take in life. At best, it was a religion that claimed their attention, so we prayed on it and let it alone.

A few weeks after the move to the community, they gathered up their little baby, Ihsaana, our first grandchild, and drove off in the middle of the night, leaving all their belongings behind, and went back to Mr. and Mrs. Pearlee Saunders's house, to his mother and father. They didn't volunteer reasons for their actions and we didn't ask. They are still Muslims, but now they live in the suburbs with three children—Ihsaana, Muta-Ali, Jihaad—a house, and a mortgage.

Just being alive almost anywhere in this world is a challenge—especially today. Being an American is a special kind of challenge, but if you're lucky, there are perks and rewards. Being an African American, however, implies that something at the core of your existence is in crisis mode, or will be at some point in life. How do we *be* in this land? We believe Hasna and Wali were asking the questions before the crisis and bracing for the storms before they hit.

Changing our religion is only one of the moves we've made throughout our history here. We've advocated and/or tried to go back to Africa, integrate, separate, go back to God, change our names, and debated how we want to be referred to. We've fought, rebelled, protested, and turned the other cheek. There's been progress in some areas, but racism still keeps us off balance, keeps us questioning and struggling, uncertain of whether we may be standing still or going backward.

OSSIE: The five of us had a lot of fun—and a lot of anguish—just working out the myriad ways by which we belong to each other. The

(383)

sailing wasn't always smooth, and many a time, there was thunder and lightning between us. The family oath—that under no circumstances would we ever turn our backs and abandon each other—was almost stretched to the breaking point as each in turn struck out to find his or her own life, to establish their independence, based on their right, and maybe even their duty, as Ruby says, to rebel. Each did rebel, but soon, the storm was over. Forgotten now were the times when they were downright nuisances, squabbling among themselves as to whose time it was to ride in the middle in the backseat of the car.

Over the seasons, in spite of everything, a burgeoning sense of family bonded us together, flowering into a sort of dinner table democracy, later joined by Mama and the grandchildren, enlivened by running debates on everything before us or by opinions constantly revised and readjusted. The dawn of the decade found us all safely ensconced behind a common front.

RUBY: Emmalyn II Productions was engaged in six major ventures: *With Ossie and Ruby,* coproduced with KERA-TV in Dallas; *Zora Is My Name!; A Walk Through the Twentieth Century; Pioneers in Black Business; With Ossie and Ruby No. 2,* coproduced with WHMM-TV at Howard University; and *Martin Luther King: The Dream and the Drum.* Nora, Guy, and Hasna brought their special talents to Emmalyn and we all learned to work together. Not only were we a family, we were a corporation, we were a team.

Almost immediately, a different kind of opportunity presented itself. Ossie had been invited by Bob Ray Saunders, general manager of KERA, the Dallas/Fort Worth public television station, to narrate a program called *Here's to Your Health.* Bob Ray had heard our Kraft-sponsored radio show, syndicated on the National Black Network. His conversation with Ossie led to an offer for us to do a similar show on public television. Here's the beauty part: Fund-raising would not be required of us. Double Beauty Part: The first thirteen shows were almost laid down in my head before the ink was dry on the contracts.

Through Bob Ray, we met David Dowe, who was precisely the kind of director this assignment needed, depending as it did on funds from public television. He was versatile, sensitive, energetic, and creative; I can't think of any part of the process he couldn't handle. Oh yes, he was white, but what the hell, we liked David, and his skills helped us stretch the dollars and find ways to accomplish some artistic objectives that we couldn't have afforded without him.

Bob Ray and David traveled back and forth to New Rochelle, and we plotted the first thirteen segments for our new TV show, *With Ossie and Ruby*. I was like a bug in a rug, a rabbit in a briar patch, a frog on a log—I mean, I was excited. Finally, I would have a chance to explore my gifts as a conceptualizer, to demonstrate what I'd discovered from my first falling in love with authors.

At first to fall in love meant that a particular writer's words walked around in my head. I would have to commit something to memory, to keep the author close. It meant I would have to read, reread, dream, and sometimes to begin to put the work into a play or a film script, especially if there was a role in the story I wanted to play. Public television gave me an outlet for years of such contemplation.

As with the radio show in the 1970s, each half hour featured a guest artist, and in some instances, we could tailor the program to fit the artist. When we weren't dramatizing short stories, featuring a poet or a novelist, we would have glorious, relaxed conversations with well-known people outside the arts. What a joy to present a story by an author just as it was written. For example, I didn't adapt the story or do a story based on the work, say, of Langston Hughes. I got a chance to use *all* the words, swinging between the prose passages and the dialogue, trimming only to fit the time requirement.

I believe that prose is as distinct as an author's fingerprint, revealing personality, character, style, thought, rhythms. Prose lodges in the mind and curls around the senses in ways distinct from that of most dialogue. It is where the heart and soul of the writer live. By way of prose, the storyteller weaves the magic that captures our imagination. The adapter generally omits these narrative passages, substituting his or her personal interpretation, which seldom lives up to the richness of the original.

Short stories were perfect for our TV show, which first aired in February 1981. Langston Hughes, Ann Petry, Toni Cade Bambara,

Ernie Brill, James Allen McPherson, and William Branch were some of the authors whose works were interspersed among our original stories and skits. Sometimes we would build a show around poets such as Gwendolyn Brooks, Bob Kaufman, Sonia Sanchez, Amiri Baraka, Nikki Giovanni, Alice Walker, and Carolyn Rodgers, all of whom I had loved a long time. Oh, how wonderful it was to share them with a wider audience on a show of our own.

Most of the prominent people who appeared on *With Ossie and Ruby* did so primarily because they could afford to, and because we asked them to. The financial arrangements were extremely modest. To Della Reese, Robert and Kevin Hooks, Billy Taylor, Max Roach, Samm-Art Williams, Billy Preston, Roscoe Lee Browne, Anthony Zerbe, E. G. Marshall, Beverly Banfield, Estelle Parsons, Tyne Daly, Vine De Loria, and N. Scott Momaday, we are forever indebted for their expert help, and for being part of this very special time.

I even want those gone and buried (or cremated), like Sterling Brown, John Henry Faulk, and James Baldwin, to know somehow, even through the ether, how very much we appreciated their participation. To have filmed Bob Kaufman, a poet from the Beat Generation; Grace and James Boggs, activists and authors; Lerone Bennett and Haki Madhubuti, authors and publishers; Gil Scott Heron, music man and poet—what could have been more satisfying than that?

OSSIE: One segment called "Kneeslappers" written by Samm-Art Williams, which featured Guy, was about the dying folk art of telling lies. It gave us a chance to reunite with John Henry Faulk, the humorist from Texas whom Ruby had met during the McCarthy days when they had both been accused of being Communist sympathizers.

John Henry, who was fired from his job as a radio personality at CBS, sued his accusers all the way up to the Supreme Court—and won! Throughout the whole ordeal, ol' John Henry never stopped taking the hides off witch-hunters, and he never stopped telling lies, which he looked upon not only as an authentic American art form, but also as his First Amendment right.

~ ~ ~

James Cheek, who became president of Howard University in 1969, well connected in Washington, D.C., Republican circles, was a man with big ideas, especially when it came to broadcast television. At a society dinner, he had met Mrs. Katharine Graham, who owned *The Washington Post,* and knowing that she had a television station she wanted to be rid of, suggested to her that such a station was just what the university was looking for. Mrs. Graham agreed and transferred ownership of WHMM-TV to Howard University.

Dr. Cheek's idea was that WHMM-TV would be a teaching station where students might get hands-on training in every aspect of television broadcasting. In addition, the predominantly black population of Washington, D.C., could get public broadcasting that was more reflective of black needs and interests than was currently available on the regular PBS station. Dr. Cheek created the Office of Theatrical Productions and invited Professor James W. Butcher—my old friend, Beanie, of my war years in Liberia—to be the producer for WHMM-TV. A damned good actor himself, Beanie had helped to form the original Howard Players, and had led them all the way to Moscow.

Beanie asked me if there was anything we could offer that might help him meet his programming obligation. Ruby had an immediate suggestion: Why not produce something from the works of Zora Neale Hurston, one of Howard's most distinguished alumnae?

I was much too busy to be of help in the planning stages, but I said yes, yes, yes! I have always felt a sense of obligation to Howard University since the days of my youth when it had taken me in, had given me an education, and put me on the road to a career in the theater. This would be a chance for me to give something back.

There was something else that we found most attractive. Black performers in America, no matter how good, are outsiders by definition, migrant workers in the vineyards of entertainment, coming and going as the seasons of acceptance or denial wax and wane. Sometimes, as with the blaxploitation films in the seventies or the Harlem Renaissance in the late twenties, black creative genius may be all the rage; then just as suddenly the door is slammed in our faces, and we are strangers again. By offering the black performer a refuge and a haven—a place where our artists could feel at home and could experiment—WHMM was an alternative to the cynicism of Hollywood and Broadway.

Ruby and Ossie would be the first to come and take advantage. Ruby's idea set us on the way. It was called *Zora Is My Name!*

Zora Neale Hurston, anthropologist, novelist, short story writer, and master raconteur, had been one of the glories of the Harlem Renaissance. Only now is the general public beginning to recognize her works as literary classics. Ruby's teleplay was perfect. Using Zora's words entirely, it was drawn from *Dust Tracks on a Road,* her autobiography, and *Mules and Men,* Negro folktales she had collected on a field trip to the South. It would feature six performers: Lynda Gravatt, Joe Pinckney, Helena Wright, Ruby, Guy, and me. And it was Ruby's first major directing assignment. Celia Bryant, who had done costumes for us in Nigeria and then again in Dallas, dropped everything and came with us to Washington. Beanie and the Office of Theatrical Productions provided the other elements of the production, and the rest was up to us entirely.

We moved to Washington, D.C., and lived with Essie, my sister. Dr. Vada Butcher, Beanie's wife, who was also dean of the College of Fine Arts, was herself an expert musicologist. She went to the Library of Congress and brought us tapes of some of the songs and music Zora had recorded, which we turned over to Guy.

We rehearsed for two weeks, then in the midst of a heavy snowstorm in February 1983, presented the show to a full house for two nights running at Cramton Auditorium. The next day, we shot some scenes in close-up for the benefit of the camera; then the whole thing was cut together in the editing room. We were highly pleased with what we had accomplished. So was Beanie and WHMM-TV.

When Ruby and I were doing publicity for *Purlie Victorious* back in 1962, we had appeared on a talk show called *PM East,* hosted by Mike Wallace for Channel 5, an independent TV station in New York. The show included Burt Lancaster promoting his *Birdman of Alcatraz* and Barbra Streisand, who was appearing on Broadway in *I Can Get It for You Wholesale.*

The producer of the show was Mert Koplin, who later left TV

programming and became an independent producer. He had remained a friend over the years, so we were not surprised when he invited us to his office in 1984, told us how much he enjoyed *With Ossie and Ruby,* and asked us to join him in his new project, *A Walk Through the Twentieth Century with Bill Moyers.* What did surprise us was the check for $10,000 he passed across his desk, asking us to get started right away.

Each weekly episode, one hour in length, was to be shown on PBS. He wanted two of those episodes to be on the Black Experience in America, and he wanted Emmalyn II to produce them. Once again we assembled our creative team in New Rochelle, including David Dowe, who took a leave of absence from his job at KERA.

We decided that our two segments, which we called "The Second American Revolution, Part I and Part II," would begin in 1900 when Booker T. Washington, the most powerful black man in America, was invited to dinner at the White House by President Theodore Roosevelt. It would continue through Washington's Great Debate with W.E.B. Du Bois—which, for the next fifteen years, was the centralizing intellectual drama in the black community. We would also include Marcus Garvey, Malcolm X, and Martin Luther King, ending with the March on Washington in 1963, the day after Du Bois died in Ghana.

Fay Boulware was hired to begin research, while Ruby and I started reading background material and working on the script. Nora was pregnant, but we were lucky enough to have Cheryl Borde, a friend of Nora's from film school who had a master's degree in communications, as our associate producer. She and David began preproduction. Black history has always been a favorite interest of mine, so it didn't take long to come up with a shooting script, and we hit the road again.

At each location, David would set up his camera and his sound equipment, and Ruby and I would stand in front of a selected building, monument, or other historic spot, explaining why this particular place was so important and talking about the people who made it so. This time, we decided to start at the birthplace of W.E.B. Du Bois in Great Barrington, Massachusetts. There we found nothing at all to show that this was where one of America's greatest intellects and creative agitators had been born. Just an empty, overgrown lot with a hole in the ground where the chimney once had been. Nothing in the dialogue we recorded could describe the sadness and embarrassment we felt.

It was altogether different at Tuskegee University in Alabama where we were permitted access to Booker T. Washington's house, which had been well preserved and is open to the public as a museum.

We visited Harper's Ferry, where John Brown had fought and been captured, to talk about Du Bois and the Niagara movement. We also went to Dexter Avenue Baptist Church in Montgomery, Alabama, where Martin Luther King was minister when Rosa Parks sat down on the bus. We talked with E. D. Nixon, the man who got Martin involved in the bus boycott in the first place. In Washington, D.C., we went to the Supreme Court building, to Howard University's School of Law, to the Lincoln Memorial, and also to Arlington National Cemetery.

Back home, we shot along Fifth Avenue in New York, where the much decorated black troops of the 369th Regiment, returning from France after World War I, marched from Battery Park, where they had just disembarked from the troop ship, all the way up to Harlem. In Harlem itself, we shot on Strivers Row, and at the church where Marcus Garvey made one of his earliest speeches. We interviewed Kenneth Clark, who told us about the experiment with the dolls he had used in the breakthrough Supreme Court case *Brown* v. *Board of Education. A Walk Through the Twentieth Century* aired in April 1984.

Earl Graves, publisher of *Black Enterprise,* a monthly magazine devoted to black business, and a friend of ours, wanted a twenty-five-minute documentary, a capsule history of black business in America, from the days of slavery to the latest start-up in Silicon Valley, to be called *Pioneers in Black Business.* He wanted it to be shown in his office as a video display. Production would take place along the same lines as *A Walk Through the Twentieth Century.* We called David in Dallas and told him what we had in mind. He excused himself from his work at KERA and came north again to join us.

This time, Hasna was hired to help with the research, and Cheryl Borde went on the road with us to handle details. Our travels, this time, took us from Fraunces Tavern in New York's Wall Street financial district to Atlanta, where we interviewed Herman Russell, one of the black builders of the International Airport in Atlanta; to Birmingham, where we talked with A. G. Gaston, who had started an insurance company in 1923; then to Chicago to talk with John Sengestack, publisher of the *Chicago Defender*. We went to Hampton University to talk with the first black man to secure a catering contract with an airport, and to Silicon Valley in California to talk with Frank Greene.

Those who know him well hold this truth as gospel: Earl Graves is known to practice what he preaches. And Emmalyn II Productions found it out the hard way.

Our last interview was to be with Earl himself in the boardroom of his office down on Fifth Avenue. Ruby and I had arranged to meet David early in the morning, giving him time to get there first and set up the equipment. When we arrived, we found the place in an uproar: There was nobody black on the camera crew and Earl refused to cooperate until that situation was rectified.

These were matters we left completely up to David, who apologized profusely, that in his haste, he had hired the first assistant available, who happened to be white. Earl was adamant: Either put somebody black on the camera crew or the shooting was off. Ruby and I were thoroughly embarrassed—such a thing had never happened before. David sent for a black technician, and only when he came did Earl allow us to proceed with the interview.

In 1985, PBS asked us to produce another thirteen segments of *With Ossie and Ruby*. We accepted the offer, but only if they would let us do it at WHMM. PBS agreed, and it seemed our hopes of establishing a media home base for the black performer was getting closer.

Ruby's idea this time was to showcase not only black and Caribbean authors, but also Latino, Asian, and Native American writers. What happened when they, too, became part of the American melting pot? And who better to bear witness than their writers? PBS liked the idea and gave us half the funding. We'd have to come up with the rest, which was customary. Normally, we would have waited until we had the additional funding locked before we started, but we didn't.

David had quit his job at KERA and formed a loose association as a line producer with Emmalyn II Productions, and he was confident that we could raise the additional funding from other sources that he knew. Ruby and I had never been charged with obtaining backing, and there was nothing to indicate that we were being unwise, or that job opportunities such as *Zora, Walk,* and *Pioneers* wouldn't keep pouring in.

Soon the house in New Rochelle was humming like a beehive, and we had purchased the rights to works from authors including Kim Yong Ik, a Korean American, and Frank Chin, a Chinese writer whose grandfather had worked on the railroads with thousands of his immigrant brothers. We made contact with Carlos Reyes, a Latino writer in Los Angeles, and Charlie Hill, a Native American stand-up comic, who'd been on the Johnny Carson show. He came to visit us in New Rochelle.

David came up from Texas again, Ruby and I moved into an apartment in Northeast Washington, and Nora and Bill were housed nearby. We were given office space at the station, some WHMM personnel, including students assigned to the project, and we began production immediately.

Our relations with WHMM were not easy. The station, though independent, was something of a personal project of Dr. Cheek's, and we had to report to Dr. Owen Nichols, a vice president. Neither of these gentlemen knew very much about television production, and though we were given a free hand, there were times when we had to run the bureaucratic gauntlet for basic necessities. Everything from paper clips and light bulbs to toilet paper had to be requisitioned, and there was no guarantee that what we needed would be delivered on time. Still, we managed to produce two of our best works there.

Fussell's Landing was a piece I wrote about the sad state of black agriculture in America today. An old black farmer whose ancestors had left him a large piece of valuable farmland in south Georgia wanted to pass it along to his own son as an inheritance for his grandson. He sits all alone, waiting for the bankers to come and dispossess him because he cannot pay his debts. Also we did *The Eighty-five-Year-Old Swinger,* starring Scatman Carrothers, which Ruby directed.

Meanwhile, the additional funding we had counted on to produce the rest of the series fell through, and we had to shift gears in the middle of the operation. Our relations with WHMM-TV became even more strained. David, who had been with us from the beginning of *With Ossie and Ruby,* left the show and went back to Dallas. It was the end of a relation with a very gifted man. The bottom line was that neither David nor we knew how to go out and raise money. It gradually became apparent that the Office of Theatrical Productions did not have the support needed to make its way through the academic bureaucracy, and, in addition, Beanie was ill.

President Cheek managed to come up with an additional $200,000, out of which we produced two other episodes. *A Letter from Booker T.* was written by William Branch, a playwright, friend, and neighbor. It was based on the famous struggle between Booker T. Washington and W.E.B. Du Bois, and its effects not only on the lives of two distinguished African Americans, Mary Church Terrell and her husband, Robert, but also on the entire black community. We had no David now, but Ozzie Brown, a young publicist who had worked on *Cotton,* came down from New York and joined our production team. Directed by Bill Pratt, it turned out to be one of the best things we ever did on tape.

We left Howard disappointed at not having accomplished our other vision for WHMM-TV and the university as a haven for the African-American artist. The glorious decade of Emmalyn II Productions was rounding to an end.

For our final segment, Nora, Bill, Ruby, and I traveled to Sarasota to do *Crown Dick,* Ruby's adaptation of a short story by Kim Yong Ik, which I directed. It was about a black man who, when he went to Korea as a soldier, performed as a clown for a local teacher and his class. In later years, when the teacher comes to visit the circus at Sarasota looking for his friend, Dick, he finds out that Dick hadn't been a clown after all, only a black roustabout who cleaned up after the elephants. Why? Because Crown Dick, as the Korean children mispronounced his name, would not have been allowed to be a clown because he was black.

Ruby made choices, pointed us in new directions, to ways and means of presenting a story I'd never heard before. Where did it all come from?

RUBY: Rhythm and music. I find myself talking a lot about words in terms of rhythms and music. What I wanted from "Solo on the Drums," for example, the Ann Petry story, was more than a duet between Max Roach and Billy Taylor, as the drummer and pianist around whom the story is based. I wanted to explore the people rhythms as well as the music rhythms, and how they fed into and out of each other. Make sense?

OSSIE: Yes, it does. But why the love affair with these particular authors? You didn't seem to hassle, or struggle, or doubt yourself. How could you be so sure?

RUBY: An idea, a story swirls around in my brain. Then before long, how it should be handled suggests itself to me. Respect for the author, enthusiasm for the material, and joy at the prospect of seeing it all come together brings a profound clarity, which pleases me enormously.

OSSIE: Quite a time it was on PBS. Our only charge was to come up with good programming. And I understand that we were well received.

RUBY: It was a sheltered opportunity to be able to work the best you know how—with no strings attached. What more can an artist ask for? We should've fallen down all over our knees thanking God. Did we remember to do that?

OSSIE: Didn't have time. The blessings kept us too busy.

RUBY: O-O-O-O-O, Ossie, God's gon' get you for saying that.

OSSIE: Aw, c'mon now. I think She can take a little joke.

RUBY: All kidding aside, those times made the words "happy" and "successful" meaningful to us.

OSSIE: Our final production was *Martin Luther King: The Dream and the Drum,* which aired in 1985. It was, in a way, one of our most ambitious efforts, and one of our most bitterly disappointing.

RUBY: No, Ossie, I think you are mistaken to say that. It was an unusual piece, and we did have some difficult moments trying to pull it off, but a lot of people found it compelling, especially since it involved the talents of some very gifted performers: Sweet Honey in the Rock, Theodore Bikel, Kim Hunter, Michael Wright, Miriam Colon, Freda Foh Shen, and Max Roach.

OSSIE: Anyway, we took the assignment because our friends at PBS, who had always supported us so enthusiastically, asked us to. It was a project already in progress with a portion of the budget already spent before it was taken away from the original producers and given to us, with three stipulations: It had to be done in New York, with and by "minority" producers, and the subject matter had to be Martin Luther King. I was in it and also had to direct it because the budget was too tight to hire a director.

The idea was to excerpt the eloquence of Martin's words, using commentary and observations from other sources. There was a long poem by Sonia Sanchez, a shorter one by Ruby, a poem called "Peace" by the French poet Paul Eluard, and music by Sweet Honey in the Rock and Max Roach. I wanted all those elements to be woven seamlessly into a threnody of words and music, evoking the tragedy and triumph of Martin Luther King.

The concept required more space and elevation than the production could afford, and just one more day of shooting would have enabled me to at least move the camera more. In spite of the physical limitations, I admit there were parts that worked exceptionally well: Ruby's rendition of the Eluard poem; Max's fiery thunder on the drums; and the extraordinary, bitter, sweet, astringent sound of Sweet Honey in the Rock.

The Dream and the Drum was a fitting swan song to the golden age of Emmalyn II Productions as television producers. The emphasis of the company then shifted closer to enterprises that served the interests of all the family.

CHAPTER 35

Going Through the Fire

OSSIE: Emmalyn II Productions was not the only activity that kept us busy during the eighties. In 1982, Ruby went to Canada to do a television production of Eugene O'Neill's classic play, *Long Day's Journey into Night,* with Earle Hyman. Nora and Bill and their children left New Rochelle and moved to Atlanta. Bill, who had been on staff at the Studio Museum in Harlem, had been invited by the city of Atlanta to open a gallery for them, and Nora would later take a post as a college administrator. Hasna was hard at work on her doctoral degree, Guy began playing his guitar regularly—and for pay—at a nightclub in the Village called Mostly Magic, and in 1986 I went back to Broadway in *I'm Not Rappaport* with Hal Linden.

Every role can be a learning experience. The special challenge for me in *I'm Not Rappaport* was how to play an old man with thick glasses and cataracts. It took thirteen months on Broadway, and even then, it was only after I left the Broadway production and went to Jupiter,

Florida, in April 1988 to do the role in Burt Reynolds's Dinner Theatre that I finally got the hang of it, knowing at last—not only in my heart and in my head, but also in my guts—what Dick Campbell, Harry Gribble, Howard Da Silva, Lloyd Richards—and Ruby Dee—had all tried so hard to teach me.

It wasn't a matter of whether I had the talent, but of whether I was free enough, strong enough, bold enough, and confident enough to use it—to summon up at will, from memory or from imagination, the authority and the power to assert myself, to stop hiding behind the ready smile of a free and easy good nature, as Paul Mann once accused me of doing, and dare to become the man I was meant to be—Kince Davis's eldest son from Cogdell, Georgia. Such is the redemptive power of trying to become an artist. I couldn't be an artist unless first I became a man!

RUBY: The decade of the 1980s acted as if it were in a hurry to join time past, to belong to the ages. It lingered a moment and was gone in a finger snap. It was like a strong but fickle wind, sometimes blowing hot, then blowing cold, at my back, then in my face almost taking my breath away.

During one of those winters, after an argument with Ossie over God knows what, on an *I'm Not Rappaport* Saturday matinee day, I stormed out for my walk, slipped on the ice, and broke my left ankle. I'll never forget how God sent a lady in a taxi to this quiet street where I had never seen a taxi before or since to pick me up and take me home.

Later in the decade I had a dream about Howard Da Silva in which he's trying to get me to follow him somewhere to a body of water and I refuse because I know he's dead and I'm not ready to go there yet. In real life, it was 1988, and I was performing in Ron Milner's play, *Checkmates,* on Broadway. That Wednesday during a matinee, I slipped on something that felt like a banana peel, or a blob of grease, and broke my left wrist. I don't believe there was anything on the floor—it was a very spooky experience to say the least. I finished the show in a sling, was rushed to the hospital where the hand was set back onto the wrist but not exactly straight, leaving my left arm permanently swollen after the cast was removed. It's a wonder I didn't develop a phobia about matinees.

One day in September 1987, when I was in Washington, D.C., as part of an awards ceremony honoring distinguished crafts people from various parts of the country, my house caught on fire. This led to having to move to the rental of another house, year-long fire damage repairs— unsupervised too much of the time—incredible expenditures, and my almost being jailed for attempting to permanently polish off a contractor with my bare hands. (I believe I would have, too, had he not got going in a very fast trot.) I could just see the headlines in the *Standard Star:* "Rooty, Tooty, Big Bad Rooby, Beats up Contractor Instead of Shooty!"

I was truly feeling " bad" during those months. I even wanted to take on death a number of times, not only after my brother and sister passed, but also after a lot of people who had become friends and part of my dreams for the future had died, like John Oliver Killens, whose novel *Youngblood* was among the first books for which I'd tried to solicit interest in turning into a film, and from which later I'd selected readings to do on tour and on television. Oh, Jesus! And Jimmy Baldwin left, too. As did Hazel Bryant, who finally got me past my reservations about portraying "the black version of this and that" to do Mary Tyrone in Eugene O'Neill's *Long Day's Journey into Night,* which brought me much praise and an ACE Award; Julian Mayfield, with whom I'd collaborated twice as a writer and worked with as an actor in *Up Tight!;* Owen Dodson, whose *Confession Stone,* about the life of Jesus, I'd gotten permission to present as an Easter offering, but which never got off the ground; Roger Furman, whose New Heritage Theatre remains one of the bright spots in Harlem; Osceola Adams, my Delta soror, friend, and teacher from the days of the American Negro Theatre.

One day I looked up and saw James Van Der Zee, who photographed so much of black life that may have otherwise been lost. He "captured" Ossie and me one afternoon in a portrait, and almost before we could complete an expression of profound gratitude, he was gone. He joined the people to whom I'd begun writing tributes in the sixties.

The list now is long, too long. It's almost time for a book devoted entirely to tributes. The eighties also took Abram Hill, who founded the American Negro Theatre. I also wrote about William Morgan, Ossie's brother-in-law, one of those black men who seemed to live in the shadows and on the sidelines. I wrote as well as about Essie, Ossie's sister, who did extraordinary work as chief of socioeconomic rehabilitation in the Bureau of Veterans Affairs. So many. So many.

The worst of it was, in July 1988, losing my beloved brother, Edward, and my precious baby sister, LaVerne, in June 1989.

I couldn't reckon with the fact that our lives together were over. Death was something I had not accommodated in my thoughts about them. I realized how much I am like everybody else in the world when the inevitable comes as a surprise, bringing with it all kinds of useless contemplations.

I remembered other funerals, seeing loved ones throw themselves on the coffin and cry, and the look of incredulity on the faces of the people watching the mourners. I never borrowed such behavior for myself, but I understood it completely when those moments came for me.

When my siblings and I grew up and went our separate ways, we didn't see each other often enough—except for LaVerne and me. We always stayed close and in touch. My brother seemed to be off in other places—at war, then at work, and with his wife and their children. For many years, he worked as an engineer for IBM, where he received numerous citations and small bonuses for his inventions. Years later, when he got sick, the company seemed genuinely concerned. They were generous, prompt, and personal as they explained and set in motion his entitlements, and extended his sick leave. By this time, he had divorced and remarried, and had settled with his new family in the Philippines.

Edward was also an artist, and I still have some of his mad drawings. There was a guilelessness about him, too, as if he always had one finger on the divine pulse. I truly believed the angels took care of him.

LaVerne had been a laboratory technician for many years. As diagnostic practices advanced and became computerized, many of her coworkers left or were fired and replaced by those who were younger and trained in new techniques. She began to feel that she, too, would be fired. One night, however, something went wrong with the electronic system and there were several medical procedures in progress that needed lab support. Doctors needed reports immediately. Wasn't there anybody around to do the tests the old way? LaVerne came to the rescue that night. After that incident, she never again feared that she would lose her job.

The contentment she sought in her life, however, seemed to elude her. I believe she looked for love through three marriages. I know for a fact that she had some good friends, though, who loved her. Anyway, I was her big sister and she was my most solid friend.

My sister Angelina lives in Canada with her husband, Carl Roach, who was a top engineer at IBM and is now retired. He was involved in the design and construction of IBM manufacturing plants where semiconductors were first introduced into computer components. Angelina was a kindergarten teacher and now I call her a servant of life. She loves working in the ground and tending her estate in Quebec. These days, she won't travel, so the family goes to see her and Carl. One of her chief values is that she gives the family a foreign country to visit. They have four children: Kylas, Brian, Celeste, and Paul. They are planning with our children and Edward's children, Sharón, Tommy, Gail, and Dana, a cousin convention for the year 2000.

The contemplation of that kind of coming together fills me with hope and makes me feel good. However, the inevitability of sorrow, of bad stuff getting out of the sack and dogging our heels and squeezing our hearts is not something we can speak about in comparative terms. If so, I need to keep my mouth shut. No. I cannot say, as Zora Neale Hurston wrote, "I've been in sorrow's kitchen, and licked out all the pots." I've tasted from the pot enough to know something about truly deep sorrow, however, and to want to offer comfort, and lend strength to those who are still in those kitchens, elbow deep in those pots.

OSSIE: The worker was using a blowtorch in the attic to melt the ancient paint from the outriggers that adorned the roof. A few days earlier, Ruby had cautioned a worker, offering to buy a liquid solvent.

But what the hell does a woman know about scraping paint? Sparks fell on some shavings and soon a fire started. The worker, instead of sounding the alarm, came downstairs to get the garden hose, but by the time he got back upstairs, it was too late, and the fire department had to be summoned.

I had just gone to the airport to put Ruby on a plane to Washington, D.C. When I got back to the house, the fire had engulfed the attic and the roof, and was still burning. They finally put out the flames, taking every care to contain the conflagration. Even so, the damages from fire and water were considerable. Thank God for Dolores Bartlett, our office manager at the time. She and Cheryl Borde acted quickly to save valuables from the top floor on down.

RUBY: In perusing items after the fire, Guy discovered some old programs and newspaper articles Mother had saved years ago. In them, I had been mentioned for something I'd written or recited when I was nine years old on a program sponsored by the James Weldon Johnson Literary Guild at the public library. And there on that same platform listening to me perform were Zora Neale Hurston and Dorothy West, literary giants whom I now look upon as almost holy. I nearly fainted. I still can't believe that I have no recollection of having been in the presence of Zora Neale Hurston.

Would that I could recall the times, so that I could fall at her feet, hug her, and kiss and thank "My Zora" for having written, for having urged on—me and so many—for having lived on earth and breathed the same air.

New Delhi, Calcutta, Trivandrum, and Bombay were the cities we would travel to in India as delegates to the Black Film Festival in January 1989. William Greaves had arranged it all and invited Donald Bogle, Ivan Dixon, Cicely Tyson, Michelle Parkerson, and me.

The film industry there is one of the most prolific in the world. It was exciting to visit a film set and the homes of the directors and other people associated with the business. As in other countries, the sights, sounds, the smells in the different cities and in the countryside, as well as the diversity of people, were most distinctive. I wonder if people who come to the United States for the first time find that there is a special smell here as well.

Eyes could not focus fast enough, nor could the senses embrace all the impressions that our short visit afforded. There seemed to be a rhythm to the poverty, as if the same ritual with the same people had existed forever. Should they decide to change the pattern of their lives, I felt, they could. Look how many poor there are! On second thought, history, tradition, and habit would first have to be addressed. Reincarnation, I thought, could just be a part of the everyday reality. You could die, perhaps, and in time return to the same living space. Begging also seemed a way of life, startling to a newcomer.

Once as I looked past faces that came to all the windows of the car, I saw a woman, seemingly with all her belongings at hand, bathing a baby under a slow stream of water from a broken fire hydrant. For all such sights of poverty, there was a sense that everything was under control, that people accepted the way things were and had been for centuries. To inquiries into the politics behind the poverty, I found no satisfactory explanation.

Above all, the chance to visit two places that Mother Teresa had established to care for the poor, and to meet Mother herself was a profoundly moving moment. Mother Teresa, gregarious and most pleasant, passed the few minutes with us as relaxed and joyous as if she had all day. She wanted to know about the festival. A couple of us took pictures; then she was gone.

Cicely, her assistant, Barbara, and I—we shopped. The fire and water damage at home had been extensive, so I bought furniture, most of which arrived in New York about two months later.

On my first trip to the city after my return, I looked again at the many people living on sidewalks and in doorways, at those pushing their belongings in carts from the supermarkets meticulously going through trash baskets on streets, and I concluded that these people were truly poor. It was a clanging poverty that had no good justification—that had no rhythm to it that would keep it bearable.

I was riding with Hasna, my daughter, in the front seat of her car, and as we were nearing a tollbooth, she realized she didn't have any money.

She asked Ihsaana, her eight-year-old daughter sitting on the backseat, to lend her some change that she knew Ihsaana had.

Ihsaana said, "No, Ummi, I need my money for my life. Ask Ruby, Ruby got money, honey!" (The grands started out calling me by my first name due to a misunderstanding; I'll explain about that in a minute.)

My brother had known I had money when he wanted to buy a house. Now my granddaughter knows I "got money." It took me a long time to stop worrying about impending poverty, to have faith that money would not be something I'd have to worry about as I'd seen people do as a youngster growing up in Harlem. To this day, I continue to struggle with a basic "making ends meet" mentality that has left me with a few deep regrets.

One such regret revolves around a letter I received from Fannie Lou Hamer. Many a night I've wished I had personally answered her letter and replied to her request instead of sending it to a surrogate. At the time, we were receiving so many funding requests that we formed a relationship with a woman affiliated with a domestic workers union to screen such requests. Mrs. Hamer is dead now but that incident has enabled me to see that one of the main benefits and joys of having money is to learn how—and to whom—to give some of it away.

And as for my grandchildren calling me Ruby, this was the misunderstanding. Before my daughter got married, I was trying to assure her that there was no pressure from me for her to marry and become a mother. I said, "I don't want any children calling me 'Grandma' until you get through school." She thought I was averse to the title, but I was illustrating my point about her priorities. Well, when the grandchildren came along, she remembered what I'd said and instructed them to call me Ruby. Even after I clarified the matter, they held on to the habit, but it just didn't sound right. I finally had to put my foot down. Now they call me Gram Ruby.

CHAPTER 36

My One Good Nerve

RUBY: The year 1990 gave birth to the millennium mind-set. Looking forward, looking back, there was much reckoning with the past in
order to be ready for the future. In January of that year, Ossie was
featured in the groundbreaking eight-part documentary *Eyes on the
Prize*. The next month, American Playhouse aired *Zora Is My Name!*
on PBS, this time with Louis Gossett, Jr., Flip Wilson, Beah Richards,
Lynn Whitfield, Paula Kelly, and Guy. That same year, I received an
ACE award nomination for my work in *The Court-martial of Jackie
Robinson,* which featured Andre Braugher. And as if to mark my fiftieth
year in the business, I won the Emmy award for Outstanding Supporting Actress in the *Hallmark Hall of Fame: Decoration Day.*

   This was the year of Nelson Mandela's release from prison. Yes,
the New World was coming, but not without perplexity. It was the
beginning of the decade in which America struck down affirmative
action, made prison-building a stock market commodity, raised up a
rash of child murderers, and downsized the workforce out of one side

of its mouth, while celebrating welfare-to-workfare as a way out of poverty out of the other. Makes you wonder what God has in mind. . . .

Our son, Guy, while working in the daytime series *One Life to Live,* invested in one of Spike Lee's earliest films, *She's Gotta Have It!* Spike went everywhere and gave people like Guy a chance to become big spenders by becoming investors. Guy went deep into his capital and came up with $500. I love the fact that had it been five dollars, I think Spike would have accepted it and put his name on the screen right along with the others who were expressing, with much heavier bread, their belief in this strongly motivated director/producer.

How thrilled I was when Guy told me one day, "Ma, I got another check from Spike." *She's Gotta Have It!* paid off, and Spike paid the people back with interest who had trusted him. I'd never heard of anything like that. "Creative bookkeeping," where projects made money but rarely showed a profit, seemed to be the rule.

I don't know if anybody ever got rich in a Spike Lee movie except in satisfaction, maybe. There is an excitement in being in a "Spike Lee Joint," however, where the people who work with and for Spike are of all sorts, all races. Mistakenly, I got carried away with imagining other possibilities in the script of *Jungle Fever.* Spike looked so young and vulnerable with his big eyes, so I thought he needed me to help rewrite the role he had cast me in as Lucinda Purify. I sent some pages suggesting changes, but he never wrote back. I think he just didn't receive my improvements. I also wanted to change the names of the sons of Lucinda and the Good Reverend Doctor Purify, the role Ossie played. I thought Spike made a mistake to name them Gator and Flipper. I should have learned from the days of *Do the Right Thing* that Mr. Spike Lee has strong ideas and will discuss anything, but relies mostly on his own sensibilities.

Get on the Bus, his 1996 film in which Ossie worked, is among his films that confirm in my mind his belief that art must be a responsible factor in the quality of our lives. Inadvertently, by inviting me to work in two of his films, he thrust me into the line of vision of another generation, thereby underscoring something in my personal career agenda, and I liked that.

OSSIE: Ruby and I were playing at the Village Vanguard in 1963, doing our usual readings and recitations for an enthusiastic crowd each night. Max Gordon, the producer, decided to back us up with four jazz musicians, each well-known in his own right, one of whom was a bass player named Bill Lee. The music was great, it added a kick to our style of presentation, and all of us worked quite well together. That's the way it was for the two weeks we worked in the Village, and then it was gone.

Years later, we received a letter from a film student at New York University, who promised that one day he would make a film with Ruby and me. It was a good-natured letter, such as we constantly receive and file for future reference. The young man identified himself as Spike Lee, the son of Bill Lee, who had worked with us in the Village. We wrote him back, wished him well, and promptly forgot the whole episode. Sometime during the mid-eighties, while we were attending an event at the Studio Museum with Guy, Guy approached us and said, "Mom, Dad—I want you to meet somebody," and he introduced us to Spike.

One day in 1988, after I had flown down to Atlanta to do a cameo appearance in *School Daze,* I was rummaging around on my desk among the old unanswered correspondence with which it is loaded, and I came across Spike's original letter. My intention was to give it back to Spike, so I put it carefully away among some other papers on my overloaded desk, just for that purpose. I haven't seen it since.

~ ~ ~

RUBY: Among some things I would like a retake on is my relationship to Adrienne Kennedy and her work. When I first read her play *Funnyhouse of a Negro,* I didn't understand it, and chose not to do it. When I was invited in 1992 to do the role of Suzanne Alexander in *The Ohio State Murders,* which Gerald Freeman directed at the Great Lakes Theatre Festival in Cleveland, I realized that indeed one of the reasons I was born was to perform in plays written by Adrienne Kennedy. I feel that we have a spiritual and artistic kinship that escaped me at the time. Her characters have, in a sense, been warped by racism. They seem off center, askew. They are people I now recognize immediately not only from intuition, but also from experience.

I'm glad Pearl Cleage was on my dance card to meet as an author and to know as a friend. Rick Khan invited me to perform at Crossroads Theatre in *Flyin' West,* her play about spousal abuse, and about some of the black women who went west to claim land and settle on it. Since it dealt with such an important slice of American history, I wanted it to have an extended run. The play was well received by audiences at Crossroads and at the Kennedy Center Eisenhower Theater.

Diane Houston, I believe, is another one of the people born with the big bold print on their personal direction manual. Ossie and I had tried to present the short story, "A Summer Tragedy," by Arna Bontemps, during our last days on public television while we were at Howard University's WHMM, but we simply didn't have the funds. It is a story about an aging couple—the husband played by Bill Cobbs—whose circumstances lead them to a drastic conclusion. Years after this attempt, Ms. Houston adapted this story and called it *A Tuesday Morning Ride.* Diane became the only black person to be even nominated for an Academy Award in 1995.

I've promised myself that I will write an article on some memorable moments as an actor, and when I do, I'll tell about what happened in the film *Just Cause,* released in 1995. Sean Connery starred and was one of the producers; in what I thought was a desperate moment in the film, he whispered between takes, "Ruby, my dear, breathe." It was a scene in which I was trying to get Connery to represent my grandson, played by Blair Underwood, who was accused of murder. Before the next take, quite out of character as Blair's grandmother in this disturbing film, I howled.

Afterward, I thought of the many times while conducting acting workshops at Howard University, Hunter College, and later at Pratt, I had stressed breathing techniques as one way to relieve tension beyond what the scene required. Sean had reminded me that I was definitely not practicing what I used to preach.

I might also include in such an article an incident involving *Evening Shade,* the CBS-TV series in which Ossie played Ponder Blue from 1990 to 1994. In one episode, as Ossie's ex-girlfriend, I simply couldn't get my lines together. It had been a very hectic week for me. There had been no time to get hair done, nails, etc., let alone to learn lines securely enough so that, in a panic, they wouldn't all fly out of my head on camera. Well, Burt Reynolds, who was directing, during the set-up for the next scene, wrote all my lines on different pieces of paper and showed me how to place them where I might need them. I thought it was so sweet of him.

Some people think about retirement when they reach a certain age, but actors never retire, unless their faculties are beyond repair. In 1992, Ossie reprised his eulogy in voice-over in Spike Lee's film *Malcolm X,* and also published his book for young adults, *Just Like Martin.* That year, he joined with Danny Glover and others to mobilize support for the Arts Visitation Program, to bolster arts curricula in historically black colleges and universities. In 1993, the year both of us lent our support to David Dinkins in his mayoral campaign in New York City, he was featured in *Grumpy Old Men.*

For me that year, a career-long dream became a reality. Invited by Karen Baxter, the producer and managing director of Rites and Reasons at Brown University, to work on one of the ideas I'd been nursing for a long time, I immediately obtained the rights to Rosa Guy's novel *The Disappearance.* I'd been intrigued by this murder mystery since its publication in 1979. And I was eager to return to the process I had begun to explore during the three seasons of our show, *With Ossie and Ruby,* for PBS. This process of adapting novels for the stage was driven by the impluse to explore the rhythms of ideas, personality, action, speech, places—even silences—as they relate to music.

Again, I wanted to present the story as written, prose and all— not an adaptation or my interpretation of her story. Even so, the task of preparing the book took several months. In the process of creating a two-hour performance text, I had to decide which parts had to be left out. It is a tightly written work, so choices came hard. I also had to rearrange passages to make up for the omissions, and to cut internally the sections retained. Fortunately, one of the aspects of the project was the privilege of working with Rosa Guy. We had been friends a long time and she participated in and approved the changes and the choices; she also made invaluable and sweeping suggestions in the interest of time and clarity.

Reading aloud to an audience is an art, and I wanted the book itself to be the centerpiece of the evening. Had there been a curtain that opened to reveal the stage, I would have liked it to replicate the dust jacket of the book. The presence of the book on stage, and the actors reading from the book, would serve the illusion that the words were coming to life, and the story was coming off the page.

In much of my work in presenting other authors' material, I have tried to wed the idea, the word, and the acting dynamic to music, to a beat heard or felt. There is melody to our experiences. Even the cacophony is scorable. I met the composer H. Q. Thompson at Brown and we began to collaborate. I gave each of the principal characters a color, and H.Q. developed a theme for them. His music helped to evoke two of the locations featured in the story—Harlem and Brooklyn, as well as interior settings.

It was a busy time for me as an actor, but that was understood from the beginning of the project. Elmo-Terry Morgan was more than an assistant. As one of the founders of Rites and Reasons, he himself was a director and understood what I was trying to achieve. In my absences, he worked with the talented student company and helped with the staging. I was eager to share in the process because—with all the books I wanted to mount—I anticipated needing the help of people who would be tuned in to my concept.

At Brown, *The Disappearance* was a well-rehearsed and well-choreographed concert reading. I rimmed the stage with music stands, from which the actors moved to a minimal set to play the scenes. Books in manuscript form were strategically placed and boldly used.

I'd seen the technique on Broadway—for instance, in the mesmerizing near-eight-hour production of Dickens's *Nicholas Nickleby*.

I called my use of the technique "Books with Legs"—a term borrowed from the film industry to describe a film that has a long run at theaters. The term also became a metaphor for books that march off the bookshelves into production, perhaps as plays or films, or are presented as I envisioned *The Disappearance*.

About seven months after my residency at Brown University, Ricardo Khan invited me to bring the performance to Crossroads Theatre as part of the Genesis Festival, where I continued working with the book itself and H.Q. continued developing the music. Avery Brooks and Phyllis Yvonne Stickney were among the actors who helped us pull it off.

Shortly thereafter, Ricardo Khan decided to give *The Disappearance* a major production at Crossroads. It became one of the most satisfying experiences I'd ever had in theater. The superb cast included Carl Lumbly, Khalil Kain, Marie Thomas, Lynda Gravatt, Frank Adu, Venida Evans, Sharon Hope, Conrad Roberts, Tonia Rowe, Isiah Whitlock, Jr., Kharisma, and Joseph McKenna. It was directed by Harold Scott and H.Q.'s score hit a new high. Through the music, we knew when we were in Brooklyn and·when we were in Harlem; we saw the prison and heard the subway and all the city noises, as well as the emotional tones of the characters' inner lives.

I don't know how Rick and Crossroads managed to get Theoni Aldredge to do the costumes and John Ezell to come up with the miraculously simple and complex set that metamorphosed into whatever location was needed. Of course, he had done the multimedia set design for *Nicholas Nickleby*.

It was Sydné Mahone, however, who helped me articulate and describe my particular vision for myself as well as for the program notes excerpted here:

"Books with Legs" involves, in a symphonic relationship, reading, dramatization, screen techniques, stylization, and whatever other elements it takes to weave the magic of compelling storytelling. It is about marrying rhythms—thought rhythms, word rhythms, people, and life rhythms. I love the idea of actors responding almost as musicians to the author's style and to the varying impulses as the story unfolds.

Every writer, like every painter, has a unique style, a distinctive spirit that comes to us only as we experience language as the author wrote it. Pictures are not always adequate substitutions for words. Often we're cutting to the chase with predictable images, reducing language to minimums, and human experience to monotones. We have even taken the sting out of cuss words.

Perhaps one of the reasons rap is so popular is because at the core

of us as human beings is a yearning and need for rhythms. Rap is bla-
tantly poetic and the rhythms please us.

It may not be a totally new way of "seeing" a novel, but we believe
that "Books with Legs" calls imagination into more vivid explorations,
makes us feel and think in more dynamic dimensions, and restores language to more accurate and satisfying proportions. The authors we want
to present are those who spell us and the worlds we inhabit with giant-
sized capital letters. *The Disappearance* leads us off.

It was an incredible production that firmly planted Books with
Legs in the forefront of the rest of my creative life.

Further along in the decade, in 1997, Ossie was in *Miss Evers'
Boys,* which aired on HBO, and in Showtime's *Twelve Angry Men.* As
he describes that experience, the ensemble work was extraordinary,
reminding him of his days in the theater.

The year 1997 was also when Betty Shabazz died. Ossie and I
together delivered the eulogy at the Riverside Church, where the memorial service took place. It was a numbing time for people all over
the nation. Ossie spoke for so many as he opened, "This is the day of
Harlem's lamentation. Great is our grief, and great our cause for grieving." I tried to voice the collective bewilderment: "What is your
snatched life trying to make us see about our times, our minds, work,
love, and above all else, about our children?" We shared the reading
of "Dear Sisters," a poem by Hasna: "Our arms are wrapped around
your arms/and we will never let go." How could we comfort the sur-
viving five daughters and the troubled grandson of Malcolm and Betty?
Yet they stood together, and as Attalah, the eldest, spoke to mourners,
it seemed to comfort all of us. They embodied grief, but above all,
strength, power, and hope. Through them, the spirits of Malcolm and
Betty were among us.

Sometimes the elements that make up a life are so scary or suddenly
depressing, magical, overwhelming, or sinister that more than breathing
comes hard. Speaking of age, I am reminded of the time when I was
preparing for the role of Mother Abagail in *The Stand.* Mother Abagail

was 106 years old. I had stopped coloring my hair, hoping to help shorten the three-hour makeup job required for a younger actor like me. During the transition, I wore wigs and scarves most of the time.

One night, however, while scurrying from activity to activity, the hair rose all over my body as, in the half-light, I encountered a white-haired creature coming directly at me, mouth open and garments flapping. I stopped. The creature stopped. I turned, the creature turned. It was I! I was looking at myself in the mirror that had been installed on the landing in my absence; I'd ordered it long ago and had forgotten about it.

I saw something in that mirror that I had never seen before. I had become all the old ladies I'd ever seen, written, or read about. Witch, angel, hag, grandmother sitting in rocking chairs on porches, crone, senior citizen, bag lady, Elder of the Tribe. The staring apparition began to giggle, so I giggled, too, and bounded down the steps to tell Ossie of the fright I'd seen, and how that old lady in the mirror had scared the hell out of me. We laughed and laughed and then I cried— cried because here I was, living longer than my grandmother, my mother, all my aunts, father, brother, sister! I cried also with joy because that old lady in the mirror and I—we'd made it!

How lucky, how marvelous not to be dead yet. Fear. Oh, it will all soon be over. Death. Let it do its own advertising, I thought. I'll spend these last few minutes kicking up my heels, writing about the contradictions, absurdities, joys, and responsibilities of living long, and let the permanently horizontal mode and intimations of mortality take care of themselves.

My One Good Nerve, the book I had published in 1987, happened something like that. Too often I find myself facing the opposites of beauty, grace, truth, peace, joy, and love, leaving room for panic and confusion to enter. Something in me cannot believe in the total reality of demons, however. So, when I look at terror, I must pluck it from my eyes, and let mind and soul dish it up again in manageable proportions. Something in me needs to suck substance from the funny folk—Mother Goose, Zora, Langston, Sterling Brown, Bootsie—needs to dip the blade in humor before sticking it to some of the demons that louse up paradise, struggling for their shot in human affairs.

Some of the most satisfying episodes in my life have resulted from people who wouldn't take no for an answer. Taro Meyer is one of those people. She is an actor who also directs the reading of books and had recommended me to Harper Audio to record Hurston's *Their Eyes Were Watching God.* It is one among the assignments of which I am most proud. Later I also audiotaped excerpts from her *Mules and Men.*

A few years earlier, Taro had seen me in a workshop performance consisting of selections from *My One Good Nerve.* The performance, directed by Lynda Gravatt, was presented at Crossroads Theatre in the Genesis Festival. When Taro called in 1995 to tell me about her friend, Peggy Shannon, the artistic director at ACT in Seattle, who wanted to do more material involving women, to whom she had suggested my performance of *My One Good Nerve,* I couldn't hide my lack of enthusiasm. In the first place, Rick Khan, the artistic director at Crossroads, decided to produce another piece I was putting together with Ossie and Guy called *Two Hah Hahs and a Homeboy;* and second, the idea of going solo in a theater run didn't appeal to me.

My self-confidence was in need of repair. It had been too long since I had first written the material, and besides—all the way to Seattle?! When I started hemmin' n' hawin,' I heard through all else that Taro was saying, "Ruby, go already." I couldn't have made a better move.

In 1998, Woodie King took the performance to the Sylvia and Danny Kaye Playhouse at Hunter College for four weeks. Charles Nelson Reilly, the very gifted actor and director, helped me add a new dimension to the offering as well as much new material.

My One Good Nerve, the book, came out without any fanfare or attention that might establish me as an author. When I began reading from it occasionally, however, people laughed at and with the humor, and that encouraged me. I told Ossie, "Maybe I'll become a comedian."

"No, Ruby," he said. "You are a humorist. There's a difference."

I have rewritten much of the original book and it looks as if the performance may last into the next millennium if I so decide. The invitations are numerous and I am the leading and only performer.

It is satisfying, too, because I can address so much that concerns me—that concerns us all—love, politics, murder, race, spousal abuse, racism, hope, nonsense, and work. People laugh, and I'm told that sometimes they cry. *My One Good Nerve* is also being published again—the new and improved version—by John Wiley and Sons.

I don't suppose we ever get over or through or around dealing with the dynamics that define who we are and life is too short, complex, precious, mysterious, and challenging to be slung casually over our shoulders, like a duffel bag that we live out of haphazardly. At this point in my journey, perspectives, goals, summations seem uncertain, because the warranty and directions that came with the package of me in that long-ago transition from heaven to earth was mislaid.

It probably stated, "Now, Ruby, I need you to be a woman, to be born black; I need you to be an actor, one who can become an instrument through which I get my messages out. I'll give you a great man, beautiful children, and good friends, but I'll need you to live in the United States, a racist location with some heavy problems, but struggling to overcome. Can you deal with that?"

Now here I am, still trying to rein in from galloping off in every direction at once, without a map, huffing and puffing up to exam time without having taken many notes along the way. I guess He'll know that mostly I have been winging it, that He will have mercy, and just let me fly on through.

CHAPTER 37

Now That We
Are Elders

RUBY: From time to time, Ossie, I wish I could call back the day, like a farmer recalls his hogs: "Yo! Wait! Reverse. Get on back here, Day! You're gone before I'm through with you. Hold your horses! I need to turn you around. Do you over again!"

OSSIE: You mean just one day? Why would you want to do that? Would one day make that big a difference?

RUBY: Matter of fact, I'd better make that two days. The first one would be when I bought Mother a tape recorder, and I asked her to talk about her life from the beginning as far back as she remembered. I didn't have the sense to realize that showing her how to operate the thing was the least of it. I should have conducted the journey, asked her questions, prodded her memory. There was so much I wanted to learn from her, about her and Daddy. So much she never told me. Things a daughter needs to learn from her mother.

OSSIE: Hindsight. Nothing like it. Notice, though, that God put eyes on the front of people. Wouldn't make sense—eyes in the back, steady keeping track of where you "wuz." The importance of what you were asking hadn't sunk in yet, that's all.

RUBY: Yeah. It just felt like something I needed to do. Same thing with Daddy. I was growing up, busy, not thinking about the fact that the world, important people, places—the Struggle—didn't get started just for my benefit.

OSSIE: Maybe you needed to tell her why you needed to know?

RUBY: I wasn't sure why. Thinking of writing stories and plays, I guess. Even curiosity should have stimulated me more.

OSSIE: Continuity. History of ourselves, where we come from—the people—that's what you wanted.

RUBY: Sometimes Daddy would volunteer information, but I think maybe I wasn't enthusiastic enough in my responses to his tentative beginnings. The last time he came to the house, I sensed it was for the last time. I sensed that I'd never get to ask him all the questions to which I now wanted answers—about his childhood, his parents, his marriage to Emma—and to tell him what a remarkable man I thought he was. Neither he nor Mother ever got to talk things out with any of us. I believe it would have made a profound difference in my life and work.

OSSIE: But for agreeing to do this book, we might not have opted to investigate, to write about, to put our lives in a kind of perspective for our kids, either.

RUBY: They know us, I feel. We've shared and kept them close—reasonably—don't you think?

OSSIE: What about their children? If there is one thing that I wish could have been different, it is that I wish I could have had a better relationship with my grandchildren. I think we owe them—what?

What else, besides a home and a business, do we owe the children—the grandchildren especially—and the family? Having to do with who they are in the first place. . . . How do we give them Kince, and Marshall, and Emma, and Mama when she leaves? What about stories? Br'er Rabbit, the traditional survivor, as against Bugs Bunny, that other rabbit, a materialistic hustler? How will they know the difference if we don't tell them?

RUBY: If they are to survive here in the race-conscious U.S.A., how will they know the defensive ways of being black, the subtle craft, the art and science of it, without some grandpa—and some grandma—standing by to tell them?

OSSIE: I am, of course, such a grandpa, and have reached the age where my grandchildren are the only peers whose judgments I truly fear. To be accepted into their forgiveness and understanding is for me now what heaven used to be. I need them for my continuity—and they know it—but how do they feel about me and my self-appointed duties?

An ancient head have I—and an old man's heart—crammed full with formulas, prescriptions, recipes, ghost stories, games, and gossip, all fading day by day, all withered, fit for a life that has died before I have died. No more like olden times when grandfather and griot meant the selfsame thing.

RUBY: A grandfather's challenge in the past was to be capable of instant recall, ready at birthdays and funerals and holidays with the family assembled, to stand and deliver . . . to gather a cousinly tribe of youngsters at his feet, open the family vaults and bring out the stories—stories about the time when he was as young and bright and devilish as they are.

OSSIE: Folkways, happenings, customs—a way of life that was stable, and enduring, and seemingly set forever, now has gone with the wind, without even saying good-bye. Grandfather's defining function is going, too, usurped, if not rendered irrelevant, by television and electronic games and MTV and other various and sundry baby-sitters.

I could hardly wait till Muta' Ali, my first grandson, was able to walk before I taught him how, with newspaper, string, and little pieces of balsa wood, and flour from the kitchen, and water to make glue, to put together a kite that could fly hundreds of feet high if the wind was strong. Or how—from a wooden box, a couple of two-by-fours, some metal curtain rods, and a set of wagon wheels about ten inches in diameter we got from the Salvation Army—to build a go-cart. It was a beauty, with everything—except for motive power. Or how to thump a watermelon in the supermarket to see if it is ripe.

These memories, so precious to me, mean absolutely nothing to them. They and I have so little life in common. They smile; they love me, and give me as much of their attention as they can spare, but the clock is always ticking, and time is running out. And Grandpa is just playing out the string.

RUBY: To believe, though, that you as grandfather and I—our whole generation—could be expendable, Ossie, is like believing a fireman could scale a tall building on a ladder with missing rungs. I don't want to excuse myself from life because I don't have an E-mail connection, can't access the Internet, or get information on the computer about anything from anywhere it exists. How blessed we are to have children like Nora, Guy, and Hasna. How lucky we are that they married caring, sensitive people like Bill, Dorothy, and Abdul Wali.

They are our continuity. They do understand the difference between Br'er Rabbit and Bugs Bunny, do appreciate the folklore and the storytellers, who can so thump a watermelon. They've picked up a lot from both of us, and especially from you.

OSSIE: It takes so much money to pay rent and put food on the table, let alone buy a house. Not only does the money system under which we live demand that both parents work; it is often necessary for the grandparents to work also. We live in an economic, cultural, and social environment that—no matter how folks pretend and profess love for the American family—is definitely at the root of the family's greatest distress. When our children and many of our friends' children tried to strike out on their own for the first time, we had to do a double take because they couldn't make it. They had to come back home, rethink, regroup, and plunge out again. What we paid for our modest two-family house when we started out couldn't pay today for an economy car for our offspring.

RUBY: Grandparents must be increasingly self-sufficient. Often with working people, like you and me, access to the grands is limited. Our independence dictates that we forfeit a consistent closer relationship with them. We don't see them often enough. We don't know them as well as we'd like to. We comfort ourselves with the thought that their parents are among the concerned and loving, and that through them, their kids are ours, too.

OSSIE: What I believe all seven of our grandchildren need from us, in addition to more time for get-togethers and theater and attendance at birthday parties and gifts and talks about aspirations and hugs, kisses, and good-byes, are some elementary conversations about the nature and necessity of struggle.

RUBY: As I watched them talking among themselves in the driveway on the way to the cars after a visit including dinner and much laughter and glorious conversation, I felt good. I began to reflect on the various stages of growing older and especially on the arc of childhood.

Childhood seems shorter now, and thicker, crammed with so much more to learn and to experience before the onslaught of adulthood and responsibility. Arrows point in conflicting directions. Time for beauty, enthusiasm, anticipation, trust, hope, time to go fishing, listen to crickets, contemplate things, is being cut short.

One of our proudest moments as a family occurred when Abdul and Hasna bought a used car for cash that turned out to be a lemon. They demanded another car or a refund, but the dealer kept giving them the runaround. Finally, we took the whole family, drove to the dealer, and told him we were going to sit in his office until he gave them their money back. After we occupied his office and had much discussion, he did. That was Struggle. That was the family in action.

OSSIE: Yeah, but Struggle isn't only a matter of action, it also involves thinking, knowing about things—like power, for instance, about money, about the way the world actually works.

RUBY: True. I've heard you talking to them about the stock market, and explaining the principles of the economy.

OSSIE: I was only trying to suggest ways to make money in case the job market dried up—you know how people are being constantly laid off, industry by industry, these days. Work is going to the countries where wages are the lowest and benefits are unheard of.

RUBY: We need to be talking about finding a better way altogether. We're headed back toward a kind of feudalism where the—

OSSIE: —rich get richer and the poor get poorer.

RUBY: And fewer and fewer people control the lives of more and more people worldwide. A new kind of slavery. . . . Thanks to you, our grands know more about the stock market than I realized. But it's strange, the way you make them think about the glories of the market and the free enterprise system—capitalism—when I know deep down you believe in a system that could be closer to socialism.

OSSIE: They've got to know about it all. That's the only way they'll ever be able to make choices, know their options. We'll be talking socialism and capitalism—and the history—just not all at once. They've got time.

RUBY: I think these kids everywhere—all of us—need a whole lot of prayer because, as you know, honey, this world is getting scary. I'm worried that they don't have a clue to what's in store for them.

OSSIE: Well, you lost me. I'll pray with you, but be I'll damned if I'm gonna worry. Praying and worrying don't go together. Here, I've brought you some wine. If you're going to sit out here and cogitate.

~   ~   ~

RUBY: I watched the grands shoot some baskets, laughing and having fun as Hasna and Nora and Bill and Guy and Dorothy leisurely worked to round up everybody for the trip up to Hasna and Abdul's house where they were to spend the weekend. As I watched the familiar family maneuvers of "Let's hit it! Let's get the show on the road," I found myself turning in circles between the outside door and the opened inside door, whimpering, like I had heard dogs in trouble do. Ossie calls from somewhere in the house, the kitchen I think, "They're beautiful. Some beautiful people. Know how lucky we are?"

I don't answer because, as I watch them all outside, my mind takes off and goes places, and I start out again talking to Ossie at first.

The stock market. You know that now prisons are on the stock market! Maybe you should teach them how to invest—how to become class-A-number-one capitalists.

OSSIE: First, who is going to teach me?

RUBY: Did you see that graph in today's paper? Tax dollars going down, down, down for improving and expanding public schools, for preparing these children for the twenty-first century, but there's much more for building prisons. Prisons are privatizing, becoming big business, plums for the privileged. Could we lose a grandson on trumped-up charges to fill the prison quota? You know, if prisons are on the stock market, they are looking to show a profit. That means somebody stealing a bicycle or caught with a nickel bag is going to be arrested and warehoused.

The powerful ones tap the public till at will, or by decree, dump their obscene debt on all of us—black, white, Asians, Native Americans—and leave us calling each other names, as the really big criminals

(421)

strut away scot-free. But what do they, my grandchildren, know about Struggle?

OSSIE: Look at the funeral business. For years, the black dead were handled by independent undertakers. Today, your black butt belongs more and more to the conglomerates. The megabuck boys are taking over the world we tried to build a place in for our children. What scares me is that it's happening now. Now!

RUBY: I want to say to those grands, "Don't let them do it. Turn off that TV. Put down that pizza. We got to get off our asses, get out in the street. Scream; sound alarms. Democracy is in danger! Demagogues and demons are in cahoots—mouthing Jesus slogans and wearing the Nazi boots. They are suiting up against blacks, against Jews, and especially against the poor. Don't let them do it!"

I want to shout to each and every one of them everywhere: "Take off those designer duds. Read. Look. See what's going down in this world. Don't let it catch you, hat on backwards, in droopy drawers."

How will you babies be able to maintain, educate, form, and nurture a family—the most endangered arrangement on the planet Earth—if you don't latch onto what is really happening and get ready for some struggle? Family is on the block—hustling jobs and time, squeezed, hassled, and beat down just for space to live in—hurting. Mama and Papa—day shifts, night shifts—tempers, meals—so much to do to pay the bills—no money, no time. Gangs are made up of those with hope misplaced, and jobless, who seem resigned to becoming convenience packages for jailers who run the shiny new warehouses.

OSSIE: Workers are forced to compete for jobs worldwide. Will we cut each other's throats to compete for crumbs? Will the tide turn and workers here be the new Third World contenders? Will we learn the new power games and unite for strength all across the world? Can paradise be behind locked doors tended by snarling wolves?

OSSIE: Global money. Global work. Take it where it costs less to do. Never mind the rain forests; pledge allegiance to the global dollar sign, they say.

RUBY: I want to tell it, yell it. "Don't you believe them. We got to wake up. We got to protest. We got to work. We got to love each other. We got to struggle. We cannot become pit bull contenders for the amusement of the greedy, global big spenders. The bottom line cannot, must not be the dollar sign."

OSSIE: Not money alone, but Struggle; that's pretty much all we've got to leave you—the unending war between good and evil. Struggle—that's where God comes from.

∾   ∾   ∾

RUBY: These are some of the thoughts that crowd my mind, that instruct what I write, that inform whatever humor escapes from me, and that I hope my grandchildren will investigate while they are young.

As senior, now, as mother now of the tribe, I feel that we can't just run off and leave it to the children. We who helped to create this mess still have an obligation. We must ring the bells, call attention to the dangers that stride in full daylight because too few are rehearsing the ways of Struggle and drawing up the demands of victory. It is time now for envisioning that vastly different future, where food, clothing, and shelter can be taken for granted as we get on with that next revolution—the revolution that speaks to the largely unexplored divinity within us, that would relegate all other revolutions to precursors of the main event. Martin wouldn't have mentioned nonviolence if he had thought that we were just a higher form of the animal kingdom.

The army of the envisioners that would usher in the new times could be from among those sixty-five years old and older. Their main requirement would be good minds set on educating, displacing, or destroying the greedy globe gobblers in order to give all children a better chance at peace, love, and understanding. My army would be set, too, on undoing past neglects, where the ferocious beasts, spawned in vanity and indifference to decent values, stampeded into our lives and encouraged us to keep ourselves in mirrors, monitoring our beauty and our money, as they made off with our children.

We will not be afraid. Let fear itself be afraid to accompany us as we, with our medication, false teeth, and pacemakers, take to wings— or to wheelchairs and walkers—to do battle, if we have to, for our children and their families. What would we have to lose? Our jobs? Our lives?

I might try to qualify as some lower-ranking officer with a degree in advanced creative agitation. A desk job, perhaps, since too little of my time in the Struggle has been on the front lines. But by then, who knows, there might be such a shortage of old-timers that I could start off as at least a first sergeant or a second lieutenant.

That scenario springs from years of kitchen conversation with you, Ossie, in which I got a Don Quixote complex. Unlike the Don, I wouldn't go up against windmills; I'd wrestle with the global bullies until I changed their minds. That's what the Struggle really is all about. Don't you think so, Ossie?

He doesn't answer. I really didn't expect him to. I think he's gone upstairs, maybe to bed. It's getting chilly now. I finish my wine, lock up, and go upstairs. Damn. Already dark. God, help me. I must have been running my mouth for hours.

CHAPTER 38

Love, Marriage, and Struggle

OSSIE: We've been on the road thirty years going to colleges, and in the beginning, the kids on the campuses wanted to know, "How do you get into the theater? How do you get to Hollywood? Should I go to New York?" But little by little, as we stayed out there, they began to ask, "How did you stay married so long?"

RUBY: In other venues as well, people would say, "Tell us, what's the secret? Hope we last as long as you two. . . ." At first, I didn't believe the questions.

I'd answer, "Day by day, like one foot in front of the other, and before you realize it, the years pile up. I don't know. It doesn't seem like we've been married that long." If the time caught me impatient, maybe I'd reply as I'd heard Bette Davis say, "You've got to have two bathrooms—one apiece." I've added, "Three at least if you have kids." In a macabre frame of mind, I'd say, "God grabs my arm every time I get ready to swing the ax as he lies sleeping after a hard day of aggravating my very soul. That way I feel lucky not to be on death row, and I cross myself, hug him, and go for marriage one more day."

OSSIE: Finally, Ruby said, "These children are asking serious questions and we can't keep telling them jokes. We've got to say something serious to them." We had to. I was prepared to go through life and not bother with it too much, to accept that it was just something we had found. But I'm persuaded now to be honest, to share, at a time when the institution of marriage has to justify itself. Whether marriage will exist as an institution recognizable to us, we don't know.

RUBY: Just as every cell in our bodies mirrors the universe—the planets, the stars—so I think one marriage has to be a reflection of all marriage, just as we are a reflection of each other.

As with the germs in our bodies, we're healthy because we don't give those deadly germs a chance to develop and destroy us. This is how I feel about life and marriage. We don't let the murderer in us, the deceiver or the whore come to the fore. We have within us that which is good and also its opposite. What we allow to come forward, what survives, attests to the fact that its opposite has somehow been held back, not that it doesn't exist.

OSSIE: You've chosen this against that.

RUBY: Yes. The world is full of beautiful people, for instance. There's no sense denying that, or saying you don't notice them just because you're married. You're going to find people you admire and love until you die, but you're also married to a person whom you admire and love, so you have to choose. If you felt you had to act every time somebody admirable and marvelous came into your life, there would be no stability. You'd tear yourself apart.

There comes a point when you discover what love really is. You don't really know it beforehand. You arrive at a point when you can say to the other, I want you to be the best person you can be; when you can ask, What is it that fulfills you as a human being? Why are you on this earth? You have to go through the resentment, the feelings of neglect and jealousy, and all sorts of emotions before you're free, before you can let somebody go toward their fulfillment. When you're able to let go, and not feel helpless and abandoned, you rejoice in the fact that they are on the road they need to be on. I think this is the beginning of love.

I don't think you can love somebody when it's a matter of "I love you for what you do for me and how you make me feel" and "You are my dream girl" because all those reasons wear thin. We will get old, fat, sick, ugly. Loving somebody means finding that reason for being. That's the beginning of the love process, I think.

OSSIE: It's the maturing of the best stage of it. You can keep the strict law and continue to live with somebody who no longer interests you—all the fire has gone, but that's life, you say, and you've got the children. You can stay there and be quite true to the code in that way. Or you can begin to sneak out and have extramarital affairs, and experience the guilt and the self-hatred for being weak, and the contempt for your partner for believing the damn lies you tell. How could you not destroy all possibility of any kind of relationship if that's a part of it? So you either have a deeply discounted affair, a distorted and thwarted affair, and you give yourself credit for bravely living through the whole thing. Or you find a way to keep the relationship truly alive.

There's a basic aspect that has to do with men as sexual partners, and how we develop or we don't. If the culture doesn't teach us, we're pretty much at the mercy of our own impulses. We satisfy ourselves and we hope that the partner is satisfied. It doesn't always happen that way.

At the beginning of marriage, here is this woman; she is iridescent as a sexual object, the center of all your passion. Through time, repetition, experience, and changes of roles—wifing, motherhood, etc.— that object moves from the center of your sexual attention. You don't know it. You certainly don't invite it, and yet it happens. One of the ways to move that object back to the sexual center is that that object should be proven to be attractive to somebody else. Now why this is so, I don't know, but it is deeply so.

With Ruby, this dynamic extended beyond the sexual plane.

When I met her, for instance, I had not known that she was a writer and humorist; I had not thought about her being the kind of performer she is until other people—critics and so forth—expressed their appreciation of her. Others' appraisals of her stimulated another kind of interest. It's a process of discovering the other dimensions of your mate.

I don't think you can get there just by thinking it, or by accepting the boredom of continuity. She's a mother, she's a drudge, she's a housewife, she has to teach you things, remind you of your failings. At times, you think, "God, this is somebody I love?" Then she becomes attractive to someone else, and you say, "Oh, don't go yet. Let me take another look at you." And you appreciate her in a new way.

The minute the partner comes back on the sexual plane, the husband has a motive to try to understand, to learn, not just to indulge his training, but to augment it. It becomes a challenge, but the challenge would hardly arise if the partner wasn't a love object again. You have to compete, and you compete by studying and asking questions of yourself: How do I appreciate her? How do I sexually express without being selfish? The object then is, I've got to keep this woman; I've got to win this woman. She's not my property. I can't let her get away.

I know how precious she is, so I'm impelled to do those things that say, "Heh, count me in. Give me another shot at this thing!"

RUBY: The letting go opens rejoicing in somebody else's glory and fulfillment. You learn to do that, and it becomes as important as your own fulfillment. So marriage becomes a process rather than an accomplishment or a fact. It goes on and on. You keep on getting married.

OSSIE: Having come to that understanding, having the capacity to practice truth in your relationship to your mate, the basis of friendship is established. When you've had to recompete for the woman you've got—good God, what a woman! So we can be partners, with a sense of equality that we never would have achieved automatically.

RUBY: There's the fear of being diminished by somebody else's success. You arrive at the elimination of that. I'd like to say to all the bigots, to those who feel superior, "If only you could just come to know that your happiness, your own satisfaction, does not depend on diminishing somebody else."

OSSIE: We're augmented by augmenting somebody else.

RUBY: We have to take a stand in this world. If we let the negative forces disquiet us too much, we will abandon our own belief. Those of us who believe have to get out there and campaign. Our lives have to become the campaign.

Love is struggle. I cannot help but do all I can. I take the risk even that you might leave me. You know, when you talk about that wife who puts that man through school and helps him to achieve some goal, and he might leave her, but that's love. You can't spit on it and live. You can't turn your back on it and not suffer. You can envy or resent or compete; that's just love strengthening itself. You've got to find out about love, how not to envy, because it's hard not to feel less than somebody who seems to be moving way ahead of you, for example.

I think about sensuality and struggle, about not having orgasm, looking for it, and being jealous of men, scrambling, going through my animal turns, getting all confused; but the animal turns are all part of it.

OSSIE: It's the animal necessity that nature imposes on us. We came here because of that necessity and it is one of the things that nature wants us to get involved in.

RUBY: The animal necessity is sensation, the exhilaration in struggle, like in sports—to win. It translates into a desire to see everybody win.

Love, marriage, relationships, staying together—ain't easy. I was looking into the eager young face of a woman after one of our performances on a campus, when I found myself trying to articulate what I really felt about marital longevity beside "Don't go to bed angry," or "You've just got to keep God in the equation," or "Try to remain attractive to each other." Ossie and I *had* gone through some rough times. Emotions that affect most married people—resentment, anger, impatience, jealousy—had affected us, too. How to ride the rough waves in a relationship long enough for the waters to get calm? When does it sink in that overcoming difficult times gets easier with practice? How do you drag some of the good feelings, good times vibrations into the stormy places? To love someone long and deep is a "consummation devoutly to be wished"!

Hey, maybe I could come up with "An Anatomy of a Long Marriage." Maybe a lot of people *do* want to know, to get an idea, to read about and take courage from such a scenario. Besides, as elders of the tribe, we need to acknowledge and reclaim our responsibility to our children. The privilege of a long life demands at least that we share whatever wealth of mind and resources that by God's grace we've accumulated. This is no time for "aw-shuckin'-and-jivin' " false modesty. Besides, you don't really own something until you can freely share it. You don't really know something until you can teach it. Our children are looking for answers! Somebody better come up with a few!

Some of what I've already alluded to is valid. It *is* day by day, one step at a time. It may not mean two bathrooms, but just some space— for some privacy, some area to be alone. It is a necessity for every human being, especially in apartments where there is no outlet to the sky, trees, and the earth. Poverty and overcrowding compromise dignity, strain love, nerves, and peace of mind.

This letter to Ossie is an effort to put something about love and marriage under a microscope and into at least some elementary perspective.

Dear Ossie,

I appreciate and acknowledge the fact that you are a good husband. For a while, though, I believed that a truly nice husband could not be achieved without a lot of hard work—if the sista is lucky and the brotha is intelligent and flexible. That such creatures couldn't even be born is due perhaps to some trauma in the birthing process of your gender. After the first several of our fifty years together, I was convinced of it. The idea that a good marriage is made in heaven and swung down on a golden cord like a gift from God did not coincide with my lifelong observations. Yes, the wedding can be a beautiful, exciting, expensive event, or it can be a handshake, or a jump over a broom—but it is just that—an event, the one that precedes the marriage.

I maintain, however, that this oneness, this coming together under one roof "until death do us part" is a challenging proposition. Unlike the wedding event, that takes place in a day, marriage is a long process that goes on at some level every day for the rest of your life. You divorce or marry around some issue constantly. The percentage of days married determines success. We have to *learn* how to live together. Oh, well. That shouldn't be too tough if you love somebody.

I thought I loved you, Ossie, when we got married, but as I see now, I was only in the kindergarten of the proposition. To arrive at love is like working on a double doctorate in the subject of Life.

I already had myself to take care of; now, with this wedding, there is *my*self and *your*self. Already a hard worker, I could do a little more, I resolved. It wouldn't kill me. After a while the drudgery of double duty and babies and more responsibility, and even after we could afford help, and I graduated to supervising drudge, I felt sorely tested in the love department. You could be more free than I to travel and write and pursue your heart's ambition. With a wife, the small details of life no longer concerned you—meals, laundry, paying bills, shopping for clothes, etc. I, on the other hand, had to strain and sweat bullets, huff and puff, and be in charge of everything. Something like peace and respite came for a little while, when I would get a job out of town, or went to have another baby.

I used to want to shout, "Help me! Help me! Can't you see? So much to be done. You're not a guest here in this house! I'm not running a hotel!" Resentment. Anger. It's not fair! Being a woman is too damned hard. Marriage is for men. A man can take so much for granted. "So tell me, what's in the newspaper? Can't you see I have no time to read one?"

After some threats, arguments, tantrums, and tears, Ossie, you began to understand. I found out you listened. You just hadn't paid attention to how lopsided the equation was. You began to say, "I'll make breakfast. I'll wash the diapers. You stay in bed. The children and I, we're going for a walk, maybe to the movies, or to the museum. Take the day, Ruby. Relax. We'll go to church. Then Sunday School. Surprised you? Didn't know I could clean so well, huh? Can't compare me now to the Collier brothers found dead knee-deep in waste and debris.

Call me godly, if that's what cleanliness is next to. I'll take care of this, and this, and this—hold it. I'll do that." I found myself smiling more and thinking up surprises.

Then, like a quickened pulse beat, the levels of concern in our life together rose, reached through us, took us to a higher level, and hooked us to a deeper Blackness, connected us to families just like us, and to all those threatened by the newer and scarier dangers, and to how the world is wobbling now, being so bombarded by rampaging progress. Both of us already had our feet in the hot waters of Struggle before we even met. As we moved out together to follow those we admired, already way ahead, we plunged in even deeper. We wanted to give a hand, help those on the front line make Justice just, and to be part of whatever the Struggle was all about.

Breakfast became more than just a time for food. We eventually learned how to pray together every day, even if only by phone. I don't remember when current political, economic, and social matters became our favorite topics, but I do remember how they stimulated us, especially you. How you love history, and cross-referencing and comparisons. How, when the children were very young, you told stories and jokes, and spread your spirit over me, too, like a warm blanket on a cold night. How the newspapers and magazines would accumulate because there was so much to catch up on, and to share. More and more, you and I became part of the Struggle and the Struggle became a part of us.

How lucky we are with Nora and Guy and Hasna. They are our greatest achievements. Concerned, considerate human beings who understand the necessity of Struggle. How proud I was when you and Guy sat in at the Draft Board, and stood up for what you believed even though you got arrested. How victorious we felt when Hasna joined the teachers in her union in protest over delayed contract negotiations.

Even last year, at an affair honoring Michael Manley, in Washington, D.C., I remember how moved I felt as you shared your knowledge and appreciation of the man and what he meant, not only in the Caribbean, but also in the world. You spoke with quiet passion about the ramifications of his political and economic philosophy, about his desire to truly serve and to empower his people, to help position the Caribbean on the road to greater self-reliance, and of what it had cost him as a man with vision who had not foreseen the tremendous obstacles that would undercut that vision, leaving him, in a sense, naked and bleeding before the waiting vultures. You made me, all of us, *see* the man and his struggle. You humanized the history and connected us profoundly to the person of Manley, to each other in that audience, to our times, and to all the struggles for justice, compassion, and common sense everywhere.

I have admired your capacity to interrelate, to see the long arc of events, sometimes in awesome detail, marrying the mundane and the majestic, the beginnings reflected in the ends. As I listened, I reminded myself again how deeply I love you. Not only because I believe you value me, but also because I believe we have both arrived, finally, at what love is. When you want and pray for someone to be all God created them to be, despite any personal sacrifice it might entail, that is love. Love is overcoming. Love is passion clothed in infinite patience.

There is a magnetism about those who love, who know things, who see, make connections, and are committed to the struggles for the wider victories in the world. There is a sensuousness about them, too—as if struggle itself is an aphrodisiac. During your Manley address, the silence in the place was so loud. I felt you walking in my secret soul, and that night we had to make love.

Good sex, feeling loved, admired, etc., is like a pat on the back, a "go get 'em, girl." A nudge to some victory from God, letting you know—sense—that now you're free to get on with the divine assignment, the mission message, with heeding the revelation of why you're here in the first place. You want to spread the good feeling, want everybody to be happy because that want rounds out your circle, fulfills your equation, says "yes" to your life. It banishes fear and envy; an insurance policy maturing in joy, security, and assurance that you've done your job, and all is right in the universe. It frees you to stretch, look around, and love beyond your circle.

You can talk now about—think now about—the welfare of others, think of worthy ideas to feed into the emotion and information systems. You can feel the world spinning, out and up from the self to the many, and to the children that are truly precious. You can love a sunset and watch a sunrise and help feed the hungry and protect the tribe because you understand love and how it erupts from the deep quiet of ecstasy to the service of divine intentions. . . .

Dear Ruby,

I, Ossie Davis, am hammered out of the same hard-shell Baptist rock that gave the world Kince Davis, a wonder to white folks and a hero to his peers; made in his image, according to Bible specifications (King James Version). Whatever I did had to square with the Ten Commandments. That's what it meant to be a Christian—as Daddy saw it—and a man. Now the Ten Commandments are a hard task-master, but Jesus, by his death, could get you a pardon for every transgression except two: Thou Shalt Not Kill and Thou Shalt Not Commit Adultery. Violate these, you wind up doing time in the deep-est pits of hell—as Daddy saw it. Ruby, you were and are my love, the chosen of my heart; but how could I marry a woman who had been divorced? That was committing Adultery, according to Daddy and the Ten Commandments.

Although the war years had seen me estranged from God—I didn't feel I owed him anything—marriage was a decision not easy to be made. Not God and the Ten Commandments, but Daddy—that was the prob-lem—a powerful river I didn't know how to cross. The woman I loved versus the father I respected, admired—and feared. I searched my soul, but my soul wasn't talking, either.

It didn't occur to me to talk to Daddy—even to Mama—about my moral dilemma, nor did they expect me to. I was a man, and strictly on my own. A long and lonely road I had to walk between opposing incli-nations in myself, with only martinis to guide me. Not to measure up as a man—and as a Christian—to Daddy's expectations would put me under the reproach of my conscience for the rest of my life, I told myself. And downed another drink.

But for me, it was you or nobody, and I had no right to ask you to wait forever. So finally, biting the bullet, I sent you a wire from Chi-cago, and you said yes.

We married, and I waited for Daddy to blow—to come barreling down God's mountain, spouting His holy fire and hellish brimstone. It didn't happen. He never said a mumblin' word. Never once did he question my choosing, or make you feel anything less than welcome, not to my knowledge. In fact, Daddy and you—divorced or not—wound up showing a great regard for each other. As for God, I'm not sure He even noticed. All those months of sweat and perturbation, for absolutely nothing. No. If indeed I do wind up in hell, it will not be Daddy and his God who sent me there; it'll be because I sent me there myself.

The great thing about marriage is that it gives a man time to find out what love is all about. Love, in the end, is the object of existence. Sex threads the needle that stitched we twain together, but only love could make time in the corset worthwhile. Sex is always in a hurry, but the making of love takes time.

Fifty years of being married, and what have I learned from it all? I say to my fellow husbands—whose eyeballs may be covered with lust—that the way to possess all women is to love one woman well.

Love? I have had the honor, the good fortune, and the common sense to have been in love with as much as my heart could carry and my mind conceive—Beauty, Art, Power, Knowledge, Women, God, Flowers, Food, Music, Poetry—I have loved them madly all my life. Sex is an errant stroke of God's most choice lightning—wild horse beyond control—its own excuse for being; having no allegiance, playing by its own rules with loaded dice. Love, on the other hand, is the maker—and keeper—of our humanity, to be trusted above all other instincts, nurtured, worked at, molded, shaped, then remolded . . . a garden where we labor against rocks which in time become flowers; one life held in common, rosebush, thorns and all. But marriage is the place which love calls home.

To love a woman, it is not necessary—at first—to understand her; education will come, but only if you give it time. You, Ruby, for example, are brilliant, but nonintellectual . . . there are too many blank spaces and missed connections in your memory for that. Yet given time, you fashion your own category, original in thought and creative enough in ideas, to startle an unsuspecting, patronizing lover. You retreat too much, putting your own interests last, allowing yourself to be overlooked—even put down—but not for long. Perceptive to a fault, you are extremely sensitive to detail, seeing intricacies in human motives discernible to few others than you. You will apologize if you think you have offended—even if you haven't. And you always worry that you haven't tipped the waiter, or the cabdriver, or the maid quite enough. You deeply fear the possibility that you have hurt somebody's feelings. Yet you have a temper—a sudden blast of fury can open up the ceiling, but at the same time, you are one of the most compassionate, understanding, and ultimately forgiving persons I have ever known. The perfect find, if anyone ever needs a friend and a defender.

But being married isn't always just about peace. There are arguments and battles and confrontations, when all of holy hell breaks loose! It helps a lot knowing how not to win, rather to hop in the bed and work out a compromise. That way, we both can have the very last word, which is often all that was at stake in the first place. But there is always one more river to cross.

I always thought, for example, that by leaving you alone—especially on matters of how you run the house, or raise the children, or the clothing that you wear—I was doing you a favor, giving you freedom to be yourself without any interference from me. It took me the longest time to understand that that's exactly what you needed—interference from me. But you don't want to be left alone; you want involvement—my hand in the diapers and dishwater, right next to yours.

There are times when it's wise for a man to be ignorant—"things without remedy should be things without regard." But you insist on my opinion anyway, and will not rest until I come up with one. You'll tell me what you want, but not directly, rather by innuendo and verbal camouflage. You'd rather me understand what was on your mind than to have to tell me, like the character in a Jules Feiffer cartoon who crouches under a desk, crying to the world outside, "If you loved me, you would find me." It's not easy to know always what you're really thinking, but time has proven it's worth my while to find out.

Yes, in the beginning, before we were married, and then in the early, male chauvinistic years, I did take you for granted. I know now that that is a definite no-no for anybody. Still in temperament and taste, we came into the marriage much alike, and that has been an advantage to us both. I never felt the necessity to explain, and certainly not to apologize for whatever it was I was up to. There were many times in our marriage when I should have consulted you before I took a tack that affected us both, like with the film *Countdown at Kusini,* but I didn't.

The world was a man's responsibility just like Daddy said it was—not a woman's. And that was that. Or so I thought until you taught me better. Luckily, I have always been flexible in my opinions—easy to make adjustments and to change. Nothing you have ever asked of me

has seemed outrageous, or ridiculous, or a threat to my delicate ego—
so give me a minute or two, or a day or two, and I can swallow it whole.

We always have been in basic agreement about money, the world,
the Struggle, how to raise the children, and what black folks must do in
order to survive. The Struggle sometimes demanded our full attention,
leaving no time to stop and worry and wonder if we were happy. Too
much work to be done, so let's get cracking. Still, there were those rare
occasions when your temperament and mine ran headlong into each
other—and the fight was on.

You know that I am, essentially, a loner. Most of my life takes
place inside my head, in my imagination—stress-free, awash in moth-
ering tides of mental self-indulgence—having the time of my life, cooking up plots and stratagems for whatever it is I am writing; which means
I don't need psychiatrists or vacations or other diversions, only time to
follow my darling thoughts to their own conclusions, paying as little
attention as possible to the world as it passes me by. I know how to
sleep on planes, and I write on the back of envelopes, napkins, and other
people's scripts. Sometimes, when my imagination is red hot and pregnant with a fascinating idea, I forget completely what I'm supposed to
be doing and where I am.

Like the day we went to La Guardia Airport to catch the shuttle
to Washington, D.C., to meet with Beanie Butcher. I dropped you off
and went to park the car. The flight was so full that two sections were
required to handle all the passengers. I forgot to meet you at the gate
as I had promised, but, busy with my thinking, I boarded the first section, found a seat, and sat down. Missing me in the hubbub, you
waited—and waited—and waited. When they started loading the second
section and I still hadn't shown, you began to worry. Then a gate attendant told you that I had boarded the earlier flight.

Furious, you caught the second section, which happened to arrive
before the first one, so you were waiting at the baggage claim when I
arrived. You grabbed me and started beating me in the chest with fists
that felt like Joe Louis was behind them. Strong as a bull when you're
angry, it was all I could do to stay up on my feet. It was a long time
before your rage was vented and you finally stopped. I didn't apologize
or try to explain—how could I?—that I was so deep in my thinking, I
completely forgot about you. Then you might have killed me.

But where I really failed you was in those areas where you, because of your own doubts and hesitations, needed reassurance, encouragement, and little husbandly pats on the back. Like the time you were invited to come to London and perform. There, of course, were the children: Either you would have to be away from them a long, long time or we'd have to pack up the family and take them with us. We discussed it briefly, just as when we had the chance to take *Purlie Victorious* out on a national tour; but you and I agreed—completely, I thought—that home and family were too important for us to move to London.

What I didn't know was that you wanted desperately to go, but didn't dare to consider putting *your* career ahead of home and family. I would have said yes in a minute and stayed home with the children— we could have worked it out, I'm sure of it—but you didn't know how to ask me. And I, of course, wasn't listening. Who knows what a starring role—such as Tony Richardson, the English director was offering— might have done for your career?

Every December the ninth, you and I go out and buy the biggest, most beautiful poinsettia we can find. Christmas, New Year's, Mother's Day, Father's Day, your birthday or mine, none of these will matter after that; no other presents, no cards, no furs, no smoking jackets, no diamonds, and no yachts—only this one, solitary commemoration of our wedding anniversary. That is the only gift we give each other during the year. Not only does that save us from the hype and hoopla that have swallowed up the meaning of our holidays, but also we know that the only true gift is yourself—your undivided attention, for richer, for poorer, in sickness and in health, till death us do part—and time on the cross together, and listening, and silences together, and wishing the best for each other . . . and willingness to learn and stand corrected. The rest? The rest is not for us.

I look back now, in praise and deep thanksgiving to you, Ruby, the woman I love, seeing not two of us, but one—not certain where I end and you begin. One thing is certain: The best of me has been subsidized by the best of what you are. I have no hungers that you do not feed. And only this poinsettia—the biggest, prettiest, most expensive in the house—can say that for me.

Ruby, marriage with you was always much more nest than prison, with no desire from the inmate to escape. Filtered infidelities might satisfy curiosity, but love was always waiting in the bedroom. Wasn't that gift enough between two sinners?

Still, there was always that one thing that stood beyond the reach of poinsettias: your need, Ruby Dee, for a gift that only you can give— the need *to believe in yourself*! To give yourself permission to excel! So it was when I met you, and so it is to this day. A fact I shall ponder till the day I die.

> And so, Best Friend of All, these final
> words: There are some doors to you I
> cannot pass,
> Nor ever could, some places where you
> hide the wounded child you were, and
> sometimes are.
> Some parts of Ruby which, in spite of
> love, and care, never found a welcome as
> a child. Trammeled, even now by
> expectations which did not die with the
> expectors—Mother, Father, who loved you
> but never remembered to hug you.
> I wish that I could do it in their stead
> —give you approval from the dead-and-
> gone—who did their level best,
> but failed to hug and kiss, or tickle
> you under the chin and press you to
> their bosom and say, "Well done!"
>
> Oh, that I, who know so well your
> thirst for reassurance,
> could open your darkest doors,
> could reach with healing hands, into the
> cage behind your doubts and fears . . .
> help find your wings, lift you up, point
> you toward the sun, and say with all the
> love at my command: "Fly, Ruby, fly!"

CHAPTER 39

A Bridge to Ourselves

RUBY: In 1993, Mama arrived at her ninety-fifth birthday. The children rented a tent, pitched it on the lawn, and gave her a party. Hasna was in charge with Nora, Guy, and their fellow grandchildren and great-grandchildren as co-conspirators. It was a catered affair, with Sharon Arthur, who was our executive assistant and one of Mama's fans, presiding. They also hired a family friend as videographer to come put it all on tape. James and Essie were dead, but both of Ossie's remaining brothers, Willie and Kenneth, and their families came. The music was provided by Guy, Wali, and friends. Several of Mama's close friends were also there, as were a clutch of preachers for whom Mama seems to have a special fondness, and they in turn have a special attachment to her. There was joking and joshing, eating and drinking, and cousins meeting cousins, some for the first time.

OSSIE: There was Nora singing "Will the Circle Be Unbroken, By and By, Lord, By and By"; there was Hasna reciting her poetry; then everybody there got up and spoke into the microphone, including Ruby and me. There were blessings and praying and plenty of laughing remembrances. And then, of course, there was Mama.

Mama was dressed like a young and glowing bride, except that her gown was made of pink lace. And she wore a small corsage of flowers on her wrist. She rose and worked the tables as she spoke, the eyes of the children sparkling—and the clergy sparkled, too. Laura's speech was Laura's masterpiece. She spoke of God, whom she thanked, of Kince, whom she fondly remembered, of her children, her grandchildren, and her great-grandchildren. This whole splendid garden affair was as much for them as for her.

RUBY: I watched it all: the generations bonding, this affection flowing among us; this "circle," that was a metaphor for family. Where else can the grandchildren get the fullest sense of who they are—except from Grandma—and us, Ossie and me?

OSSIE: It was Thanksgiving, 1995, two years after Mama's birthday party, and the time had come to introduce the family to Cogdell, the place where I was born.

Nick Fluker, an old family friend and schoolmate, who worked with Ora Lee Bolden to plan everything, was waiting for us in Waycross with his wife, Johnnie Mae. He warned us not to eat till dinnertime. On, on to Cogdell, twenty-three miles to the west, but Cogdell wasn't there anymore, and hadn't been for many and many a year. There was only the old store and a few scattered houses hidden away from each other by growths of bushes and trees. There was no pretense whatsoever that what I had come back to had ever called itself a town. Gone. Especially gone was the Waycross and Western railroad that my father had helped to build, which once had run straight through the heart of Cogdell. Cogdell, with its four hundred people, most of them black, was not only no longer a fact; it wasn't even a memory.

RUBY: Still, the crowd was already gathered, waiting to greet us as we clambered out and soon found ourselves swallowed up in welcome, Southern style. Some of the people who used to live there, their chil-

dren and their children's children, had come back—thanks to Nick—
just to greet the Davis family. A tent had been set up, and the smells
of pine smoke, barbecue, and Brunswick stew hovered over the feast
that was already in progress. We were soon busy fellowshipping, meeting and greeting, and shaking hands, making small talk with a mouth
full of beans and rice and corn and succulent spareribs.

OSSIE: The people, white and black, mingling so easily together, as
if the past had never happened at all, were truly glad to see me. To
them, I was the one on television who had done great honor to them,
and they were grateful and proud.

RUBY: Later, we drove some farther miles to Valdosta, to the cemetery where Kince is buried, gathering there, holding hands around his
grave just as the sun was setting. Mama and Guy hadn't come, but
there was not the slightest doubt among those of us who had made it
that indeed "the circle was still unbroken."

∽   ∽   ∽

OSSIE: When I left home in 1935 on my way to college, the rich and
wonderful life I had spent with my siblings came to an end. I enjoyed
the fact that I had escaped the segregated South, but I missed completely what happened to them after that. Correspondence was not our
way—seldom we wrote, making little effort to stay in close contact with
each other. So I finished growing up up North, all by myself; while
they stayed behind down South, with Mama and Daddy, and we siblings gradually lost track of one another.

Kenneth was, and still is, handsome, well dressed, charming, and
good-natured, a good laugher, with a prodigious sense of humor. I
never saw him angry in my life. He is a registered pharmacist, having
graduated from Xavier University in New Orleans.

William, or Willie as we called him, was the most independent—
almost eccentric—of the children. Strong-minded, determined, deeply
set in his ways, he was a self-starter. After he spent time in the Army,
he went to Talladega College and majored in chemistry. He earned his
doctorate in agricultural chemistry at the University of Idaho, and he

is now chairman of the Department of Natural Sciences at St. Philips College in San Antonio, Texas.

I hardly knew my baby brother, James. He was only "knee high to a grasshopper" when I left home. He became an educator, teaching at Benedict College, among some others. He, too, was a laugher, but after he served in Korea, he came back home a confirmed alcoholic. He'd become sober in his final years, but ultimately died of his affliction in 1969. He is buried in Valdosta beside Daddy.

Essie, whom I have saved for last, was the most complicated of us all, the most ambitious, the most achieving—but the least fully realized and self-satisfied of us all, having risen to distinction as the Chief Social Worker of the Continental U.S., the highest post held by a woman in the Veterans Administration, at the time of her death in 1990.

Her childhood affections were concentrated on Daddy, as were ours; but seeing ourselves as men, we unthinkingly formed a greedy circle that effectively shut her out. Her very spunk and sparkling aggressiveness—and she was certainly the brightest of us all—made it all but impossible for us to see how much she was vying with us for Daddy's acceptance. It took Ruby, an outsider herself, to point out, years later, that we boys—happy residents of a world where God gave men all the marbles—had made our sister an outsider, too, barred from access to Daddy—because she was a woman.

Hasna says in one of her poems, "We touch so many with our mistakes." We most certainly do.

Whatever Mama does, it seems to keep her spry and active, and even combative. She was one hundred years old on July 9, 1998. The children and grandchildren planned a great big party. The first person Mama invited was President Clinton.

～　　～　　～

RUBY: There comes a time when you know that the play is over, even if the curtain is still up and the audience still applauding. There's no further use for you at center stage. How, now, to make a graceful exit, removing yourself from the scene without bumping into the furniture as you depart?

OSSIE: Sent back from the ardent vortex, now that the whirlwind is over, knowing that your moment in the great parade has come and gone. A proper time to think of death and dying.

RUBY: Both Mama and Nora are laughing people, especially when it's time to update Mama's funeral—a production for which they have been in rehearsal for about twenty-five years.

OSSIE: Nothing, except God's timing, has been left to chance. What Mama will be laid out in has long been decided, music has been selected, dignitaries have been designated to bring the spoken word; but thereby hangs the rub: Mama tends to outlive the speakers of her choice. One by one, the cast of characters keeps dropping dead and changing. Mama and Nora spend time checking off who's still alive, then auditioning replacements for those who are not. My job, when the proper time comes, will be to supply the eulogy at my own mother's funeral. That, of course, puts me in a bit of a bind.

I told Mama I didn't feel it proper for a son to do the eulogy at his mother's funeral. Especially me, since there is always the danger that right in the middle of whatever it is I am trying to say, I would break down and cry. But Mama was adamant: "You did the eulogy for Malcolm X, and you didn't break down and cry. Why can't you do it for me?" So. It's all set. If I'm still around when Mama passes on, dry eyes or wet, I do the eulogy.

RUBY: Ossie and I have also made arrangements. Cremation after a public ceremony, and then, into the urn. A special urn, large enough and comfortable enough to hold both our ashes. Whoever goes first will wait inside for the other. When we are reunited at last, we want the family to say good-bye and seal the urn forever. Then on the side, in letters not too bold—but not too modest either—we want the following inscription:

RUBY AND OSSIE—

IN THIS THING

TOGETHER

OSSIE: We are outside the urn at the moment, busier than ever, but still not satisfied. Like most of our peers and comrades in the Struggle, we honor a cease-fire that we never called, an armistice that we never accepted. We are part of the general strike against the New World Order and the Global Market. We toothlessly protest the injustices we perceive still up and growing, but not in the same bold and impetuous way. We say we are in the Struggle, but mostly now on standby, not on guard.

RUBY: The largest piece of unfinished business before humankind is, in our opinion, poverty, spiritual as well as material. Racism, yes, and sexism, too; unemployment, drugs, child abuse, black boys too much in prison—oh, yes, Struggle is all there is, and we are still committed. And even if, from time to time, it finds us slow or absent, we ask the Struggle to accept our children. To give them meaning and purpose just as it did us. To make a place for them in the line of march.

OSSIE: We want them to remember something of what it was like to have been black for most of the twentieth century, something of what the Struggle meant to us.

RUBY: The taillights from the kids' cars have disappeared long ago, but our thoughts trailing them have no end. We want them to know that black is a dynamic identity. Black people in America have helped give life to the Constitution. We have helped make it a pulsing, living document. We put justice on the map. We've kept the whole question of human rights alive for this country. We want them to glory in their blackness, knowing that we have important work to do for ourselves and for this world. We want them to believe that unimagined miracles are in the wings preparing for an unprecedented entrance onto the main stage of human affairs; and we pray each one of them will be in the vanguard.

OSSIE: We want them to know that the essence of human history— the meaning of existence—did come to tarry awhile in our home, in the bosom of one particular family; that the glory of God, and the cumulative light of all knowledge, the summing up of the entire human experience—civilization itself—shone at its brightest there. We want them to know that, if only for one lifetime, under that one roof, all meaning came to rest. Time ran its endless circle through our living room; all space extended there. That our little band, happy for the most part, but crying together too, spent time at the center of Creation, right next to the throbbing heart of God Himself.

APPENDIX

THEATER CREDITS

*written by Ossie Davis
†written/adapted by Ruby Dee
**Ossie Davis stage manager

OSSIE	OSSIE/RUBY (JOINT APPEARANCE)	RUBY
Joy Exceeding Glory (Rose McClendon Players, 1939)		*On Strivers Row* (American Negro Theatre, 1940)
On Strivers Row (RMP, 1940)		*Natural Man* (ANT, 1941)
Booker T. Washington (RMP, 1940)		*Starlight* (ANT, 1942)
Black Woman in White (RMP, 1941)		*Three's a Family* (ANT, 1943)
		South Pacific (Cort Theatre, 1943)
		Walk Hard (ANT, 1944)
	Jeb (Martin Beck Theatre, 1946)	
	Anna Lucasta (Mansfied Theatre and Tour, 1946–47)	
A Long Way from Home (Maxine Elliott's Theatre, 1948)		*The Leading Lady* (National Theatre, 1948)

OSSIE	OSSIE/RUBY (JOINT APPEARANCE)	RUBY
The Washington Years (ANT, 1948)	*The Smile of the World* (Lyceum Theatre, 1949)	
Stevedore (Equity Library Theater, 1949)		
The Wisteria Trees (Martin Beck Theatre, 1950)		
The Royal Family (NYC Theatre Co., 1951)		
Green Pastures (Broadway Theatre, 1951)		
Remains to Be Seen (Morosco Theatre, 1951)		
	*Alice in Wonder** (Elks Theatre, 1952)	
Touchstone (Music Box Theatre, 1953)		
*The Big Deal** (Yugoslav Hall, 1953)		
	The World of Sholom Aleichem† (Barbizon-Plaza Theatre, 1953)	
The Wisteria Trees— revival (City Center, 1955)		
No Time for Sergeants (Alvin Theatre, 1956)		
Jamaica (Imperial Theatre, 1957)		
	A Raisin in the Sun (Ethel Barrymore Theatre, 1959)	

Appendix

OSSIE	OSSIE/RUBY (JOINT APPEARANCE)	RUBY
	*Purlie Victorious** (Cort Theatre, 1961)	
*Curtain Call, Mr. Aldridge, Sir** (Henry Hudson Hotel, 1963)		
Ballad for Bimshire (Mayfair Theatre, 1963)		
	Broadway Answers Selma! (Majestic Theatre, 1965)	
The Zulu and the Zayde (Cort Theatre, 1965)		*The Taming of the Shrew* (American Shakespeare Festival, 1965)
		King Lear (ASF, 1965)
		The Oresteia (Ypsilanti Greek Theater Festival, 1966)
		The Birds (Ypsilanti Greek Theater Festival, 1966)
		Boesman and Lena (Circle in the Square, 1970)
		The Imaginary Invalid (Walnut Street Theatre, 1971)
		The Wedding Band (Public Theater, 1972)
		Hamlet (N.Y. Shakespeare Festival, 1975)
	Take It from the Top!† (Henry Street Settlement, 1979)	
		Bus Stop (Drury Lane, McCormick, 1979)

Appendix

OSSIE	OSSIE/RUBY (JOINT APPEARANCE)	RUBY
	Zora Is My Name!† (Howard University, 1983)	
I'm Not Rappaport (Booth Theatre, 1986) *I'm Not Rappaport* (Burt Reynolds Jupiter Theatre, 1988)		*Checkmates* (46th Street Theatre, 1988) *The Glass Menagerie* (Arena Stage, 1989) *The Ohio State Murders* (Great Lakes Shakespeare Festival, 1992) *The Disappearance*† (Crossroads Theatre, 1993) *Flyin' West* (Crossroads/Kennedy Center, 1994)
	Two Hah Hahs and a Homeboy (Crossroads Theatre, 1995)	
		My One Good Nerve† (A Contemporary Theatre, 1996; Danny·Kaye Playhouse, 1998)

FILM CREDITS

*Film version of *Purlie Victorious,* screenplay by Ossie Davis
†directed by Ossie Davis
**co-written by Ruby Dee

OSSIE	OSSIE/RUBY (JOINT APPEARANCE)	RUBY
		The Fight Never Ends (1947) *That Man of Mine* (1947)

OSSIE	OSSIE/RUBY (JOINT APPEARANCE)	RUBY
		Love in Syncopation (1947)
		What a Guy (1947)
	No Way Out (1950)	
Fourteen Hours (1951)		*The Tall Target* (1951)
The Joe Louis Story (1953)		*Go, Man, Go* (1954)
		Edge of the City (1957)
		The St. Louis Blues (1958)
		Our Virgin Island (1959)
		Take a Giant Step (1959)
		A Raisin in the Sun (1961)
		The Balcony (1963)
	*Gone Are the Days** (1963)	
The Cardinal (1963)		
Shock Treatment (1964)		
The Hill (1965)		
A Man Called Adam (1966)		*The Incident* (1967)
The Scalphunters (1968)		*Up Tight!*** (1968)
Sam Whiskey (1969)		
Slaves (1969)		
Cotton Comes to Harlem† (1970)		
Kongi's Harvest† (1971)		
Black Girl† (1972)		*Buck and the Preacher* (1972)
Let's Do It Again (1975)		
	Countdown at Kusini† (1976)	
Hot Stuff (1979)		*Cat People* (1982)
Harry and Son (1984)		
House of God (1984)		
Avenging Angel (1985)		
School Daze (1988)		
	Do the Right Thing (1989)	
Joe Versus the Volcano (1990)		*Love at Large* (1990)

OSSIE	OSSIE/RUBY (JOINT APPEARANCE)	RUBY
	Jungle Fever (1991)	
Gladiator (1992)		
Malcolm X (1992)		
Grumpy Old Men (1993)		*Cop and a Half* (1993)
The Client (1994)		*Just Cause* (1995)
Get on the Bus (1996)		
I'm Not Rappaport (1996)		*A Simple Wish* (1997)
Doctor Dolittle (1998)		*Baby Geniuses* (1998)

TELEVISION/RADIO CREDITS

*co-authored by Ossie Davis
†written/adapted by Ruby Dee

OSSIE	OSSIE/RUBY (JOINT APPEARANCE)	RUBY
	Radio	
		"New World A-Coming" (1946)
		"The Story of Ruby Valentine" (1954)
		"This Is Nora Drake" (1955)
	The Ossie Davis and Ruby Dee Story Hour (1974–78)	

Television: Movies and Teleplays

OSSIE	OSSIE/RUBY	RUBY
"The Emperor Jones" (1955)		
	"Play of the Week: Seven Times Monday" (1960)	
	"Camera Three: Actor's Choice" (1960)	
		"Play of the Week: Black Monday" (1961)
		"Frontiers of Faith: The Bitter Cup" (1961)

Appendix

OSSIE	OSSIE/RUBY (JOINT APPEARANCE)	RUBY
"Catholic Hour: The Sign of Fire" (1962)		"Alcoa Premiere: Impact of an Execution" (1963)
	"The Great Adventure: Go Down, Moses" (1963)	
"The Outsider" (1967) "Teacher, Teacher" (1969)		"Armchair Theatre: Neighbors" (1966)
"Night Gallery" (1969)		"Deadlock" (1969)
	"The Sheriff" (1971)	
		"To Be Young, Gifted and Black" (1972) "It's Good to Be Alive" (1974) "Wedding Band" (1974)
	"Today Is Ours" (1974)	
"Billy: Portrait of a Street Kid" (1977) "A Piece of Cake" (1977) "Freedom Road" (1979)		"I Know Why the Caged Bird Sings" (1979)
"Don't Look Back" (1980)		
	"All God's Children" (1980)	
"For Us the Living"* (1983)		"Long Day's Journey into Night" (1982) "Go Tell It on the Mountain" (1985) "Zora Is My Name!"† (1990) "The Court-martial of Jackie Robinson" (1990) "Decoration Day" (1990)
	"The Ernest Green Story" (1993)	
		"A Tuesday Morning Ride" (1995)

Appendix

OSSIE	OSSIE/RUBY (JOINT APPEARANCE)	RUBY
		"Mr. and Mrs. Loving" (1996)
		"Captive Heart: The James Mink Story" (1996)
"Miss Evers' Boys" (1997)		
"Twelve Angry Men" (1997)		"The Wall" (1998)

Television: Miniseries, Documentaries, and Specials

	"Stage 2: Of Courtship and Marriage" (1964)	
	"The Creative Person" (1965)	
"History of the Negro People" (1965)		"The Fight Against Slavery" (1976)
"King" (1978)		
	"Roots: The Next Generation" (1978)	
"Here's to Your Health" (1979)		
	"A Walk Through the Twentieth Century with Bill Moyers: The Second American Revolution" (1984)	
		"The Atlanta Child Murders" (1985)
	"Martin Luther King: The Dream and the Drum" (1986)	
		"Gore Vidal's Lincoln" (1988)
		"Windmills of the Gods" (1988)
"Alex Haley's Queen" (1993)		
"Baseball" (1994)		

Appendix

OSSIE	OSSIE/RUBY (JOINT APPEARANCE)	RUBY
	"The Stand" (1994)	
"Thomas Jefferson" (1997)		

Television: Series, Regular or Recurring Roles

OSSIE	OSSIE/RUBY	RUBY
"The Defenders" (1963–65)		"The Guiding Light" (1967)
		"Peyton Place" (1968–69)
	"With Ossie and Ruby" (1981–82, 1987)	
"B. L. Stryker" (1989–90)		
"Evening Shade" (1990–94)		"Middle Ages" (1992)
	"African Heritage Movie Network: Movie of the Month" (1993–)	
"NBC Friday Night Mystery Series" (1994–95)		
"The Client" (1995–96)		
"Promised Land" (1996–)		

Television: Series, Guest Appearances

"Big Show"	"Beulah"
"Cavalcade of America"	"The Big Town"
"Car 54, Where Are You?"	"The First Year"
"East Side/West Side"*	"The Nurses"
"Doctors and the Nurses"	"The Fugitive"
"Slattery's People"	"East Side/West Side"
"The Fugitive"	"Tenafly"
"Run for Your Life"	"Police Woman"
"N.Y.P.D."	"Spenser: For Hire"
"Bonanza"	"China Beach"
"Hawaii Five-0"	"Evening Shade"

Appendix

OSSIE AND RUBY WRITING CREDITS

OSSIE

RUBY

Fiction, Drama, and Poetry

Alice in Wonder (1952)
Purlie Victorious (1961)
Curtain Call, Mr. Aldridge, Sir (1963)
Escape to Freedom: A Play about Young Frederick Douglass (1978)
Langston: A Play (1982)
Bingo! (1985)
Sybil (1990)
Just Like Martin (1992)

Glowchild and Other Poems (1972)
Take It from the Top! (1979)
Zora Is My Name! (1983)
My One Good Nerve (1987)
Two Ways to Count to Ten (1988)
The Disappearance (1991; adapted from the novel by Rosa Guy)
Tower to Heaven (1991)

Essays, Articles, Publications

"Purlie Told Me!" International Library of Negro Life and History (1967)
"The English Language Is My Enemy," *Black Language Reader* (1973)

Freedomways, contributing editor (1970)
"Swingin' Gently," *New York Amsterdam News,* column (1978)
"Tattered Queens" International Library of Negro Life and History (1967)

Appendix

SELECTED AWARDS AND HONORS

OSSIE	OSSIE AND RUBY	RUBY
First Mississippi Freedom Democratic Party citation (1965)	N.Y. Urban League, Frederick Douglass Award (1970)	Emmy Award nomination—"The Nurses" (1964)
Emmy Award nomination—"Teacher, Teacher" (1969)	Actors Equity Association, Paul Robeson Award (1975)	Obie Award—*Boesman and Lena* (1970)
Antoinette Perry Award nomination—*Purlie* (book for musical—1970)	Volunteers in Service to America (VISTA) Arts Award (1980)	Drama Desk Award—*Boesman and Lena* (1970)
Emmy Award nomination—"King" (1978)	NAACP Image Awards Hall of Fame (1989)	Operation PUSH Martin Luther King, Jr., Award (1970)
American Library Association, Coretta Scott King Award—*Escape to Freedom* (1979)	National Academy of Television Arts and Sciences, Silver Circle (1994)	Drama Desk Award—*Wedding Band* (1973)
Jane Addams Children's Book Award—*Escape to Freedom* (1979)	National Medal of Arts (1995)	ACE Award—"Long Day's Journey into Night" (1983)
Neil Simon Awards' Jury Award—"For Us the Living" (1983)		Theater Hall of Fame (1988)
NAACP Award—*Do the Right Thing* (1989)		NAACP Image Award—*Do the Right Thing* (1989)
Theater Hall of Fame (1994)		Literary Guild Award—*Two Ways to Count to Ten* (1989)
Emmy Award nomination—"Miss Evers' Boys" (1997)		Emmy Award nomination—"China Beach" (1990)
		Women in Film's Crystal Award (1991)
		Emmy Award—"Decoration Day" (1991)
		N.Y. Women in Film and Television, Muse Award (1997)

Appendix

VIDEO AND AUDIO TAPES

Video

Hands Upon the Heart, Vols. I and II, Emmalyn II Productions

Audio

Emmalyn II Productions
  Holy Bible (15 cassettes)
  Book of Matthew (2 cassettes)

Caedmon
  Poetry of Langston Hughes
  To Be a Slave
  Tshindao and Other African Folktales
  Up from Slavery
  The Rain God's Daughter—African Folktales
  Why Mosquitos Buzz
  A Raisin in the Sun

Harper Audio
  Black Pearls
  How to Succeed in Business Without Being White
  Mules and Men

HarperCollins
  Their Eyes Were Watching God

INDEX